Konpa Encyclopedia

A LOOK AT KONPA MUSIC AND KONPA ARTISTS
FROM 1955 TO DATE

A reference book about Konpa music

By Professor Jean Claude Vivens

Order this book online at www.trafford.com/07-2922
or email orders@trafford.com

Most Trafford titles are also available at major online book retailers.

Note for Librarians: A cataloguing record for this book is available from Library
and Archives Canada at www.collectionscanada.ca/amicus/index-e.html

Printed in Victoria, BC, Canada.

ISBN: 978-1-4251-6368-6

*We at Trafford believe that it is the responsibility of us all, as both individuals
and corporations, to make choices that are environmentally and socially sound.
You, in turn, are supporting this responsible conduct each time you purchase a
Trafford book, or make use of our publishing services. To find out how you are
helping, please visit www.trafford.com/responsiblepublishing.html*

*Our mission is to efficiently provide the world's finest, most comprehensive
book publishing service, enabling every author to experience success.
To find out how to publish your book, your way, and have it available
worldwide, visit us online at www.trafford.com/10510*

www.trafford.com

North America & international
toll-free: 1 888 232 4444 (USA & Canada)
phone: 250 383 6864 ♦ fax: 250 383 6804
email: info@trafford.com

The United Kingdom & Europe
phone: +44 (0)1865 722 113 ♦ local rate: 0845 230 9601
facsimile: +44 (0)1865 722 868 ♦ email: info.uk@trafford.com

10 9 8 7 6 5 4 3 2

INTRODUCTION

The rhythm that we affectionately and simply call "Konpa" today was named "Compas Direct" by its creator, "Nemours Jean-Baptiste". Nemours was a great saxophonist, an innovator, and a charismatic band leader.

Most people used to call Nemours' band "Compas Direct" even when they actually knew that the official name of the band was: Super Ensemble De Nemours Jean Baptiste.

In 1955 Nemours changed the beat of the Dominican Republique rhythm "Meringue" by simplifying the conga tempo to what we all know today as Konpa. Later, Nemours added to his drum line the floor tom and the cow bell percussion. Haitian musicians call that set "The Gong", and the musician playing the set is called a "Gonguist". That metronome is found only in "Konpa", thus making Konpa a unique form of music.

To promote his new creation and to raise public awareness Nemours criticized through his songs the 1950s most popular band of Haiti ", Jazz des Jeunes". He called "Des Jeunes" old school and told them that it was time to leave the musical scene to the young people.

In 1960, the saxophonist Webert Sicot created his own band. He modified the conga beat of Nemours' Compas to what he called "Cadence Rampa".

With this new challenge Nemours got what he really was looking for, a group of musicians of his generation that he could compete with. Thus began the rivalry Nemours – Sicot.

Although Nemours and Sicot have been dead for some time now, the culture of bands rivalry is still going on among Haitian musicians and may continue for many years. It's an unfortunate characteristic in the Haitian music industry. It was passed on to the Mini Jazz in the 1970s, and continued today. Konpa fans still remember the rivalry between Difficiles and Gipsies, which later became the rivalry of D.P. Express - Scorpio in the 80s. Even in the U.S. the tension was high between Tabou Combo and Skah Shah. In the 1990s to the 21st century, Sweet Micky and T. Vice made song after song calling each others names that were not always pleasant to the average listener. T. Vice and Djakout continued with even more unpleasant attacks, sometimes even naming family members in their lyrics, especially during the carnival season. By the same token, it's no secret that whatever the generation, they kept the rivalry only in their songs. The musicians are good friends and they often participate together on all-star collaboration albums. They travel together, they joke around a lot and they get on stage at each other's show, or do concerts to raise funds for Haiti especially after a natural disaster like Hurricane Jeanne in 2004.

However, to some people, the musical rivalry is one element that gives the Haitian musician the strength to get up and work hard, because he wants to excel, to produce more and more than the competitor.

Konpa has dominated the Haitian and French Caribbean music scene for decades and it is getting a lot more recognition in many countries. Over the years, many people have tried to modify it, but they always go back to basics by playing the rhythm just like Nemours intended for it to be played.

In the mid 1960s, we saw the revolution of a new generation of musicians. It was called the "Mini Jazz" movement. Indeed, at that time the Nemours' generation felt it was a step back for Haitian music, because the new formations actually removed some essential wind instruments to reduce the 15 to 20 piece band format into six to eight member groups. On top of it all they were "jazzing" instead of using musical sheets and young people felt that was cool. The musicians of Nemours and Sicot felt it was a lazy form of music, but unfortunately for them, they could not keep up, and the Mini bands took over the airwaves of Haiti and the French Caribbean countries, and a new buzz was created.

Since one no longer needs to know how to read music in order to perform, many young men were simply "ad lib" in creating new songs. Thus, a new trend started in the country, especially in Port -au -Prince, the nation's capital. People were learning of the creation of some new musical groups in almost every neighborhood. Certain bands even added to their titles which neighborhood they were from, like Tabou Combo de Petion-ville, Les Fantaisistes de Carrefour, Les Legendaires de Delmas, Les Pachas du Canapé Vert to cite a few. Soon after, there were too many to identify them by neighborhood. They simply came out with the name of the band without adding which area they were from: Samba Creole, Bossa Combo, and Les Loups Noirs etc…. Other bands used to add the name of the owner/investor to identify the group, like Les Shleu Shleu de Dada Jacaman or les Vikings de Georges Saieh.

Many of them did not last long, and very few of those musicians are still part of the Haitian music industry. The only band of the Mini Jazz era that made it to the 21st century is "Tabou Combo". Tabou Combo, which was created in 1968, had to make many changes over the years, including the addition of wind instruments in the late 1970s and keyboard in the early 1980s in order to keep up in this demanding Konpa field. It is also the band that has traveled the most around the world to make people hear and dance to the Haitian music.

In 1975, another form of revolution took place in the Konpa world. The other French Caribbean bands, especially "Exile One" of Dominica and "Les Aiglons" of Martinique, came out using horn instruments in their lineup along with the piano synthesizer. Their sounds were not only different; they were also new and sweet to the Haitians' ears. The generation of the 70s wanted more of that musical form, so Tabou Combo, Skah Shah, Bossa Combo, and

Les Loup Noirs, in order to keep up with the market, had to make the necessary changes by adding a horn section and a piano synthesizer to their lineup. Skah Shah, Bossa, and Loup Noirs used to play with an alto sax player, but they were force to add a trumpet, a trombone, and a tenor sax. Tabou Combo had never used any horn instrument prior to 1978.

With the addition of new members some groups in Haiti found it necessary to change their names entirely, thus Les Difficiles de Petion-ville became "D.P. Express" and Les Gypsies became "Scorpio".

In the early 1980s, once again the other French Caribbean countries were advancing musically. In Martinique, Guadeloupe and Dominica musicians were moving from the traditional Compas Direct of Haiti and their own Cadence Lypso by increasing the tempo and by adding other flavors to the drums line. A new rhythm was born in the Caribbean, and Haitian musicians felt once again the blow." Zouk", as it is called is still a form of music that is getting a lot of attention on the airwaves and in nightclubs around the world, especially among French speaking African countries and the Caribbean. Nowadays the Zouk tempo is not as fast as it used to be. The slower form of the Zouk is called "Zouk Love", but Zouk fast or slow is still a product created from the roots of Konpa.

Just like Aiglons and Exile One in the 70s, the Zouk virus was being transported to Haitian ears everywhere, especially by "Kassav", one of the most popular Caribbean bands of the 1980s. It was being played at every party (private or public) and by many radio stations in Haiti. The mid-1980s was the hardest time ever for the Konpa artists and for Haitian music in general. One could easily hear 10 to 15 Zouk songs on some radio stations before one Konpa song. Many musicians felt that it was the end of Konpa, but some stood still and believed that all they needed to do was to work harder, to produce more and to improve the quality of their products. While some bands were adding a little Zouk flavor to their repertoire, many great Konpa artists never lost faith, and held on to the heritage left by Nemours Jean Baptiste.

In 1986 another change occurred in the Haitian Music Industry (H.M.I). The departure of President Jean Claude Duvalier led to a series of apparitions of new musicians eager to sing about the changes and the beauty of Haiti. A series of music competitions were held throughout the country, notably "Mwen Renmen Haiti", which gave birth to a new generation of musicians who simply call themselves "Nouvel Jenerasyon".

Nouvel Jenerasyon musicians at first did not intend to play Konpa, they were so eager to change everything about the country that they felt that the traditional way the Konpa was being played needed to be changed too. They based their style mostly on the way they sing rather than on the conga/gong metronome. Some groups like "Zekle" in Haiti and "The Partners" in the U.S. made you wonder sometimes if you were listening to a Haitian band. The style was completely different from the traditional pure Konpa band like Les Frères Dejean, Loups Noirs or Bossa Combo.

Another change that took place at the same time was the introduction of the electronic drum machine, the clapper, and the sequencer in the business. Musicians who were "computer savvy" quickly got the edge over those who were not, and the band "Top Vice" surfaced in the market once again with limited personnel, this time with even fewer musicians than the bands of the Mini Jazz era. The difference this time was the fact that unlike the Mini Jazz one could enjoy the sound of a complete horn section without ever seen a sax, a trumpet or a trombone in the room. It was also the same with regard to the drum set. Top Vice managed to do with three musicians (keyboard, guitar and a singer) almost the same job that Nemours used to do with more than 15. Later on, a fourth member (bass) was introduced to their lineup.

Soon, this formula was being copied by other young men, and in the late 1980s and the 1990s groups like Sweet Micky, Digital Express, T. Vice, Konpa Kréyol, and many others were created in Haiti and in the Haitian diaspora. This form is called "Digital Band". Although popular, it is still not appreciated by many music lovers. Some musicians, even if they are making money doing it, still feel that the right way to play Konpa is with a "full live band", or what Haitians simply call "Jazz Normal". In other words, what a Konpa band should normally be.

Little by little, the Nouvel Jenerasyon musicians went right back to the basic of Nemours' Compas Direct in order to make the people dance and to satisfy the public. At the turn of the century, one could notice that most bands were using live horns and live drum sets in their lineup. Some bands, like "Zin" in New York "K-Dans and Mizik Mizik" in Haiti, don't use the live horn, but they played with a full drum set including the conga and the gong. So even though few are still using the computer to work, basically every single one of them is playing the Compas Direct of Nemours Jean Baptiste.

In 1999 the production company Noel Cecibon organized the Haitian Konpa fest in Miami to celebrate the anniversary of the creation of Haitian flag. Haitians from everywhere traveled many miles to participate at the festivity, to wave their flags and to listen to the best Konpa band in the market. The Konpa fest, which is now held annually in Miami, has been listed as one of the top 10 music festivals in the East Coast of the United States.

As a member of the industry, I have contributed over the years in many ways to the promotion of the Haitian music.

As a musician, I have entertained thousands, and have proudly represented Haiti and its Konpa at many international events, especially in the Washington metropolitan area, notably at the D.C. Caribbean Carnival, The Baltimore Museum of Art, The Kennedy Center, The D.C. Caribbean Festival, The Baltimore Caribbean Carnival, The Organization of the American States

(O.A.S) and many other festivals in Washington, D.C. and in Maryland.
As a show producer, I have promoted many artists and many Konpa bands in the Washington D.C. metropolitan area for more than two decades. I have awarded many artists for their contribution to the Haitian Music Industry. My company JCV Productions does many concerts, picnics, cabarets, festivals and dances in the Washington Metropolitan area to entertain music lovers.
As a television producer, show presenter, and radio announcer, I have for decades made our Konpa heard by millions. In 2003 & 2006 my T.V show 'Haiti A Suivre" received the Best International T.V. Show Award in Maryland. As a writer and educator, I contribute to the online Konpa community via Haitinetradio.com, Konpatv.com, Kompamagazine.com, Opamizik.com and Basekompa.com under the name STaFF PoZé, by writing Konpa news, anecdotes, Konpa history and stories.
Today my contribution to the Haitian Music Industry, to the public, to the fans and to the generations to come is this reference book about Konpa music and its artists.

Jean Claude Vivens

A

A.A Express - Band
This band was created in New York by the drummer Yves Arsene Appolon in the late 1970s after Arsène left Skah Shah. The initials A.A stands for Arsene Appolon. Later the name of the band was changed to Astros

Abel, Yves - Bass
One of the best bassists in today's Konpa community, Yves had his best years with Tabou Combo in the 1990s. At the end of the decade, he left Tabou to join Cubano's Skah Shah for a brief period. He also contributed to the formation of the band New York All Stars. Yves Abel is also known in the business as an arranger and an artist who take part in many studio projects. Yves Abel eventually returned to Tabou Combo and continued to tour the world with the popular band.

Abelard, Faresse - Bass
Faresse played with Missile 727 in the 1990s

Abelard, Lyonel -Trombone
Lyonel played with Missile 727 in the 1990s

Abellard, Alex - Singer / Guitar / Keyboard

Alex is the son of Alexandre Abellard, a well-known Haitian musician. Alex is the band leader and co-founder of the New York based band Zin. Alex is also the owner of the record company Alabel Mizik.

Abraham, Joseph –Trumpet
Played for most of his career with the band La Ruche de Léogane

Abraham, Norcis -Trumpet
Musician of Tropicana - He is the uncle of the talented drummer Shedly Abraam.

Abraham, Raphael - Trumpet
Musician of the band Tropicana; he is the father of the talented drummer Shedly Abraam.

Abraham, Shedly – Drum

Shedly is a talented drummer who immigrated to America with the band Lakol du Cap. The son of Raphael Abraham, Shedly is one of the best Konpa drummers in the New York City Konpa world. Sheldly has helped many musicians in their solo projects. He has also substituted for many drummers at countless live performances. He presently owns a studio in New York where several artists have recorded many hit songs. Shedly uses the collaboration format that producer Fred Paul used to do in the 70s & 80s on the Mini Records projects by asking his fellow musicians to do all-star albums under the name Djaz La. Unlike the Mini All Stars and the *Haiti Twoubadou* projects which also featured musicians of different bands, Djaz La never actually goes on an organized tour.

Absolu, Louimane (Mamane) - Bass / Guitar / Drum
Louimane is also one of the musicians who participated in many studio recordings with different artists. He played with Digital Express and Strings in his career. He is presently the bassist of Djakout Mizik.

Accolade (Accolade de New York) - Band
In the late 70s a group of musicians left Bossa Combo, one of Haiti's hottest bands at the time, to create the band Accolade de New York. The band stormed the Haitian diaspora not only with the hit songs of Bossa, but also with a series of new and good Konpa hits like *"La Foie"*, *"Accolade la rive,'* *"Madan Jules"*, to name a few. The name **Accolade** was also the name of medley song by Bossa Combo. Jean Robert Damas (sax/band leader),Jean Claude Dorsainvil (singer),Jules Pagee (sax) Claude Degrottes (bass) were among the superstars that left Bossa Combo to immigrate to New York and created the band Accolade.
In the 1990s a reunion with some members of Bossa Combo, who had immigrated to New York some 15 years after the first squad, gave birth to the BossAcolade project. As many people in the business anticipated the band

didn't last long, as at that time the famous superstars of the 70s & 80 couldn't keep up with the powerful stardom of the new generation movement.

Adam, Napoléon - Conga
Napoléon is the first conga player of Super Ensemble de Webert Sicot

Adhémar, Frantz - Bass
Frantz played with Septentrional du Cap.

Adolphe, Charles - Drummer

Adolphe, Patrick - keyboard

Adolphe, Reynold - Singer
This singer is one of the pioneers of the Mini Jazz era in the 1960s. He left Haiti at first to immigrate to Europe, and later he moved to New York.

Adonis, Christo - Guitar
Christo played with Digital Express in the 1990s.

Afro Combo - Band (1)
Mini Jazz of the early 70s in Haiti that introduced the talent of the guitarist Réginald Benjamin.

Afro Combo - Band (2)
This band came out strongly in the late 1970s in Boston at a time when the Konpa was not doing well in that part of the Haitian diaspora. The song *"Requin"*, released in 1976, became an instant hit, and also introduced the tenor voice of singer Chrisostome Bazile (Chris), who later left the band to join Volo Volo.

Al-Khal, Jessy - Band Manager
Jessy Al Kahl is the manager and part owner of T.Vice. She is also mother of two of the founding members Roberto Martino (guitar) and Reynaldo Martino (Keyboard). In the H.M.I many people simply refer to her as "La Madre"

Al-Khal, Pierrot - Band manager
In the 1970s, it took the courage of the young impresario Pierrot Al Khal to create the the band Gypsies. He negotiated contracts and record deals for the band and he managed to take the band on international tours. In the mid 70s, when the band leader Robert Martino and some other musicians moved to the U.S many people thought that it was the end for Gypsies in Haiti, but Pierrot quickly introduced in the market Claude Marcelin and Ti Polis, two young

guitarists who would later become Haitian superstars as Les Gypsies de Petion Ville released the album *Loa Baron*.Pierrot who was at the time about the same age as his musicians also appeared on the album cover, laying on the ground and surrounded by his peers.

Robert Martino eventually went back to Haiti where he started his new band Scorpio once again under the supervision of Pierrot Al Khal.

In the 1990s Pierrot became the road manager of T.Vice. His experience has contributed to the success of his nephews Roberto and Reynaldo Martino.

Albert, Pascal - Singer
One of the best products of the 1970s, Pascal's voice was heard on radio stations throughout the country in the super hit songs of "Les Ambassadeurs", especially the slow ballades like: "*Dis, Sans toi, Revers de la médaille*". The super singer of the band has also proved himself in songs like: "*7em flotte, Ti fi ya, and Port-au-Prince.*

In the 1980s he had a brief success with the band D.P. Express when he was chosen to replace Antoine Rossini Jean Baptiste (Ti Manno) While in D.P. Express; Pascal sang the popular early 1980s song "*Grace*" later on he performed in New York with the bands Sakad and Klinik. In 2001 he released a solo album with some old hits songs.

Albin, Wilson - Bass
Wilson played with Meridional des Cayes.

Alcé, Daniel - Saxophone
In Haiti, Daniel played with Les Diables Bleus du Cap Haitien.
In New York he became the leader of the band Les Astros after the departure of the drummer Arsene Appolon.

Alciné, Frantz (Fanfan Epav) Singer
Musician of the band Gabel

Alcindor, Antoine - Drum
Antoine played with Latino, a Haitian band based in New York City in the 1970s.

Alcindor, Jean - Piano
Just like Cubano and Shoubou Jean Alcindor is a product of Port de Paix. His best years in the Konpa world were with Skah Shah in the 1980s. He excelled in songs like: *This Is It, America* and the song *Forever # 1*. He also participated in the Fred Paul Mini All Stars project, "The 15 Best Golden of Nemours Jean Baptiste".

Alcindor, Rodrigue - Keyboard

Alexandre, Alain - Guitar

Alexandre, Harry - Conga

Alexandre, Jackson - Conga

Alexandre, Martine - Singer

Alexandre, Stephane - Singer

Alexis, Antoine * - Singer
Antoine Alexis had his best years with Les Pachas du Canapé Vert in the Mini Jazz era.
After a long period away from the musical arena, he reappeared in the Washington D.C. area in 1982 with the band Les Pachas de Washington, a band created by Richard Baltazar, the bassist and leader of the popular Pachas du Canapé Vert, in the early 80s with some ex-musicians of the Washington D.C. based band Choc Combo. Antoine, who died in Maryland in the 1980s, is remembered for his performance on the hit song 'La Messe sou Boulevard" by Les Pachas du Canapé Vert.

Alexis, Jean Dieuseul - singer

Alez - Band
In the summer of 2007 the band System Band was getting ready to go on a tour in Haiti when four musicians including one of the singers Dabenz Chéry decided that they will not travel until they can settle their differences with the band's management. When a solution couldn't be reached the musicians moved on by creating the band Alez with the help of the singer/drummer Michel Blaise who had left System a year earlier.

Ali, Daroud Salim - Guitar
Daroud is better known for his contribution to the band Delta Force.

Alliance, Casimir - Singer
Casimir is a singer who will put on a good show regardless of the number of people in the audience. One of the first singers of Channel 10, Casimir had his best years when he joined Les Frères Dejean in the 1980s.

Alien, Michael - Guitar

Almatas, Jean Marie (Pokito) - Bass
Pokito replaced the bassist Mario Germain in Gemini of Ti Manno. He later performed with Magnum band. He is today a freelance musician.

Almeus, Fritz - Bass

Almeus, Jocel - Keyboard
Jocel is a music composer, arranger and producer. His recording studio in New York is one of the most used by musicians working in the Haitian diaspora.

Alnatas, Wilfred - Trombone

Alouchesse - Band
This band came out in the neighborhood of Fontamara in the mid 70s with the voice of Raymond Cajuste on lead. The band didn't last long, unfortunately, as Raymond moved on with his life and found fame with the popular band Bossa Combo.

Alouidor, Elliot - Singer

Alphonse, Lesly - Bass

Alphonse, Yves – Bass
Yves did his best recording with Jacques Sauveur Jean in the album 'Kriye Chante'.

Althema, Andy -Trumpet
Andy played with Septentrional du Cap.

Althema, Miloux - Drum
Miloux had his best years with Missile 727 in the early 1990s.

Althenor, Rigord – Bass
Rigord played in New York with System Band, he was among the musicians who left System in the summer of 2007 to create the band Alez. In April 2008, Rigord moved to Florida to join the band 5 Etoiles.

Althenor, Rony - Conga

Althéon Yvon - Producer /Promoter /Videographer

Yvon started his career as a show promoter, and a T.V show producer in Boston. He moved on to the production and the selling of Haitian videos and soon after, he became known in the Haitian community as "Yvon Video". Later he became one of the greatest Haitian movie distributors via his company Télé Diaspora.

Altidor Garry - Promoter/Producer

Altine, Eddy - Guitar
Eddy was the popular rhythm guitar player of Les Shleu Shleu in the early days of the Mini Jazz era.

Altino, John Jube (Papa Jube) - Guitar / Bass / Keyboard / Singer/Producer
Papa Jube played mostly in the New York City area. At one time he was the manager of Haitian superstar Emeline Michel. In the early 1990s Papa Jube played Konpa often mix with the Ragga style. He became the manager and booking agent of the popular New York City club SOB's and with his busy schedule, he stop performing live, but is helping many artists as a music producer and mentor.

Alvarez, Jose Perez - Singer
Best years with D.P. Express in the 1980s. He has the ability to sing in French, Créole and Spanish very well. In 1985, Alvarez moved to Maryland with the squad from D.P. Express that created the band G.P. Express in Washington D.C. however, he moved to New York after a very short stay in the D.C. area. He also joined System Band for a short period before leaving the music business.

Ambassadeurs (Les Ambassadeurs) - Band

Ambassadeurs was one of the most recognized bands of the Mini Jazz era. Compared to Fantaisites, Shleu Shleu and the others, Ambassadeurs had more people in their lineup because they had three singers and an organ player. The band started in the town of Port de Paix under the name Fontana. When the Menelas brothers moved to Port-au Prince they changed the name of the band to Les Frères Ménélas, and soon after to Les Ambassadeurs, on July 23, 1966.

Their music was well written, the lyrics made sense and they used to sing more love songs (Bolero) than the other groups of their generation.
The style of Ambassadeurs was adopted by Les Loups Noirs and Les Lionceaux des Cayes. After their first tour in America, the airport in Port au Prince was crowded with fans waiting to see the superstars getting off the airplane. Musicians like Ricardo Frank alias Ti Plume (guitar), Pascal Albert and Essud Fung Cap (singers) Reynold Menelas (sax) were the sensation of the time. Songs like *Fini, 7em Flotte, Bobine, and Romeo & Juliette* remain as enjoyable today as they were in the 1970s.

Ambians - Band

Ambroise, Alix - Saxophone

Ambroise, Jacky - Singer / Guitar
Jacky played in Haiti with a few bands in his early career including Bossa Combo. As Haitian music was taking a turn with the digital movement, Jacky Ambroise, who was living in New York in early 1990s, started a program in a Long Island bistro and called himself "Jamming Jacky". With only his guitar and a sound man (Gary Mauzoul) Jacky rocked the place weekend after weekend in a one man show. Soon after, he went back to Haiti and came out with an album with the song *"Ti Dous"*. After a period of silence and non performance except some shy apparitions with some carnival songs, he created in 1996 the band "Strings" a group composed of guitarists and percussionists. With the guitarists Ralph Blanchard, Philippe Augustin and the drummer Joel Widmaier working under the leadership of Jacky, Strings became an overnight success, traveling outside of Haiti, entertaining Haitians and non-Haitian equally. It's amazing that stardom was awaiting Jacky in a

style that is completely new to Haitians, after trying so many avenues over the years.

Ambroise, Rony - Guitar
Rony played with Gypsies de Queens and the band Wanga Negess. Later in his life he left New York and moved to Los Angeles, where he was still performing.

Ambroise, Wilkens - Singer

Améde, Momo - Singer-
He was the singer of the popular Mini Jazz Super Soline, prior to Super Soline he played with Les Vautours, which became Samba Jazz.

Anatal, Daniel - Singer

Andal, Patrick - Singer
Patrick played with the new generation style band Skandal in the 1980s.

Anderson, Brégard - Radio Personality
Popular radio announcer and host of the show "Canal Musical" on Radio Caraïbes FM or www.caraibesfm.com

Anderson, Prosper - Singer / Guitar

André, Georges Osse - Keyboard
Osse is one of the musicians of the Mini Jazz era. He was the first keyboardist of the band Les Ambassadeurs. He didn't last long with the band and was replaced by André Bellegarde (Dedy).

André, Herlex - Keyboard

André, Raymond - Drum
Raymond played with Les Legendaires de Delmas in the 1960s. He was replaced by Yves Arsene Apollon. He later performed in Canada with the band Tchaka.

André, Rodrigue - Singer
Rodrigue played with Septentrional.

André, Yvon (Kapi) - Gong / Singer / Keyboard
Kapi is one of the original musicians of Tabou Combo, the most popular Haitian band. He acquired the name Kapi because his father was a captain of

the Haitian army. Kapi, for his entire musical career, only played with Tabou Combo. He also has produced a couple of solo projects. He is also a mentor and producer to other artists.

It was in 1968 when then 15 year-old percussionist Yvon Andre, known to all as Kapi, became a member of Tabou Combo. Back then the young musician had to sneak out of his family's home in Petion-Ville to play with the band due to the fact that his parents were determined not to let their son become a musician. However, his love for music was too strong to be stopped. Kapi said he could have become anything, but he chose to be a musician because he loves music. It is that love that has motivated him to stay with Tabou Combo for so many years. Kapi is not just a percussionist; he's also a pianist, vocalist and songwriter. Kapi has penned many of Tabou's hit songs. He has also written most of the band's Spanish songs including Fiesta and Panama Querida. The latter he co-wrote with Fanfan. Kapi was discovered by Albert Chancy, the band's founder, while he was playing the drums with a local band named Les Diplomates de Petion-Ville. Albert saw an already accomplished musician, who would fit quite well with Tabou Combo, so he invited him to join the band. Kapi said his most memorable moments as a member of Tabou were in 1998 when he traveled to the Ivory Coast to receive a lifetime achievement award on behalf of Tabou Combo, and again when RFO (French radio/television) honored Tabou Combo in Martinique. Those, he said, were historical moments.
Part of this bio is from: www.taboucombo.com

Andrévil, Danilo -Trumpet
Danilo played with Septentrional.

Angibeau, Eric - Saxophone.
Eric played in Washington D.C. with the band Washington Express in the 1980s.

Animateurs (Les Animateurs) - Band
Animateurs was one of the Mini Jazz groups that didn't have a long journey. Based in Carrefour, the 1970s band didn't get the support of the Carrefour population like Fantaisistes of the 1960"s. Although Animateurs music had nothing to envy in the other 1970s bands, they simply didn't get enough airtime to be recognized by the Konpa mania. Animateurs' song *"Ti Machine"* is one of their best. They are the band that came with the 70s slogan *"Ou la la"*.

Anjou, Raphael - Singer
Raphael played with Septentrional for only a short period.

Anselme, Endrick - Gong

Anselme, Marie Aurel - Singer

Anson, Patrick - Producer
Patrick Anson is known as one of the first Konpa record producers.

Anson Records
Haitian owned record company.

Ansona Record
Haitian owned record company.

Antidote - Band
Konpa band based in Montreal Canada

Antilles Mizik
Haitian owned and managed record production and distribution company.
Antilles Mizik is one of the top Haitian record producers since the early 90s.

Antoine, Felder - Bass
Although the best years of this talented bass player are still ahead of him, he had some successful live and studio recording at first with the band D-zine and later with Nu Look.

Antoine, Frantz - Bass
Frantz is one of the first bassists of the 1960s Mini Jazz movement. He played with Pachou Combo, and later he joined Les Shleu Shleu.

Antoine, Joanne - Singer

Antoine, Mitag - Congas

Antoine, Patrick - Trombone

Antoine, Roselin - Keyboard
Roselin played with Septentrional.

Antoine, Serge - Gong
Serge played with Shupa Shupa in the Mini Jazz era.

Antoine, Yvon - Bass
Yvon was the notable bass player of Shupa Shupa during the Mini Jazz era.

Apocalypse – Band
This band was created by guitarist Evens Ignace (Penm) after he left D.P. Express.

Appolon, Yves Arsene - Drum/Guitar
Arsene started his musical career in his native Port-au-Prince at an early age. As an adolescent, he was seen playing the drum on the float of the 1960s top carnival band Cadence Rampas. He soon became the most in-demand drummer of his generation, playing at first with Les Legendaires de Delmas and later with Les Loups Noirs before becoming the star drummer and composer of the second version of Dada Djacaman's band Les Shleu Shleu. He filled the position left by the popular Smith Jean Baptiste of the first version. Other members of the second squad include the saxophonist Loubert Chancy, the guitarists/cousins Mario Mayala, and Jhonny Frantz Toussaint (Ti Frè) as well as the singers Jean Elie Telfort (Cubano) and Jean Michel St Victor (Zouzoule). In 1974, it was that same squad that became Skah Shah # 1 of New York. With the creation of Skah Shah, Arsene proved to be not only a great drummer, but also a great Konpa composer with super hits like: *Haiti, Le Jour, and Regret* among others. After many years of power struggle with his colleagues he left Skah Shah to create his own band "A.A Express". The initials A.A stand off course for his name Arsène Appolon. The band that later became known as Astros. Arsène later left his own band to rejoin Skah Shah for a short while. He left New York and went back to Haiti where he created the band Skah Shah #1 Plus which did not have the success of the New York based band Skah Shah #1. Back in New York in the 1990s Arsène tried diligently to have his own Shah Shah in New York. Recently he has worked with several French Caribbean stars on other projects. He also works with Skah Shah upon his availability.

Appolon, Patrick - Drum
Patrick followed the footsteps of his older brother Arsene by becoming another great Haitian drummer in 1980s. He played with Shoogar Combo and later with Scorpio in Haiti. He reached his stardom when he became an active member of Zin a popular New York based band. Patrick has managed to come out with an album in duo with his fellow Zin member, the percussionist Romeo Volcy.

Arman, Camille - Congas
Although Camille was not one of the founding members of Skah shah, one can

say that he has been the most loyal member of the band. Since he joined the band, he had the most perfect attendance. You wouldn't see a Skah Shah show without Camille Arman. When the band split, and members were taking sides, he continued to perform alongside the singer Cubano. Many artists performing in the New York City area have solicited Camille's talent in their albums. Camille moved to Florida, where he is working as a freelancer and mostly performing and traveling with Magnum band.

Arnauld, Gertho - Bass
Gertho became popular in the field in the 1980s playing with the band Shoogar Combo.He was among the members of the group who collaborated with the drummer Yves Arsène Appolon in the formation of the band Skah Shah #1 d'Haiti. In the 1990s he became the bassist of the New York based band Gran Pan Pan.

As (Les As de Pétion Ville) - Band
Band of the Mini Jazz era created in 1963.
In the early 1980s a collaboration of popular Konpa artists of the town of Pétion-Ville also came out with a record under the name Les As de Pétion Ville.

As (Les As de la K-Dans) - Band
This band came out at the turn of the century, their album *Mizik* was released in 2001.

Ascendas - Band
That band was based in Cap Haitien.

As Nash (Les As Nash de Turgeau) - Band
This band came out in 1974, in the neighborhood of Turgeau in Port-au-Prince. One of their songs was used as the theme song for a popular radio show on Radio Haiti by the comedian Fritz Polynice, also known as Fito Popo. Many can remember the catchy phrase *"Eské nou paré - Wi Nou Paré"* every weeknight on Radio Haiti in the late 70s. Some people used to write the name of the band as Les Asnashes de Turgeau, but the proper spelling is "As Nash".

Astros
This band was created by the drummer Arsène Appolon, first under the name A.A Express, which was later changed to Astros. When Arsène left the band, the saxophonist Daniel Alcé (Ti Sax) became the band leader. Well-known musicians like the singers Antoine Rossini Jean Baptiste (Ti Manno), Ernst Letemps, the percussionist Fritz Frederique (Ti Mitou), and the guitarist

Ronald Smith were all part of Astros.

The song *Bingo* remains, even today, the greatest hit of Astros. Ti Manno added part of the song to the famous medley *Ensem Ensem* which he did with D.P. Express in the early 1980s. It is important to note that in the original version it was the singer Ernst Letemps who sang *Bingo* in Astros, and not Ti Manno.

Athis, Lemerque - Keyboard

Atho, Jean Baptiste - Saxophone
Jean Baptiste played tenor sax for the band Jazz Capois.

Atkins, André -Trombone
André plays different types of music including Pop, R& B, Soul, Blues, Funk, Jazz, Classical, and Caribbean. He has played with the likes of David Linx, Aretha Franklin, George Benson, Luther Vandross, Magnum Band, Phantom, Soulive, Groove Collective, Dizzy Gillespie, Wynton Marsalis, Roy Hargrove, David Murray, Seattle Youth and Senior Symphony, Seiji Osawa, Yo Yo Ma, and many more.
Bio based from info on www.taboucombo.com

Atomik Konpa - Band

Attilus, Herald - Congas

Aubin, Fritz Gerald - Guitar
Fritz is a very talented guitarist living in the Washington D.C. area.

Aubourg, Louis Carmel - Keyboard

Audain, Patrick - Keyboard

Audatte, Géhu - Guitar
Gehu played with Safari Combo, which later became Super 9.

Auguste, Bob - Bass
Bob played with Jazz Des Jeunes and Panorama Des Cayes.

Auguste, Eddy – Keyboard

Auguste, Emmanuel - Singer
Emmanuel did not play much Konpa during his time since he was a star

singer in the 1950s and 60s. He played with Jazz Des Jeunes. His voice was heard all over the country in songs like *Celina, San Manman, and 20 Juin 4 Avril.*

Auguste, Franky- Singer
Franky played for the band Les Beatniks de Queens in the Mini Jazz era.

Auguste, Gerard - Singer
Gérard played with Etoile Du Soir in the 1970s.

Augustin, Dieujuste - Drum
Dieujuste played with Panorama des Cayes.

Augustin, Joel – Keyboard

Augustin, Kelly - Saxophone
Kelly played with Panorama des Cayes.

Augustin, Marcel - Bass
He is the first bass player of the Konpa rhythm to play an electric bass guitar. Marcel, of course, played for the band Super Ensemble de Nemours Jean Baptiste.

Augustin, Philippe - Guitar
Musician of the band Strings, alongside Ralph Blanchard and the band leader Jacky Ambroise, he formed the trio that changed the world's perception about the ability of Haitian guitarists.

Austin, Ronald - Guitar

Avin, Frantz - Gong
It is at the house of this left-handed gonguist that "System Band" was created in the late 70s. Fanfan Avin was known in the business as "The Black Chinese" for his oriental look. He was, however, not the only gonguist with Chinese features. A man named Ludovic Savius (Chinois) who played for Channel 10 in Haiti in the 70s and later in New York with Les Shleu Shleu in the 1990s, also looks like a black Chinese.

Azerot, Nestor - Singer
Nestor is a French Caribbean star singer of the 1980s who has lived in Haiti for many years and has performed with the Magnum band.

B

B - Tops - Band
This group was created by popular singer/guitarist Ricardo Frank (Ti Plume) after he left the band Les Ambassadeurs.

Babillards (Les Babillards) - Band
Mini Jazz created in 1973.

Baby, Eddy - Guitar
Eddy played for the band Les Beatniks de Queens in the Mini Jazz era.

Baby Jazz - Band
Band of the Mini Jazz era based in Pétion -Ville.

Back Up - Band
Konpa band based in Haiti

Badette, Jean - Singer

Badette, Maxon (Max Badette) - Singer
Born in Cayes, Max started is musical career as one of the singers of Les Lionceaux des Cayes. He joined Les Gypsies de Pétion -Ville in 1972 when Bob Neff, the singer of the band, did not return to Haiti from a U.S. tour.
In the early to mid-70s he sung super hits like: *LaTulipe, Reproche and Patience*. In the late 70s he moved to New York where he played with Djet X. There, he sung many hits like "Love *to love you baby, Nostalgie, Rossignol* among others". In 2003 he released his solo album "*Sweet Boleros*".

Bailly, Gilbert - Singer

Balan, Gerald - Guitar
This calm and excellent guitarist participates in several Haitian music projects in New York. Well-known for the song *Ti pa ti pa* of the band Suspense, Balan also played with Lakol and other bands on live performances as a freelance guitarist. In 2006, he joined Jean Max Valcourt and Armstrong Jeune in the creation of the New York-based band DoLa.

Baltazar, Jean Robert (Bob) - Promoter
In 1985 the promoter Bob Baltazar moved eight musicians of the band D.P.

Express to Laurel MD a suburb of Washington, D.C. and created the band G.P. Express.

Baltazar, Richard - Bass
Richard was the bassist and band leader of Les Pachas du Canapé Vert in the Mini Jazz era. He left Haiti to study in Venezuela, and after his studies he moved to the U.S. to the state of Maryland, where he is working as a specialist in different hospital's radiology department. In the 1980s he tried diligently to bring back to life the Pachas project in Maryland with veteran singer, the late Antoine Alexis and some former members of the band as well as some local talents like the singer Jean Claude Vivens.
In the 1990s Richard was known in the business as one of the best sound engineers. He used to travel with his sound system to mix bands in almost every city on the East Coast corridor. Unfortunately, his truck, loaded with musical instruments, was stolen from the parking lot of a Philadelphia hotel where he was resting after a show.

Banges (Les Banges) - Band
This band came out in 1972, in the Mini Jazz era. It is the band that helped discover the talent of the singer Assade Francoeur.

Baptiste, Georges - Gong

Baptiste, Idomène - Trumpet
Idomène played with Jazz Capois.

Baptiste, Jacques Yves - Gong
Jacques played with Les Shleu Shleu.

Baptiste, Jean Robert - Singer
Jean Robert played with Samba Creole and Panorama des Cayes.

Baptiste, Loubert - Guitar
Musician of Tropicana

Baptiste Willy - Bass
Willy played with the band Washington Express in the 1980s.

Barbot, Jacques - Congas
Jacques is a member of Zin.

Barbot, Myriam - Singer

Barbot, Richard - Bass
Richard played with Zèklè and Caribbean Sextet.

Barnave, Carl - Trumpet
Carl played with Djet - X.

Baron, Mario - Gong
Mario played with Shupa Shupa in the Mini Jazz era.

Barrateau, Destinoble * - Saxophone
One of the great Haitian saxophonists of all time, Destinoble was born in 1915 in Cayes where he learned to master the instrument. He was first the band leader of Meridional des Cayes and later the band leader of Panorama des Cayes. He continued to play in his old age especially on special occasions in and out of Haiti, until his death on March 31, 2001 in Cayes.

Barthelemy, Champy - Guitar

Barthelemy, Cyrus – Gong

Basekompa.com
Basekompa is a popular online magazine where Konpa fans discuss issues regarding Konpa music on a daily basis. It reports Konpa news 24/7 on the website forum "Music/H.M.I news" as it happens. It is owned by radio personality Jean Berdy Pierre Louis.

Bastien, Lucien - Keyboard
Lucien played most of his musical career with Shoogar Combo. He was also one of the Shoogar members who helped Arsene Apollon in the creation of Skah Shah d'Haiti.

Bastien, Réginald (Ti Régi) – Keyboard
Ti Régi revolutionized the music of Djakout Mizik at the turn of the century, as he used the guitar sound directly from the keyboard and took charge of the band's most solo part. That formula has been used ever since by many other Konpa bands. The formula is called the Keytar among Haitian musicians. Ti Régi is also the musician in charge of sequencing the songs of Djakout Mizik. He is one of their top songwriters and hit makers.

Batista, Michel - Singer
This Haitian/Dominican singer took the Konpa world by storm with his ever

strong voice. His best moment was in the 1980s with the band Superstars. With that group he sings super hits like *"La Familia"* (not the 2001 hit music of Djakout music) and *"Alpha"*.

When the band was dismantled in Haiti, Batista joined his band leader Adolphe Chancy in New York where they reappeared under the name Superstars of New York. The band later moved to Miami. Batista returned to Haiti, where he also had some great moments with the band Digital Express in the 1990s

Bautrau, Jean Carol - Drum/Singer
He was the drummer of Les Loups Noirs in the Mini Jazz era. He later moved to New York, where he performed with gospel bands, He also has a few solo albums under his belt as a singer. He was, in the 1980s the singer/drummer and composer of the Brooklyn based band "Gospel Force".

Bayard, Kiki - Guitar

Bayard, Pierre Richard (Pépé Bayard) - Piano /Accordion
Pépé is one of the pioneers of Haitian musicians performing in New York. With his band "Pépé Bayard and His Orchestra", many Haitian artists including Gary French were able to showcase their talent in the Big Apple. As a businessman Pépé Bayard also introduced the Cuban style shirt (Guayabera) in Haiti with the imprint Pépé Bayard on the shirts.

Bazelais, Casseus -Trombone

Bazile, Chrisostome (Chris) - Singer
Chris gave the people of Boston a complete revival by filling the missing space left by Antoine Rossini Jean Baptiste (Ti Manno). Just when the people were worried that the Konpa was going to die in Boston, Chris came with his great tenor voice in the band Afro Combo de Boston. His best hit at the time was the song *"Requin"*. Chris later joined the band Volo Volo de Boston.

The following is a bio of Chris Bazile as it appeared on Haitinetradio.com in May 2007.It was written by Paul Henegan aka Léon Azul.
Courtesy of Paul Henegan

Chris Bazile was born in 1953 in Petion-ville, Haiti, and spent his school years there. He early on distinguished himself as a singer in the choir that regularly performed at Eglise St Pierre. At this time, Chris became friends with many of the musicians of the era, in particular Les Frères Dejean and Isnard Douby. Other influences from that time include jazz singers such as Nat Cole, Johnny Hartman, and Tony Bennet, as well as popular Haitian artists of the time, such as Tabou Combo, Roger Colas, Gerard Dupervil, and of course Guy Durosier. While his family was supportive of his appreciation of music and the arts in general--they were, after all, frequent visitors to the Dejean household the typical admonitions against adopting music as a full time profession applied. This was to change rather abruptly in 1973 when Chris visited his sister in Boston. Instead of going directly from the airport to her house, they went out to dinner at a nightclub where Volo Volo was performing that evening. Among other people at the club was one of Chris' former teachers from high school, who just happened to be playing drums in a newly-formed Afro-Combo de Boston. Chris was recruited on the spot, attended a rehearsal with them the next afternoon, and was immediately instated as the lead singer for Afro Combo de Boston.

Afro Combo de Boston continued to grow both musically and in popularity, resulting in the release in 1976 of Stylistique, Page 1. Besides receiving critical acclaim in its day, this recording has never been "out of print", and has become arguably one of the best selling Haitian recordings of all time.

There was never to be a Page 2. By 1978, three of members had relocated to other cities in pursuit of other opportunities. Chris and several other former members of Afro Combo de Boston became successfully assimilated into Volo Volo. They continued to perform and release significant recordings well into the 1990s.

Bazile, Felix - Flute / Baritone Saxophone

Bazile, Jean Eddy - Promoter

Bazile, Michel Ange - Songwriter
His best Konpa hit is *Cézar*, a song that he wrote for System Band.

Bazile, Pierre - Bass

Bazilik - Band
This band came out under the leadership of the trumpetist Eddy Brisseau.

Bazilik Kréyòl - Band
Konpa band based in Haiti

Bazouka - Band
Bazouka was created in New York in the 1990s by a few musicians that left Skah Shah. With Jean Michel St Victor (Zouzoule) on lead vocal, the band played mostly the old hit songs of Skah Shah. Unfortunately, Bazouka only lasted for a couple of years, as they were not able to create a hit music of their own.

Bazz see: Laurore, Edzer

Beatniks de Queens - Band
This band came out in the 70s in Queens, N.Y.

Beaulieu, Jacky - Congas
Jacky played with Djet X in the 1970s.

Beauvais, Léon - Congas
Léon had his best years with Shoogar Combo in the 1980s. He is one of the few percussionists who had the ability to play Konpa with three congas. He was also one of the members that left Shoogar Combo to join Arsene Apollon in the creation of the band Skah Shah #1 plus.

Beauvil, Liza Williams - Singer
Born in the town of Port de Paix, Liza's best song remains *"Siw té connen"*. She is mostly known to the New York City Haitian community.

Bel Jazz - Band
During the summer 2007 tour of the band Hangout in Haiti the lead singer Eders Stanis (Pipo) decided to leave the band. Upon his return to the U.S. he came out with his own band Bel Jazz, and on Nov. 22 the band released their first single entitle *"La Femme De Mon Patron."*

Bélizaire Arkinson (Zagalo) - Radio/T.V Personality

Bélizaire, Clement (Kéké) - Guitare / Bass / Keyboard
Next to Fabrice Rouzier, Kéké Belizaire is credited for his contribution to the success of Mizik Mizik and the reincarnation of the twoubadou style in the music industry. Music lovers will forever cherish the sound of his guitar in songs like *Blackout, 4 kanpé,* and the 2003 carnival of Mizik Mizik.

Bélizaire, Jean Délouis - guitar
Délouis played with Scorpio.

Bélizaire, Leniel -Trombone
Leniel played with Les Loups Noirs.

Bellande, Jacques - Singer
Jacques played with Blousons Noirs in the Mini Jazz era.

Bellegarde, André (Dedy) - Keyboard
Star keyboardist of the 60s and 70s, Dedy played with the band Les
Ambassadeurs.

Bellegarde, Serge - Keyboard
Younger brother of Dedy, Serge played in the Washington D.C. area with
Masterful Band.

Belliard, Brave *- Saxophone
Brave played with the band Jazz Capois. He died at a young age in a boat
accident after a show.

Bélo see: Belony, Jean Murat

Bélony, Jean Murat (Bélo) - Singer
This artist was discovered by the producer Fabrice Rouzier. In 2007 Bélo won
the first place of the Radio France Inter organized in Cameroon Africa. His
album Lakou Trankil, based mostly on Reggae beat, became an automatic best
seller.

Belot, Almajik - Bass
Almajik played with Combite Creole in Haiti. For the past decades he has been
living in New Jersey with his wife and his two daughters. His brother Marc
Orel Belot is one great guitar player who never played with any band. His
nieces, Emmeline and Edeline Belot (twin daughters of Marc Orel) had a brief
appearance in the business with the band Maniak in Brooklyn.

Belot, Edeline - Singer
Edeline played with the New York based band Maniak in the early 90s next to
her twin sister Emmeline. In 2002, Edeline left New York and moved to
Maryland with her sister.

Belot, Emmeline - Singer
Emmeline played with the New York based band Maniak in the early 90s next
to her twin sister Edeline before moving to Maryland in 1994.

Bénito d'Haiti See: Philogène Bénito

Bénito, Raphael - Singer
He played with the band Etoile Du Soir alongside his friend Momo. Benito also had a great time with Coupé Cloué in the group "Trio Select".

Benjamin, Ernst - Bass
Ernst is the bassist of Zenglen.

Benjamin, Fresnel - Keyboard

Benjamin, Jean Lucien - Keyboard

Benjamin, Lyonel - Singer
Lyonel Benjamin only did a few Konpa songs. He is mostly famous for his solo albums, his Christmas songs and religious songs. He played with Caribbean Sextet and Les Frères Dejean during his Konpa career. His other contribution to the industry is his beautiful and powerful voice as a Konpa show broadcaster, especially in the radio Metropole show *Tam Tam 129* in the 1970s. Today Lyonel Benjamin is known as an actor playing in movies like *Cicatrices 2* and *Le Miracle De La Foie* among others. Lyonel Benjamin is the father of Michael Benjamin singer of the band Krézi.

Benjamin, Michael - Singer
Michael Benjamin is the son of Lyonel Benjamin. He is best known for the song "Ou Pati". In 2005 Michael became the lead singer of the band Krézi.

Benjamin, Michelot - Singer
Michelot was the original singer of the band Los Incognitos, which later became Tabou Combo.

Benjamin, Réginald - Guitar
In Haiti, Réginald played for an underground Mini Jazz band named Afro Combo before becoming full time musician of Les Frères Dejean. He played in New York with the Déjean brothers in the mid 70s. During a tour, some members of the band were arrested at the U.S./Canada border due to the expiration of their visas. The band went to Haiti, but several musicians could not return to the U.S. after the tour. Réginald was among those who returned to start System Band with some Déjean members like Ernst Vincent, Isnard Douby and Harold Joseph.
Réginald who learned some of his techniques from the late guitarist Ti Polis

has electrified the Konpa world over the years with his style and innovative sound with the assistance of Ronald Smith, who has played with him for more than two decades. Réginald Benjamin has developed a style that is today imitated by many Konpa guitarists. He is the maker of many hits songs including the unforgettable *Anita*.

Benoit, Glenny - Guitar
Glenny was the band leader and guitarist K-Dans. He later moved to the U.S. where he joined his former K-Dans members in the band Carimi.

Benoit, Joel - Singer
Played with Les Loups noirs in the 1970s

Bernadin, Jacques - Saxophone

Bernard, Jean - Keyboard

Bernard, Robert Cenatus (Bono) - Singer

Bernard, Serge (Ti Aigle) - Congas
Ti Aigle played with Coupé Cloué most of his career. He and the late bongo player Jean Pierre Pétion were the two men who conducted with great chemistry the unique style of the Compas Manba of the band Ensemble Select de Coupé Cloué. That style is still today the choice of many Haitian musical groups.

Bertin, Jimmy - Drums
Jimmy played with Shupa Shupa in the early 70s.

Bertrant, Jean Georges - Keyboard

Besson, Byrneste (Youyou) - Guitar
Youyou was one of the original members of Les Fantaisistes de Carrefour, one of the pioneers of the Mini Jazz era.

Betiz - Band
This band is based in Atlanta, Georgia.

Bi-Tops - Band
This band was created by the guitarist Ricardo Frank (Ti Plume) after he left Les Ambassadeurs.

Bichote, Carmin - Saxophone
Carmin was one of the original members of Les Fantaisistes de Carrefour.
Carmin is one of the pioneers of the Mini Jazz era. He also played with Les
Morphees and Les Diplomates.

Bideau Victor (Vicky) - Singer

Bien - Aimé, Antonio - Gong

Bien - Aimé, Bob - Bass
Bob played in the Mini Jazz era with the band Les Manfoubens.

Bien - Aimé, Lubens - Bass
Lubens played with Super Soline, and later with Channel 10 in his early
career.

Bigaud, Martial - Congas
Martial Bigaud is a member of System Band.

Bilade, Jean Charles – Guitar

Bizi - Band
Konpa band based in New York

Bizou - Band

Black Alex see: Pierre James Alex

Black Parents – Band

This band came out in Montreal in the 1990s. They are for the most the children of the famous artists of the band Les Frères Parents, of the 70s and 80s. Black Parents really got some momentum with the song *Sensuel*. In 2005 they released the album *Obligé*.

Black Shu Shu - Band
Discography includes: *Christelle* and *Salutation*

Blagueur see: Lainé Joseph

Blain, Pierre - Singer
Born in Cuba, Pierre Blain is one of the pioneers of the Konpa music. He played with the band of Murat Pierre and with Jazz Des Jeunes before joining the band of Nemours Jean Baptiste. Pierre Blain was the first singer of Nemours' band with the nasal sound in his voice. Nemours always looked for singers with that nasal sound ever since. Pierre Blain reappeared in the Haitiando #3 record at the beginning of the century.

Blaise, Carlo - Guitar
Carlo played with the band Accolade de N.Y in the early 1980s.

Blaise, Michel - Singer
Michel played with many little groups as a drummer before joining Bazouka as a singer. He later joined System Band, where he excels not only as a drummer, and a gonguiste, but also as a singer. Blaise is also a composer. His solo album "*A l'aise comme Blaise*" is more than a testimony to his musical talent. His favorite color is obviously white, for he is known for wearing it all the time.

Blaise, William -Trumpet
William played with the band Norma de Léogane.

Blanc, Max - Drum

Blanchard, Ralph - Guitar
Ralph is one of the original member of the group Strings alongside Philippe Augustin and Jacky Ambroise.

Blanchard, Yves Andre - Congas

Bléus, Hervé (Boulou) - Singer
This singer captivated the Konpa mania as the first singer of D.P. Express in the mid 70s. Soon after Ti Manno joined the band, Boulo moved to New York, where he performed on Loubert Chancy's solo album. He retired from the Konpa world at a very young age. Many will always remember the voice of Boulo in songs like *Libèté, Grand vent, Zèl Sapate* etc...

Block, Daniel - Saxophone
Daniel is a non-Haitian musician who has played Konpa music with several Haitian bands in Haiti and in the Haitian diaspora.

Blousons Noirs - Band
Band of the Mini Jazz era, created in the mid 1960s.

Blousons Verts - Band
Band of the Mini Jazz era, created in the early 1970s.

Boirond, Joseph - Singer
Joseph played with Les Frères Déjean in the 1980s.

Bonheur, Fritz - Gong / Congas / Sound Engineer
Fritz played with System Band as well as Zin as a back up percussionist, and also as a sound engineer for those bands. For many years now, he has been the sound engineer of the band T. Vice. He is a well-known personality in the Haitian music world.

Bonne Année, Wilfrid - Bass

Bonnet, Stephania - Singer

Bono see: Bernard, Robert Cenatus

Boron, Ali - Saxophone
Ali played with Latino in the 1970s.

Boulou see: Bléus Hervé

Boura, Taniah Guerin - Singer

Bourjolly, Eddy - Guitar

Bossa Combo - Band

On Aug. 15, 1968, in the neighborhood of Wahney, in the locality of Carrefour, a group of young men put together a new Mini Jazz under the leadership of their congas player, Max Lévy aka Totòs. That new band was baptized under the name Bossa Combo. At that time, an employee of the National Palace name Lemaire asked Jean Claude Duvalier the son of then-president François (Papa Doc) Duvalier for his used instruments, which were given to the new band. Soon after, the band started to get notice due to some very good songs like *Hugette, and Vacances*. Because the band was using the instruments that came from the national palace and because of their relation with Lemaire, many macoutes as well as the National Palace employees made Bossa their band of choice as the word got out that the son of the president was happy that the band he supplied with musical instruments was doing well. As soon as the band started to gain some success, a macoute named Olaf and a soldier of the presidential security unit name Romulus became instant supervisors of the musicians and called the shots. Many of the original members like the singer Raymond Cajuste (who would return to the band later), the drummer Almando Keslin, the congas player Totòs, the bassist Ernst (Nènè) Volcy, the saxophonist Emmanuel Figaro and some others were all replaced by some new musicians in the early 1970s. The new squad consisted of musicians like the saxophonist Jean Robert Damas, the gonguist Jean Michel Ulcena, the guitarist Bertholini Jean François (Berto) the bassist Claude Desgrottes from a band from the Place St Anne neighborhood called Latino d'Haiti, as well as some other talented musicians like the singers Fritz Coq and Jean Claude Dorsainvil (Charlie), the latter left medical school to become a full-time musician of the elite band. Also were added the drummer Harry Sylvain (Tico), and a macoute/musician, Alfred Michel, who was named as the new band leader ironically. When Jean Claude Duvalier became president in 1971, Bossa Combo played at most of the government organized parties and also received new musical instruments upon request. Thus, the band became known to the public in general as President (Baby Doc) Jean Claude Duvalier's band.

With the hit song *Bossu,* most people started to believe that the musicians, despite their privilege, did indeed have some talent. By the mid 70s Bossa Combo proved that they could be a first division Konpa competitor with the hit song *Te Quero.* As many bands were adding a full horn section, Bossa added the saxophonist/trombonist Jules Pagié and Manes Dérices on trumpet as a support to saxophonist Jean Robert Damas.

With this new lineup and the reintegration of the singer Raymond Cajuste, as well the addition of newcomers like Frantz Joseph (Fanfan Kè Kal) of Samba Créole on congas, and the replacement of Tico Sylvain (who moved to the U.S.) by Mario Volcy on drums, Bossa Combo, with a rhythm line well directed by its two original members, (the guitarist Rodrigue Toussaint and the keyboardist Adrien Jeanite) did a series of super Konpa hits. Those songs are today still the favorite songs of many people. Songs like *Permanente, Te Quiero, Chère Madame, Racine, Accolade,* and the carnival song *Correction Majeure* will never be forgotten.

Despite their popularity Bossa Combo was always afraid to perform in the Haitian diaspora, fearing that people would not welcome them as musicians, but as a product of the Duvalier regime. With the success of the album *Accolade* in the early 1980s, the band finally decided to tour the U.S. and as they predicted, many people took offense in their visit. Some of their shows were the subject of political demonstration and disorders like the incident at a Brooklyn nightclub called Coconut Grove.

A year after the tour the band went back to New York, but that time to record the album *Racines.* When a group of musicians choose to stay in New York, they created the band **Accolade de New York**, a name based on Bossa Combo's hit song *Accolade.*

Bossa Combo survived by recruiting new musicians like the singer the late Joel Théodore, the gonguist Louis Lafontant and the bassist Harold Mathieu. They added Bernard Dorsainvil and Renaud Casseus on saxophone as well as Phaton Jeune, who played both trumpet & trombone. The administration of the band now tried to have substitute musicians for almost every position. For instance, the drummer Mario de Volcy shared his stool with the drummer Jean

Claude Jules. With a roster of so many musicians, the band became known by 1983 as the Big Band Bossa. With hit makers Mario de Volcy, Raymond Cajuste as well as Frantz Joseph (Fanfan Kè Kal) from Samba Créole in the lineup, Bossa Combo came out with the album *Religion,* quickly followed by the album *Big Apple* and *A la Plage.*

After Jean Claude Duvalier left the country many musicians of Bossa moved to the U.S. In 1988 an attempt was made to recreate the band in New York and in Miami, but it was in vain because time had changed and so did the public. In the 1990s some of Bossa Combo's musicians collaborated with some members of Accolade de New York and created the band BossAcolade. However, BossAccolade was unsuccessful and the musicians eventually scattered here and there around the world, with a few in Haiti and many in the Haitian diaspora working in other fields to support their families.

In Nov. 2007, after a decade of silence, Bossa Combo announced that they are back in business with most of the musicians of the 1980's.

The discography of Bossa Combo includes but is not limited to the following albums: *Haiti Que J'aime* which was released in 1969 *De port Au Prince A Acapulco* released in 1970 followed by many albums like *Te Quero ,Bossa De Haiti ,Ague Taroyo , Accolade ,Racine, Lessentiel, Ambiance D'été, Premiere Communion,Chalpapa ,Fanm Sa, Religion,Konpa Kè Kal,Haiti, In The Big Apple,Deuxieme Independence,Haiti Eté 91, Arrosoire,Big Band Original* and some live and compilation CDs The band also did some albums backing up other artists in their solo projects, like the singer Guy Durosier, and their drummer Mario de Volcy.

Bossa Combo is

BossAccolade - Band

This band came out in New York in the 1990s with a combination of some former musicians of Bossa Combo and Accolade de New York trying to work out a collaboration which, unfortunately, didn't go as planned.

Boulou see: Bleus Hervé or Valcourt Henriot

Bouzi, Ulrick (Touco) - Drum / Producer

Touco started to play the drums at a very young age. He played in Haiti with a second version of Les Fantaisites de Carrefour. He then became a member of Shupa Shupa, Bossa Combo, and Les Alouchesses de Fontamara, respectively. In the mid- 1970s Touco replaced Arsene Apollon in Skah Shah #1 of New York. He distinguished himself in the album *Message,* which also includes the hit songs *Zanmi and Yahweh.* It was the first album of Skah Shah with trumpet, trombone, a sax tenor, and a keyboard. Unfortunately he was released by Skah Shah when Arsene the original drummer decided he wanted to return to his job. Soon after, Touco was called by the Déjean brothers to replace Ernst

Ramponeau.
He was the drummer of Les Frères Dejean when, for their visa status, some musicians couldn't return to the U.S. after the band was stopped at the Canadian border. Touco made the choice to stay in Haiti with les Frères Déjean. He played in Haiti for a few years with Les Frères Dejean before creating his own band, "Dixie Band".
Dixie Band was one of the bands that dominated the music scene in the mid 1980s especially during the carnival period. The band moved to Canada in the late 80s, lost momentum and finally broke up.
While residing in Canada, Touco became the producer of the album series "*Les Rois du Compas*", a project that includes other artists. With the Dixie Band, Touco had produced more that 20 albums. In 2005 he collaborated with the singer Carmelo Frederique (Freddy) in the band Top Vice.

Bovano, Bob – Guitar
If you like Rodrigue Milien and his Combite Creole, then you need to know that the man who was bringing you the sweetest guitar sound was none other than Bob Bovano.

Brasserie Créole
Haitian owned restaurant/nightclub in Queens N.Y.

Briet, Jean - Guitar
Jean played with La Ruche de Léogane.

Brifils, Henry (Henry de Brenfenchen) - Singer
Henry played with Les Gypsies de Queens.

Brisseau, Eddy - Trumpet
Eddy had his best years with Les Frères Dejean.
Eddy is known as one of the greatest Haitian trumpet players. His solo albums *Bazilik* are highly recommended. Eddy is now a music distributor and record store owner. He also sells CDs in his well-decorated and organized super mobile van.

Brouard, Angelau – Keyboard

Brown, Juliana - Singer
Juliana did background vocal for Les Beatniks de Queen in the Mini Jazz era

Bruce, André Robert - Saxophone

Brutus, Jean - Vocal

Brutus, Michelet - Singer
Michelet played with the band Missile 727. He moved on to be the lead vocalist after the departure of Joseph Dieudonné Larose.

Burr, Renaud (Freddy) - Gong

Butoix, Joseph - Saxophone

Button, Sharon -Vocal
Sharon played with Phantoms. Her best performance is in the song "*14 Février*". She also has a solo album titled "*Sharon's Best*".

Buzz - Band
This Konpa band was based in Montréal, Canada with Haitian and Canadian musicians.

C

Cabane Créole
Popular club in Port-au-Prince that has contributed to the success of the bands Combite Créole and Les Lionceaux des Cayes.

Cadence Rampas - Rhythm created by the legendary band leader and saxophonist Webert Sicot. The name Cadence Rampas is also used by many people to refer to Sicot's band Super Ensemble de Webert Sicot.

Cadet, Carlo - Guitar

Cadet, Dudley - Keyboard

Cadet, Frantz (Bab) - Singer
This singer is mostly known as the (maternal) brother of Shoubou, the famous singer of Tabou Combo. Bab was one of the first singers of Les Frères Déjean. He was, for a short while, a member of the early days of System Band in New York.

Cadet, Frontline (Lèlène) - Singer

Cadet, Loubert - Singer / Guitar

Cadet, Marcel - Conga / Drum
He started as the conga player in the Original Super Ensemble de Nemours Jean Baptiste, replacing Claudy Jean. Ti Marcel later improved from congas to drum replacing Ti Charles on the drum set.

Cadet, Rodly – Drum

Cadet Moïse – Bass
Moïse played for the band Les Beatniks de Queens in the Mini Jazz era.

Cadet, Victor – Bass

Cajou - Band

Cajuste, Clark - Keyboard / Singer

Son of Raymond Cajuste, his best song is "*I Promise*" with the band "Summer" in the year 2000. He joined the Florida based band Hangout in 2004. In September 2006, Clark left Hangout and moved on with his musical career.

Cajuste, Claude Jeffrard - Guitar

He was the first lead guitarist of Gemini All Stars de Ti Manno. Later, with his wife Sandra Jean, (one of the singers of the all female cast band "Riské"), Ti Claude came out with his own band, "Caress".

Cajuste, Pierre Nesly - Conga

Cajuste, Raymond - Singer

Raymond Cajuste is known as one of the best compas singers in the Haitian music industry. He sang many hits while playing for Bossa Combo, especially in the late 1970s and the early 1980s. Raymond was the star composer of the group, especially after most of his colleague left to create Accolade de New York.

Raymond could sing in Spanish as easy as he could sing in French and Creole. He can animate the public whether he is singing a slow song like *Caroline* or a hot hit like *Correction Majeure (Le majeur)*.

In the early days of Bossa Combo Raymond was not the band's star singer the spotlight was taken by the late Shubert Géhu. When some people close to President Jean Claude Duvalier took over the administration of the band, Raymond Cajuste was let go and Raymond moved on with his own band "Alouchesses" in his neighborhood of Fontamara.

Alouchesses didn't last long, as Raymond moved on to play with Les Difficiles de Petion-Ville next to the superstar and band leader Henry Célestin. There again, Raymond was playing in the shadow of a more popular artist.

However, the only sentence Raymond Cajuste was given by Henry to sing in Les Difficiles album, "*Enfant ne court pas si tu cours tu tombes si tu tombes tu pleures,si tu pleures je te bas,si je te bas je te bas fort*", was going to be one of the most catchy tunes of the Mini Jazz era. Raymond Cajuste became a household name in the country with a single part of a song. Soon after he was called back by Bossa Combo where he forever marked the Haitian music world with his unique and remarkable voice in hit songs like *Accolade, Johanne, Sempre En Domingo, Racines, Mission Impossible, Chère Madame* among others.

In the 1990s Raymond Cajuste moved to Florida, where he tried his best to bring back to life Bossa Combo as a top band in the Haitian diaspora. He even tried to collaborate with the musicians who left Haiti in the early 1980s to create the band Accolade de New York in the BossAccolade project in New

York in the mid 1990s. However, the market was going through some serious changes and producers and promoters were mostly interested in working with more stable bands like Tabou Combo & System Band, or with new and more in-demand bands and groups with fewer musicians. In other words with the reduced digital format like Sweet Micky, Top Vice and T. Vice, than dealing with reviving the Big Band Bossa with aging superstars.

Raymond Cajuste made several appearances as a guest artist on several albums and fund-raising concerts in the Diaspora while enjoying his retirement and finally accepted the fact that Bossa Combo is a band of the past. His son Clark Cajuste is an active musician in the Haitian music industry who has over the recent years played in New York with the band Summer and with the Miami based band Hangout.

Raymond Cajuste is living in the U.S. with his family. In 2007 he was invited by System Band to take part in the album *Nan Building Nan* where he delivered one line in the song *Homage à Ti Mitou*. Despite his old age, Raymond Cajuste showed to the world that he still has one of the best voices ever in the history of Konpa music. In November 2007 Bossa Combo announced that they are back in business with Raymond Cajuste as their lead singer.

Cajuste, Sheila - Singer

Cameau, Anderson -Trumpet
This Haitian musician can read and write music very well. He started at the St. Jean Bosco School in Haiti and later he was an active member of the fanfare of Lycée Pétion. At a young age, he became a member of the Conservatoire de Caserne Dessalines. Before Anderson left Haiti for French Guyana, he was seen playing the trumpet in different Compas band like "Cobra, Formule H, and Shoogar Combo".

He was the founder of the band 'Les Vautours" in Guyana. In the 1980s, after a few performances with System Band, he became an active member of Skah Shah. With Skah Shah, he remade some memorable albums like: *America, This is it*. His solo project "Kalalou" did not last too long, but had some wonderful songs. Anderson left the Konpa scene and moved on to playing Gospel music.

Cameau, Frantz - Drums

Cameau, Roland - Guitar
Roland played with "Lov" a New York-based band that did not last long in the 1990. Prior to "Lov" Roland also played with "Magnum Band".

Camille, Yves (Doudou) - Guitar
Doudou played with 'Super Soline, Les Fantaisistes d'Haiti and Samba Jazz.

One of the best of the 70s, Doudou is to many musicians a role model. If Nemours has invented the rhythm Compas Direct, Doudou is described by many as the man who invented what Haitians commonly called the "Siwèl". In Siwèl (see well) at one time while the music is playing the guitar or the keyboard take the lead with a solo (often with a pitch sound) that can make one extend both arms with pleasure. Siwèl is a rare small seasonal fruit found in Haiti, like mango it is green but turn yellow when it's ripe. It is considered by some people as a small plum. How, and who came up with the term Siwèl in the Haitian musical world still remains a mystery. It's often described by fellow musicians as music with no or little substance.

Camille, Yvon - Saxophone
Yvon played with "Les Vikings". He is one of the saxophonists that, once you hear the sound, you can automatically recognize the band and his signature.

Campagna, John - Saxophone

Candio, Jean Kenny - Drum

Cangé, Réginald - Singer
Réginald is one of the two singers who replaced Gracia Delva in Zenglen. In 2007 he created the band Fasil. Reginald Cangé is also an actor.

Cantave, Joubert - Congas

Cap All Stars - Band
This band came out in Cap Haitien in the 1980s under the direction of maestro Roselin Antoine who is a former keyboardist of Septentrional.

Captain Jean see: Provilus James

Caribbean Sextet - Band
When many of the musicians of the popular New York-based band Ibo Combo returned to Haiti in the mid-70s, they were scattered here and there doing their own things until a meeting was called by some members to put the band back together under a new name. The Caribbean Sextet was created in 1977. The singer Boulou Valcourt was already working at Télé Haiti doing his T.V show "Boulou show" and playing with the band "l'Horizon 75", when he was called to join the new band of his ex-partners of Ibo Combo the saxophonist Edgard Dépestre (Gaguy), the Keyboardist Réginald Polycard, and the drummer the late Jean Alix Laraque (Jean Jean).
Philippe Laraque (Toto Laraque), the younger brother of Jean Jean, became the

new guitarist of the band and the singer Lyonel Benjamin was added next to Boulou on lead vocal. The bassist Alix Corvington, the congas player the late Claudy Jean filled up the "band dèyè", while the trumpet player Jacques Fatier gave support to the sax and flute of Gaguy Dépestre. With a regular show at the club "Dingeling" in Delmas, the band quickly gained confidence and the appreciation of music lovers.

By the end of the decade the music of Caribbean Sextet was already on the airwaves all over Haiti with the release of their first album *Forte Dose*. It included *Tante Nini*, describing a nosy old lady who can't stay away from other people's business, and *Kòk Gauge*, which is still being played by today's band. Most Konpa lovers may know the catchy tune "*Ma chè Ginette ouvri pou mwen, lè ya rivé fòk mwen alé*".

In the 1980s Caribbean Sextet was one of the favorite bands of the Haitian elite. Their regular show at the club "l'Auberge" in Kenscoff was one of the most successful programs of the decade. At this time the band also experienced some changes in personnel as some new members, like Arius Joseph (who played the congas after the death of Claudy Jean), guitarist Toto Laraque became more involved in singing and was also trying to entertain with the style of Coupé Cloué by coming up with some tunes with daring and vulgar lyrics, in songs like *Chatte Fifi* and *Madougou*.

By their fourth album popular musicians like the guitarist Claude Marcelin, the bassist Joe Charles ,and a solid horn section with Lyonel Simeon on trombone, and Eddy Brisseau on Trumpet took the Caribbean Sextet to the level of one of Haiti's most popular bands. There again the voice of Boulou delivered another memorable hit in the song *La Pèsonn*.

After his death, the original drummer of the band Jean Jean Laraque was replaced by the singer/drummer Joel Widmaier. For some reasons the albums that followed were released as *Réginald Polycard et le Caribbean Sextet*. In the fifth album, with songs like *Decidéw* and *Lésém viv*, the public got to discover the talent of Joel Widmaier not only as a drummer but also as a talented singer who will forever put his signature on the Haitian music world.

By the time Réginald released the sixth album, *Vini Avèm*, Caribbean Sextet was no longer a performing band, and the public got the message that Réginald Policard was definitely a solo artist and that Caribbean Sextet was a band of the past.

Carimi - Band

This band came out in the Haitian diaspora when three members of Haiti's popular band K-Dans moved on to study in the U.S. where they met and created the band. By using the first two letters of their first names, the new group was baptized Ca Ri Mi, as **CA** for Carlo Vieux **RI** for Richard Cavé and **MI** for Michael Guirand.

With Richard and Carlo both playing the keyboards and the charismatic singer Michael Guirand, the band became overnight the new sensation of Haitian music after the release of the songs *Pozé* and *Haiti bang bang*, which also helped discover the talent and the rocky style of guitarist Steve Dérosier. However, when Glenny Benoit, the former guitarist and band leader of K-Dans, moved to the U.S. the founders didn't waste a minute in replacing Steve with their former leader and friend. Carimi, which started with the digital format, has been increasing its personnel. First, they added a drummer and, little by little introduced other musicians, moving away from the out-of-style digital formal. Their discography includes *Bang Bang Nasty Business* and *Are You Ready* as well as some live recordings.

The following is an unedited biography of Carimi...source Carimi.com

Half a decade ago, three friends, who had worked together in some arena of music, almost simultaneously made the decision to further their education. Knowing that the state of their homeland, Haiti, was unsure and insecure, Carlo Vieux, Richard Cavé, and Mickael Guirand each decided to leave and set their sites on the United States. Always driven by their passion for music, this small group of guys reunited in New York to touch upon making their current past time a potential career.
Soon they found themselves surrounded by sound proofing foam, extended boom mics and a mixing board. To their surprise each had the same desire to pursue music and by taking the first two letters of their first names, CaRiMi was born. Drowning themselves in the studio in the hopes of creating a new sound, one that was uncommon in the Haitian Music Industry at the time, the guys found themselves putting to paper some profound, socially charged lyrics that encompassed the troubles in their native land.
"Ayiti Bang, Bang" was released in the summer of 2001. Instantly, CaRiMi became a household name. They are known as one of the first younger generation digital bands to put out music that touched upon the political pressures and the deteriorating security of Haiti. They had mass appeal to the Haitian Diaspora who fled the country and through their allure lyrically, musically and of course physically as eye candy for the ladies, CaRiMi has thrived throughout the years.
Receiving accolades from the International music scene, including Best Album Of The Year, CaRiMi has risen to the top of the charts across Billboards best in Haiti, Guadeloupe, Paris, Guyanne Francaise, Canada and parts of Europe.
Be it with a love story of betrayal or desire being sung by Richard Cave, a song about jealousy and possessiveness vocalized by lead singer Mickael Guirand, a passionate dedication to loyalty harmonically displayed by Carl Vieux, a deep felt note composed by Noldy, a tap of the snare drum by Stanley, or a melodic groove off Glenny's strings, this dynamic cluster, has proven that talent is not only a gift but a necessity in making all your dreams a reality.

Carlito Coupe see: Francois Carl

Carré, Claude - Guitar

Caress - Band
This band is also known as K-Res.

Carriès, Frantz - Trombone
He played with System Band, Phantoms, Magnum band, Skah Shah, Djakout and other groups respectively as a freelance musician. He is well-known and much solicited by bands and artists for live and studio recordings. Frantz knows his Konpa. He is like Lyonel Simeon and Reynold Menelas, one of the few trombonists who can improvise an excellent solo during a Konpa performance.

Casimir, Frantz (Fanfan) - Singer
Fanfan played with Superstars in Miami, and with Les Shleu Shleu New York.

Casimir, Fritz - Singer
Fritz played in Haiti with "Super Chocoune" and in New York with "Tropical Combo" de Ti Jacques.

Casper, Chris - Trumpet

Cassagnol Garry - Bass

Cassamajor, Gregory - Bass

Casseus, Hervé - Keyboard
Played with Tropicana

Casseus, Jacques - Bass

Casseus, Patrick - Drums
Patrick was one of the young musicians brought into the business by Antoine Rossini Jean Baptiste (Ti Manno) in his band Gemini All Stars. He moved to the U.S. in the mid 1980s and in 1986 he was the drummer who replaced Edner Couloute in the band G.P. Express in Washington, D.C. Patrick did not live long in Washington. He moved to Boston where he became the drummer of Volo Volo. He is among the best drummers in the business although he retired from Konpa at a very young age in a Boston suburb.

Casseus, Wilson - Keyboard

Cassy, Jean - Guitar
Best years with Missile 727 in the early 1990s.

Castel, Jean Robert - Guitar
Jean Robert was next to Ronald Smith the guitarist of the band Les Beatniks de Queens.

Castelli, Myote (Yoyo) - Keyboard
He was the band leader of the Mini Jazz "Les Jokers" in the Mini Jazz era

Castera, Maxime - Congas

Catan, Eddy - Congas
Eddy played with Volo Volo de Boston.

Cavé, Georges Alan - Singer

AC is, without any doubt, one of the best composers of his generation. He came out like a storm in 1985 with the appearance on the market of the group Zin as the leader of the *Nouvel Jenerasyon* (New Generation) movement. It took the voice of Alan Cavé to bring the trust to many artists of his generation. With Alan Cavé and the group Zin, many young Haitians living in the Diaspora started to attend Haitian parties. Until then, Haitian parties in the Diaspora were mostly attended by older, nostalgic Haitians.

In Alan Cavé, young High School and college students could identify, and eventually blend into the movement. The Zin song *Fèm Volé* was the vehicle that introduced the voice of Alan to the world and before long; Alan Cavé became the most successful rising star of New York. The song *Ma Rose*, which came out in his first solo album, took Alan Cavé to the status of Haitian superstar, and he became by far the best composer of the group Zin. His solo album *"Sé pa pou date"* really shows the world that AC is an artist that will be immortalized. He has earned his star in the imaginary Haitian Hall of Fame. His singing style and techniques have been imitated by many young artists over the years.

When the French Caribbean band "Malavoi" invited Alan Cavé to sing the Caribbean Sextet hit song *La Pèsonn* in one of their albums, it clearly sent the message that Alan Cavé is indeed one of the World Music wonders.

Alan Cave also has his own production company, called AC Production. His company not only produced albums for bands and artists but is also working as the agency representing several artists and band in the U.S.

In 2007 Alan released yet another solo album titled *De La Tête Aux Pieds.*

Cavé, Richard - Keyboard

He is the "RI" of the band Carimi, as the name of the band bears the first two letters of the founders Carlo Vieux, Richard Cavé and Michael Guirand's names. As a music producer and a hit maker, he has helped bands and artists like K-Dans and King Posse since the mid-1990s. Richard Cavé moved to the U.S. where he was reunited with his partners from the band K-Dans and created the band CaRiMi, which became one of the most in-demand bands in the Haitian music market.

Cavé, Syto Jr. - Keyboard

The older brother of Alan Cavé, Syto played with Lakol alongside Tantan in the 1990s

Cayo, Valérie - Singer

Valérie played with Riské, the 1990sall female Konpa cast of New York.

Caze, Florence (Zshéa) - Singer

Zshéa is one of the most vibrant Haitian singers in the business. She uses her skills as a folkloric dancer to entertain those who have the chance to see her live. She did some times with Zin, Phantoms, Papash and Riské, to name some popular bands that have used her talent and charisma over the years. Her album *Débodé* generated much recognition in the French Caribbean countries. The video released for her 1994 song *Konpa Z* is one of the best ever released by a female Konpa star.

Caze, Mario - Guitar

Caze, Ralph - Singer

Caze, Sheila - Singer

Cazeau, Castro - Bass

Cazeau, Micheline - Singer
Micheline played with the group "Triomex".

Célestin, Gary - Guitar

Célestin, Gardy * - Singer/Promoter
Gardy played with the band Maniak in the late 1980s in New York. In the late 1990s he purchased the club Imagine and changed the name to Planet Malibou.

Célestin, Henry - Guitar - Singer
The founder of the band Les Difficiles de Pétion Ville, Henry Célestin came out with a unique voice and style that made his mark, not only in the 70s, but forever in the history of the Haitian music. If Difficiles was such a great band in the Mini Jazz era, they really owe it to the talent and mega hits of their founder Henry Célestin like *Bèl Balé, Les Ombres du Temps, Sé Lavi, I'm Sorry, Jambé Baryè Cash Cash Lubin* and *Tuyé Lamp"*.
When Henry Célestin retired at an early age in the mid-70s, he asked firmly that his friends and fellow musicians never ever use the name Les Difficiles anymore. The squad moved on with the name D.P. Express with the **D** for Difficiles and the **P** for Pétion Ville.

Célestin, Jean Marie - Guitar

Célestin, Nadia - Singer
Nadia played with Riské in the early 90s.

Célestin, Serge - Gong

Célestin, Yvon - Saxophone

Celine Records
Records production company

Céran, Lucien - Saxophone
At a very young age, Lucien Céran was discovered by the Déjean Brothers while he was still in high school in Rockland County, Spring Valley, N.Y. Fred

and André Déjean basically taught him the Konpa techniques. In 1979 he played with them on the album *L'Univers*. He became an original member of System Band. He had also worked with the band Accolade de New York in the 1980s, but he spent the rest of his musical career with System Band. He also released an album that contains the songs that he had contributed with in System band's numerous albums.

Césaire, Makarios - Guitar
In the 1990s Makarios Césaire established himself as one of the distinguished Haitian guitar players. He participated in several shows and albums in the Haitian diaspora, particularly in New York with Skah-Shah and the band New York All-Stars, among others.

Césaire, Michael Ange - Keyboard

César, Pédro - Keyboard

Chadavoine, Jean - Keyboard

Chalmers, René Max * - Bass
One of the best in the 70s, René Max Charles played with "Les Gypsies de Pétion Ville and later in New York with Djet X.

Champagne, Emmanuel (Manno) - Singer / Gong
Manno played with the band Les Astros in the late 1970s.

Champagne, Sarita - Singer
Sarita played with the band Jam in the 1990s.

Chancy, Adolphe (Doff Chancy) - Bass / Producer
Adolphe is the younger brother of Albert; he is also one of the founders of Tabou Combo. He left the band to go to college in Puerto Rico. During his absence he was replaced by Yvon Ciné. Unlike his brother Albert, who did not join the band in the diaspora, Adolphe Chancy had his best years playing in New York with Tabou Combo. He was for a long time the band's leader (maestro) and one of the Tabou Combo's managers and composers. In the 1980s, he became the owner of Chancy Records, and he produced several Haitian albums in the 1980s. He left Tabou Combo at the end of the 1980s and moved back to Haiti, where he created the band "Super Stars". The band moved to New York and later to Miami where it finally broke up.
Adolphe returned to Haiti in the 1990s where he faced some troubles with the law and was arrested. Upon his release Adolphe moved back to the U.S.

where he put together a new band based in Miami Fl. under the name "T.Tabou".

Chancy, Albert - Guitar / Singer

Albert Chancy is one of the founders and the first band leader of 'Tabou Combo" in 1968. He is the creator of hits like *Natasha, Bonne Anniversaire*, among others. When the band was re-created in New York in the early 70s, Albert was not part of the new squad. He was replaced by André "Dadou" Pasket. Albert never played with any other Haitian band. He simply moved on as a solo artist. He sings and plays the piano at special function in Haiti.

Chancy, Alix - Gong

Chancy, Jacques Ardouin (Doudou) - Saxophone

The younger brother of superstar saxophonist and Skah Shah's band leader of Loubert Chancy, Doudou Chancy made a name for himself mostly by playing solo. He played for a few years with Skah Shah, either next to his brother or replacing him. Jacques Chancy has a B.S. degree in music. He is living in New Jersey with his family.

Chancy, Loubert - Saxophone

Loubert Chancy started his musical career with Les Consuls, one of the first bands of the Mini Jazz era, based in Carrefour. In the early 70s, he was chosen by maestro Serge Rosenthal (the band leader of the second squad of Les Shleu Shleu) to be the saxophonist of the popular band. In 1974, the band moved to New York. Since there was already a Shleu Shleu in New York, the new squad called themselves Skah Shah #1.

He is also a very good composer and did horn arrangements on other artists and bands projects, including for the longtime rival band Tabou Combo.

In the 1990s Loubert moved to Florida, where he created his own band, Krik Krak which didn't last long. Soon after he worked with the band Scandal, but once again, his heart was still with Skah Shah, so he joined some ex-Skah Shah of members, like singer Jean Michel St Victor (Zouzoule) and guitarist Johnny Frantz Toussaint (Ti Frè). They came out with the band Bazouka, playing the hit songs of Skah Shah. In the meantime the singer Jean Elie Telfort (Cubano) was still performing and releasing records under the name Skah Shah. At the turn of the century, Loubert once again became the band leader of the "re-united" Skah Shah with the original members of the 1974 roster including the singer Cubano. In September 2006, the band released the album "Lagué Jazz La."

Chancy Records

Haitian record label own by Adolphe Chancy.

Channel 10 - Band
This band came out in 1975 in Port-au-Prince. Apparently Channel 10 wanted to follow the footsteps of Frères Dejean because their style was extremely similar to the Compas played by famous Déjean's brothers. When their song *Sabrina* came out in the late 70s many Konpa lovers thought that it was another hit of Les Frères Dejean. Other songs like *La Police, A La Chaleur,* and the Carnaval song *Zorange* really got some airtime in the late 70s and early 80s Channel 10 song **SABRINA** was apparently made from the template of **MARINA** one of Les Frères Déjean's mega hit of the 70s.
Apparently the brothers were aware also that the not-so-popular Channel 10 had the formula because when they got in trouble during their tour, and some of the musicians returned to New York to create the group System Band, the brothers went to the Channel 10 camp to get the lead singer, Casimir Alliance. He later became Déjean's star singer of the 1980s and 1990s. Over the years the remaining members have tried other unsuccessful attempts, like the creation of the bands Super Channel 10 and Universal Channel 10.

Charité, Ferry - Keyboard

Charlemagne, Edzer (Ti Pouch) – Bass / Guitar / Keyboard
Ti Pouch is best known for being one of the talented musicians of Djakout Mizik. He started his musical career as a gospel music bass player. He played with Boulou Valcourt as a guitarist, but he found fame when he joined the band Djakout Mizik as a keyboardist.

Charles, Adolph - Drummer

Charles, Carlo - Gong

Charles, Claude Cinna Octavius (Ti Blan) - Sax
One of the most popular Haitian saxophonists of the past decades, Ti Blan was also a renowned soccer player in the town of Cap Haitian. However, he took the sax over the round ball and spent his entire musical career with the band Tropicana. He's one of the most recognizable musicians of Tropicana, and he made and arranged many songs for the band over the years.

Charles, Derly - Guitar

Charles, Eddy - Guitar

Charles, Edner - Gong

Charles, Emmanuel - Guitar
He played with the band Les Difficiles De Pétion-Ville during the Mini Jazz era.

Charles, Eric - Singer
Eric Charles was first noticed by the Konpa Mania when he joined DP Express in the 1990s. Later on he excelled with the band Mizik Mizik in the song *"Blakawout"* and all the latest carnival songs of Mizik Mizik. In the Haiti Twoubadou record he proved that he is a talented singer for his delivery in the song *"4 Kanpé"*.

Charles, Gersaint (Mama) - Bass
One of the first bassists of the Mini Jazz era, Mama played with Les Fantaisistes De Carrefour.

Charles, Jean Loner - Singer

Charles, Joseph (Joe Charles) - Bass
Joe Charles is known as one of the top bassists in the Konpa music arena. His jazzy style impressed, motivated and inspired bassists of his generation to learn other styles and to research other avenues to master their game plans. In effect, Joe had the ability to adapt to the style of any band when one considers his days from Tropical Combo de Ti Jacques, Wanga Negess of Assade Francoeur to a complete u-turn in the bands Lakansyèl, Zèklè, Caribbean Sextet, Tabou Combo, and the Miami Top Vice.

Charles, Joubert – Promoter/Producer
Joubert Charles has been over the past decade one of the greatest producers in the Haitian Music business. He produced albums under his label Nouvel Jeneration Records in New York. He later relocates in Haiti where he becomes one of the top show producers of the country and also works as an agent and manager for some bands and artists.

Charles, Judes - Guitar

Charles, Lesly - Gong

Charles, Lyonel - Guitar
He is the older brother of Joe Charles.

Charles, Louis Benoit (Youyou) - Keyboard
He played with the band Super Ensemble de Nemours Jean Baptiste.
Charles, Marc Nicolas - Gong

Charles, Philippe - Bass

Charles, Pierre (Pèdè) - Bass
One of the first bassists of the Mini Jazz era, Pierre played with Les Fantaisistes de Carrefour. Pierre and Mama were the two bassists of the band.

Charles, Reynold - Guitar

Charles, Tony - Guitar
Tony Charles played with the band Les Vikings in the Mini Jazz era. Tony was in a class by himself. He was especially appreciated in the French Caribbean islands. His style was one of the reasons why Les Vikings stand out in the 70s.

Charles, Wesner - Congas
Wesner played with the bands Zenglen Plus, D Zine, Nu Look and T. Vice.

Charlier, Alexandre - Bass

Charlier, Camille - Gong

Charlier, Erick (Manatan) - Congas
Manatan played with Astros in the late 1970s.

Charlier, Jophet -Trumpet
Jophet played with the band Panorama Des Cayes.

Charlis, Cherlot - Keyboard

Charlot, Donald - Keyboard
Keyboard player, Donald Charlot (Don Dodo) is a very friendly young man whose model musicians include Ansyto Mercier and Fabrice Rouzier. Don said he considers himself a good musician and an excellent keyboard player who enjoys moving the public up and down and making them dance until the party is over. But, music is not the only thing he enjoys. He also likes movies, sports and all kind of entertainment. Don's musical training started in Haiti when he was 12. He started by learning the violin; then switched to keyboards because the keyboard has always been his favorite instrument. His first professional gig was with a band named K-Res. A couple of years later, he

joined Triomecs and stayed with them until he left Haiti for Miami.

In Miami, he met with well-known congas player, Alix Nozil, who introduced him to Massaj, which was then one of the hottest bands in Florida. One day in 2001, while he was at home practicing, he got a phone call from Kapi asking him to play with Tabou Combo. He gladly accepted.

Don said that he enjoys being a musician of Tabou Combo for various reasons. First, playing with Tabou Combo makes him feel and know that he is a big star in both the Haitian and international communities. Second, he gets to travel a lot, representing Konpa and Haiti, and, also to meet different people. Third, the musicians are confident, professional, friendly and competent. "Tabou Combo is a legend," said Don. "Haitians should be proud of themselves and thank God for having Tabou Combo to represent them worldwide."
Bio from: www.taboucombo.com

Chatelier, Jean Roosevelt - Guitar
Roosevelt played with Magic Connection and Shoogar Combo. He was one of the members of Shoogar recruited by Arsène Appolon for the creation of the band Skah Shah d'Haiti.

Charm - Band
This band based, in Brooklyn N.Y released their demo song *Lanmou Frajil* in 2006.

Chaussettes Rouges (Les Chaussettes Rouges) - Band
Band of the Mini Jazz era.

Checkers (Les checkers) - Band
This band came out in the early 70s, their album *Harry Crié Pou Poy* was released in 1974 by Shango Records.

Chelberts (Les Chelberts) - Band
This band was created in 1968.

Chérubin, Hans (Gros Bébé) - Singer
Gros Bébé was born in Port-au-Prince in 1946. The Mini Jazz movement needed a voice like Gros Bébé's to take the revolution to another level. This pioneer, who played with the popular band Les Shleu Shleu, sung some memorable hits, like *Alfredo, Dans La Vie, Haiti Mon Pays, Haiti Terre De Soleil, Boutillers,* and *Grille Ta Cigarette*. During that time he made a perfect duo next to Peddy in the front line of Les Shleu Shleu.

Chéry, Dabens - Singer
Dabens played with System Band in the years 2006-2007. After the release of the album *Nan Building Nan*, Dabens resigned on Aug. the 8th 2007, on the eve of a three-week tour to Haiti. In conspiracy with three other musicians (the bassist, the keyboardist and the gonguist) citing nonpayment, a charge that the band's management completely denied.
Dabens delivered a great job on the album and the song *Catel* was one of the most played songs in Haiti for the summer 2007. He also did a great job on the album *Happy 50 Konpa*, released by Zenglen's drummer Jean Richard Herard (Ritchie).

Chéry, Grégory - Bass / Sound Engineer
Gregory is one of the founders of the band K-Dans, he is also known in the business as a very good sound engineer. In 2007 he became another member of K-Dans to join the band Carimi. He was hired as a sound engineer and not as a bassist.

Chéry, Manno - Guitar / Singer

Chéry, Pierre-Rigaud - Guitar
Pierre Rigaud Chéry is a respected Haitian guitarist and songwriter.

Chéry, Roosevelt - Singer
Roosevelt was one of the two star singers of the band Panorama des Cayes.

Chill - Band
Chill is the band created by the singer Jude Jean after he left the band K-Dans. The word "Chill" is a reference to the popular K-Dans hit song *Nap Chill*.

Chill Konpa - Band
This band which has nothing to do with the Chill band of Jude Jean happened to release an album in 2007 titled *Espwa* with a song also called *Nap Chill*, but quite different.

Chine
In the konpa jargon the word chine is used to describe the person or people in charge of moving a band sound system from point A to point B. The reason the word is widely used is because a man named Roland who was in charge of transporting and setting up the equipment of Nemours Jean Baptiste's band had Chinese features, and the musicians used to call him "Chine".

Chinois see: Savius, Ludovic

Choc Combo - Band
This band was created in the 1980s in Washington D. C. Most members had moved on to create the band Les Pachas de Washington.

Chomeurs - Band
This band was created in 1970. However, they got the attention of everyone in 1975, when they released the album *En Vacances* with some panties on the cover, referring to their song *Chiré Pantalette La.* That cover was considered offensive at the time. Their discography also includes the album *Appuyé.*

Chouchou de Nord Est - Band
Their album *Agarou* was released in 1998.

Cicéron, Laurent - Bass
Laurent Cicéron is one bass player who has a unique style in the history of Konpa.
Although he played with bands like Les Deutz, Les Loups Noirs, he is best known as the bassist of Magnum Band.

Cicéron, Marco - Drums
Just like Laurent Cicéron, Marco has a style unique to Marco on the drums. He started at a very young age with the band Les Deutz. Soon after he moved to New York when he met Fred Paul, who made him the drummer of choice of the Mini records projects. He participated also in the memorable album G.M. Connection, by Mario Mayala, the guitarist of Skah Shah, and Gerard Daniel, who was saxophonist and band leader of Djet-X.

Cicéron, Reynold - Drums
Reynold played with Les Loups Noirs in the Mini Jazz era.

Cicéron, Serge - Congas
Serge is one of the Cicéron brothers who also played with Les Deutz. He later joined Magnum band just like the bassist Laurent Cicéron.

Ciné, André (Doudou) - Guitar
He was one of the first guitarists of Tabou Combo.

Ciné, Edva -Trumpet

Ciné, Records
Haitian owned record company.

Ciné, Yvon - Bass
Yvon Ciné played with Tabou Combo in the 1970s. He is also a well-known producer. Yvon Ciné was the master brain behind the success of the band King Posse in the mid 90s.

Cinéas, Wesner - Saxophone

Cinéus, Gérard - Guitar

Cizo - Band

Clairsidor, Martinez - Radio Personality

Claude, Jean Marie -Trumpet
Jean Marie played with the band Accolade de New York in the 1980s.

Claude, Ronald - Keyboard
Ronald played with the band Les Légendaires De Delmas.

Claudin, Carlo - Singer
Carlo is one of the first singers of the rhythm Compas
Direct that gave the rhythm a new direction by showing that he could take control if the front line, thus being a true role model. Unlike other singers of his generation, Carlo used to acknowledge the fans by incorporating their names in the songs in live shows and studio recording Thus, making him the father of shout outs.
Nemours recruited Carlo from the Band "Sublime" and used him and Arthur Lovelace as the vehicle that will forever changed the Haitian music. Many generations grew up listening to the voice of Carlo Claudin. After all he was for many years the most popular lead singer of Nemours' band. It is the style left by Carlo that is still being used today in the Konpa world. Since the 1970s Carlo has been living in the Washington metropolitan area. He is today residing in Rockville Md with his wife Marlène.

Claudin, Eddy - Drums

Claudin, Victor - Guitar

Clénador, Wilfrid (Malou) - Singer
He was the star singer of the band Les Fantaisistes De Jérémie

Cléo see: Pierre Cléona

Clergé, Rigobert - Bass
Clergé was one of the two bassists of the band "Les Lionceaux Des Cayes" He shared his position with Fred Dorlette.

Clermont, Estepherly (Big Steve) - Keyboard
Born in Port-au-Prince, he started with the band Triomex. His best years were with Papash and Lakol in the 1990s. He moved to Florida where he worked with the band Superstars. Today Steve has his own recording studio and record label called "Caribia" in Long Island N.Y.

Clermont, Jacques - Guitar
He was the artist who replaced Raymond Gaspard in the original Compas Direct of Nemours Jean Baptiste.

Clermont, Lionel (Yoyo) - Gong
Lyonel played with the band Safari Combo in the 1970s.

Clermont, Milot - Drums
He played for the band Cadence Rampa of Wébert Sicot.

Clermont, Nixon – Gong
Nixon played with the bands Pachas de Washington in the 1980s and with G.P.Express, and Zépon in Washington D.C. in the 1990s.

Clermont, Serge - Bass
Serge played with the band Scorpio Fever.

Clerveaux, Chavannes - Bass

Clervil, Eric - Trumpet

Clerville, Jean René -Trombone

Clinik –Band
That band raised the issue of domestic violence in one of their song which is supported by a well made video.

Cobra Band - Band
This band was created by the talented trumpeter Anderson Cameau.

Coby, Pat - Drums
Played with Pépé Bayard

Coffy, Jean Paul - Keyboard

Cohen, Eddy - Saxophone

Coignard, Jean - Singer
Jean Coignard played with Tropicana before he moved to Port-au-Prince to
join Bossa Combo.

Colas, Roger - Singer

Born in Quartier Morin in Cap Haitien in 1937,
Roger Colas was made popular by the great
maestro Ulrick Pierre-Louis after Ulrick heard
the 18 years old's voice in Radio Citadelle in
1955. Roger then became one of the main voices
of Septen and the most popular singer coming
from the Northern part of Haiti. He marked his
musical career by singing mega hits in different
styles, like Bossa Nova, Pachanga, Pétro, Ibo
and especially Bolero like: *Ti Yayi, 25em
Anniversaire, Toi & Moi* and the unforgettable
Frédeline, among others.

Roger also sang many hot hit songs for Septen, and he was also known for
singing easily in Spanish, especially the music of the Mexican Augustin Lara
like *Solamente Una Vez, Noche de Ronda* and *Maria Bonita.*

Like many artists, Roger left Haiti to immigrate to the U.S. At first he moved to
Florida, then to New York. Roger did a series of solo albums while living in
the Diaspora. Roger Colas returned to Haiti in the mid 1980s. On Sept. 15,
1986, after performing at a show at Club International, Roger Colas was killed
in a car accident in Petion-Ville. Besides being a musician, Roger Colas was
also a well-known tailor in Cap Haitien. He made many uniforms for Septen
over the years.

Colas, Roger Jr - Singer
The son of the legendary singer Roger Colas is mostly known for playing the
memorable tunes of his late father.

Colas, Rudy (Yanvaloo) Promoter/Photographer
Yanvaloo is known in the Konpa community mostly for snapping pictures of
Haitian stars and partygoers at different events. His pictures are posted on

several Haitian website over the internet. He is also a show promoter.

Colas, Wilherme - Saxophone
Wilherme played with Shoogar Combo and Gemini All-Stars in the 1970s.

Colé Colé Band - Band
This band was created in 1980 by the bass player Alix Jacques after he left Djet-X.

Colin, Carl - Guitar

Colin, Serge - Trumpet
His best year was with D.P. Express in the late 70s.

Combite Creole - Band

Rodrigue Milien   Toto Nécéssité

This band was created by Rodrigue Millen and Jules Similien (Toto) in 1973. Prior to creating to band, the two used to play at different concerts in Haiti, especially with "Theatre de Verdure", as they were actors of "Troupe Alcibiade". After the album "*Nécéssité*", Rodrigue and Toto moved to New York, where they performed as a Mini Jazz rather than a duo. Their song "*Loup Garou*" was an instant hit, and was being played in radio stations in Haiti as well as in the other French Caribbean countries.

After a few years in the U.S. Rodrigue returned to Haiti where he continued with the band Combite Créole de Rodrigue Milien. He did many hit songs that are still favorites. Toto stayed in New York and in the late 70s returned to Haiti where he did his own band Toto Nécéssité. In the 1980s they were once again reunited, but it was only to do a record together. Throughout their careers they both have been traveling and living in two countries, the U.S. and Haiti. Lately Rodrigue has been working as a radio personality in Haiti.
On April 4, 2007, in a radio interview on the show "Matin Caraïbes" in Haiti, Rodrigue Millien said that in the early days of the band, he and Toto were invited to play at the movie theater Bel Air Ciné. To do the show, they borrowed some instruments from friends and carried an amplifier borrowed from the band Samba Creole for more than four miles because they couldn't afford public transportation which was one Gourde (then the equivalent 20 cents U.S). Rodrigue said after the show they were paid three dollars for the two of them. He also said that they were only paid $350 for their first album titled *Nécéssité* which became one of the mega hits and best sellers of the 1970s.

Rodrigue said that he finally made some serious money in music when the singer Wyclef Jean paid him for using one of his songs in Wyclef Jean's hit *24 Hours*.

Combite Express - Band
This band was based in New York.

Combo Express - Band

Comeau, Patrick - Gong

Compagnons (Les Compagnons De La Musique) – Band

Compas
Compas is a shorter name for the rhythm Compas Direct.
The word Compas is also used to describe the way people dance the rhythm Compas Direct. Modern Haitians choose to write it in their native Creole language as "**Konpa**" instead of the French version "Compas". Because Creole is a phonetic language the letter **K** replaces the **C**. The letter **S** is also dropped, and in the Creole grammar, the rule of **M** before the letters **B** and **P** doesn't apply.

Compas Direct - Rhythm invented by Haitian saxophonist Nemours Jean Baptiste. After Nemours introduced his new band "Ensemble Nemours Jean Baptiste" at a small park across the street from the St. Anne church (Place Sainte Anne) in Port-au-Prince on July 26, 1955, many people simply chose to call the new band "Compas Direct", thus making that date the anniversary of Compas.

Compas du Sud - Band

Compas Express - Band

Compas Manba - Band
In the last days of Coupé Cloué, some members created the band Compas Manba in Port-au-Prince, but when the keyboardist Guy Montreuil died at a very young age, the project failed and most of the musicians moved to the U.S.

Compas Manba - Band
This band was founded in New York by Yves Léon Paul (Ti Guy), former singer of the band Ensemble Select de Coupé Cloué. In the late 1990s he changed the band's name to Lojik Compas.

Concept records
Haitian owned record company.

Condé, Ralph - Guitar / Singer
Ralph Condé made a name for himself in the Konpa world when he appeared as the lead guitarist and singer of the band Papash in the1980s. Soon after, Ralph moved to New York, where he created the band Vag. The band did not last long in the demanding New York Konpa market and Ralph joined Lakol and later Tabou Combo. Ralph had his best years with Tabou Combo. At that time Ralph also had a recording studio in New York. While working one night, he was assaulted, robbed, and ended up in the hospital. After that incident, he left New York and moved to Montreal, where he created the band Banjo, which also had a very short life.
He then moved to Florida, where he joined Top Vice as the replacement for Robert Martino, who was then playing with Sweet Micky. When Robert Martino reconciled with his partner Robert Charlot and created the band Nu Vice, Ralph quietly moved on with his life and joined the band Nu Look and managed his own recording studio. In the fall of 2006 Ralph stepped away from New Look and he continued to work and to travel the world as a freelancer with other bands, especially Tabou Combo.
In 2007 he released his solo album Akoustik Kreyol.

Confidents de Boston - Band
This band was created in the late 70s by some former member of Volo Volo.

Connecticut All Stars (C.A.S) - Band
This band was introduced to the market in August 2007 in a well-organized show in Connecticut.

Constant, Lesly - Drum
Lesly played with the band Les Astros in the late 1970s.

Consuls (Les Consuls) - Band
Band of the Mini Jazz era, based in Carrefour in the late 1960s, with Loubert Chancy on saxophone.

Copins (Les Copins) - Band
This band came out in the Mini Jazz era.

Coq, Fritz *- Singer
The late Fritz Coq played for many years with Bossa Combo next to Raymond

Cajuste and Jean Claude Dorsainvil. When he moved to New York in the 1980s he joined Accolade De New York. Fritz Coq was known for always wearing hats during performances. Fritz Coq died in New York.

Coriolan, Pierre Gramont (Pè Kòy) - Saxophone / Drums
Pè Kòy played with the band Washington Express in the 1980s in Washington, D.C.

Corvingtons (Les Corvingtons) – Band
Band of the Mini Jazz era, the band was created by the Corvington Brothers.

Corvington, Alix - Bass
Alix played with the band Les Corvington and also with the band Caribbean Sextet.

Corvington, Michel - Guitar
Michel played with the band Les Corvington and also with the bands Tropical Sextet and Ibo Combo.

Cougars (Les Cougars de Pétion Ville) - Band
This band came out under the name Super Tabou and later became known as Les Cougars de Pétion-Ville.

Couloute, Edner - Drums
Edner Couloute, a very popular artist in the town of Petion-Ville, is known to everyone as "Couloute". He played with Super Tabou, Les Cougars de Petion Ville and had his best years with D.P. Express when he replaced Almando Keslin in the mid-1980s. Couloute was among the eight musicians of D.P who left Haiti to create the Washington D.C./Maryland-based band G.P. Express. He did not stay long in Maryland, and he returned to Haiti, where he joined Doff Chancy and Jean Claude Jean in the creation of the band Superstars. Edner Couloute left his mark in the Washington metropolitan area with songs like *Pa wè clè*, and *Kasé ponyèt*.

Coupé Cloué - See: Henry Gesner

Courtois, Frantz – Guitar

Courtois, Herby - Bass

Crékel, Jean Claude - Drums
Jean Claude played with Combite Créole in the 1970s.

Créon Records
Haitian record label

Crève Coeur, Edouard * (Doudou) - Accordion
He played for the band Les Manfoubens, which later became Les Shleu Shleu.
Unfortunately, the young Doudou passed away in the Fort Dimanche Prison.

Crossover - Record Label Company

Curtis, Robert (Bob) - Saxophone
Bob is another non-Haitian musician who contributed to the horn section of
Magnum Band.

Curve - Band

Custom Band - Band

Crystal - Band
This band was based in the town of St. Marc.

Crystal Band - Band
This band was created in New York by Skah Shah's famous gonguist Rodrigue
Gauthier (Ti Crann) after the break up of the original Skah Shah # 1.

Cyriaque, Alex - Gong
Alex played with the band Septentrional. He was the first gonguist of the band
Septentrional du Cap.

D

D.P. Express - Band

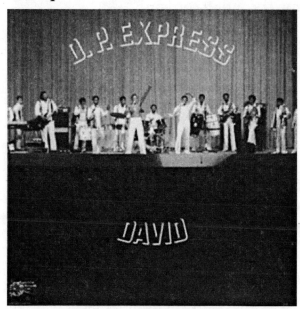

One of the most popular bands of Haiti, D.P. Express rocked the nation, the Caribbean and the Haitian diaspora from the mid 70s to the mid 90s with mega hits like "*Pa pran contact, Libèté*" (sung by Hervé Bléus) "*David, Corrigé, Ensem Ensem*" (sung by Ti Manno), and *Grann Nanna* and *Négrié* (sung by Dieudonné Larose).

The band was created on July 17, 1976 after Henry Celestin, the leader and singer of the popular band Les Difficiles de Pétion Ville, decided to call it quits and requested that the name Difficiles not be used in his absence. The band manager, alongside with members like the guitarist Eddy Wooley, the bassist Jean Robert Herissé (Porky) and the gonguist Philippe Denis moved on with the name D.P. Express in 1976 with the letters D for Difficiles and P for Pétion-Ville. They teamed up with the guitarist Claude Marcelin, and the drummer Almando Keslin and the congas player Pierrot Kersaint completed the percussion line. The band introduced a horn section with Frantz Pierre Gilles and Serge Colin and keyboards played by Claudy Fremont and Raoul Denis Jr, with some new and innovative sounds putting an end to the Mini Jazz movement with the addition of so many members.

The band presented itself as an Express train, taking on more passengers at every stop. With the catchy voice of the singer Hervé Bleus so new and entertaining, the band captured the attention of a crowd in search of something new.

In 1976 the band released their first album, *M'Pa Pren Contact* with a total of six songs. All of the songs: *M'Pa Pren Contact, Deception, Pren Sanw, Aprann Palé, Sensib Pa Joué* and the carnival song Souké *Kow* were being played on radio stations in the country. In 1977 the band released their second album *Palé Palé Ou* with six more hit songs including *Liberté* and *L'Amiral* followed in 1978 on their album *Zafew*. During that period some members of Gypsies the rival of the band Les Difficiles decided to follow the route of D.P. by adding the same group of instruments that was working for D.P and they too had a name change. The public was introduced in 1977 to the band name Scorpio and suddenly the train had a dangerous animal in its path, ready to bite the passengers and turn them into followers of the scorpion.

Thus began, in the late 70s, the famous polemic D.P./Scorpio that forever left its mark in the history of Haitian music. The bands rivalry was so deep that the government tried to manage to put the bands far apart in the carnival parade to avoid any physical confrontation between the fans of the Green & White (D.P.), and the Bleu & White (Scorpio).

In 1979 the band Astros was on tour in Haiti and their lead singer Antoine Rossini Jean Baptiste (Ti Manno) joined D.P. Express. It was the best marriage that ever happened in Konpa Music, as it was the perfect fit. By the fall of 79, Ti Manno was already the sensation of the country and the neighboring islands as the new conductor of the train, leaving his mark in the songs *Min Zin* and *D.P. Fever* also called *M'enragé*. The band was in demand all over the country and in the French Caribbean Islands.

During the 1979 summer tour the band was caught in the middle of a hurricane in the island of Dominica. They feared for their lives, thinking that they would all die in a foreign country. That incident inspired them to do the song *David* (based on Cyclone David), one of the greatest Konpa hits ever made. The D.P. Express album *David* released in 1980 with the hit songs *EEEE, Corigé, David, Ensem Ensem* and the carnival song *Cèso*, were so successful that the band had sold out shows at all their events in Haiti and in the Haitian diaspora.

At the 1981 carnival in Haiti the band introduced the song *Biberon* which had the whole country singing and dominated the parade route as if everyone wanted to be in the same band. The popularity of the lead singer Ti Manno was without precedent and the trouble started as Ti Manno asked for a bigger piece of the pie than what he was receiving. When his demands were not met, he decided to move on by creating his own band Gemini All Stars.

D.P. in the meantime, hired Pascal Albert, the star singer of the former Mini Jazz Les Ambassadeurs. Although Pascal had what it took to keep the train moving, and did his best in the band's 6th album titled *Réfléchi* especially in the song *Grace*, many fans did follow Ti Manno wherever Gemini was playing, and the attendance of the Express train continued to drop.

In the years that followed, D.P. Express tried its best to stay on track as they move some of their back up singers like Perez Alvarez and Lesly Dauphin on to lead vocals. They also hired Benito Philogène (also call Benito d'Haiti) a singer whose voice reminded the public of the legendary Ti Manno. During that period of the 80s D.P. released the following albums *Pran Plezi Nou, Bariè,* and *Tête Calé.* The management of the band worked on hiring some new stars out of other bands and keeping new young faces in the band, like the keyboardist Ansyto Mercier and the bassist Mario Germain who they got from Ti Manno's band, ironically. They also acquired the talented trombonist Lyonel Siméon, and the guitarist Denis Nozile (Ti Polis), and the public started also to notice the talent of the gonguist Marc Bellande Jacquet (Choupitte), With a new drummer Edner Couloutte, and the band was once again the crowd pleaser of the 80s and with carnival songs like *La Mort De La Bète* and Min *Siga'w*

Despite the up and down seasons, D.P. Express never stopped being one of the giants of the carnival season in Haiti, keeping the public tuned in with many polemical songs against their rival Scorpio.·

After the carnival of 1985, eight members left the band and moved to Laurel Md a suburb of Washington, D.C. to create the band G.P. Express. The immigrated members were Ti Polis, Mario, Ansyto, Lyonel, Choupitte, Edner, Alvarez and Pierrot. Their argument was that bonus money given by then President Jean Claude Duvalier for the band's performances in front of the palace during the three day carnival parade was mishandled by the management team. Once again the management was in a position to do some damage control and they got some musicians from other bands that were eager to play for a band of the caliber of D.P. Express including Dieudonné Larose the singer of the band Shoogar Combo.

During the live shows Larose proved that he is a charismatic singer by keeping the public tune in. He delivered a great job in the album *Anba Anba* which was released in a hurry and containing only four songs to include the hit *Tou Lumin (Anba Anba)* a song that the public also called *Grann Nan Na.* That album also had *Maladie Damou* and *Négriers.* The band, however, no longer had the hit makers or the chemistry of the late 70s and early 80s, and the public also stayed home due to the political movement of the post-Duvalier era of the late 80s.

Despite the return of Ansyto and Choupitte to the band the best gigs for D.P. was at the Ansyto fan club on Sunday afternoon. All the best shows and gala nights were given to other bands like Tabou Combo and Zin coming all the way from New York. D.P. Express would suffer yet two more serious losses. The singer Larose moved to Canada where he found success with the band Missile 727. In Haiti, Ansyto had revived the hit song *Exactement* by adding some super keyboard solo and groove as well as a new chorus part that got the crowd chanting the word "Digital". With that success, he moved on by creating his own band call Digital Express.

In 1991 D.P. Express released the album *D.P. Tounin* meaning D.P. is back.

However, the passengers of the train had moved on with other interests, like following younger artists and the new trend of the digital bands like Sweet Micky, T. Vice and others putting an end to the route of the famous train despite a last try by singer Eric Charles. At the end of the ride, both Eric and Choupitte were rescued by Fabrice Rouzier. In the mid 90s, he saved their career, by adding them to his band Mizik Mizik a band that managed to keep alive some of the memories of D.P. as they played on March 16, 2007, at their 20th Anniversary party in Miami the song David, to the delight of the fans.

D'alphonse, Patrick - Bass
Patrick played with Septentrional.

D'arbouze, Frantznor - Horn

D'Sire

Female Konpa band base in Florida

D'Zine – Band

This band, which was created in the 1990s in Florida by some ex-members of the band Zenglen Plus, was made popular by an unfortunate event. An underground record label released an unofficial live CD of the band. Soon after, the existence of the band, and the artists Gazzman, Deli François, Zagalo and Arly Larivière were no longer incognito. After a few years of success, the band split-up as some of the members created the band Nu Look.

D-Zèl - Band
This band was created from a collaboration and partnership of former musicians of the band D-Zine and a band named Zèl based in Florida.

Dabady, Frantz - Gong / Congas

Dabens see: Chéry Dabens

Dadou Pasket see: Pasket André

Dalcé, (Ti bass) - Bass
Daniel started his career with the band Super Choucoune. He moved forward in his career as composer and bassist of Ensemble Select de Coupé Cloué.

Dalder, Philippe - Keyboard

Dalencourt, Gerard – Saxophone

Dalzon, Max Sam – Promoter / Producer
Max Sam Dalzon is one of the most popular personalities in the Haitian community of Boston Massachusetts. He is known as a show promoter and a record producer. His record store is one of the spots known not only for the selling of new releases and rare to find albums but also as one of the main locations to purchase tickets for Haitian shows in the Boston area.

Damas, Jean François - Guitar

Damas, Jean Robert - Saxophone
Jean Robert is known to many simply as Damas. He was the lead saxophonist of Bossa Combo. Damas was among the members of Bossa that created the group Accolade de New York. To many people, Jean Robert Damas sounded almost like the legendary Webert Sicot.

Damas, Joe - Radio Personality
Joe Damas is a popular radio host and actor who have contributed in the promotion of Konpa music over the years.

Damelus, Jean Junior (Mass Doudou) - Singer
Musician of the band Take Off, he previously played with the band Imaj Konpa.

Damour, Jean Riché - Guitar
Jean Riché played in New York with the band "Lov."

Daniel, Gérard - Saxophone
Gérard Daniel is one of the best Haitian saxophonists in the Haitian music industry. He started his professional career with Les Shelberts before becoming a regular with Les Pachas du Canapé Vert. After the departure of Loubert Chancy, he was called to feel the vacant saxophonist position and became one of the members of the 3rd version of Shleu Shleu. He led Shleu Shleu until he moved to Brooklyn, N.Y in the mid-70s. In New York he had his best years as the band leader of Djet-X. Ti Gérard as he is known in the Konpa world also acquired the name "Préfè de Brooklyn". He did an album under the name G.M. Connection with his friend, the late guitarist Mario Mayala of Skah Shah, with the G for Gérard and M for Mario. Gérard Daniel is one of the musicians who left his mark in the Haitian music world for his unique sound on the saxophone.

Daniel, Jimmy - Drum

Daniel, Joseph Almatasse - Saxophone
Joseph played with band Les Virtioses de St. Marc.

Dantus, Carl - Gong /Congas

Darcy, Jean Musset (Vava) - Singer
Vava played with Shoogar Combo in the 1970. He sang a few hit songs like the unforgettable "*Matinette*". He later moved to New York after an attempt with the band "Les Loups Noirs", who was trying to make a comeback in the early 1980s. Vava simply vanished and apparently retired.

Darléus, Sylvie (Sylvie d'Art) - Singer
Sylvie was one of the remarkable singers of the gospel band "Les Etincelles de L'évangile" before joining the band Caribbean Sextet for a short while. She collaborated later with Master Dji on some rapping tracks and live shows. However, the song *Mandela Lagué,* made with Mario de Volcy's band "Mirak", remained one of her best performances. At the end of the 20th century Sylvie released a solo album titled *Tous Les Deux.*

Dary, Daphney (Queen Dada) - Singer
Dada played with the band Suspense in New York before having her best years with Zin in the mid-1990s.

Dauphin, Lesly - Singer
Lesly sang a few songs as a lead vocalist for D.P. Express. Over the years he was mostly used as the background and a substitute lead vocalist. Among musicians he was known as a good lyricist and the man who created the best lines for the carnival songs of D.P. Express.

Dauphin, Melissa - Singer /Guitar

David Sextet - Band

David, Thomas - Singer
Played with Septentrional, but started in the band Septen Junior.

Davis, Rick – Trombone

Dayard, Jérome (Tibobdenazareth) – Singer
Ti Bob played shortly with the band D-Zine before becoming a gospel singer.

De Laleu, Bob - Congas
Bob de Laleu played for the band Les Beatniks de Queens in the Mini Jazz era.

Décius, Sergo François - Congas
One of the best in his field Sergo, not only played the instrument, he is also a well-known conga instructor in Haiti. Sergo played Konpa with bands like Ozone, Papash and Zenglen.

Dee, Ronnie - Radio Personality
Popular broadcaster in Montreal, Ronnie has contributed to the promotion of Konpa music in Canada as a radio announcer and as a live show producer.

Défailli, Fénel - Bongo
Fénel played in the U.S. with K-Sou Coupé.

Déga - Band
Konpa band based in Haiti

Dégand, Billy - Gong
Billy played with Gypsies in the early 1970s.

Dégand, Joanne - Singer

Degree - Band
Konpa Band based in Florida

Déjean, André - Trumpet /Trombone
André is one of the famous Déjean brothers. A product of the Lycée
Petion-Ville Fanfare, André has the ability to play many instruments besides
the trumpet and trombone, including the guitar. He is also one of the artists
that have made many Konpa hits. He has also arranged many songs for other
Haitian and French Caribbean bands and many of solo artists. His reputation
as a great Haitian musician goes beyond the borders of Haiti. In 2006 he
became a musician of Magnum Band.

Déjean, Camille - Gong
He was mostly known for hitting the floor tom really hard. Sometimes during
performances he could do some serious damage to his instrument. He was
also known for wearing large hats while performing.

Déjean, Fred - Saxophone
Fred became the band leader of the group Les Frères Déjean when Lyonel, his
older brother, moved to the U.S.

Déjean, Gerard - Congas
Gérard played with Magic Connection in the 1980s.

Déjean, Lyonel - Saxophone
The founder of the band Les Frères Déjean, he moved to the U.S. before the
band made it big. He passed the leadership to his younger brother Fred who
did a very good job making Les Frères Déjean one of the best bands in the
history of Konpa with the collaboration of his brother André.

Déjean, Philippe * - congas
One of the famous Déjean's brothers, Philippe died in 2003 in Haiti.

Déjoie, Nazaire - Saxophone
Nazaire was the founder of the band Shooblack. He got his experience with
the band Super Ensemble de Webert Sicot.

Dekwochay - Band
This band came out in New York in 2005

Delaravin, Lyonel - Congas
Played in New York with Shleu Shleu in the 1990s

Delbrun, Harry – Gong

Played with Les Vikings in the 1970s
Delcis, Eddy - Radio Personality

Délice, Farelus - Congas

Delinois, Pascal - Congas

Delisca, Lorifis -Trumpet
Lorifis played with the band Norna de Léogane.

Delmas Jean Arnold - Saxophone

Delmas, Wins - Saxophone
Wins Played in New York with Skah Shah and System band in the 1990s.

Delva, Garcia (Graciadelva) - Singer

Garcia left his first band Gerostar and emerged as the lead vocal of Djakout Mizik in the 1990's. Later he moved to Miami where he found success with the band Zenglen at the end of the decade. He excelled in songs like *5 Dwets, Flanneur Femèl,* and *Do It Right* among others.

While returning to the U.S. after a show in France in 2002, Garcia faced problems with the U.S. immigration for his visa status. He returned to Haiti, where he eventually started his own band, Mass Konpa. In April 2008 in an interview at Radio Vision 2000, he said that he made a difference between Garcia and Gracia.

Delta Force Compas - Band
When Ansyto Mercier left his band Digital Express to join Sweet Mickey, the other musicians moved on with the name "Delta Force Compas".

Delta Record
Haitian record label

Démesmin, Gabriel - Bass
Gabriel played with La Ruche de Léogane in the 1970s.

Démosthènes, Jean Robert - Trumpet
Jean Robert played with Gemini in the 1980s.

Denard, Lesly - Gong

Dénatus, Guerino – Congas

Denis, Jacqueline - Singer
She played with the bands Caribbean Sextet and Zèklè in the 1980s and 90s.

Denis, Mario "Ti Chouk" *- Trumpet
Mario started to make a name for himself in the Petion-Ville based band
Channel 10. He later joined Scorpio in the early 80s after the departure of
Reynold Menelas. He was one of the leaders of Scorpio until he left Haiti to
join System Band in New York. He did not stay long in America, and returned
to Haiti, where he died in 1985.

Denis, Philippe - Gong (Percussion)
Philippe had his best years with Les Difficilles and D.P. Express. In the late
1970s he stopped playing, and he was replaced by Marc Bellande Jacquet
(Shoupitte). Philippe then became the road manager of the band.

Denis, Raoul - Producer

Denis, Raoul Jr - Keyboard
Raoul grew up in a house where music was king. The son of the famous
pianist Micheline L Denis was a well-known and respected artist in Haiti.
Raoul became popular in the Haitian music arena when he joined D.P. Express
as the second keyboardist next to the talented Claudy Frémont in the late
1970s. Later he became the keyboardist of the band Zèklè, before engaging in
his solo project where he gave the nation and music lovers all over the world
the super hit of the 1980s Sukaina.
Raoul is credited by many as one of the pioneers of the Nouvel Jenerasyon
movement which took place in Haiti in the mid 1980s.

Denis, Robert - Drums
Played with Les Corvingtons in the 1960s, he later became the sound engineer
of choice of the Mini Jazz era and beyond.

Denis, * - Guitar
Sergot played with many bands from Haiti to New York in his career. In
Washington, D.C. he did some of the songs of the band Washington Express in
the mid-1980s. Sergot Denis died in Florida.

Denis, Seymour - Guitar

Dénizar, Jacques - Keyboard

Dépestre, Edgard (Gaguy) - Saxophone - Flute
Gaguy played with Skah Shah for a short time while he was in New York in
the mid-70s, but the man born in Jacmel was mostly known in the Haitian
diaspora in the band Ibo Combo.
Gaguy was one of the first musicians of Ibo Combo to return to Haiti. He also
played with the Caribbean Sextet during the good years of Caribbean at
L'Auberge in the Boutilier neighborhood.

Derenoncourt, Henry - Promoter
In the mid-70s Henry left his electronic store business to open the nightclub
Creole Paradise in Queens N.Y with his partner Frantzy Théodule. After a few
months the club was destroyed by a fire and they opened the club Imagine in
Long Island N.Y in the late 1990s. Imagine was later sold to the late Gardy
Célestin who changed the name to Planet Malibu. Henry took a step back in
the Haitian music scene only to reappear in 2007, as he helped his friends
Frantzy and other partners, to open the club Djumbala in Brooklyn N.Y, on
Sept. 12, 2007

Derenoncourt, Ronald - Singer / Percussion

Dérices, Manes - Trumpet
Manes played with Bossa Combo.

Dérisier, Jean - Drums

Dérissaint, Jean Brutus - Guitar /Singer
As the new generation movement was gaining momentum, the band Zenglen
came out with the song *Fidel* to signify what the Konpa revolution was all
about. The public also met, at the same time, the guitar works of Brutus in the
album *An Nou Alèz*. After the success of the album, Brutus moved to the U.S.
Without their leader, the band didn't last long.
He eventually put another Zenglen together in Miami, after several attempts
and a couple of solo projects, which include Brutus *X-Tra*. The band struggled

until a complete overall was made with the addition of the drummer/producer Jean Herard Richard (Richie) and the charismatic singer Gracia Delva. The band came out with hit songs like *5 Dwets, B.S Production, Tempo, and Flanneur Femèle* among others.

Today, Brutus really shows that he is not only a good musician and a hit maker, but also a true warrior devoted in keeping alive the mission of Zenglen to stay forever "Fidel" to the Konpa by creating and designing new routes for generations to come. Brutus, a very humble individual, is still today a true role model who believes despite his fame that he is not bigger than anyone else and not bigger than the music.

Dérodèle, Edva - Congas
Edva played with Les Vikings in the Mini Jazz era (1970s).
Deroncerey, Jude (Roupy) - Radio Personality

Dérosier, Jean Claude - Drums

Derosier, Jensen – Drums

Jensen is one of the original members of "Partners", a New York-based band in the 1980s, which later become 'Phantoms". Jensen is known in the business for his cool demeanor. He used to play with two bass drums with the picture of a large skeleton head on each of the base drums. For a while, he has been the P.R. person of the band as well as one of the songwriters.

Dérosier, Steve - Guitar
He played with the band Carimi and he is the leader of the band Nomad.

Desgrottes, Claude - Bass
He is the son of the legendary musician Michel Desgrottes. Claude had his best years with Bossa Combo. In the early 1980s he moved to New York with some members of Bossa Combo to create the band Accolade de New York. Later on in his career, he joined the band Skah Shah. He also did a solo album in which he honored his father's work.

Desgrottes, Michel - Trumpet
Over the years he has been a role model for many Konpa musicians.

Desgrottes, Shirley - Singer

Konpa mania discovered the talent of Shirley Desgrottes when she joined the group Jam. Later on, she joined the popular band Zin for a few years during the 1990s.

Désilus, Pierre - Singer

Désir, Colbert - Congas

Désir, Gatien - Singer
Born in Saint Raphael, Gatien became the star of the neighborhoods Bas-Peu-de-Chose and Carrefour Feuilles as the singer of the band Shupa Shupa in the Mini Jazz era. His voice took Shupa Shupa to another level with songs like *Vacances, Epòk Chalè*, and *Voisine Carme*.

Désir, Gérald - Congas
Gérald played with Les Shleu Shleu in the Mini Jazz era. Gerald is today known as one of the best sound engineers in the Haitian diaspora. He has been living in New York with his family for many years.

Désir, Jean Claude - Guitar
Jean Claude is the older brother of the singer Gatien Désir.

Désir, Jude (Zagalo) - Gong / Percussion
Zagalo is one of the most popular gonguists. He is a charismatic musician who can bring the crowd up to their feet with his savoir faire. During his time with D-Zine he was known for taking over the show at times.

Désir, Louco - Radio Personality

Désir, Moïse - Saxophone
Moïse played the saxophone for the Boston based band Volo- Volo.

Désiré, Harry - Drums
Harry started his career with the band Super Ensemble de Webert Sicot. He also played with the band Combite Créole de Rodrigue Millen in the 1970s.

Désiré, Welton - Bass
Welton has been for the past decades the bassist of choice of the entertainer Michel Martelly.

Desmangle, Jean Claude - Keyboard

Desmangle, Kennedy - Congas

Desmangles, Kenny - Singer

He started his career in the New York based Band Siwèl in the early 1990s.

He became one of the founders of the band N.Y. All Stars in the late 1990s. At the turn of the century, he moved to Florida where he became the singer of the band "509"until he was recruited by Zenglen on Nov. 18th, 2006.

The following is an article on Kenny Desmangles...courtesy of Opamizik.com

Dated Nov. 18, 2007

In many music industries you have three types of artists; those who are very talented and receive instant notoriety, those who get lucky by force of nature and then you have Kenny Desmangles the one that has to go the extra mile to get the proper recognition. Kenny recently joined one of the top Haitian bands today, Zenglen in November 2006 after the sudden departure of the band's two lead singers, Fréro Jean Baptiste and Réginald Cangé. Some people might not have heard of Kenny before this event or heard about him but not in depth.

Born on the 28th of November in Cap-Haitien, Haiti, Kenny Desmangles moved to the United States at the age of 13; however, it was in Haiti Kenny realized his talent and love for music with the help of his cousin who introduced him to all of the old school Haitian bands like Tropicana, Bossa Combo, DP Express, Scorpio, Septen, and many more by playing their songs around the house. Like most Haitian families, Kenny's family wasn't too happy about him becoming a musician and encouraged him to pursue a professional career to secure his future.

In order to please his family, Kenny decided to put away his dreams and continue on with his education. After immigrating to the U.S. with his family in 1988, he attended Louis D. Brandeis High School in Manhattan. He developed an immediate interest in sports. He joined the school's soccer and basketball teams, but those extra curricular activities soon came to a halt after being attacked by a gang. It was during the time when Haitian students were tormented in school because of their nationality. Kenny decided he was going to stand up and defend his fellow Haitians, a decision that almost proved fatal as he was stabbed and wounded after being attacked by 15 students. He was rushed to the hospital where he spent over a month and underwent surgery to survive his wounds. He spent his birthday in the hospital, a birthday he will never forget. His English teacher, who came to like him because of his academic excellence, bought him a piano along with his home work and told him to use it so he can make the time go by faster.

After recovering from that experience, Kenny went back to school but carried his piano with him wherever he went. One day while walking, he met a young man by the name of Rudy Appollon who asked him if he knew how to play the piano and he hesitantly replied "No, I just mess around with it, can you play?" The young man took the piano from him and started playing it and after finding out they attend the same church, Holy Name, in Manhattan, which Kenny was already a member of the church's choir and so was his new friend; they became the best of friends. They later on formed a band called "Zouke" and performed at the church's talent shows just around the time "Nouvel Jenerasyon" music were emerging.

After graduating from high school in 1993, Kenny decided to pursue his dream. He attended Hunter College and earned a business degree. During his college years Kenny became a part of a band called Seewell with Ralph Menelas (Zenglen) and Theo (Kreyol La). The band started performing for his school's Haitian Club which expanded to other colleges. They released an album titled Zepon (1996). After Seewell separated due to members graduating and going their different ways, he received a phone call from Rigaud Simon who got in contact with him after Armstrong Jeune personally requested him to join a band they were putting together called New York All Stars, a New York based band with Armstrong Jeune, lead vocalist, Makarios Césaire guitarist, Shedly Abraham drummer, Yves Abel bass player and Welmyr Jean Pierre on keyboard. Kenny became the band's vocalist.

In the year 2000, New York All Stars released the album "Pou La Vie", which consists of ten songs in which Kenny wrote 4 songs; Kago Konpa, One More Chance, Ou Ka di'm Sa which he sung on the album and *Nap Fe Yo Sezi* sung by Armstrong Jeune. While traveling to Florida with NYAS, Kenny met his old Seewell band mate Ralph Menelas and started working on a collaboration project. New York All Stars never really took off despite releasing one of the best albums during that time. While going to Florida back and forth with NYAS, Kenny grew fond of the Florida weather. He later on gave NYAS his letter of resignation and joined Ralph Menelas in 509. The collaboration project turned into full band project for 509.

Like NYAS, 509 too never got off the ground. "Till this day I can't explain it... maybe one day I might be able to sit down and talk about it but for now I really don't understand why 509 never really took off." Kenny Desmangles. Despite releasing a very well-known song *Fake*, which other upcoming band interpreted during their live performances, 509 was never accepted among the popular bands circle.

Then came that faithful day in November when Kenny received a call from long time friend Brutus of Zenglen who called him in an SOS mission when both of the band singers decided to leave the band. Kenny, without any hesitation came to the rescue. His decision to join Zenglen has proven to be the best in his career's history. Today, Kenny is enjoying the spotlight that he's not only deserved but rightfully earned. "Konpa Direk" is moving Kenny's way at this moment!

Opa Mizik would like to congratulate and thank Kenny Desmangles for being our artist of the month.

Did you know: 1-A side from singing, Kenny knows how to play the piano. He took piano lessons while he was in High School. 2- Kenny wrote and produced for Zshea (one of he first female singers in the group Zin) 3- He filled in for Kino of Phantoms on two different occasions and Alan Cave of Zin while Alan was on his Se pa Pou dat tour 4- He produced Je t'aimerai toujours and co-produced Selebre, from Alan Cave Se pa pou dat album and co-wrote Kouraj on Zin's album titled Sa Zin Gen La. 5- He sung in countless albums both as lead and background vocals. 4- Kenny is a proud Parent of a little boy.

Desramaux, Caleb - Show host /Radio and T.V Personality

Désormeau, Kesner - Trumpet

Desrosiers, André - Percussion

Desrouleaux, André - Bass
André played with Super Ensemble de Webert Sicot.

Destin, Charles - Singer

Destin, Jean Duval - Singer/Guitar

Destin, Weiner - Singer
Weiner was one of the star singers of the band Les Vikings in the Mini Jazz era. He is best known for his work on the hit song *Teuleuleu*.

Destiné, Frantz -Trumpet

Détour - Band

Deutz- (Les Deutz de Delmas) - Band
This band did very well in the mid 70s in Haiti with songs like *Courage, Conseil,* and *Réalité.* It is also the band that introduced the talent of the Cicéron Brothers.

Devalcin, Jules - Trombone

Desvarieux, Patrick - Journalist
Patrick is the owner and administrator of the popular Kompa Magazine, an internet site that reports news on Konpa music as it happens. Patrick started the magazine in print in the 1990s and he later changed it to an internet site, attracting Konpa fans all over the world.

Diables Bleus (Les Diables du Cap Haitien) – Band

This band came out in the Mini Jazz era. While most Mini Jazz was concentrated in Port-au-Prince, Diables Bleus was the most recognized mini in Northern Haiti. Some of their best known hits are: *Etoile La Filé* and *Plaisir Vacances.*

Diables du Rythme (Les Diables du Rythme de St Marc) - Band
This band became popular in the Mini Jazz era. However, the band was created a decade earlier in the town of St. Marc on April 24th, 1958. We can easily name *Tounen Lakay* and *Yole* as some of their hit songs. However, the song *Pa Apiyé Sou Do Mwen* will always remain their most memorable song ever.

Diamants (Les Diamants) - Band
This band that came out in the early 70s was actually the first band of the late guitarist/Bassist Luckner (Kiki) Dor, who later became one of the star musicians of Djet - X.

Diaz Julio –Trumpet

Didi Santana see: Fontaine Dukenson

Difé - Band

Difficiles (Les Difficiles de Pétion-Ville) - Band

One of the top bands of the Mini Jazz era, Les Difficiles gave the Konpa society some of the best musicians out of the town of Pétion Ville. The band that would later be known as D.P. Express was created by the singer/guitarist Henry Celestin. When Henry retired from the band, he requested that the name Difficiles not be used anymore. Les Difficiles leave us with some memorable songs like *Janbé Baryè, En Septiemme, Cé La Vie, and Viré Rond,* among others.

Digital Express – Band

After many years of playing for other bands like Gemini, D.P. Express and G.P. Express, star musician Ansyto Mercier came out with his own band, Digital Express in late 1980s. The name Digital was chosen from a D.P. Express hit song of the same name. Digital stopped playing when Ansyto joined Sweet Micky in the late 1990s. Soon after, his son Ti Ansyto came out with the band "Top Digital" to keep alive the Digital Express project.

The legacy came to an end in 2005 when Ti Ansyto became a member of the band Kréole La, and in February in 2006 Daddy Ansyto also joined the Kréole La squad.

Dimanche, Léon – Singer

Léon Dimanche took over the Haitian musical scene in the southern part of Haiti especially in the town of "Les Cayes" in the 1970s. He is still today the greatest star that Les Cayes has known. Léon did not waste time getting recognition all over the country and in the Haitian diaspora. The band "Les Lionceaux des Cayes" was getting so much airtime that anyone in Haiti could recognize Léon's powerful voice just by hearing one note. Songs like *Nostalgie, Vas-t-en*, and *Maman* will always be memorable to the 70s generation.

After the band's first tour to the U.S. the town of Les Cayes was paralyzed the day the band returned. Almost everyone was out to greet the musicians. Léon sings mostly love songs, songs that make people think, songs that are charming.

Léon was a great fan of the band Les Ambassadeurs, which is reflected in his songs. He got the attention of Ernst Ménélas the band leader of Les Ambassadeurs. When Ernst asked him to join Les Ambassadeurs, Léon simply replied "I understand that you need a singer, but I can use you too as a saxophonist for Les Lionceaux, and Ernst Ménélas just walked away.

Léon moved to New York where he resided for many years. Today he is living in Port St. Lucie Fl. with his family. Léon Dimanche is also the owner of a recording studio. He continues to sing, but mostly as a guest star in concerts and festivals. Léon also did a series of solo albums over the years, but his best years still remain those he spent singing for the band Les Lionceaux des Cayes.

The following is an unedited version of Léon Dimanche biography from Leondimanche.com

The baby of a family of 8, Leon grew up listening to the guitar playing and singing of big brothers, Robert and Gabriel. Too young to be involved in this kind of activity, he used to be kept away when family members and friends got together to have fun in the family's house. First born brother Raphael did not want him around so he would not develop an early taste for this kind of events, worrying he might neglect his school works and also develop an addiction for alcohol. He and other brother Jean were able to benefit from the knowledge of Gabriel a poet and Raphael a judge who almost every day would talk for hours about literature, history among other things. Early on, he would start writing poetry himself, and since he was not allowed to play guitar, he would hide at a friend's house (Oswald Genois) and teach himself to play. He was only 16 when he wrote one of his best hits "Va-t-en". The lyric for this song was so deep that people from his town would say the song was written by Brother Gabriel the poet, and later by another of the town composer, Jean Ledans. In the years to come, a lot of our media's writers would still wrongly give credit to Leon's works to Jean Ledans, may be because Leon sang one of Jean Ledans' song "ma vie, une vallée de douleurs" on one of his albums. One of them would write that Jean Ledans has written Leon Dimanche's songs, when in fact Leon would release only one of Jean Ledans' song mentioned above and another one "Pourquoi la rose "was released by Les Lionceaux Des Cayes

Leon started singing at a very early age. At 6, he was already a member of his school choir (Frères Oblats Du Sacre Cœur), but he really started his solo career, only at 13, after his older brother Raphael heard him sing while showering. He joined the group « Les Black Boys des Cayes » at 15 during the summer, at end of school, since he was not allowed to play during the school year.

A year later, still during the summer, he was found playing with a new band "Organ Combo", under the direction of Pierrot Leger. He was with that band for 2 years and right after finishing high school, the band was dismantled and a new one formed under his direction, when **Organ Combo** was forced to perform in "Adults environment not suited for these young musicians", by a powerful Tonton Macoute, who was angry because he felt they were playing for a selected class of people. Pierrot Leger thought, by making a teenager the leader of the band, the man might leave them alone. It worked and he left him alone. Within a few months, the new group "Les Lionceaux Des Cayes" became the town's favorite, and was being sought all over the south side of the country.

In 1971, Marcel Mathieu, Director of "**Radio Diffusion Haitienne**" one of the leading radio station of Port-au-Prince, was passing by his town, heard of him, and came to one of his performance. He asked him if he could record some of his music to be aired on his radio. He agreed and he recorded "**Va-t-en, Nostalgie, Pourquoi la rose**", and a few other songs, which within a month were on every body's lips in the Capital.

Early in 1972, Leon received a signed contract from Mrs. Odette Winner of Bacoulou Night Club in Petion Ville to come and play for her on Saturdays. "Les Lionceaux"performed the first night in that magical ambiance of Petion-ville, the next day, a Sunday morning, Marcel Mathieu introduced Leon Dimanche And "**les Lionceaux Des Cayes**" to the youth of Port-au-Prince in a live and covered event. It was an unbelievable day which's still on the mind of many. Within weeks, every single radio station of Port-au-Prince was airing Leon's music and offers to perform were coming from all over the Country.

After releasing his first 2 albums in 1973, he was named the best singer, composer, and vocalist, and was presented by Pierre Edouard Domond, the director of one the Capital best Social Institution, a medal at a live event in Rex Theatre where he and his band performed every Saturday at 6 & 8 PM for the entire year to a sold out crowd.

He went on to play in every famous night club in the Capital, notably the **Rond Point Restaurant**, where he performed every Saturday night after leaving the **Rex Theatre**, and **Cabane Creole** on Sundays to an always impatient crowd who would show up sometimes hours before the event.

There are many famous moments in his career, but one he seems to remember clearly, was when he went to perform at morning concert in **Cine Lido** one Sunday morning, he got to the place at 9:30, when the show was supposed to start at 10:00, there were hundred of people wanting to get in, outside the theatre, when he finally made it to the gates, he was even more surprised, because there were no room for him to get in. The 2 aisles leading to the stage was crowded and there were at least 200 people on the stage alone. When they saw him, and since there was no room for him to make his way to the stage, the crowd lifted him up and passed him hands to hands all the way to the stage.

He Traveled to the US and Canada and played everywhere for the Haitian Community. He can't even count the amount of awards he received over the years. He is now working with young talents and is still performing all over. This is of course a short version of his career. There are so many stories about him some he does not even know about, that could fill pages of paper, but surely you have heard some....

He recorded 20 albums both with the **Lionceaux** and Solo, the last one a Gospel CD which according to many is a work of art. He went on to perform in many famous theaters notably **Place des arts in Montreal, BAM and Carnegie Hall in N. Y.** etc. He is happy recording albums and writing songs for others, and he is determined with God's blessing to stay around and keep playing for you all for many years to come.

Dimanche, Frantz - Singer
Frantz played with the band Méridional des Cayes.

Diogène, René - Trumpet
Legend has it that at François Guignard's house, the respected musician René Diogène, creator of the L'Orchestre Citadelle, was teasing Nemours Jean Baptiste that the new style of music that Nemours was playing was nothing but a "Compas". Nemours used that word ever since to describe his style and added the word Direct making it "Compas Direct". He popularized the word by using it as a reference in many of his songs. During the carnival seasons, he used the name Compas Direct as the band's name in the parade.

Diogène, Ricot - Percussion

Diplomats (Les Diplomats) - Band

Band of the Mini Jazz era and author of the songs *Trou Métro, Rose Marie and Controle.*

Divers, Pierre Raymond (King Kino) – Singer

One of the most charismatic and popular singers of the past decades, Kino started his career in the mid 1980s with an unknown band in New York named Moon Foo Band. His first hit song, *Sa Fèm Mal*, however, came out in the early 1990s with the band Cajou. When the band Partners changed name and became Phantoms with a new management, the voice of Jean Claude Provilus (James) was replaced by the talented Kino who took the lead in the band with his attitude and professionalism. In the mid-1990s Kino changed his hair to the dreadlock style and, at the same time, gave himself the title of King Kino. His unique voice and style will forever mark the history of Konpa with songs like *Vagabon and Haiti en Cowboy* among others. He tried to leave music for an unsuccessful political career, a move that affected both him and the band. In 2004 King Kino reappeared in the musical scene with the project *"King Kino Mové Mové"*. Once again the King couldn't do it by himself as the public barely answered to his invitations. In 2006 King Kino was reintegrated in the band Phantoms.

Divine, Marc Evans (Ti Marco) - Guitar
He came out in the early 1980s as the rhythm guitarist of Gemini All Stars de Ti Manno. On the band's first album he showed his talent as a singer in the

song *Homage à Bob Marley.*

Dixie Band - Band
After he left Les Frères Dejean star drummer Touco Bouzi came out with his own band, Dixie Band. The band had many good songs but they really lacked a major hit song. The original name of the band was Dixie Land Band. Dixie Band was also known in the 1980s as a band with very good-looking uniforms. The discography of Dixie Band includes but is not limited to the following: *Malouines,Roulé ,Bel Carnaval, Abu, Andréa, El Unico, La Bande à Touco ,La Ki Na Na, Voyé Monté, Bayo Bayo, Pretty Lady, Ti Yaya, Lolita, Kenbé Compas Ou,* as well as some live recordings and some albums with the band's best songs.

Dixie Land Band - Band
The band name was changed to Dixie Band prior to the release of their first album.

Djackaman, Hugues (Dada Djackaman) - Band Manager/Owner
Dada Djackaman was the man that gave life to the Mini Jazz movement. He encouraged the ambition of some young men in the Bas Peu De Choses neighborhood by helping them in the creation of the band Les Shleu Shleu. The Haitian Jewish businessman took it upon himself to find jobs for the young musicians and, one day, Nemours Jean Baptiste agreed for the band to play during his break time at a show at Cabane Choucoune. At the time the mini skirt was in style in Haiti and Nemours said to Dada, "You like my band so much that you created a mini version of it because what I see there is a Mini Jazz".
In the late 60s some of his musicians moved to the U.S. and Dada quickly replaced them with a second version of Les Shleu Shleu. In 1974 the second version followed the footsteps of their predecessors by moving to the U.S. where they created the band Skah Shah # 1. Once again, Dada had to do some damage control by creating a third version of Les Shleu Shleu, and believe it or not he had to create later a fourth version. Nevertheless, he mentored over the years many musicians that we have come to know as some of the greatest superstars of the Haitian music industry.
Dada's name became a household name in Haiti in the 1960s when the first version of Les Shleu Shleu did the song Dada 4/3. His name was also heard on the song *Tête Chauve,* a song made about a baldheaded man in New York name Franky. Dada worked hard, and he was respected by the artists who have worked for him over the years. His picture is also on some of Shleu Shleu's albums.

Djakout Mizik - Band

The name Djakout Mizik was first made public in 1986 at the American Airlines music competition when Guitarist Hans Peters came out under that name as one of the finalists.

The group eventually became a Konpa band after a few years with a completely different squad over the years to include the guitarist Ti Claude Marcelin and the singer Gracia Delva. Ironically, the band saw its best days only after the departure of Gracia and Ti Claude as musicians like Ti Pouch, Roro, and Shabba stepped up as the main performers.

They also acquired Ti Régi, a young keyboardist who initiated a new sound in Konpa call the "Key-Tar", which consist of playing a well-advanced guitar sound on the keyboard. Ti Régi's style as a musician and a composer and the entertainment provided by Shabba, Roro, Ti Pouch and the lead singer Pouchon were the ingredients that took Djakout Mizik to another level.

With songs like *Konpa U.S., La Familia, Manigetta (Money Getter), Saw Méte* and *Biznis Pam,* among others, Djakout, which in the early 1990s was often playing for an almost empty room, has became one of the most in-demand and most entertaining bands ever of the Haitian music industry. At the end of 2006 Djakout released the album Jistis.

Djet-X – Band

This band came out in the 1970s in New York with superstar singer Max Badette and saxophonist Gerald Daniel.
In no time Djet-X became one of New York City's greatest Haitian bands. With hit songs like *Love To Love You Baby, Rossignol, Rét Sézi*, and *O Mayéyé* among others, Djet X became one of the most in-demand bands on the market. Soon the public discovered other stars in the group, like guitar player Roger Jean Baptiste (Ti Yale) bass player Alix Jacques and, of course the band leader/saxophonist Gérard Daniel and the talented singer Max Badette.

Djo Gong see: Durandis, Joseph

Djo Light see: Tabutau, Joseph

Djoubap's (Les Djoubpa's) - Band

Do Ré Mi Jazz - Band
This band of the Mini Jazz era came out in the 1970s.

Doane, John * - Keyboard
The late John Doane was the leader of the band Skandal.

DoLa - Band
Created in 2006, this band is based in Brooklyn, N.Y. with the singer Armstrong Jeune and the keyboardist Jean Max Valcourt as the leaders. In 2007 the band released the album *Brassé* with 16 songs.

Doctor Black see: Washington Andrew

Dominique, Gérard - Drums
Played with the band Norma de Léogane.

Dominique, Hans - Drums / Congas

Dominique, Jean - Promoter / Band Manager
Jean Dominique is known as one of the promoters and investors in the Konpa community of New York City.

Dominique, Wesner - Trumpet
Wesner played respectively with Latino, Sicot and Nemours

Domingue, Liautaud * (Yaffa) - Saxophone
While most people know about Nemours Jean Baptiste as the leader and saxophonist of the band Compas Direct many don't know that next to Nemours was the great Yaffa, who used to do some solos on his alto sax as well. Yaffa was also the composer of a few hit songs of the band, including Minou.

Dor, Luckner * (Kiki) - Guitar / Bass
At a very young age Kiki played with the band "Les Diamants". That band never had the chance to record an album. Later in his career, in New York, Kiki joined the band Djet X.

Dor, Serge - Bass / Percussion

Doralus, Luc - Singer

Dorcé, Jacques - Congas
Played with the band Sakad

Dorcélien, Bellerive * - Guitar
Star guitarist of the band Ensemble Select de Coupé Cloué throughout his career until his death.

Doré, Joe - Singer
Joe played with the band Sakaj.

Doriscent, Jean Joseph - Congas

He played in New York with the band Tropical Combo de Ti Jacques.

Dorismond, André - Singer
One of the stars of the 1960s, André Dorismond sang most of the hit song of Webert Sicot's legendary band, Cadence Rampa.

Dorival, Altiéri * - Singer
Altiéri became popular in the late 70s with the song *Carole* of his Konpa/Troubadour band Ensemble Le Progres. His album *Ca* was released in 1979 under the label Marc Record.

Dorlean Records
Haitian-owned record label

Dorlette, Dieujuste - Bass

Dorlette, Eddy - Saxophone

Dorlette, Frantz (Fanfan) - Saxophone

Dorlette, Fred - Bass
Fred was one of the two bassists of the band Les Lionceaux Des Cayes. He used to share his position with Rigobert Clergé.

Dorméus, Ralph Albert - Guitar / Bass

Dormus, Raymond - Singer
Played with the band Diables du Rythme de St. Marc in the 70s

Dorsainvil, Bernard - Saxophone
Bernard played with the band Bossa Combo in the 1970s and 80s.

Dorsainvil, Jean-Claude (Charlie) - Singer
Charlie's voice was, for a long time, one of the most heard voices in Haiti, especially in the 1970s. He created some of Bossa Combo's greatest hits, songs like "*Te Quero*" and "*Permanente*", which will always be in the hearts and minds of Konpa fans all over the world.
Charlie was also among the members that left Bossa Combo to create the band Accolade de New York. He reached his stature of stardom by becoming one of the most popular voices of the 1980s, singing super hits like *Madan Jules, Latiamimi,* and *La Foie* among others.

Jean Claude Dorsainvil, who was once a medical school student, chose a career in music in the early 1970s by joining Bossa Combo. In the 1990s he became a bus driver in the Linden Blvd. corridor in Queens N.Y. After several attempts to bring the band Accolade de New York back to life, and an attempt to reunite with some former members of Bossa Combo in the project BossAccolade, Jean Claude finally called it quits and realized that his life as a musician was behind him.

Dorsainvil, Nicholas - Keyboard

Dorsillome, Smith - Drums
Smith played with the band Diables du Rythme de St. Marc, which later became Les Virtuoses. In the 1980s he joined the band Scorpio Universel.

Dorval, Hilario - Trumpet

Dorval, Loulou - Singer
Loulou played in the Mini Jazz era with the band Les Jokers.

Dorval, Mann - Trombone

Dorval, Omane -Trombone
Omane played with Scorpio and System band, among others. He is living in New York with his family.

Dorvilien, Fritz - Trumpet
Fritz played with the band Scorpio Universel in Haiti then he moved to NY where he joined the band Astros in the late 1970s.

Dorville, Jean - Singer

Douby, Isnard - Singer /Trumpet
Isnard Douby is one of the Haitian music industry's top superstars. He sings and played the trumpet for Les Frères Dejean in the early days of his career. When the band was forced to stay in Haiti during a tour due to some of the members expired visas, Isnard started the musical group System Band in New York, also assuming the role of band leader. During that time because of problem with his neck his doctor ordered him to abandon the trumpet. Isnard is extremely popular in the Caribbean, particularly in French Guyana. Besides being a good Konpa singer, Isnard has the ability to sing very well in Spanish. He is also known for creating many slogans in the Konpa world. While the music is playing you can hear Isnard saying things like: "*Maché*

Maché Maché, Eske'm dan lair, Ayi Manman, Voyé Konpa monté ak dé men nou" and many more. He is also known for calling the name of the fans and members of the media attending the shows. Isnard is one of a kind when it comes to entertaining the public. Songs like *Marina, Coté Ménage ou, Arête, Débaké, Gladia,* and *Naïdé* were some of Frères Dejean hits sung by Isnard Douby. Songs like *Anita, César,* and *Bam Passé* are some of System Band's memorable music that made Isnard Douby an immortal Konpa superstar.

Douby, Leslie - Singer
Lesly is the younger brother of Isnard Douby. He played with Les Frères Déjean in the 70s and System Band in the 1980s.

Dougé, Jules - Singer
Jules started his career with the band Jazz des Jeunes before becoming the star singer of the band Diables du Rythme de St. Marc.

Douyon, Antoine - Guitar
Antoine played with Webert Sicot's band in the 1960s.

Dozz - Band
Discography includes *Dominé* and *Ou Sé La Vie*

Dragon - Band
Former band of the town of St. Marc

Dragonaire - Band

Drice, Chantale - Singer

Drouillard, Kerly - Percussion

Dubois, Michel * - Conga

Dubuisson, André - Singer
André played in France with the group Vega Band.

Dubuisson, Durcys - Guitar

Duclair, Marie Maude - Singer

Duclervil, Adam - singer
Adam played with the band La Ruche de Léogane.

Dugué, Charles - Singer

Dugué, Dieuville - Trumpet

Dugué, Jean Enock - Bass
Enock played with Zenglen and later Ozone.

Dugué, Nixon - Gong / Percussion
Dullon, Joseph - Saxophone

Dupermé, Sadrac – Saxophone

Duperval Lyonel * – Promoter / Producer / Radio Personality

Duperval, Sebastien – Keyboard

Dupervil, Gérard - Singer * Singer / Keyboard / Trumpet / Guitar

Born in the town of Miragoane in 1932, Gerard Dupervil played in his early musical career with a series of bands including his Trio Les Gais Printemps, Conjunto International of Nemours Jean Baptiste and Septentrional. He was well-known in the music scene of the late 1940s and early 1950s as a great singer, and a gambler and undisciplined individual. However, he quickly gained the status of one of the greatest stars ever in the history of Haitian music when he joined the popular band Jazz des Jeunes not only as a singer but also an arranger and a writer. His voice has, for more than four decades, dominated the airwaves wherever Haitian music is played in hit songs like *Fleur de Mai, Maman, Des Roses Pour Des Coeurs, Je N'avais Que Toi, Comme Jadis,* and *J'ai Péché.*

He also wrote the song *Denise* for President François Duvalier's daughter Marie Denise Duvalier who, according to popular belief and people around the band, was like many young women of the 60s in love with the popular singer. No relationship ever evolved between the two however.

Gerard Dupervil left Haiti and moved to the U.S. where he did a couple of solo albums with memorable songs like *Haiti, Désiré* and *l'Amour Est Il Un Mal.*

By the 1980s Gerard Dupervil lost his sight, and he became a gospel singer. He later moved back to Haiti, where he devoted the rest of his life to helping needy children until his death in 1994.

Dupervil, Gina - Singer
Gina is the daughter of the legendary singer Gerard Dupervil. On her first album she did a re-mix of most of her father's songs.

Dupervil, Sebastien - Keyboard

Duplan, Lyonel * - Bass
Lyonel played in the New York based band Thamad Fever. Lyonel was also a star volleyball player in Haiti in his teenage years.

Dupoux, David – Keyboard

David really made a name for himself when he created, with his partner and best friend Djo Zenny, the band "Konpa Kréyol" which came out in Dec. 3rd 1998.
While on tour in Florida, an argument occurred among the members of the band, and upon their return to Haiti the band was split in two. The singer Joseph Zenny Jr. came out with the band "Kreyol La" and David moved on with his new band "Krézi". David is an excellent keyboardist, a great Konpa composer and the leader of the band Krézi.

Dupuy, Adrien - Guitar
Adrien's talent started to show in the band Shooblack, but he became a star guitarist in his years with Shoogar Combo.

Dupuy, Jean Yvon - Keyboard

Dupuy, Sarah - Singer /Guitar /Percussion

Durand, Alliette - Singer
Alliette did background vocal for Les Beatniks de Queen in the Mini Jazz era

Durand, Billy - Bass

Durand, Cécile - Singer
Cécile did background vocal for Les Beatniks de Queen in the Mini Jazz era

Durand, Georges - Bass
Georges played with the band Norma de Léogane and later with Les Ambassadeurs.

Durand, Robert - Keyboard

Durand, Osvald Jr. - Saxophone / Flute / Guitar
He is to many musicians a great arranger on their solo projects.

Durandis, Joseph (Djo Gong) - Gong
Djo Gong played with Shleu Shleu and Skah Shah D'Haiti among others.

Duroseau, Harold - Keyboard
Harold played most of his career with the band Les Lionceaux des Cayes. Harold also played with the bands Washington Express and G.P. Express in the Washington metropolitan area; although he never did record any albums with those D.C. based groups. Harold can, at times, have a bad temper, and can be a difficult person to manage. He is, however, a very talented keyboardist and a great musician.

Duroseau, Jacky * - Keyboard
Jacky played with Les As, and also Ibo Combo in the Mini Jazz era.

Duroseau, Kesnel - Bass

Duroseau, Kretzer * - Congas
Played with Nemours Jean Baptiste in the band Aux Calebasses, and stayed with Nemours in the creation of Compas Direct. Kretzer is credited for the congas beat being used by all the Konpa congas players until today. Apparently while Nemours was trying to find a new style to distance himself from his previous group and to show something new about his new band Super Ensemble de Nemours Jean Baptiste, Kretzer had some problems following the tempo imposed by the maestro. So Nemours had to simplify the beat in order to accommodate Kretzer's style and the rhythm Konpa, as we all know it today, was born.

Duroseau, Maurice - Keyboard

Duroseau, Mozart * - Keyboard
Music instructor and music sales person in his late adult years, Mozart was a real Haitian Mozart when it comes to playing the piano. One of the star musicians of the band Aux Calebasses, Mozart can also be credited with being the very first Konpa Keyboardist, playing for Nemours' band before leaving his place to his younger brother, Richard Duroseau.

Duroseau, Richard - Accordion/Keyboard
No other Haitian musician ever knew the glory at such an early age as Richard Duroseau. Growing up in a house where the Keyboard was king, his older brothers were already star musicians when he made his debut in the musical arena at the age of 14.
Too young to handle his stardom, the new found superstar of Nemours Jean Baptiste was not easy to manage. He was known for cursing and insulting others, even the club owners. However, he was so talented and such a quick learner that the maestro depended on him while making the songs and even named him as one of the best composers of the band next to himself and the guitarist Raymond Gaspard in the song *Les 3 Dangers*.
Richard was eventually replaced and Nemours had to make some serious changes in the way the band played to fill up the hole left by the legendary musician. Richard moved to New York to join his older brothers. He played in area restaurants, particularly in Brooklyn, and in the 1980s and 90s he became a regular of Skah Skah.
When Skah Shah became less busy at the turn of the century, he went right back to playing at the restaurants to entertain to make a living as a musician. Richard had, on several occasions, received some awards and trophies as well as the recognition of fellow musicians of all generations, and music and records producers as one of Konpa music's greatest musicians and a true representation of Haitian music heritage and legacy.

Durosel, Arsène - Keyboard
Arsène played with Cadence Rampa of Webert Sicot and with Les Ambassadeurs.

Durosier, Guy * - Singer/Keyboard/Guitar/Bass/Saxophone/Flute/Congas
It seems like you name an instrument and Guy Durosier can play it. Guy was mostly known for playing classical concert than playing with bands in clubs and halls. However the man born in Port-au-Prince had one of his most popular albums with the Cap Haitien-based band Septentrional, where we can find some of his songs like *Tambour Frappé* and *Vent Tempète*.

Duval, Felix - Guitar

Duval, Georges - Bass /Drums

Duverger, Auguste (Pouchon) – Singer

Pouchon is the singer of the popular band Djakout Mizik. Pouchon showed to the world that, despite his unknown past and lack of experience, he was able to reach stardom after only a few live performances and was able to bring the crowd to their feet in songs like *Konpa U.S., La Familia, Manigetta, Biznis Pam,* and *Loué Christ La.* He also charmed the ladies with his charismatic voice in the down tempo songs like *Ma Seule Folie* and *Love Me Girl.*

Duverger, Marc *- Producer
One of the top Haitian Records producers from the 1960s to the late 1990s, Marc was the owner and President of Marc Records. Marc Duverger worked until his death for the advancement of Konpa music, not only as a record producer but also as a show promoter. Marc Records has given exposure to bands and artists that were ignored by most producers and eventually contributed to the success of many Konpa superstars.
Duverglas, Joel - Guitar

Duverglas, Reynold - Keyboard /Accordion /Violin
Reynold received a solid musical formation at an early age. He was of course, like many people of the 60s, part of the Mini Jazz movement when he became a member of the band Les Diplomats. He later moved to New York where he was seen playing in his adult life with Djet-X and Skah Shah.

Duviella, Serge - Keyboard

Dynamite All Stars – Band

E

Eby, Curtis - Trumpet
Musician of Tabou Combo

Edmé, Marc - Congas
Marc came out in the 1960s during the Mini Jazz era with Difficiles before moving to Gypsies in the 1970s. Later he played with Scorpio in the 1980s.

Edmé, Paul - Congas
Paul played with Les Difficiles and later with Les Shleu Shleu.

Edouard, Fritz - Singer
Fritz was one of the lead singers of "Blousons Noirs" in the Mini Jazz ear.

Edouard, Jean Baptiste *- Keyboard
Edouard started to get the recognition of other musicians in his time with Les Loups Noirs, but in the late 70s and early 80s he showed maturity in the live performances and albums of Accolade de New York and System Band.

Edouard, Jean Claude - Singer
Jean Claude played with Septentrional du Cap.

Eklips - Band

El Pozo see: Florestal Rommy

El Sahied, Issa *- Saxophone
Respected musician before the creation of Konpa and a role model and mentor to countless musicians.

Elaine, Ronald - Saxophone

Eliassaint, Réginald * - Guitar
Réginald was a very good songwriter. He left the Konpa community to write songs for some of the Rasin bands like Koudjay and Rèv. His sudden death was a real shock to the Haitian music industry.

Elie, Jean Claude - Promoter

Owner and administrator of the Konpa website Rockmasters.com

Elie, Marc - Guitar
Popular guitarist and soccer player of the football team Aigle Noir in the 1960s

Elie, Ralph - Drums
Ralph played with Ibo Combo and later with Les Shleu Shleu.

Elysée, Emmanuel - Drums

Emile, Dernst - Keyboard /Guitar
Dernst Emile is a respected music arranger for many Konpa bands.

Emile, Denis* - Guitar
Denis played with Bossa Combo in the early days of the Mini Jazz era.

Emile, Erick - Bass

Emile, Frantz - Keyboard

Emile, Ronald - Singer
Musician of the Washington D.C based Trankill.

Emile, Wilner - Congas

Ensemble Aux Calebasses - Band
This band was put together by Maestro Nemours Jean Baptiste, and would later become known as Super Ensemble de Nemours Jean Baptiste, or simply Compas Direct. The band was the house band of the popular nightclub Aux Calebasses (Calabash) located in Mariani, a small town south of Port-au-Prince.

Ensemble de Nemours Jean Baptiste - Band
The band was also known as Super Ensemble de Nemours Jean Baptiste. Most people refer to the band as Compas Direct.

Ensemble de Webert Sicot – Band
The band was also known as Super Ensemble de Webert Sicot. Most people refer to the band as Cadence Rampas.

Ensemble Select de Coupé Cloué - Band
This group, which stated as Trio Select in the late 1950s, became a band in

1973. It was in the years that followed one of Haiti's most popular bands for more than two decades.

With star singer Coupé Cloué the band traveled to many countries around the world, playing their mega hit songs like *Fanm Kolokent, Madan Marcel* and *Miyan Miyan* among others.

Eperviers (Les Eperviers) - Band

Essence - Band
That band was put together in New York by Tony Moise, the former leader of Les Shleu Shleu.

Estimé, Eddy - Keyboard

Etienne, Charles - Keyboard
Charles played with the band Scorpio Fever.

Etienne, Ezekiel - Keyboard / Accordion

Etienne, Felix - Bass

Etienne, Fernande - Singer
Fernande played with the band Pyé Bèf.

Etienne, Jacqueline - Singer

Etienne, Louis - Keyboard
Louis played with Septentrional du Cap.

Etienne, Loulou * - Singer
Loulou played in the early days of the band Les Jouvenceaux de Jacmel.

Etienne, Vladimir (Katalog) - Singer
Musician of Gabel

Etienne, Weston - Singer
Winston played with Tabou Combo.

Etienne, Yanick - Singer
Yanick participated in several Konpa projects including Skạh Shah and System band among others, before coming out with her own projects. The song *Mistè Lanmou* appeared on an album arranged by her husband, the

respected composer and music arranger Dernst Emile.

Etienne, Yvenel - Singer

Etoile Du Soir (Ensemble Etoile Du Soir) - Band
Although popular in the 1960s Etoile Du Soir never really made it big like other Haitian bands of that time. The music of Etoile Du Soir was too dull for the era. However, it is a band that was unique in its style. The songs of Etoile du Soir are still the favorites of the troubadour bands.

Eugene, Bedy - Keyboard

Eugene, Fedlain - Bass

Eugene, Jean - Claude - Singer
His best hit song is *"Cecilia"*. Jean Claude moved to New York in the early 1970s and in the 90s he migrated to Virginia where he lives with his family. His new venture, "Theatre Mapou" has presented popular plays like *Mouché Défas* and *Gouverneur De La Rosée* among others in several cities.

Eugene, Roger (Shoubou) - Singer

Shoubou will be the first to remind you that he is from the town of Port de Paix. He was, with to Jean Eli Telfort (Cubano), the star singer of the band La Perle des Antilles one of the few bands of Port de Paix in the mid-60s. When he moved to Petion Ville, his mother's hometown, he joined the band Ibo Negro until he was discovered by Albert Chancy who introduced him to the members of Los Incognitos, the band that would become known as Tabou Combo.

To some of the members, who were already a clique, Shoubou was considered as an outsider. He basically had the support of the band leader, Albert, who became his protégé. His hard work, plus his strong, charming and unique voice took him to stardom with the release of the first hits of Tabou Combo in songs like *Natasha, Sépa,* and *Yapatia.*

In the late 1960s most members of the band left the country to study outside Haiti. The band was re-created in New York and Shoubou joined the squad in the early 70s where he again excelled in songs like *Kokobé, Canne à Sucre,* and especially *Bonne Anniversaire,* one of the best-known Haitian slow songs ever. While some the musicians' favorite singer was their Pétion Ville pal Sergo

Guerrier, to the public Shoubou was the star of band. When Guerrier left the band to move on with other projects, Shoubou became the only voice of Tabou Combo in the album titled *Respect*.

The song *Respect* is also the one that would make Tabou Combo one of the most popular Caribbean bands ever. Shoubou rocked anyone who had the chance to witness Tabou Combo playing live especially when he added the super jam "Fanm lan dansé kon mabouya". The band later changed the name of the song simply to *Mabouya*. On the same album the charismatic Shoubou once again shocked the world in *Plus Près de Toi,* another slow song, and the hot song *Bébé Paramount.*

From 1968 to today Shoubou has made his mark in the Haitian music industry by singing hundreds of Konpa hit songs. His stardom goes beyond the perimeters of the Haitian music industry. He has over the years, with his voice, made the crowds jump high, get down low and clap their hands under his command from his hometown Port de Paix to places as far as Japan.

On Dec., 8th, 2007 the Haitian association Nord Ouest Réuni (Northwest United) presented to Shoubou and Cubano the Haitian Music Ambassador Award.

Evans, Ignace (Penm) - Guitar
When Nemours started his band Super Combo to revive Compas Direct under new management and a new name, he called on the young Penm as the guitarist to satisfy his audience. Since Super Combo didn't have the success of Compas Direct, Penm was somewhat incognito in his early days in the music business. Later, in the late 70s, Penm joined the band D.P. Express where he finally got some fame and recognition as an excellent guitarist. After he left D.P. he tried to come out with his own band, 'Apocalypse". Unfortunately that didn't last long.

Evenaty, Heribert - Bass
Musician of the band Take Off

Exantus, Patrick (Checko) - Congas
Musician of the band Take Off, Checko played in previous years for the band Back Up.

Eventsmaster.net
Haitian owned website to promote and search for events.

Exit - Band
That band was created in New York in the early 1990s by Media Personality and show Promoter Jojo Lorquet.

Exit d'Haiti - Band
Konpa band based in Haiti

Exit entertainment
Popular Haitian T.V show broadcasted in New York and hosted by show promoter Jojo Lorquet.

Exodus - Band
This band was created in New York by the guitarist Gary Résil after he left Skah Shah in the 1980s. Their discography includes *Nou Pral Décolé, Bonjour Marie, Victoire,* and *Merci Dessalines.* The band also introduced to the market the talent of the congas player Eddy Germain, who later made a career in the band Zenglen. The singer Imgart Manigat moved from Haiti to be part of the band, and he delivered a very good performance in the song *Nou Pral Décolé.*

Explosion - Band

Ezil, Verieres - Congas

F

Fabre, Patrick –Promoter / Band Manager
Patrick Fabre is known as one of the promoters and investors in the Konpa community of Miami Fl. Patrick is the manager of the band Gabel.

Fanfan, Henry - Saxophone

Fanfan Ti Botte see: Joseph Yves

Fantaisistes (Les Fantaisites de Carrefour) – Band

One of the pioneers of the Mini Jazz era, Fantaisistes rocked the country from their creation until they stopped playing. When the first album, *Petit Oiseau d'Haiti* came out one couldn't find a song that was not a hit. The band proved itself once again at the release of the second album titled *Volley ball.*

Fantaisistes (Les Fantaisistes de Jérémie) - Band
This band, which also came out in the Mini Jazz era, was the most popular mini in the town of Jérémie in the Southern part of Haiti.

Fahrenheit - Band
Under the leadership of the keyboardist Jeff Policard and his brother Gaëtan, both sons of the respected keyboardist Réginald Polycard, the band Fahrenheit was created in New York with Elie Lapointe on lead guitar. Their discography includes *Chalè Nan Kay La* and *Difé*. In 2007 the guitarist Elie Lapointe was recruited by Djakout Mizik but Fahrenheit continued to move on.

Fassad - Band
This band came out in the 1990s. Their song *Pou Chimène* will remain a

memorable one.

Fatal, Fragile - Keyboard
Fragile played with the band Etoile du Soir.

Fattier, Jacques - Trumpet /Saxophone
Jacques is a French musician who played in the 1980s with several Haitian bands, including the Caribbean Sextet and Zèklè.

Faustin, Eric - Singer

Faustin, Harold - Guitar

Févry, Vilsor - Drums
Vilsor played with the band Panorama des Cayes.

Félix, Fritz - Gong /Percussion
Fritz played with the band Volo Volo de Boston.

Félix, Hans - Guitar
Hans played with the band Les Ambassadeurs in Haiti and later on, in the mid- 70s, he joined the band Volo Volo de Boston.

Félix, Jean (Janmò) - Singer /Drums
Janmò played with Shoogar Combo in Haiti. He is the author of the song *St.Cécile* by Shoogar Combo.
In this song he talked about how the hard work of Haitian musicians is not appreciated. He moved to NY in the early 1990s, where he joined the band Shleu Shleu. He got his nickname Janmò (Jean Mò) because he used to drive the hearse of his family owned funeral home.

Félix, Jean Claude - Singer
Jean Claude Felix is one of the first singers of Ensemble de Nemours Jean Baptiste. Jean Claude started his career in the band Les Diables du Rythme de St Marc at an early age. Jean Claude Felix is the older brother of Hans Felix, a well-known guitarist of the Mini Jazz era who played for Les Ambassadeurs in Haiti and later for Volo Volo in Boston.

Félix, Jean Wesley (Kid Ali) - Guitar /Singer
Kid Ali represented Haiti as a boxer in the 1976 Olympic in Canada.

Félix, Robert - Bass

Félix, Ronald - Bass
Started his musical career with the band Clinic de NY. In the late 1990s he played with Tabou Combo.

Félix, Wilner - Guitar
Wilner played with the band Les Vikings in the Mini Jazz era.

Féquière, Donald - Drums

Féquière, Gerald - Singer

Ferdinand Sidney - Guitar
Sidney played with the band Les Fantaisistes de Carrefour in Haiti and became a regular member of Volo Volo de Boston in the 70s.

Ferdinand, Wilbert - Singer
Wilbert played with the band Norma de Léogane.

Ferentino, Nicolina - Saxophone
Nicolina is a talented non-Haitian musician who continues to make her mark in the Konpa community with her contribution in the horn section of the band Zenglen. She is called Sweetness not only for her sweet sound on the sax but also for her kindness as a person.

Ferrere, Edouard - Guitar
Played with the band Accolade de NY in the 1980s.

Ferrier, Fritz - Saxophone
Fritz is one of the saxophonists of Nemours' band Ensemble de Nemours Jean Baptiste.

Ferrier, Jean Marco - Keyboard

Ferry, Claude - Congas

Fidel - Band

Fidele, Rigaud - Trumpet
Played with the band Jazz Capois in the city Cap Haitien

Figaro, Emmanuel (Ti Sax) - Saxophone

Ti Sax started his musical career with Tropicana, then he joined the band Super Combo of Nemours Jean Baptiste and later on became a member of Bossa Combo.

Fils, Frantz - Trumpet

Fils -Aimé, Joel - Bass

Fils -Aimé, Parisien - Band
Star singer of the band Tropicana since the 1960s.

Firmin, Gérald (Gérald Kaliko) - Promoter/Producer

First Class - Band
This band was created by the popular singer Yvon Mondésir former, singer of Tabou Combo and Magnum Band. One of their best hit songs is *"Computer"*, with the catchy phrase *"Mété'l sou Computer."* At the turn of the century another band by the same name came out in New York with a different spelling as they are known as 1st Class.

Fisher, Patrick - Guitar

Flambert, André * - Guitar

Flash - Band

Flashback - Band
This band is made up primarily of ex-members of Gypsies and Difficiles who get together to do one or two shows in Haiti especially during the Christmas season reminiscing about the good old days of the Mini Jazz era.

Fletcher, Farnah - Keyboard
Farnah played with Magnum Band.

Fleurant, Erode - Bass

Fleurima, Billy - Guitar
Billy played with the band les Stars and Scorpio in Haiti. He also participated in the Mini All Stars projects in New York.

Fleuristal, Joseph - Bass

Fleuristil, Variété - Keyboard

Fleurentin, Michel - Singer
Michel played with the band "Tropicana".

Fleury, Serge - Drum
Serge is one of the founders and original members of the band "Volo Volo de Boston" in the 1970s.

Florestal, Louis - Keyboard

Florestal, Louixène - Bass
Louixène constituted, with Ornel Henry, one of two bassists who played with Coupé Cloué and his band Ensemble Select in the last few years of the legendary superstar.

Florestal, Rommy (El Pozo) - Guitar
El Pozo has played with several bands in his career, but he became popular in the Konpa community when he joined the band Zenglen based in Miami.

Florestant, Jocelyn - Singer

Florival, Herline - Keyboard
Herline played with some respectable bands throughout her career. The daughter of a Haitian preacher, she started by playing in churches. In the 1990s she became a regular in Macho Band. She did a wonderful job on the album of the Washington, D.C. based band Zépon's and she also rocked the nation capital many times during their live shows and at the D.C. Caribbean Carnivals. She later did many live shows with the all female band "Riské" before becoming a regular in one of the latest version of "Shleu Shleu", directed by Smith Jean Baptiste. In 2006 Herline moved to Philadelphia where she plays for a Baptist church.

Florvil, Frantz - Keyboard/Bass
Frantz played for the band Washington Express in the 1980s and in 2005 he joined the band Trankill.

Fontana - Band
This band, which started in Port de Paix by the Menelas bothers, became known later in Port-au-Prince as Les Ambassadeurs.

Fontaine, Dukenson (Didi Santana) – Guitar

The public started to notice the guitar works of Didi in his days with Déga and later he moved with his career playing for K-Dans. Didi is considered as one of the best Konpa Guitarist of the new century.

Foreste, Maggy - Singer

Maggy Foreste career's only lasted a few years. She joined the band "Zin" in the second part of the 1980s but her heart was mostly to her school. While she was performing with Zin she was also pursuing a career in nursing. Today she is a full time nurse. Her best hit with Zin is the song *"All the way'*.

Formidables (Les Formidables de St Marc) - Band

Band of the Mini Jazz era that came out in the town of St. Marc, a town located in the northern part of Haiti. In the early 1970s their song *Papa Loco* was played quite often on the air. Besides the album *Papa Loco*, their discography also includes the albums *Ambition* and *Compas Sacré.*

Formule H - Band

This band came out in the 1980s under the leadership of Joseph Tabutau (Djo Light) the ex-bassist of Samba Créole.

Fortère, Jacques Maurice (Wawa) - Singer

Wawa played with Ensemble de Nemours Jean Baptiste. After Nemous, he also played with Sicot and was one of the members who created Super Choucoune after the departure of Sicot. Wawa moved to a different style of music before becoming one of the greatest singers of the Rasin music movement.

Fortère, Gerard - Singer

Fortère, Michel -Ange - Congas

Fortunat, Wilky - Singer

Fortuné, Arnold - Guitar / Bass / Singer

Fortuné, Joe - Bass
Joe did his best years with the Dixie Band in the 1980s.

Fortuné, Lenor (Azor) - Singer
Azor played Konpa music with different bands, but he didn't achieve stardom until he started to play Rasin Music. Azor is the leader of the band "Racine Mapou de Azor", representing the Haitian culture at several festivals around the world, especially in the U.S. Azor has performed many times in Europe and as far as Japan.

Fortuné, Paolo - Singer

Foucard, Mario - Congas

Foufouille see - Georges Malval

Francillon, Robens – Bass
Musician of the Miami based band Gabel

Francis Entertainment
Record and Show Production Company

Francoeur, Assade (Assali) - Singer
The public discovered the voice of Assade when the band Do Re Mi Jazz released the song *Wi Parrain*. After the band broke up he moved on with some members in the creation of the band Safari Combo, which later became Super 9.
In the late 70s he joined the band Ensemble Select de Coupé Cloué, where he forever made his mark in the Haitian music world in the song *Miyan Miyan* and *Marie Jocelyne*. The latter is a song he wrote for his wife. He later moved to New York where he created the band "Wanga Nègès". Since the band couldn't make it in the difficult New York market, Assade returned to Haiti. Depressed about the way his career was heading, he became mentally ill. When he recuperated from his illness he converted to Christianity and today he is only performing as a gospel singer.

Francois, Carl (Carlito Coupé) - Singer
Carl Francois better known as "Carlito Coupé" got this nickname for his

ability to sound like the legendary Haitian singer Coupé Cloué. Carlito's best hit ever is the song *"Boujon Bourjoli"*. Carlito 's voice resembles Coupé Cloué's voice so much that for a long time radio announcers all over Haiti and in the Diaspora had to repeat the singer's name every time his songs were played in order to make the public aware that it was not Coupé Cloué on the air. He had many successful tours in the mid 1980s and a few other good songs, but none had the success of Boujon Bourjoli.

François, Delcarme - Keyboard

François, Delly - Singer
Delly played with the band Lakol D'Haiti in his native town, Cap Haitien, before moving to Florida, where he became one of the vocalists of the band D'Zine. When the band broke up and some members moved on to create the band Nu Look, Delly who was not part of the squad experienced a period of silence. Later he moved to New York where he became for a while a member of System Band.
His journey with System didn't last long and he returned to Florida where he tried to put the band D Zine back together. Once again, that was a failed project. In 2007 he reappeared with the band Pozé in Miami.

François, Eddy - Singer
Eddy François started his professional singing career with the Konpa band Superstar Music Machine in 1988, and he moved on to the music rasin genre when he joined Bookman Eksperyans in 1989. In 1993 he created his band Boukan Guinen and in 2007 he became a solo artist.

François, Jacques (Ti Jacques) - Singer / Trumpet
Ti Jacques started his career as one of the showmen of the band Septentrional in the city of Cap Haitien. When he moved to New York in the 1960s Ti Jacques wasted no time and started his own band, Tropical Combo, playing in Haitian restaurants in Queens and Brooklyn, where he made his mark as a singer.

François, Jacques Arthur * - Saxophone
Arthur played with "Tropicana".

François, Joseph Duphène - Trumpet

Francois, Kenny (Chapotol) - Congas
Kenny played with Scorpio and Les Frères Dejean in the 1980s and 1990s.

François, Wilner - Singer

Frank, Fresnel - Guitar
Excellent guitarist of the 70s who played with the band "Do Ré mi Jazz Simalo" which later became "Safari Combo" the name was changed again to "Super 9".

Frank, Joseph (Kayou) - Guitar
Kayou, the father and mentor of Ricardo Frank (Ti Plume) played in his glory days for Ensemble de Webert Sicot.

Frank, Ralph - Bass
Ralph played with the band "les Loups Noirs. He is the brother of legendary guitarist Ricardo Frank (Ti Plume)

Frank, Ricardo (Ti Plume) - Guitar / Singer
Born in Port-au-Prince, Ti Plume was one of the greatest guitarists of the Mini Jazz era and a member of the popular band Les Ambassadeurs. His father, Joseph Frank (Kayou), who played for Sicot's band was essentially his mentor and music professor.
When Ti Plume left Les Ambassadeurs he was one of the first of his generation to come out with a Troubadour style solo album titled "Jovial Ti Plume". He also had his own band, Les *Bitops* in the mid-70s. As the Bitops project was not successful, Ti Plume joined Les Loups Noirs, where he worked not only as a guitarist but also as a vocalist in songs like *Roi* and *Lajan ak Zanmi.* In the mid-70s he rejoined Les Ambassadeurs, where he excelled in the song *King à La Ganache* again as a guitarist and on lead vocal.
In the 1980s Ti Plume stayed in North America, particularly in Canada, and later in New York where he created his band "Makumbe". When the band once again couldn't make it in the New York market, Ti Plume became, for a short while, a member of the band Accolade de New York.
Then, surprisingly, Ti Plume retired from playing live Konpa shows and for the rest of his musical career he only played acoustic guitar as a one-man show. He also, at the end of the 20th century, released his classical guitar project in an album called *Touch of Class.*

Frédérique, Carmelo (Frédy) - Singer
Proud of his native town "Léogane", Frédy was, at a young age, a fan of the band La Ruche de Léogane, which inspired him to become a musician. When he moved to the Washington, D.C. area with his mother and younger brothers Gino Mathurin (actual owner of the site Echo d'Haiti) Jean Michel Mathurin (now a popular DJ and a satellite radio announcer), he met his mentor Michel

Pressoir, who let him join his band and showed him some vocal techniques. Unlike Haiti and other communities of the Diaspora, in Washington it was O.K. in the 70s to play the songs of other bands. Since the community didn't have an active and popular Konpa band, the public was happy to have a band that could remind them of their favorite songs.

In the mid 1980s Frédy moved to Florida where he took that idea to his partners Robert Charlot and Robert Martino and the band Top Vice was created. They played the music of other popular bands in the market without shame. This formula was later followed by Michel Martelly and many other bands thereafter.

Frédy like many popular singers released a solo project which unfortunately didn't get the success of the songs he did with Top Vice. In 2005, after he had a dispute with his partners, the band members moved away by creating the band "Nu Vice". Frédy recruited some more musicians, like the veteran drummer Ulrick Bouzi (Touco), to keep Top Vice alive as a performing band.

Frédérique, Fritz* (Ti Mitou) - Singer /Gong
One of the best Haitian Gonguists, Ti Mitou has also managed to have one of the most well-known Haitian voices in the Konpa world. His voice has a pitch that makes you wonder whether you are hearing a man or a child singing. Mitou played with Djet X and Astros in the late 1970s. He excelled however in the business when he joined System Band in the 1980s, replacing Frantz Avin (Fanfan) who was System Band's first Gonguist. While playing his instrument "The Gong" he will intervene in the middle of some songs with some interesting lead singing parts, like his famous line *"Man ni gette sou Man ni gette"*. Soon, he was getting more and more lead part as a vocalist, and in the 1990s he completely stopped playing the gong and was moved to the front line of System Band as a singer next to Isnard Douby. In the late 1990s, while touring in Haiti, Ti Mitou had a mild stroke that essentially put an end to his musical career. Sometimes he was seen at Haitian parties in the public, just watching his fellow musicians doing what he loves to do best, or what he used to do best. Fritz Frédérique died on Feb. 20, 2007 at the age of 47 years old. He was the role model of many Gonguists in the Konpa music business. He will always be remembered for his live performances with System Band, especially in songs like *"Assorossi, Ann Fè Lanmou, Pilon, Moun Sou Moun and JPP"* among others. In his days in Astros, Ti Mitou made the famous trio with Lesly Jean and Eric Charlier (Manatan) not knowing that he will later be part of a trio that was going to be even more popular playing next to Martial Bigaud and Jean Mathurin.

Frédérique, Jean Willy - Congas

Frédérique, Marc - Gong
Marc played with Djet-X. He is known for being a very disciplined musician.

Frederique, Walter - Trumpet

Freedom – Band
This band came out in the town of Les Cayes in 2003, but was not know by many people until their wonderful presentation at the eight edition of Music En Folie in Haiti on Nov. 18, 2007.

Frédy see: Frédérique Carmelo

Frémont, Claudy - Keyboard
Claudy is a very talented keyboardist who used to rock music lovers all over the world in the glory days of D.P. Express in the 1970s. He was later joined by Raoul Denis Jr.

French, Gary - Singer
One of the star singers of the 1950s, Gary French played with some unknown groups until he became a member of the band "Orchestre Latino". He had his best years when he became one of the lead singers of the band Ensemble de Webert Sicot. His charming voice made him one of the most popular musicians among women of the 1960s. In the 1970s Gary rocked the world of the Haitian diaspora as the lead singer of Pépé Bayard's band. He later released some solo project singing in French, English, Spanish and Créole.

Frère, Rony - Keyboard

Frères Déjean – Band

Created on July 13, 1963 in Petion-ville this band consisted of the Déjean brothers and their friends. The band really had its big break with the song *Marina*.
Marina was also the song that put Isnard Douby on the Konpa map. The brothers made hit after hit in the Haitian music industry. In the 1970s they were known as the international Frères Dejean. André Déjean is one of the most respected musicians in the Caribbean,

and to many people the best Haitian trumpet player of the Konpa community. He also has the ability to play many instruments. Frères Dejean was not only a band, it was considered as a Konpa School by many Haitian artists.

In the late 70s the band moved to New York where they made a serious impact in the Big Apple. After a successful tour, the band found difficulties returning to New York due to some of the members expired visas. Some musicians were obligated to stay in Haiti because of their visa status, the rest of the band

returned to New York, where they created System band. In Haiti, the brothers continued to make history by composing some of the most beautiful Konpa songs. Later, the group was split once again; this division gave birth to a band called Dixie Band.

Once again, Les Frères Dejean prevailed. They hired new musicians and the band continued to work in Haiti until they went back to the U. S. as a group. In the 1990s they were living in Miami, and sometimes played at some oldies and goodies parties in the Caribbean and the U. S. In 2003 the family lost one of their famous brothers as the congas player Philippe Déjean died in Haiti. In 2006 André started to play with Magnum band, a clear signal that the Band Les Frères Déjean was no longer with us.

Fréro see: Jean Baptiste Jean Edouard

Frisson - Band

Freycinet, Gary - Bass

Fukuhara, Ado - Keyboard
This Japanese woman is a very active member of the Konpa world who has worked with some of the top Haitian bands, including Tabou Combo and Skah Shah. She also took part in some of the Mini All Stars project.

Full Stop - Band

Fung Cap, Essud - Singer
This star singer of the band Les Ambassadeurs was born to Chinese parents in Haiti. It was amazing to see a Chinese man singing in a Konpa band. With Ambassadeurs super hit of the 70s, like *Anaïla* and *Romeo et Juliette*. Fung Cap became a household name in the whole country and people traveled from far

away to see the young entertainer.

In the late 1960s, he left the band and moved to the U.S. where he later became a member of the Magnum Band where he delivered once again, two of Dadou Pasket's greatest hits of the late 70s, *Experience* and *Magnum Déyò*.

Living now in Atlanta, Ga. with his family Essud Fung Cap is also one of the best known Haitian painters in the planet. His art works are sold all over the world and have been part of countless expositions.

His name Essud (Est-Sud) was chosen by his father because the family is from the Far East and he was born in the South side of Port-au-Prince, the nation capital of Haiti.

Fwèt - Band

This band was created in New York by the guitarist Edouard Richard.

G

G - 5

Band based in New York. This band was created by the drummer Guitary Roche aka Pè Gigit after a misunderstanding with his former partners of the band 718 Boys. When 718 split some members created the band Tempo and Guitary called his band G – 5, (Grenn 5").

G.M Connection - Band

That band never played any live show. It was a record project that was put together by 'G" (the saxophonist Gerard Daniel) the saxophonist and leader of Djet X and "M" (the guitarist of Skah Shah Mario Mayala), who were two icons of the Haitian music industry and superstars of the 1980s.

G.P. Express - Band

In 1985 eight musicians left D.P. Express, one of Haiti's most popular bands at the time, to create the band Gemini Plus Express or "G.P. Express" in the Washington metropolitan area, particularly in Maryland. The band was composed of not only the members of D.P. like Pierrot Kersaint, Marc Bellande Jacquet (Choupitte), Edner Couloutte, Dennis Nozil (Ti Polis), Perez Alvares, and Lionel Simeon. It also included the Bassist Mario Germain and Keyboardist Hans Mercier (Ansyto), who were ex-members of Gemini All Stars de Ti Manno and were new in D.P.

The expenses for the creation of G.P were covered by show producer Jean Robert Baltazar, who felt that it was time that Washington, D.C. got its own band. Mario Germain was chosen as the band leader.

Soon after their arrival, other musicians of Gemini already in America, like singer Imgart Manigart and guitarist Claude Geffrard Cajuste joined the squad. The band quickly went into the studio to record their first album, but before the recording was completed Pierrot (conga), Couloutte (drum) and Choupitte (gong) went back to Haiti, and Alvarez and Claude Cajuste moved to New York.

Patrick Casseus (drum), another Gemini musician, was called from Boston to replace Couloutte and to complete the album. After the release of the album, local musicians Jean Claude Vivens (singer) Nixon Clermont (gong) and Robert Richard (guitar) replaced those who left. In 1988 Ansyto returned to Haiti and the band recorded a second album with some more beautiful songs that never got any exposure. After the release of the second album Patrick Casseus, moved back to Boston where he joined the band Volo Volo de Boston, Ti Polis moved to Miami, and in 1992 the remaining players of the band created the band "Zépon".

Gabel - Band
The band Gabel came out in Miami Florida with a total of eight musicians fairly new to the Konpa music arena and they are: James Momplesir (Ti Linet) Maestro, keyboard player Jean Junior Marcellus (G Money) Lead Vocals Vladimir Etienne (Katalog) Lead Vocals Frantz Alcime (Fanfan Epav) Percussions Jacques Joseph (Becken) Drums Edner Jean Francois (Bob Doll) Guitar Guerino Senatus (LP) Congas Francillon Robens (Ti Paul) Bass.

Gabriel Guy - Bass
Guy played with Les Frères Déjean in the 1980s.

Gamma Express - Band

This band was created by D.P. Express star conga player Pierrot Kersaint. Although the albums were very good and got a lot of recognition and airtime on the radio, Gamma never made it big as a performing group.

Gaspard, Raymond * - Guitar

Some people play music, but others have the chance to be innovators. Before Raymond Gaspard, Haitian guitarists only played acoustic guitars. Raymond was the first to introduce the new and sweet sound of the electric guitar to the Konpa world.

He was with the accordion Player Richard Duroseau, the right and left arm of maestro Nemours Jean Baptiste, in putting together some of the best songs of the band Ensemble de Nemours Jean Baptiste in the 1960s, and in shaping the style of music that we all know today as Konpa.

Nemours refer to the Trio (Nemours, Raymond, and Richard) in a song as *Les 3 Dangers*.

Raymond Gaspard, who has entertained countless people, left Haiti in the late 1960s and moved to New York where he quietly lived with his family until he died in 2000.

Gaston Jean Adler (Top Adlerman) Singer

One of the pioneers of the ragga movement in Haiti in the late 1990s, Top Adlerman manages to become one of the most popular Haitian artists of his generation. His album *Watcha Krazem* released in 2004 came out as a complete surprise with some of the best songs of the year and a supporting video for the Konpa song *Problem mwen*.

Gauthier, Frantz (Ti Fanfan) - Singer

Played at first with Channel 10, and with Les Frères Déjean, and was part of the team that created Dixie Band with Touco Bouzi. Frantz made his mark for singing the controversial Dixie Band song *Malouïnes*, in which he sings *Solda mouri Officier decoré* lyrics that were hard for the Haitian Army to digest. He also proved himself in the hit song *Lolita*. Ti Fanfan left Haiti and moved to Paris. He didn't stay long in Europe because he continued his career by playing and producing in the French Caribbean islands, particularly in Martinique.

Gauthier, Rodrigue (Ti Crann) - Gong / Drums

The public first met Ti Crann in 1974, when some members of Les Shleu Shleu created the band Skah Shah in New York. His unique style and charisma made him one of the most noticeable musicians of Skah Shah. After many years with the popular band, Ti Crann career also suffered from the band's mismanagement and irresponsible acts of the superstars who couldn't agree on minor details and were constantly fighting for the band's leadership. In the middle of all the breakups and the creation of several Skah Shah Ti Crann hopped between one and the other and at one time created his own band, "Crystal Band", where he performed as a drummer. At the turn of the century the band Skah Shah finally, after almost two decades put away their differences and started to record and perform live with members of the original squad that gave Ti Crann the opportunity once again to showcase his talent on the gong.

Gay, Emilio - Trumpet
Emilio is from Jérémie, but he played most of his career in Port-au-Prince alongside the best musicians of the 50s and 60s, like Michel Desgrottes, Edner Guignard and Nemours Jean Baptiste.

Gay, Henry Wilgem - Congas

Gédéon, Marc - Drums
Marc played with the band Les Gitans

Géhy, Shubert - Singer
Shubert played with Bossa Combo next to Raymond Cajuste. Shubert was known for his ability to sing easily in Spanish.

Gelin, Saur (Samsonito) -Trombone
Respected Trombonist of the 1980s, he played with Scorpio when Reynold Menelas moved to New York.

Gemini All Stars - Band
This band was created by Antoine Rossini Jean Baptiste better known as "Ti Manno", when he left D.P. Express. At first Manno hired a group of star musicians, but he soon realized that well-known artists would be difficult to manage, so he let them all go.

When the band finally came out the public was amazed to see that they were very young, very good and very new in the business. Songs like *Lagent, Exploitation,* and *Mariage d'Interet* were over night hits in the country, in the Caribbean and in the Haitian diaspora.

Gemini One - Band
One of the first Konpa bands based in the town of Boston with Robert (Bob) Nerf on Drums with the Raymond Brothers Max on Guitar and Claude on Sax. Most of the brothers were former musicians of Super Soline a well-known Mini Jazz of the 1970s.

Généus, Roosevelt - Bass

Les Gentlemen – Band

Georges, Bellande – Promoter / Band Manager
In his early days in the H.M.I Bellande represented many bands in Florida including Tabou Combo. He did several successful shows and contributed to the promotion of the Konpa music. In the 1990s, he was for several years the manager of Zenglen. Bellande is the owner of the record store and production company La Perle Production.

Georges, Ernst * (Ti Gé) - Trombone
His best years were with D.P. Express in the late 70s.

Georges, Stanley - Singer

Germain, Eddy - Congas
Eddy is also a very good accordion player. He showed his talent in the album of the band Exodus out of New York, but it took the albums 5 Dwets of the band Zenglen to show to the rest of the Konpa world that the man playing next to Richie is one talented musician. Eddy is also a great barber.

Germain, Gardy - Congas
After Pierrot Kersaint move to Washington D.C. to create the band G.P. Express with 7 other members of D.P. Express who left Haiti after the 1985 carnival. The management of D.P. quickly called on the help on Gardy Germain, the young cousin of bass player Mario Germain, to replace the legendary, the late Pierrot Kersaint.
Gardy moved to America, where he played with Bazouka, Skah Shah, and G.P. Express among other bands. Gardy quietly retired from the Haitian musical scene and is living in New Jersey with his family.

Germain, Jacob - Singer
Jacob played with "Septentrional du Cap".

Germain, James - Guitar/Singer

Germain, Mario - Bass/Guitar
Mario, who at an early age used to play in Catholic churches in his Petion Ville neighborhood, first appeared in the Konpa world in the shadow of Jean Robert Herissé (Porky) as a back-up bassist for the band D.P. Express.
However when Ti Manno left D.P. Express he hired Mario as his guitarist, but after a couple practice sessions Mario made the choice to be the band's bassist instead, leaving room for Marc Evans Divine and Claude Geffrard Cajuste to shine on guitar.
After the release of the first album of Gemini All Stars de Ti Manno, the name Mario Germain became rapidly know to almost everyone in the Konpa society due to his touch on songs like *Lagent* and *Unissons Nous*.
After the release of the second Gemini album, *Exploitation*, Mario left the band and became the lead bassist of D.P. Express putting Porky on the back burner by playing all the band's recordings and most of the songs during the live performances. He also during that period took part in several music projects

of other artists and has played live also with bands like Exodus and Gamma Express.

In 1985 eight musicians left D.P and moved to Maryland at the invitation of producer Robert Baltazar to create the band G.P. Express. It was under the leadership of Mario Germain that the band was able to put out hit songs like *Pa Wè Clè* and *Kassé Ponyèt*. After G.P. Express' second album titled, *An Alé*, the band lost its momentum as some of the musicians moved on to other towns in America.

Mario, while still trying to manage his band's crisis by adding new members, also played and toured the world with many African bands and artists, including Jean Papy, M'bila bel, Itady and others.

In 1992 he managed to create the band Zépon, thus giving the Haitian community of Washington D.C. and Maryland another professional Haitian band representing the Konpa and the Haitian culture at countless festivities in the Washington metropolitan area. Zépon performed at the Smithsonian Institute festivities and at the Baltimore Museum of Art, among other festivals and international shows.

Under his leadership Zépon has rocked the D.C. Caribbean Carnival for more than 10 years and has won more than a dozen music trophies and awards.

Today Mario Germain is a music producer, a recording studio owner, a music arranger, and a Haitian CD and video distributor in the Washington, D.C. metropolitan area. He performs as needed with the local bands and at times will assist visiting artists.

Géronimo see: Raphael, Géroboam

Géronimo Records
Haitian record labels.

Gérostar – Band
Gerostar was basically the band that introduced Gracia Delva to the public. Their album *Mizè Fanm* was released in 1991.

Gerrin, Tania - Producer
Tania was the first manager of the band Carimi. She was replaced by Fritz Yacinthe also know as Fito Farinen. Her remarkable marketing work for the band Carimi was noticed by all the people interested in the Haitian music industry.

Les Gilbreteurs - Band
 This band was created by Serge Simpson in the 1960s.

Gilio, Jean Raymond - Percussion

Gilles, Anderson - Congas
Anderson played in the Mini Jazz era with Les Loups Noirs.

Gilles, Georges - Trumpet
Georges played with the band Norma de Léogane.

Gilles, Henry Magloire - Guitar

Gilles, Marcel - Keyboard
Marcel played with the band "Septentrional" and later with "Septen Junior".

Gilles, Stephane - Keyboard
Stephane is one of the musicians of the band "Groove La" who also played with Sweet Micky for a couple of years.

Gitans (Les Gitans) - Band

Glémaud, Guy * (Ti Guy) - Congas
Guy played in New York with the band "Djet-X" in New York.

Gondré, Guy - Guitar
Guy played with "Volo Volo" de Boston.

Gonel, Paul - Accordion / Keyboard
Paul played with Les Corvingtons and Tabou Combo.

Gornaille, Jean Robert – Promoter/Club Owner
Jean Robert Gornaille in the late 70s and early 80s owned two of the most popular Haitian nightclubs in Queens N.Y. The nightclubs "Chateau Royal" located on Jamaica Ave and "Le Flamboyant" located on Francis Lewis Boulevard were only a few blocks apart.

Goudet, Jocelyn - Saxophone

Goudin, Tricoulere - Bass
Tricoulere played with Les Frères Déjean.

Gouin, Gerard - Gong
Gerard Goin played with Samba Creole in the 1970s. He moved to New York in the 1970s.

Gran Pan Pan - Band
New York based band playing the style of Coupé Cloué.

Grand Pierre, Fritz (Fito) - Bass
Fito is one of the first bassists of the rhythm Konpa who played with Nemours Jean Baptiste. Fito who was also called Ti Bass also played with the Carrefour Feuilles band "Sublime" in his glory days.

Granfort, Carmelle * - Singer

Gratia, Rodney * - Singer
Rodney played with Septentrional du Cap.

Gravois, René - Saxophone
Played with the Sicot brothers in the 1960s

Grégoire, Alan - Sound Engineer
Alan has worked for the Miami-based bands Zenglen and Nu Look He died of a heart attack at his home in Florida in September 2007.

Gros Bébé See: Chérubin, Hans - Singer

Groove Kréyol - Band

Groove La - Band
This band came out in Miami at the turn of the century.

Guanel, Jean Luc - Singer
Another non-Haitian Konpa singer who played in Haiti with Arsène Appolon's band Skah Shah d'Haiti in the late 70s
Guerrier, Serge (Sergo) - Singer
Sergo Guerrier was the star singer of the band Les Corvington and later became the singer of choice of the band Tabou Combo de Petion-Ville in 1968. The man basically rocked the festivals of Ciné Paramount with his sweet, noticeable and charming voice in the song *Ghislaine* which became one of Tabou Combo's first hits.
After the band broke up in Haiti, he took part in the reconstruction of Tabou Combo in New York as their only singer until Shoubou came from Haiti. In 1972 he delivered, with his charming, voice the hits *Manou, Konpa Flonn* and the slow song *Je T'ai Perdu*.
He eventually joined the U.S. army and moved on with his life. At the end of

the 20th century he finally let his voice be heard once again in Herman Nau's solo project, *A la Source*.

Guilbaud, Pantaléon (Pantal) - Singer
Pantal was, along with Max Badette, the singer who charmed the world in the early days of the New York based band Djet-X.

Guillaume, Barbara - Singer
Barbara is also an actress.

Guilàume, Donald - Drums

Guillaume, Gashford - Drums

Guilaume, Jean Claude - Singer

Guillaume, Jephté - Bass
Well-known Haitian professional bassist based in New York.

Guillaume, Phillippe - Guitar
Musical arranger

Guillaume, Raoul - Saxophone
Superstar musician and innovator of the pre-Konpa era, Raoul Guillaume has been a mentor, professor and a role model to many Konpa artists. His super hit songs like *Crème A La Vanille, 40 En Ro 40 En Ba, Sé Léon,* and *Joseph,* among others. In 1964, in the middle of the super rivalry of Webert Sicot and Nemours Jean Baptiste, the talented composer did the song called *Vive Le Football* and a remix of that song in which he invited the sportscaster Serge Ambroise to do an imaginary football (soccer) game between Nemours and Sicot's bands.
Today, more than 40 years later, that song is still being used by many sportscasters as the theme song of many sport shows. Many found that this idea was a genial one.
Raoul also wrote three carnival songs for the band Ti Ta To and one of them won first place in the annual musical competition.
He left Haiti in the 1960s, only to return in the late 1970s. He became at that time the Music Director of the government run T.V. station, "Télé National". He also presided over the jury for the most famous Haitian musical competition of the 80s, the famous American Airlines "Konkou Mizik".

Guillaume, Raymond - Saxophone

Raymond is the brother of Raoul Guillaume. He played in New York with the band Ibo Combo in the Mini Jazz era.

Guillaume, Roland - Saxophone
Brother of Raoul Guillaume.

Guillaume, Vaval -Trumpet

Guillaume, Wilner - Trumpet

Guilliaume, Lyonel - Congas

Guillautau, Adolphe - Guitar

Guillet, kénold -Trumpet

Guillet, Shiler - Bass

Guinard, Edner - Keyboard
Edner is one of the greatest and most respected Haitian musicians of all time, a role model, instructor and mentor to several musicians.

Guinard, Felix - Keyboard /Accordion

Guirand, Gervais (Tiboul) -Trumpet
Ti Boule played next to Sicot in the 1960s in Haiti. After living in the U.S. for a while, he moved to Martinique where he became a music instructor.

Guirand, Franky - Gong / Congas

Guirand, Michael - Singer
Michael Guirand is the star singer of the band CaRiMi. He is one of the members who came from the band K-Dans. He is very charismatic and has the ability to make the crowd follow his instructions without any hesitation.

Gutieres, Hernandez - Keyboard
Although he was not from Haiti Hernandez played some serious Konpa under the leadership of Dadou Pasket with the Magnum Band for several years.

Gypsies (Les Gypsies de Petion-Ville) - Band

Created in Petion-Ville in the early 1970s by Robert Martino and Pierrot Al Khal, Gypsies wasted no time becoming one of Haiti's most popular Mini Jazz groups. Just like their counterpart Les Difficilles, the band got a lot of airtime, especially on Radio Haiti and Radio Metropole.

Gypsies was indeed a very good Mini Jazz and up to now songs like *La Tulipe, Patience* and many more still bring the best memories to Konpa lovers all over the world.

Les Gypsies de Queens - Band

After the success of Les Gypsies de Pétion-Ville, a group of young men created their own Gypsies in Queens, N.Y. in 1974, where a Haitian community was growing in the 1970s.

Among them were some musicians that had a past in the Mini Jazz movement, like Edward Richard, ex-member of Shupa Shupa, and other musicians like Gary Résil, who will later put his signature on the Konpa world with Skah Shah and Tabou Combo.

H

H.M.I - An abbreviation for Haitian music industry

Haiti Records
Haitian-owned record company

Haitinetradio.com
Haitinetradio.com is a popular online magazine where Konpa fans discuss issues regarding Konpa music on a daily basis. It reports Konpa news 24/7 on the website Art Music and Entertainment forum as it happens.

Hall, Kesnel -Trumpet

Halloum, Nassim (Papite) - Band owner / manager
Papite Halloum was known to everyone as the owner and manager of the famous band D.P. Express.

Hamsters - Band
Their album *Hamsters Frappé Compas* was released in 1976 under the label "Brothers".

Hangout - Band

This band came out in Florida at the turn of the century under the leadership of Ernst Vincent, former bassist of System Band. With a solid vocal line that includes Eders Stanis (Pipo), who has previously played for Passion de Montreal, as well as Georgy Metellus (former star singer of Zin), and the addition of Cléo, who has played for the all-female band D-Zire. The fact that the two female singers never seems to be on the same page has brought much drama to the band, however no one can contest that on stage they always deliver the best shows and are always in sync with their dance moves.
In 2006 Cléo decided to quit the band and moved on with her career. She was replaced by a newcomer in the business, a model named Mei Mei. After the

arrival of Mei Mei, Georgy decided to leave also, and in September 2007, after the Haiti summer tour, the singer Pipo made it public that he too was leaving the band to move on with other projects. He was replaced by Fréro Jean Baptiste.

Hangout is known for wearing nice uniforms on stage.

Hans, Henry - Bass
Henry played with the band Volo Volo de Boston.

Harden, Russ - Trombone
Russ, who palyed Magnum Band for many years, is another non-Haitian musician who contributed to the horn section of the band.

Harmonic 5 - Band
Toto Laraque performing band in Montreal Canada

Harmonik - Band
In spring 2008, the keyboardist Nickenson Prud'homme surprised the Konpa world when he introduced his new band as Harmonik with Mac D on lead vocal as he released a single titled *Jerem*.

Harsh, Mark - Keyboard
Non-Haitian musician who took part in some Haitian music projects, including the Loubert Chancy and Friends record.

Henegan, Paul -Trumpet
Paul is a talented non-Haitian musician who played with several Haitian bands and artists in his career.
Henry, Fils Luckner - Drums

Henry, Gesner (Coupé Cloué) - Singer /Guitar

Jean Gesner Henry, who was born in 1925, left his hometown of Brache, a suburb of Léogane, at an early age and moved to Port-au-Prince, the nation's capital. He joined the school "Centrale Des Arts et Métiers", a school that specialized in the formation of young children by teaching them several trades, including music. Jean Gesner Henry learned cabinetry and for his music lessons he learned to play the trumpet and the clarinet.

As he became a teenager, Jean Gesner Henry joined the football (soccer) team 'Hartley Bacardi'. His skills as a defender caught the attention of the members of the team "Aigle Noir", who made him one of their starters. On the football field he was hard to compete against and most of all, he developed a style that impressed not only his teammates, but also everyone who had the chance to watch him play.

Jean Gesner had the ability to cut (coupé) the velocity of the speedy ball and reduce it to a full stop, and nail (cloué) it with a super kick right back to the other side. Each time Gesner made this soccer stunt he used his cabinetry jargon coupé (to cut) and cloué (to nail) to describe it. Soon his teammates and other players started to call him: Coupé Cloué.

In the mid 1950s the soccer star Coupé Cloué moved on to playing music, but this time as a guitarist jamming and serenading his friends and local businessmen with some members of the band Crystal, like René Delva and Victor Claudin.

In 1957 he came out with his own group, the "Trio Select", playing the style of Canjo, the father of the twoubadou style music in Haiti. The Trio surprised the crowd of the famous venue Theatre de Verdure at their first live performance as they were the opening act for Haiti's most popular band of the 1950s, Jazz des Jeunes. After the show all the top radio stations MBC, Radio Caraïbes, Radio Haiti and others were after the artist for interviews and recordings.

The Trio soon got momentum in the early 1960s as it got a regular Friday night show at Cric Crac Ciné as well as many gigs of the club Bamboche both venues located in the neighborhood of Carrefour.

By the mid to late 1960s with songs like *Kilibwa, Men Rat, La, Plen kay, Bambou,Chada* , and *Kousi Kousa* among others the voice of Coupé Cloué became one of the most recognizable of the airwaves even with the evolution of the Mini Jazz movement.

In the early 1970s, as Trio Select was getting more shows playing with other popular bands with heavier sound, Coupé decided to introduce more sophisticated and amplified instruments in his group by changing the Trio to a Band. This decision was one of the best by the entrepreneur as the introduction of talented musician like Bellerive Dorcélien on guitar, Daniel Alcé (Ti Bass) on bass, Jean Pierre Pétion on Bongo, Serge Bernard (Ti Aigle) on congas and Ernst Louis (Ti Nès) on drums took the band to another level.

The new band revamped songs like *St Antoine, Yéyé* and *Chanm Gasson* by adding some jokes to them like Gerard Dupervil did previously in the song *"Cout Lang"* of Jazz des Jeunes. By using that template, Coupé Cloué, with his unique style of telling the jokes accompanied by his new found rhythm based on the work of the bongos and congas combination, quickly got the attention of the public. By the mid 1970, Ensemble Select de Coupé Cloué became the band of choice of people visiting the country and a got contract to perform on a regular basis at "Le Lambi Nightclub", which is one of the most popular venues in the south side of the nation capital.

In 1976 Assade Francoeur, one of the top singers and composers of 70s, joined the band. His enormous contribution was going to take the band to his apogee with the super hit song *Myan Myan*. The voice of Assade Francoeur on the airwaves as the new lead singer of the band, playing next to Coupé Cloué created a new wave of young fans following the band. While many people knew of Coupé Cloué as a controversial singer who often used harsh words to describe the reality of the country, like in the song *Shada*, and sometimes hidden profanity (like in his songs *Map Di* and *Juge)*, or not quite hidden like in the song *Sociss*. Assade's contribution to the band was quite different as he came up with more ballades, like the song *Marie Jocelyne*, which he wrote for his wife.

The news of the band attracting so many followers and the selling of many albums outside of Haiti got the attention of show producers around the globe. By the late 70s the band was already playing in many countries outside of Haiti. While many bands were influenced by the sounds of the new wave of French Caribbean bands by adding a live horn section to their lineup, Coupé Cloué kept his originality and even was the champion of the 1980s Haiti's Carnival Parade with the song *Roi Coupé* (King Coupé), a title he kept for the rest of his life. By the early 1980s the band went to several cities in North America, many countries in Central and South America and as far as Africa, where they got the best welcome in "Ivory Coast" where Coupé Cloué was received with honor like world dignitaries.

By the end of the 1980s Coupé Cloué had so many hit songs in his repertoire that it would have been hard for any radio announcer to do a show in which they would be able to satisfy all the requests of the listeners as songs like *Fanm Kolokent, Madan Marcel, Sa Dépan, Tu Peux Mettre, Azoukenken, Kenhen Kenhenk, Gasson Colon* and many others, were super hits that were the choices of so many people in the Haitian music world.

In the early 1990s, despite all the changes happening in the Haitian music society, and the introduction of the digital bands getting most of the contracts, Coupé still kept his originality and was still one of the busiest bands in the market. However, by the mid-1990s the deaths of some of his musicians and the departure of others, who decided to leave the country to reside elsewhere, often in the U.S., took a toll on the King. The band was mostly performing his former hits and was not coming up with new hits except for the song *Donki* in which some people were able to see an aging Coupé Cloué with a few words in the video.

In the years that followed he was even absent at some of the live performances and had also stopped performing outside of the country as he became ill and too old for the night performances in the demanding Haitian music industry. In 1997 he was invited to the Brooklyn Academy of Music in New York where the producer of Haiti Focus presented him with the Lifetime Achievement Award. Also in Haiti he was later honored by his fellow musicians, the media and the public in general at a ceremony which was televised nationwide. Coupé Cloué one of the most popular Haitian artists of all time, died on Jan. 29, 1998 leaving behind many memories, many hit songs and a style of music called the Konpa Manba that is even now being played by many bands around the globe.

Henry, Gesner Junior - Singer /Percussions
Junior is the son of the legendary singer Coupé Cloué. He is trying his best to keep the rhythm created by his father alive and well.

Henry, Onel - Bass

Hérard, Estavil - Guitar

Hérard, Georges Lys (Master Dji) * - Singer / Rapper / Radio Announcer
Master Dji is credited for starting the Rap Movement in Haiti in the early 1980s.
In 1987, he came out in second place, with his song *Sispann* at the "Concours Découvertes", a music contest organized annually in different countries by Radio France International (RFI). In the years that followed he was employed as a correspondent for international radio stations in Asia, Europe, and Africa. He also has worked in Haiti for popular stations like Radio Port-au-Prince, Radio Metropole and, finally, Radio Tropic F.M. where he promoted many Rap Artists through his show, "Rap Nation".
On May 21, 1994 the Rap movement lost one of the best leaders that they had in Haiti. The funeral of the young artist has attracted too more people in the streets than the police could handle. Master Dji is remembered by his hit songs *Politik Pam, Manmzel, Sispann,* and *Tann Pou Tann*

Hérard, Jean Richard (Richie) - Drum / Singer

Richie is known as one of the best drummers and Konpa hit makers of his generation. Richie became popular when he joined the Miami-based band Zenglen in the late 1990s. As the songs *5 Dwèts Flannè Femèl, Easy Konpa,* and *B.S Production* were getting the attention of the public, people started to find out that all those beautiful songs were the work of the band's new talented drummer. In the years that followed Richie became the force behind the band coming with one hit after another. His contribution took the band not only to the level of one of the best Konpa bands of the late 1990 and early 2000's,but has also made the band's front man Gracia Delva a star singer. In 2002, after a tour in Europe, the singer Gracia Delva was banned from entering the U.S. and moved to Haiti, where he created his own band, Mass Konpa. Zenglen replaced Gracia with two singers, Réginald Cangé and Jean Edouard Jean Baptiste (Fréro). The job of Richie was to turn the new singers into household names, and the job was done efficiently as he wrote many of the songs in an album with hits like *FKD* and *5 Etoiles*. In 2005 he released a solo album with hit songs *Pal Kokal* and *Happy 50 Konpa,* a song to commemorate the 50th anniversary of Konpa. In that album Richie made the public discover the talent of another singer named Dabens. After the release of that album Dabens was hired by System Band. In 2006 he recorded an album with Gracia Delva the former singer of Zenglen. The album was released at the end of the year. In 2006, Richie became the band leader and decision maker of Zenglen, a challenging job as Zenglen also had his share of drama. At the end of 2006 he faced his greatest challenge as both singers (Réginald and Fréro) quit the band without any notice. Diligently the leader of the band called Kenny Desmangle the singer of the band 509 to the rescue. Seeing the opportunity to advance his career by working with Richie, the singer Kenny Desmangle resigned from his ascending band 509 to join Zenglen.

Richie has also excelled in many songs as a lead singer also. To many people he is a talented drummer, a good singer, a great Konpa composer, and no one can contest his statement as a Superstar Maker.

Herissé, Jean Robert (Porky) - Bass

Porky was noticeable on stage, with his huge size and his long hair. Porky is one of the nicest Haitian musicians. He made several hit songs during his years with Les Difficiles and D.P. Express

Herissé, Stanley - Bass
Stanley is the son of jean Robert Herisse (Porky). He is one of the founders of the band Konpa Kreyol. He remained with the squad when the band divided and became Kréyol La.

Heritage Konpa.com
Popular Haitian website about Konpa music

Herivaux, Jacques - Trumpet
Hilaire, Fred - Congas
Fred is member of the band Hangout

Hillaire, Garry - Drums
Musician of the band Q - Style, Garry also played with Konpa Express - Siwèl and Les Ambassadeurs in previous years.

Hilaire, Guy - Congas /Percussion

Hilaire, Jean - Guitar
Jean played with Super Ensemble de Webert Sicot.

Hilaire, Philomé - Guitar

Hilaire, Sylvain - Guitar

Hilton, Gérard - Guitar

Horizon 75 - Band
This band was created in 1975 by the singer Boulou Valcourt.

Horse Back - Band
This band was created in the 1960s by the keyboardist Serge Simpson.

Hubel, Herb - Trombone
Herb is a non-Haitian musician who took part in several Haitian music projects especially with the Mini All Stars.

Hubert, Eddy - Gong / Percussion
Eddy played with Samba Jazz, Les Fantaisistes D'Haiti, Super Soline and Les Ambassadeurs.

Hyacinthe, Fritz - Promoter

Fito started the production company Farinen, a name based on a song by the band Mizik Mizik in the 1990s. Ever since that time is know in the H.M.I as Fito Farinen. He became the manager of the band Carimi replacing Tanya Gerrin.

Hypolite, Jean Gardy - Guitar
Gardy played with a series of bands in Haiti as a freelancer. In 2004, in Washington D.C. and Maryland with Jean Claude Vivens and the Walker Family he created the band Trankill. He later joined Sweet Micky to replace the legendary guitarist Robert Martino. His association with Sweet Micky only lasted for a while, and Jean Gardy returned to Maryland where he continues to work with the local bands Trankill and Rafrechi.

Hypolitte, Jocelyn - Singer

Hypolitte, Ralph Getho - Trumpet

Hypolitte, Steve Albert - Singer

Hypolitte, Ulrick - Singer

I

Ibo Combo – Band

Ibo Combo was one of the bands that marked the Mini Jazz era. While many bands were doing wonders in Haiti, the band was playing in the difficult New York market of a growing Haitian diaspora. When they realize that they were more popular in Haiti, most members of the band, like Réginald Policard, Boulou Valcourt and the Laraque brothers, returned to their country where they found fame as they changed the name of the band to Caribbean Sextet. The discography of Ibo Combo included *Engendré, Café,* and *La Fraicheur.* The song *Engendré* was one of the hit songs of the Mini Jazz era.

Ibo Records
One of the first Haitian record labels

Imaj Konpa - Band
Konpa band based in Haiti

Infini - Nightclub
Nightclub located in Haiti

Innocent, Ludwig - Keyboard

Israel, Luckensy - Keyboard /Bass /Guitar

Invincibles (Les Invincibles de Jacmel) - Band
This band, created in 1969, is one of the top bands to ever come out in the town of Jacmel. During the carnival season in Jacmel, many people do compare the carnival songs of Les Invincibles to their rival band Les Jouvenceaux de Jacmel. At times just like the rivalry of Nemours and Sicot, D.P. Express and Scorpio, Septen Tropic, T. Vice and Djakout, the musical competition of the two bands can be very heated. However, at the end of the 1990s, both bands had lost the momentum and their popularity in their own town. The people of Jacmel's choices increased with the invasion of the town's nightclubs by the

most popular bands out of Port-au-Prince and the diaspora, especially during the carnival season, the Christmas holidays and the summer months. Another trend that has affected Jacmel's top bands is the fact that often the visiting bands will hire the best musicians on the spot and manage to take them to the States where they often find fame and a chance to travel around the globe. It's an offer that is hard to resist by many artists living in Haiti.

J

J.D Records
Haitian owned record company

J.R.S Records
Record company owned by the singer Jacques Sauveur Jean in Miami Fl.

Jackson, Celso - Keyboard
Celso is a member of Legend.

Jackson, Ernst - trumpet

Jabouin, Patrick - Saxophone

Jackson, Pierre - Trumpet

Jacques, Alix - Bass
Alix Jacques was one of Haitian music's star bassist of the 1970s. He played with Djet-X in New York where he was one of the Haitian diaspora superstars. He came out with his band, "Colé Colé" Band, which unfortunately didn't last to long. Alix Jacques is also known as "Dr.Lulux".

Jacques, Herly - Singer
Herly is the singer of Nu Vice.

Jacques, Jean Claude - Saxophone / Singer
Jean Claude played with Tropicana.

Jacques, Joseph "Joe Jack" - Singer / Accordion / Piano
Joe Jack is a product of the St. Vincent music school of Port-au-Prince, a school for handicapped children. The man who would become the most popular Haitian accordion player of all time would never see his audience as Joseph Jacques (Joe Jack) was born blind.
Joe Jack is known in the Haitian music industry as "L'Homme Orchestre", meaning a one-man orchestra, as he has since the 1970s performed as a one-man show with his rhythmic accordion which provided a pre-recorded full percussion line. In the early 1980s he moved to New York and by the late

80s he replaced the accordion with a keyboard. His style inspired the creation of the digital bands with reduced format like the Miami Top Vice, Jamming Jacky, Sweet Micky and many others. Joe Jack retired in Canada, where he only performed on special occasions.

Jacques, Marie Josée - Singer
Marie Josée played with the band Trak.

Jacques, Pierre (Boss) - Saxophone
Boss played with Septentrional.

Jacques, Rudy – Keyboard

Jacquet, Elizabeth (Mamina) - Saxophone /Singer

Mamina is a young female saxophonist born in Martinique, but who has been living in Haiti most of her adult life. Her role model is Loubert Chancy; she is extremely popular and is known for taking part in some of the best Haitian videos.

Jacquet, Marc Bellande (Shoupitte) - Gong (Percussion)
Shoupitte replaced Philippe Denis in the band D.P. Express in the late 1970s. He is one of the most respected gonguist in the Haitian music world. His timing is on point; he hits the floor tom and the cow bell really hard, but despite the loud, sound one still can hear the "cop co dop" played by Shoupitte. When, in 1985 eight members of D.P left to create a new band in Washington, D.C. called G.P. Express Shoupitte was part of the squad, however he was also the first one to return to Haiti to rejoin D.P.
In the 1990s he became a member of the band Mizik-Mizik.

Jadotte, Théophile (Théo) - Bass /Drum /Guitar
Théo played in New York, with Lakol among others. He later joined Phantoms. It was while performing with Phantoms at a show in Paris that he

was approached by the guys of "Konpa Kréyol" to be the second bassist of the band next to Stanley Herissé.

When "Konpa Kréyol" split in two, Théo stayed loyal to the squad that revolted against the leadership of the keyboardist David Dupoux and his sister/manager Fabiola Dupoux Leger by becoming a member of the new band Kreyol la. On the early days under the new name "Kréyol La", Théo was playing the drum. Later he moved on to guitar next to the talented guitarist Ti Loulou.

Jakito see: Jean, Jacques Sauveur

Janvier, Adolphe - News Reporter
Adolphe is a well-known reporter at the newspaper Tickets Magazine.

Jasmin, Marc Anglade - Bass
Marc Anglade played with "Tropicana".

Jasmin, Rosny (Momo) - Singer
Momo was the star singer of the band "Etoile du Soir" in the 1960s.

Jazz Des Jeunes - Band
Haiti's most popular band before the Konpa era.

Jean, Béni - Singer

Jean, Claudy - Congas
Claudy played with Nemours, Ibo Combo and Caribbean Sextet.
He was actually the second congas player of Super Ensemble de Nemours Jean Baptiste replacing Kretzer Duroseau.

Jean, Clébert - Drums
Clébert played with the band Les "Lionceaux" des Cayes in the 70s, later he joined the former Septentrional trumpet player Jacques François in his band "Tropical Combo" de Ti Jacques in New York.

Jean, Clinton - Singer

Jean, Evens - Singer
Evens Jean is also known as a Konpa show host. He played with Mizik Mizik and also on some solo projects under the name Evans Jean and Friends.

Jean, Gérald - Drums

Jean, Guy - Singer
This childhood friend of both Cubano and Shoubou started his career with the two superstars in their native Port De Paix. However Guy moved on with other things in his life and spent the rest of his career in the D.C. area singing mostly the French hits of the 1960s in private parties, local shows, restaurants and bistros.

Jean, Jacques - Saxophone
Jacques played with Septentrional.

Jean, Jacques Sauveur (Jakito) - Singer / Guitar
In the 1980s the public was charmed by the wonderful voice of Jacque Sauveur Jean. The young man has captivated and won the heart of many women throughout the country and beyond the borders of Haiti. With songs like *Kriyé Chanté* and *Lanmou Doudou* suddenly, a star was born. With the innovation of music videos the artist couldn't ask for more to rise into the life reserved for the most famous ones.
At the end of the 1990s Jacques Sauveur Jean took a complete turn with his musical career. He moved to Miami Fl. where he opened his record store and music production company under the label JS Record. He produced his own records and at the same time moved away from the style of singing love songs to playing Konpa music like most Haitian bands. The man who used to be called Le Prince de L'Amour (the Prince of Love) became a Konpa star under his new stage name, "Jakito".
In 2006, he joined the political party L'espoir, the party that won the presidency. As a personal friend of President René Préval, the artist put his business up for sale, liquidated his assets and went back to Haiti to work, where he continues to perform as well.

Jean, Jean Claude - Guitar
Cool, excellent, energetic, and exciting are some of the words used to describe Tabou Combo's rhythm guitar player, Jean-Claude Jean. An original member of the band, Jean-Claude Jean has been mesmerizing fans around the world for years with his style of playing the guitar. He brings an impressive blend of talent and skills that has been driving the band's striking sound for the last 35 years. Jean-Claude has created a style that is unique, and one that has become Tabou Combo's rhythm signature by combining different styles of blues, Latin, Soukous, and funk. In addition to his excellent guitar skills, Jean-Claude is also recognized for his ability to write and produce hit songs. His most famous work was the 1974 million-copy seller *New York City* (written with Shoubou) that helped take the band from the local clubs to international

stardom. Other songs that he either wrote or co-wrote are *Bebe Paramount, Riyel, Son La Ri, Mabouya,* and many more. Jean-Claude is undoubtedly one of the most admired Haitian guitar players to have graced the world of Haitian music.

Bio from: www.taboucombo.com

Jean, Jean Robert - Guitar

Jean, Jonas -Trombone

Jean, Jude - Singer

In the 1990s a new band by the name of K-Dans came out in the heart of Port-au-Prince, introducing to many a group of young men that would later become household names. Among those young men was the famous singer Jude Jean who was a rising star. The young man didn't waste any time winning the heart of the public with his ability to sing. Jude Jean is known to be at ease with high notes as well as the low notes. He can bring the crowd joy and make them sweat in songs like *Nap Chill* as well as making people cry with the drama in his voice in songs like *Touman* and *Graduation*.

In 2005, Jude Jean, after a disagreement with his fellow members regarding the addition of a younger singer in the band, preferred to quit K-Dans altogether rather than have another singer performing next to him.

Before long, K-Dans introduced the singer Mac D and Jude Jean moved on with his career by coming out with the band "Chill". On Dec. 21, 2006 Jude Jean released his first album without K-Dans at the Club Café des Arts in Port-Au Prince.

Jean, Kébreau -Trumpet

Jean, Lenor - Singer /Congas

Jean, Lesly - Drums
Lesly was the drummer who replaced Arsène Appolon in the band Astros when Arsène moved to Haiti to create the band Skah Shah D'Haiti. Later he continued his career with Djet-X and tried out with some other bands in the New York area before fading away from the Konpa scene.

Jean, Lohman (Loulou) - Guitar

Loulou was born in Jérémi. As an adolescent he was already the family entertainer playing with a guitar he practically made from scratch. When he moved to Port-au-Prince, he became the guitarist of Crystal Secure, which he left soon after to join the band Déga.

When Konpa Kréyol was created on Dec. 3rd, 1999, they called on Loulou to lead them on guitar and the choice could not have been any better. Loulou showed a maturity and professionalism on and off stage. In 2005 Konpa Kréyol split in two groups, Loulou stayed loyal to the singer Ti Joe Zenny and bassist Stanley Herissé and they created the band "Kréyol La". Konpa Kréyol leader David Dupoux and her sister/manager moved on to create the band Krézi.

Jean, Lucien - Singer

Jean, Misterline (Misty Jean) - Singer

Misty Jean started her life on stage at an early age as she joined the dance school of Lynn W. Rouzier when she was only three. By her seventh birthday she was already singing in front of a live audience and took part at the Paul Villefranche singing contest. In 1999, she was chosen as the model to promote the phone company Haitel. In Feb. 2001 she represented Haiti at a beauty pageant in St. Martin where she was crowned "Miss West Indies". On the same year she took part on the album *Caribbean Escape* by Raoul Denis.

In 2002, she won another beauty contest "Miss De La Francophonie", in Haiti. Soon after, she left Haiti to study in the U.S. In 2003, she was crowned "Queen of Greater Miami Carnival".
In 2004, she released her album *Plus Pres De Toi* which also included the songs Cé *Ou Mwen Vlé* and *Maladie D'amour*. She received the award for "Best Female Artist" from Ticket D'or
In 2006, she released her second album *Konpa A Gogo*. Once again she was awarded "Best Female Vocalist" of 2006.
Misty has over the years performed in the U.S., in Europe and the Caribbean. She has worked with several superstars like Thierry Cham, Keysha, Ralph

Condé, Robert Martino, Top Adlerman, Nickenson Prud'Homme, Jean Claude Jean, Andre Déjean, and Roberto Martino among others.

Jean, Moise - Guitar
Moise played with the band Ensemble Select de Coupé Cloué.

Jean, Paul Edouard (Polo) - Singer
Polo played with the band Tropicana du Cap.

Jean, Pierre Robert - Drums
Robert played with Bossa Combo in the early 70s.

Jean, Ronald - Singer

Jean Roselin - Radio Personality
Roselin became popular in New York in the 1990s with the creation of the Haitian satellite radio station Radio Tropicale, however after the radio stop broadcasting from New York, Roselin went on to create his own station, Radio Pétion Ville Inter. He is also known as a live show host in the U.S.

Jean, Sandra - Singer
The younger sister of the singer Guy Jean made a name for her self when she joined the all female band Riské in the early 1990s. After the Riské adventure she married the star guitarist of Gemini All Star Claude Geffrard Cajuste and together they came out with the band Karess in New York.

Jean, Sergot - Singer
Sergo is known as one of the first singers of the Mini Jazz era. Sergot was the first vocalist of Les Shleu Shleu before joining "Les Legendaires" de Delmas.

Jean Stanley - Drums
Stanley is the drummer of Carimi.

Jean, William - Gong / Percussion
William played with Caribbean Sextet and Zèklè.

Jean, Wilson (Sonson) - Drums
Sonson is one of the musicians of the D-Zine who moved on to create the band Hangout.

Jean, Wyclef - Singer / Guitarist

Hip Hop, Rap and R& B superstar of the American music industry Wyclef Jean was born in Haiti. After his success with the Fugees next to American music superstar and actress Lauren Hill and his cousin Praz, Wyclef moved on with a successful solo career as a singer and rapper. He then did a few Konpa songs to show the world that he is indeed a full blooded Haitian. Wyclef never missed the opportunity to talk about Haiti or to wear the Haitian flag at internationally broadcast events like the award ceremonies and the 2006 FIFA world cup in Germany.

Jean Bart, Guy – Bass

Jean Baptiste, Alexandre - Keyboard
Alexandre played with the band Safari Combo which later became Super 9.

Jean Baptiste, Antoine Rossini (Ti Manno) - Singer / Drum / Keyboard / Guitar

Ti Manno was by far the most popular hit maker in the late 70s to the early 80s. He rocked many clubs and dance halls. When he said "jump" people jump when he said 'take off your shirt" people just do it.
After trying with a few bands in Haiti, Ti Manno got his break when he joined the band Volo Volo de Boston. The Volo Volo song *Carésse* released in the mid 70s was his first mega hit. By the late 70s he was the lead vocal for Arsene Appolon's new band, A.A. Express which later became Astros. While touring Haiti with Astros, he was hired by D.P. Express in 1978.With D.P. Express he made hits after hits. Ti Manno was singing what others were afraid to say in a country socially divided and dominated by repression. Hits like *EEEE, David, Corige, Ensem Ensem, Cèso* and *Biberon* will always be memorable, especially to those who had the chance to witness Ti Manno on stage.
In the early 1980s he created his own group, Gemini All Stars with a group of very young musicians like Mario Germain, Ansyto Mercier, Patrick Casseus, Imgar Manigat and Claude Geffrard Cajuste among others. The band got so many contracts that at one time they were playing 7 days a week. Songs like

Lagen, Exploitation, and Marriage D'interet were being played on the air day and night by every creole speaking radio station in the world.

Almost every show with D.P or with Gemini was sold out especially in the early 1980s.

On May 13, 1985, Ti Manno died in New York. To pay for his hospital bills many Haitian stars, producers, promoters and fans took part in a fundraising effort called "Operation Main Contré" meaning "Joining Hands Operation".

Operation Main Contré was also the title of one of Ti Manno's songs.

Many Haitian musicians have made songs to honor the work and life of Antoine Rossini Jean Baptiste alias Ti Manno.

Let's note that even though throughout his career Ti Manno used the name Antoine Rossini, his real name was Emmanuel Jean Baptiste.

Jean Baptiste, Edwige - Gong /Congas /Percussion

Jean Baptiste, Emmanuel - Congas

Jean Baptiste, Franky - Gong /Percussion
Franky is one of the pioneers of the Mini Jazz movement in the 1960s.

Jean Baptiste, Frantz - Guitar

Jean Baptiste, Gaston - Congas
Respected conga player who is able to play different styles of music Haitian and non-Haitian as well.

Jean Baptiste, Gérard - Trumpet
Gérard started his career in St. Marc, his native town, with the band Diables du Rythme de St Marc before joining successively Tropicana and Septentrional throughout his career. He is also a good composer and musical arranger who provided his services in New York to many bands, including Magnum Band and Accolade de New York.

Jean Baptiste, Germain - Saxophone

Jean Baptiste, Guy - Congas
In the 70s Ti Guy was one of the stars of the famous band Super Soline

Jean Baptiste, James - Percussionist /Congas

Jean Baptiste, Jean Edouard (Fréro) - Singer
Fréro played with the band Les Invincibles de Jacmel before joining Zenglen in

Miami Fl. At the end of 2006 he and the singer Réginald Cangé left the band to create the band Fasil in Haiti. In 2007, he became the lead singer of Hangout in Miami Fl. Fréro also has a solo album on the market titled *Frérot Sou Konpa*.

Jean Baptiste, Jérôme - Singer
Jérome is one of the star singers of the popular Mini Jazz Les Loups Noirs.

Jean Baptiste, Jimmy - Drums
Jimmy is the drummer of Septentrional du Cap for many years.

Jean Baptiste, Maquel - Guitar/Bass

Jean Baptiste, Michel (Ti Michel) - Producer
Michel is the owner of the record company Tropidisc.

Jean Baptiste, Monfort - Bass
This brother of Nemours Jean Baptiste had the chance to play with his legendary brother in the band Aux Calebasses. Unfortunately Monfort died prior to the glorious days of his brother Nemours.

Jean Baptiste, Nazaire - Congas

Jean Baptiste, Nemours - Saxophone /Guitar /Creator of Konpa Music

No one can contest that Nemours Jean Baptiste is one of the greatest Haitian musicians ever.

Just like the Heroes of the independence war liberated Haiti from colonization, Nemours Jean Baptiste delivered the Haitians from the power of the Cuban and Dominican music by creating a national rhythm and dance that every Haitian around the world can identify as something purely Haitian.

The father of Konpa music was born in Port-au- Prince in the street *Rue des Fronts Forts*. In his younger years he became friend of the Guignard family particularly Félix Guignard (Féfé). Since the Guignard family had their own band, "*Jazz Guignard* ", Nemours, the son of a shoemaker and a dress maker found himself in the middle of the music world at an early age, learning how to play the guitar and the banjo. While father Guignard was busy working performing and teaching, Nemours (on guitar or banjo) and Féfé (on accordion) would sometimes go around town, or at times, around the country serenading and charming hundreds with their musical skills.

Nemours continued to learn from the Guignard family not only how to play different instruments, but also the techniques of leading and managing a band.

One day when the music business took him to the town of Les Cayes, he met one of the greatest maestros of the country, a man not known to many, the great saxophonist Barrateau Destinoble. For some reason Mr. Destinoble must have had an influence on the young musician because ever since he played the guitar for Destinoble's band in the town of Les Cayes, Nemours Jean Baptiste have also fell in love with the saxophone. Barratole passed on to the young man most of the secrets of maneuvering and mastering the sax.

When he left Les Cayes, Nemours created a trio call *"Trio Anacaona"*. This band didn't offer the opportunity for him to do what he wanted to do, which was to play the sax in public and to prove himself as a top blower since the trio consisted only of strings instruments.

Nemours finally got his break to play the saxophone for a band when Joe Lavaud, a singer also known as *Atomik,* called on Nemours to join the horn section of his band, Orchestre Atomique. Also in this band were Nemours older brother the late Monfort Nemours on contrabass, Robert Camille on keyboard and Kesner Hall on trumpet among others. Before long, Nemours became the band leader (Maestro) of *Orchestre Atomique,* however the members had difficulty accepting the changes he wanted to bring and he was voted out of the band even by his own brother after a brawl and many words were exchanged among the members. Nemours walked away with the band's alto sax and it took a tribunal to make him return the sax by order of a judge. As soon as he left the band with all his anger and not many resources, he quickly created the band *Atomique Junior,* a band that only lasted a few days. His leadership was seen by the great Issa El Saieh, who introduced him to the band *Orchestre Citadelle.* Nemours wasted no time becoming the leader of his new friends. Nemours soon recruited some musicians of his choice also like the young saxophonist Webert Sicot and Gerard Dupervil, who both later will become well-known Haitian superstars. With the help of the legendary Antal Murat, the country soon learned of the *Conjunto International.* Once again, Nemours saw his work vanish as his friend Antal left with some of his musicians to join René Saint Aude in reinforcing the band *Jazz des Jeunes.*

Nemours was an innovator. Each time he was dropped, kicked out, betrayed or rejected or walked away on his own, he always seemed to have the energy, the will, and the determination to bounce back for the better. He also always seemed to find influential people who believed in his projects. It is by that same token that he gained the trust of the entrepreneur Jean Numarque, who let him use his dance hall in Kenscoff to work on his new project. With the help of some fellow musicians, the band started to put together some new songs and some performances at the hall. When Mr. Lumarque opened his new place called *Aux Calebasses* (Calabash) (the club ceiling was decorated with multiple calabashes of different colors) in the neighborhood of *Mariani* a few kilometers south of Port-au-Prince, Nemours' band became the house band and therefore was automatically named also *Orchestre Aux Calebasses*. As the band was getting some momentum and recognition the people who first experienced the band called the rhythm that Nemours was playing *Rhythm Aux Calebasses*.

At that point of his career Nemours was facing his greatest challenges ever. One must understand that in the early 1950s, there were almost no Haitian recordings to play on the air and on the phonographs at the private parties. Most radio stations were forced to play the music of the artists of the U.S., Europe and most of all the music of our neighbors Cuba, and the Dominican Republique. Therefore the songs of foreign artists were being marketed to millions of Haitians due to the lack of national music productions. Artists like Celia Cruz, and bands like La Sonara Matancera dominated the country. Most bands were forced to play Salsa, Merengue or other form of music that we have learned from our African ancestors like Pétro, Ibo, Yanvalou, Banda, Congo, Rara, and Rabòbay among others. Suddenly, out of the mind of Nemours was coming the idea of simplifying the Hispanic-influenced music formula by coming out with a one-two punch much easier for Haitians to dance. Nemours introduced to the percussion line the *"Gong"*, a set of instruments which is played by hitting a cowbell and a floor tom with a drum stick at different intervals. The pattern created with the Gong mixed with the Congas is unique only to Konpa music. The best thing that happened is that the public quickly found a way to move around the music and many were calling it already *Dansez Carré*, which is known today as the *Konpa Dance*. When Nemours presented his new formula which, consisted of the congas played by Kretzer Duroseau as the directive of his new rhythm to some of his friends at the Guignard family residence, a trumpet player named René Diogène, who went to see Mr. François Guignard for some correction of a music sheet, said this thing you just presented to us is nothing. It's too easy; it is direct and exact as a Compass (compas in French). While Mr. Diogène used the word "compas" as a mockery of Nemours new findings, Nemours Jean Baptiste said well that's exactly what I will call my new found rhythm **COMPAS DIRECT**.

On July 26, 1955 Nemours Jean Baptiste introduce his new band in a small, public park by the Sainte Anne Church in the heart of Port-au-Prince. The band was no longer the house band of Aux Calebasses, but was ready to travel under the new name "Super Ensemble de Nemours Jean Baptiste" around the country and around the world. The composer quickly went into some serious attacks on the country's most popular band Jazz des Jeunes, as a retaliation to Antal and René by calling them old people (vié gran moun) and telling them that it was time to make space for the younger generation. Nemours backed up his actions by introducing some innovative sounds by adding for the first time amplified instruments in the Haitian music community. No need to say that he was seen as the new best thing around the country. Before Nemours, no bands had played with an electric guitar. With the help of the guitarist Raymond Gaspard and the accordionist Richard Duroseau, Nemours dominated the Haitian music scene of the 50s and 60s as the public was also being introduced to Haitian music on (33 tours/45 tours and 78 tours) records called *Plaques* by Haitians. In the early 1960s Nemours, realizing that his friend Webert Sicot was also becoming popular, put Jazz des Jeunes on the back burner and launched his new attacks on Sicot's band.

This polemical music battle would last for most of the careers of the two musicians. Most of the songs were telling a story, sometimes the life story and secrets of the two leaders, thus becoming a real soap opera for the public and their followers. The Haitian music scene of the country was cut into two pieces. You were either for one or the other. Make your pick Nemours or Sicot, and during the carnival season sometimes the battle did become violent among the followers if the two bands happened to meet in the streets. The fans of Nemours will wear the *Red and White* color to identify themselves from the *Red, Blue, White and Black* of the Sicot fans. Later Sicot replaced the blue with green. Sometimes people used to say well I'm a fan of the *four colors* or I'm a fan of the *two colors*. In the middle of this masquerade one thing was certain, Nemours had managed, with his tenacity, his will, and his savoir faire, to put an end to the influence of Cuban and Dominican music by giving the country its own musical identity and a dance affectionately call Konpa.

In the late 1960s Nemours faced yet another challenge, as so many young men wanted to be the next Nemours Jean Baptiste. A new musical revolution had started in the country as in almost every neighborhood were emerging new musical groups with young fellows.

The new groups simplified Nemours' work by reducing the number of musicians to six to eight instead of 12 to 15 members. Since the 1960s also brought the style of short skirt call *Mini Jupe*, the reduced bands also called themselves the *Mini Jazz*.

The new groups attracted not only the new generation, but also the show producers because they were young and were willing to perform for less money. They created also a new avenue for the record producers who suddenly had more options to produce new records instead of waiting for the two leading bands and a few others to come up with new materials. So the Mini Jazz movement was an opportunity for many people to make money in the music business. Therefore many of the shows, balls, concerts, festivals and private parties that used to be played by Compas Direct and Cadence Rampas were turned over to bands like Les Shleu Shleu, Les Loups Noirs, Les Fantaisistes, Les Ambassadeurs, Bossa Combo and Tabou Combo to name a few. Nemours, who finally realized that there was no way that he would be able to compete with so many adversaries, decided to call it quits and moved to the U.S. to join some of his musicians who had already abandoned ship. In the Diaspora, with the help of the Duroseau brothers and some other ex-members of his band, he and his longtime rival but still best friend Webert Sicot and Raoul Guillaume tried their best to entertain some of their compatriots and ex-fans from the good old days in search of Konpa music. At that same time, Nemours was also losing his sight, so he decided to return to Haiti where he still tried to make a comeback by creating the band Top Compas, which he later name Super Combo de Nemours Jean Baptiste. But the real fans were no longer there to support either name, and young people had found some new leaders and younger entertainers to follow, and no one could understand that better that the man who had in previous years moved Jazz des Jeunes to the back burner.

Facing great financial difficulties by losing his band and without any pension, no retirement money, no government support, or any royalties whatsoever even when his songs were being copied and remixed by many Haitian and non- Haitian artists as well, Nemours Jean Baptiste who was once a barber before becoming Haiti's most famous musician ever had to face the reality that he would die broke. He once said to his family that people will understand and learn to really appreciate his works only after he is gone.

In an attempt to raise fund for his surgery he released an album with his friend Webert Sicot called *"Union"* to show unity among the two musical icons. Unfortunately after his eye surgery Nemours Jean Baptiste faced once again another hard reality that he was going to spend the rest of his life in the dark. On May 18, 1985 Nemours Jean Baptiste died in Port-au-Prince after suffering from prostate cancer and blindness. He left behind a multitude of hit songs like: *Ti Carole, Les Trois Dangers, Compas Cabane Choucoune, Flagrant Déli, Gaçon Nou Nan Ka, Immortel Compas, Infidélité, Rouge et Blanc, Lumière Rouge, St. Cécile, Solanges, Boule Malachon, Ginou, La Joie de Vivre, Joyeux Noel, Nou sé Chelbè, Vive Compas,* and *Universel Compas* among others.

Nemours has over the years played in many countries especially in the Caribbean Islands the U.S. and Europe. He has received several awards and most of all his music remains a model being used by millions of artists all over the world. Today the term Konpa is commonly being used by millions of Haitian as well as non-Haitians, there are several Konpa festivals organized throughout Haiti and in the Haitian diaspora particularly in Florida, New York, Boston, Washington, D.C., Canada, the Dominican Republique and the French-speaking Caribbean Islands.

Nemours is gone in person, but his legacy will last forever, after all he didn't work in vain as he left behind something that no one could ever be able to take away from him......a heritage.....a music and a dance called _**Konpa**_.....one thing that Haitians all over the globe will always be proud to claim as being _**Made in Haiti**_.

Jean Baptiste, Pierre (Baba) - Bass

This talented bassist showed a very good stage presence at an early age when he became one of the first bassist of Bossa Combo. He kept his cool appearance all the way to his years with Shooblack which later became Shoogar Combo. When Arsène Appolon moved to Haiti to create his band Skah Shah D'Haiti he called on the expertise of Baba to the rescue as the musician that can play the Konpa he was looking for. In the late 1980s Baba became a member of Scorpio for a short while before disappearing from the Konpa radar.

Jean Baptiste, Pierre Rigal - Guitar

This star guitarist of L'Ensemble Select de Coupé Cloué who played next to Bellerive as the groove master of the Konpa Manba actually started his career with the band Cadence Rampa of Webert Sicot. When Sicot left his own band to immigrate to the U.S., Rigal was one of the musicians who kept the legacy alive with the band Super Choucoune under the leadership of André Dorismond.

Jean Baptiste, Ricot - Singer

Ricot played with the band Les Papillons and Les Eperviers in the Mini Jazz era.

Jean Baptiste, Ricot *- Radio Personality

Ricot Jean Baptiste contributed to the evolution and emancipation of the Mini Jazz movement of the 1970s with his show "_Tambours Batants_" on Radio Haiti and later on the show "_Podium 129_" on Radio Metropole.

Jean Baptiste, Robenson - Drums

Jean Baptiste, Roger (Ti Yale) - Guitar

Talented guitarist of the band Djet-X, Ti Yale was for many years next to the saxophonist Gerard Daniel and the bassist Alix Jacques, one of the Konpa masters of the band.

Jean Baptiste, Roland - Saxophone
Roland played with the band Les Diables du Rythme de St. Marc.

Jean Baptiste, Smith - Drums
One of the first drummers of the Mini Jazz era, Smith indirectly started the style Bolo Bolo 4 -3 with the band Les Shleu Shleu. Many drummers and Konpa musicians played Bolo Bolo 4 -3 without ever known the name of the style of Konpa that they were playing. One of the perfectionists of that style is Arsene Appollon, the drummer who followed Smith in Shleu Shleu. In the first album of Les Astros a band that was created by Arsene under the name A.A. Express, popular singer Antoine Rossini Jean Baptiste (Ti Manno) did identify the song "Cépo" as a Bolo Bolo 4 -3.Smith spend most of his adult life in New York. On many occasion he tried to revive Les Shleu Shleu with new and sometimes former musicians of the 1960s famous Mini Jazz. In 2005 he came out with his album Smitty. Smith has relocated in Florida.

Jean Baptiste, Tony - Guitar
Tony Jean Baptiste is the band leader of "Djakout Mizik" one of Haiti's most popular bands. He is known as the mentor and instructor to many young guitarists.

Jean Baptiste, Wilfrid - Congas
Wilfrid played with Tropicana.

Jean Charles, Biladé - Guitar

Jean Charles, Gardy - Bass
Gardy was one of the first musicians of the group Zin. He was also the man who created the group Lakol with Stanley Toussaint (Tantan).

Jean Claude, Julien - Keyboard

Jean Destin, Duval - Guitar/Singer

Jean fils, Clovis - Keyboard /Singer
Musician of the band Hangout

Jean François, Bertholini (Berto) - Guitar
Berto did his best years playing with Bossa Combo in the 70s and early 80s before moving to New York. Berto is not the kind of guitarist that will move

the crowd with his solo, but he was the man holding the super groove of Bossa Combo.

Jean François, Edner – Guitar
Musician of the band Gabel

Jean Jacques, Errol - Percussionist

Jean-François, Roger - Saxophonist
Roger played with the band Septentrional

Jean François, Roosevelt - Guitar / Bass

Jean Gilles, Alfred - Bass

Jean Gilles, Georges – Drums
Georges had his best years with Scorpio playing next to his cousin the gonguist Mario Jean Gilles who later became a very good drummer too.

Jean Gilles, Mario - Gong / Drums / Percussions
Mario played with Scorpio next to his cousin the drummer Georges Jean Gilles. Mario became a very good drummer when he moved to the U.S. to play with the band Les Pachas de Washington.

Jean Gilles, Rodolph - Guitar
Rodolph is an excellent and quiet guitarist who did his work with pride and knows his Konpa very well. Rodolph has been gaining experience from the days of the Mini Jazz with the band Super 9 in Haiti. In New York he played respectively with System and Skah Shah for short periods before finally earn a place as a member of the Brooklyn based band Partners next to Lemy on lead guitar. When the band became Phantoms and getting very busy with King Kino on lead vocal, Rodolph finally get to the stardom level he always deserved from an early age as he became one of the Haitian music well-known guitarists, but still a very quiet man on stage.

Jean Lesly, Rigaud - Bass

Jean Louis, Alphonse - Saxophone

Jean Louis, Cassique - Keyboard

Jean Louis, Maggy - Singer

Maggy has a very notorious voice in the Haitian music world who did little Konpa work. Her best years as a musician are with Boukman Eksperyans.

Jean Louis, Natalio - Guitar
Played in Haiti with the band Etoile du Soir, however in New York he became the star guitarist of the group Macho Band and performed later with the band Sweet Natal trying his best to keep alive the Konpa Manba of the late Coupé Cloué in the diaspora.

Jean Louis, Nicholson - Drums
Nicholson played with Tropicana.

Jean Louis, Orson - Singer
Star singer of the band Scorpio, Orson retire from Konpa at an early age, however he marked his generation and others to come with his unique voice in some of the most memorable songs of Scorpio to include *Men Yayade La.*

Jean-Louis, Raymond - Bass
Raymond played with Septentrional.

Jean Louis, Yves - Gong/Percussion
Yves played in the min jazz era with Les Loups Noirs.

Jean Luben, Louis - Trumpet
Louis is also one of the composers and music arrangers of the band Tropicana.

Jean Luc, Joseph - Bass

Jean Marie, Alex - Singer
Alex played with the New York based band "Pèlen".

Jean Nazaire, Yvon - Guitar
Yvon played with Magic Connection.

Jean Noel, Roosevelt - Drums/Singer

Jean Phillipe, Johnson - Keyboard

Jean Phillipe, Gracia * (Ti Kit) - Singer
Ti Kit was the star singer of Scorpio in the early 1980s, at the time when Ti Manno was the king of the airwaves in Haiti. Ti Kit was the only artist that stood as an opponent in front of the popular Ti Manno.

Despite the fact that he played with some Mini Jazz in the early 70s, Ti Kit first became known to the public in the late 70s when the fourth version of Les Shleu Shleu released the song *Crapeau*. In the years that followed he was recruited by Les Ambassadeurs, but he really found fame when he joined the band Shoogar Combo which gave him the opportunity to shine in the song *Craché Difé* his second mega hit as a lead singer.

In 1980, when Olson Jean Louis left Scorpio and moved to the U.S., the staff of Scorpio called on two singers to replace the popular Olson, one of them was Maxime Mascary and the other one was Gracia Jean Philippe (Ti Kit). In the next carnival period (1981) Ti Kit rocked the streets of Port-au-Prince on the Sundays prior to the carnival and also during the parade of bands with the song *Kaskèt Sou Tète*, one of Scorpio best Carnival song ever. On the album *"Gipsy Fever"* his performance in the song *Christiane* put him on the map as one of the top Haitian showmen.

Ti Kit became the leader of Scorpio when Robert Martino left his own band after a dispute. Ti Kit called on the guitarist François M. St Preux to replace the maestro. Ti Kit literally launched an attack on Martino accusing him of not paying and mistreating the musicians in the album of Scorpio Fever titled Vacances in the song *Aprann Viv*. Ti Kit moved to New York in the mid 1980s where he put together the band Scorpio La Crème with the help of his brother/manager, the promoter and store owner Prudent Jean Philippe. Gracia Jean Philippe (Ti Kit) died in New York in 1993.

Jean Philippe, Prudent - Promoter
Prudent was a store owner in New York and the manager of his brother Gracia Jean Philippe (Ti Kit) and his band Scorpio La Crème.

Jean Pierre, Assel - Keyboard / Bass
Assel is one of the two famous Jean Pierre brothers who revolutionized the Konpa music in the New York area in the early 1990s. The brothers who are the owners of a recording company usually played different instruments on many music projects.

Jean Pierre, Francisco (Cisco) - Singer

Jean Pierre, Gracia - Singer
Musician of the band Washington Express in the 1980s

Jean Pierre, Jeff (Ton Jeff)
Jeff is the road manager and coordinator of the band Kreyol La.

Jean Pierre, Harold - Saxophone

Jean Pierre, Jowel - Keyboard

Jean Pierre, Louis - Saxophone

Jean Pierre, Patrick - Singer

Jean Pierre, Richard - Drums

Jean Pierre, Ronald - Keyboard

Jean Pierre, Welmyr - Keyboard
Welmyr is one of the most solicited Haitian musicians. He is the master brain behind many studio projects done in his recording studio especially in the 1990s. His has on of the most remarkable touch on the keyboard, and he is able to play different style of music besides Konpa. He is known among musicians especially for his jazzy style.

Jean René, Emilien - Guitar
Emilien played with Septentrional.

Jean Robert, Lestage - Saxophone

Jean Sylvio, Jean Pierre - Saxophone
Jean Pierre played with Shoogar Combo.

Jeanite, Adrien - Keyboard
Adrien Jeanite dominated the chord section of Bossa Combo for about three decades.

Jeannot, Claude - Guitar

Jeannot, Hans - Singer

Jeanty, Marc (Marco) - Singer
Marco was the partner of Manno Charlemagne who in the 1970s formed the duo Manno & Marco.

Jeanty, Rachelle - Singer

Jedeikin, James - Saxophone
James is a non-Haitian saxophonist who played with Skah Shah.

Jensen, Dave - Saxophone
Dave is a non-Haitian musician who played with Skah Shah.

Jérémie, Didi - Singer

Jérôme, Hervé - Singer
Hervé played with the band Pèlen of Spring Valley N.Y.

Jérôme, Jean Claude - Singer
Jean Claude made his mark in the 1970s by playing with Les Loups Noirs.

Jérome, Jean Céguerre - Sound Engineer

Jérome, Yvon - Drums
Yvon played with several bands to include his early days with Bossa Combo to the Nouvel Jenerasyon bands like Triomecs to recently playing with Gracia Delva's band Mass Compas. Yvon Jérome is also a radio announcer and a politician. In 2007 he became the mayor of the Carrefour a town located in the south of Port-au-Prince.

Jets (Les Jets) - Band
Les jets was a band of the Mini Jazz era

Jeudi, Frantz - Singer

Jeune, Armstrong - Singer
Armstrong is a voice that many have heard in several songs in the 1990s, finally the N.Y All Stars video *Pou LaVie* had finally put a face to the voice for those who don't go to nightclubs. He moves constantly from New York to Fl. working on his solo career and singing on other artists projects as well. He is the singer of the band Do La.

Jeune, Etienne - Keyboard

Jeune, Phaton - Trumpet / Trombone
Phaton played with Bossa Combo in the 1980s.

Johns, Norman - Bass
Musician of Gabel

Joachim, Dios - Singer

Joachim, Maxo - Keyboard

Joachim, Paul - Singer

Joanis, Jhon - Trumpet

Joassin, Fritz (Fito) - Guitar
Fito played with Les Diplomats de Petion-Ville and later with Ibo Combo in the Mini Jazz era.

Jokers - (Les Jokers) - Band
Band of the Mini Jazz era created in 1969.

Joly, Jacques Dewinston * - Bass
Jacques is one of the founders of the band Les Diables du Rythme de St Marc. He became schizophrenic and committed suicide while living in Montreal in the 1980s.

Joly, Ulrick - Bass /Guitar

Josama, Gary - Guitar
After playing with many no name bands, Gary finally got his break by joining Tabou Combo at the turn of the century. He was for Tabou a good catch by filling the gap left by Ralph Condé.

Joseph, Arius - Congas
Arius is by far one of the most popular congas players of his generation. In the 1980s he was called by many bands and artists to help in their projects and live shows. He played with Dixie Band, Lakansyèl, Ansy Dérose, Zèklè, Caribbean Sextet and in the 1990s he played with Strings.

Joseph, Auguste - Saxophone

Joseph, Carlo - Keyboard

Joseph, Carly - Keyboard

Joseph, Cassandra - Singer
Musician of the New York based band Phantoms. Cassandra is a talented and energetic young female artist.

Joseph, Constantin - Drums

Joseph, Elias - Trumpet
Elias played with the band Les Formidables de St Marc in the Mini Jazz era.

Joseph, Emilien - Guitar
Emilien played with Septentrional.

Joseph, Ernst - Keyboard

Joseph, Frantz (Vié Fanfan or Fanfan Kè Kal) - Congas
Fanfan, who was nicknamed Vié Fanfan by his childhood friends, started his musical career with the band Samba Créole in the 1970s. After the dissolution of Samba Créole he joined Bossa Combo next to the drummer Mario de Volcy also a former member of Samba Créole.
In 1983 a group of young men and women in New York known as the Agimal did a yellow T. shirt to identify the group of friends in the Labor Day parade. On the t. shirts were inscribed the words "Agimal Kè Kal". The name Kè Kal was basically from a friend of Jean Claude Vivens by the name of Yves Perpignan. One day Jean Claude was on the way to the immigration in D.C. to pick up some documentation to send to a friend in Haiti, when Yves realized that he was going to the INS he got scared and Jean Claude assured him that most people found at the INS are people without proper documents filing for permanent status. As he felt reassured Yves then said in that case *Mwen Kè Kal* (Coeur calme) meaning in a sense *I'm cool* with that. When Jean Claude told his friends in New York about the story and that he ever since that day call his friend Yves "*Kè Kal*" the group like the story so much that they make the *Kè Kal* t. shirts for the Brooklyn Caribbean Labor Day Parade.
As the shirts were being painted with spray paint some musicians of Bossa Combo on tour in New York came to the house of Alex and Edith Vivens Badeau in Cambria Heights Queens to see Jean Claude and his brother, Ambroise Vivens also nicknamed Fanfan Agimal. This is how Frantz Joseph fell in love with the name *Kè Kal.*
When Bossa Combo returned to Haiti after the tour they started to work on their carnival for the year 1984, and the word *Kè Kal* hit the streets of Port-au-Prince like fire on gas. With the success of the carnival song and since the showman Frantz Joseph (Fanfan) came up with the idea, the musicians and the public called him *Fanfan Kè Kal* ever since.

Joseph, Gérald - Congas
Gérald played with the band La Ruche de Léogane.

Joseph, Harold - Singer
Harold Joseph talent was discovered at an early age. Harold was a schoolboy when he started to play at the professional level in the band Super Prince. When he realized that Super Prince wasn't going to go far he moved to the town of Les Cayes where he joined the band Panorama des Cayes for a few months only. He switched to Les Lionceaux des Cayes which was however a Port-au-Prince based band. Les Lionceaux, with Léon Dimanche one of the top singers in the business, was a busier band and therefore gave Harold the chance to shine as a young artist. He also had the opportunity to show that he can easily sing in Spanish.
By the mid-70s the public discovered the voice of Harold Joseph when the song *Débaba* of the band Safari Combo hit the airwaves. Playing next to Assade Francoeur, he shared the front line of Safari Combo, the band that would later become known as Super 9.
By the late 1970s Harold no longer the popular pupil of the School Frères Adrien moved to New York where he joined Les Frères Déjean just before the release of the album *"l'Univers"*, there again he shared the front line of the band with Isnard Douby. When the band Les Frères Déjean was forced to move to Haiti, Harold who didn't have any problem returning to the U.S. was among the members who created the musical group System Band. With System Band he became one of the star singers of the Haitian diaspora with songs like *Chagrin Damou* and *Péyi Ya Pa Pou Vann* until he abandoned ship and went on an adventurous route with Adolphe Chancy (Ti Dof) in the band Superstars based in Miami Fl. In that band Harold's voice once again found some space not only on the radio, but this time people who don't go to live shows had a chance to see him in the video of the song *La Vi A Bel*.
By the late 1990s, Harold Joseph was no longer a name that young music followers could recognize as he quietly vanished from the musical scene.

Joseph, Jacques - Gong
Musician of the Miami based band Gabel

Joseph, Jean Arthur - Singer

Joseph, Jean Claude - Saxophone
Jean Claude played with the band Tropicana.

Joseph, Jean Yves (Fanfan Ti Botte) - Congas /Singer
A Native of Petion-Ville, Yves Joseph, better known as Fanfan, is one of the original members of the band Tabou Combo. Fanfan started with the band in 1968 playing the congas. In the 80s, he moved to the front as an additional vocalist in support of Shoubou. The two have formed an impressive singing

duo for the last 30 years. Fanfan is, undoubtedly, one of the most important and versatile members of Tabou Combo. Apart from being the band background vocalist, he's also the band's manager and main songwriter. As a teenager, Fanfan has developed a fondness for poetry and a passion for music a combination that has made him into one of the most successful songwriters and composers in the Haitian music industry. Some of the songs that carry Fanfan's signature are: *Zap Zap, Aux Antilles, Et Alors, Prejuge, Juicy Lucy, Baissez Bas*, to mane a few. Fanfan said he often hears himself in dreams singing the songs he wrote for the band. When Fanfan is not performing or composing, he's taking care of the band's business as he is responsible for most of Tabou's administrative affairs. Fanfan is a graduate (Cum Laude) from City College with a major in International Relations and a minor in Education. In the summer of 2000, Fanfan became the first Haitian artist to land an endorsement deal with a major U.S. company when he signed with Latin Percussion (LP). Fanfan said his most positive experience with Tabou Combo was when the hit single New York City was released. "It's a good feeling to hear your songs everywhere you go in Europe, in jukeboxes, major radio stations and Clubs," said Fanfan." The attention you get, the pampering and the fame is unbelievable..."
Bio from www.taboucombo.com

Joseph, Jacques (Beken) - Drums
Beken is a member of Gabel

Joseph, Joël - Singer

Joseph, Joel - Singer
Joel did his best years singing next to Coupé Cloué in Ensemble Select de Coupe Cloué, later on in his career he joined Les Frères Déjean.

Joseph, Josué (Doudou) - Bass

Joseph, Jordani - Singer
Born on October 17, 1937 in Terrier Rouge, Jordani was by the mid-1940s seen as a potential singer by those who had the chance to see the 7 years old boy on stage at the Immaculate Conception Church Choir. In 1951, his father got a job as a mechanic in Plantation Daulphin, an American Sisal Company, since the family had to move he became a regular of the church St. Thérèse, it's also in that plantation that he joined his first band Jazz Citadel under the leadership of Jacques Mompremier. There he also had the chance to meet other professionals like Joseph Manigat, Gerard Monfiston and Hervé Casséus who were from several different cities but still working at the plant.

In 1966 the plant closed down and the band moved to Cap Haitien performing in the nightclub "Le Feu Vert" until they split up in 1968. Jordani received the offer to join the band Septentrional, but he felt that Tassy and Roger Colas would have been too much of a competition. Instead he joined the band Tropicana which offered more opportunities to shine. So the man known as *Gwo Mésié* or the Big Man for his size stood tall next to the tiny Parisien Fils Aimé in front of Tropicana until he retired in the year 2001.

Jordani also excelled in the 1980s with the *Pot Pouris de Boléros* a series of medley of slow songs in French, Spanish and Créole put together by Daniel Larivière.

Jordani resigned from playing music and he is living Connecticut with his family.

Joseph, Jude James - Keyboard

Joseph, Kétel - Congas

Joseph, Lesly – Congas

Joseph, Maxen - Keyboard

Joseph, Miratel - Drums

Joseph, Pierre - Keyboard
Pierre played with Septentrional du Cap.

Joseph, Pierrot - Drums

Joseph, Ricardi (Ricky) - Singer
Ricky is a member of Trankill.

Joseph, Reynald - Bass

Joseph, Samuel - Drums
Samuel is a member of Take Off.

Joseph, Sergio - Drums

Joseph, Walter - Bass

Joseph, Wilbens - Bass

Joseph, Wilmar - Guitar

Joseph, Wuydens - Singer
Wuydens played with Papash

Josy Records
Haitian owned record company

Jouvenceaux (Les Jouvenceaux de Jacmel) - Band
This band, created on Aug. 14, 1968 has been over the years, one of the top bands that ever came out in the town of Jacmel. During the carnival season in Jacmel many people do compare the carnival songs of Les Jouvenceaux with their rival band Les Invincibles de Jacmel. At times just like the polemic of Nemours and Sicot, D.P. Express and Scorpio, Septen Tropic, T. Vice and Djakout, the musical rivalry of the two bands can be very heated. However, at the end of the 1990s, both bands had lost the momentum and their popularity in their own town. The people of Jacmel's choices increased with the invasion of the town's nightclubs by most popular bands out of Port-au-Prince and the diaspora, especially during the carnival season, the Christmas holidays and the summer months. Another trend that has affected Jacmel's top bands is the fact that often the visiting bands will hire the best musicians on the spot and manage to take them to the States where they will find fame and a chance to travel around the globe. It's an offer that many artists living in Haiti find hard to resist.

Ju-Kann -Band

Judah, Syd - Trumpet
Syd played with the Magnum Band as well as the System Band is his career. He is also known as a great music arranger and an excellent musician.

Jules, Michel - Keyboard
Michel played accordion in the band Jazz Capois.

Jules, Jean Claude - Drums
Jean Claude played with Shoogar Combo and later became the regular drummer of Bossa Combo when Mario De Volcy left Bossa Combo for his solo career.

Jules, Patrick - Congas

Julien, Frandy - Drums

Julien, Senéque Jean - Drums

Julmé, Joseph - Drums
Joseph is one of the pioneers of the Mini Jazz era. He played with Les Frères Déjean in the 1960s.

Julmiste, Gomel - Drums

Jumeau, Jean - Trombone

Juste, Eddy - Guitar
Eddy is one of the two star guitarists of the troubadour band Les 7 Vedettes.

Juste, Emile - Guitar
Emile is the other star guitarist of the troubadour band Les 7 Vedettes.

Juste, Léonel - Singer

Juste, Moise - Singer

Juste, Patricia - Singer

Patricia came out in the mid-90 with the band Lakol, getting the attention of the band's followers not only with her strong voice but with her acrobatic stunts as well. She was known to do front and back flips while performing. When she left the band she moved on as a solo artist, releasing a series of albums to include *Sa Poko Ayen, Tête Calé, Bwat Secret Ya* and *Gaçon Vicieux*. She became known as Miss Energy and made occasional appearances at some events. The once very active entertainer also released a few videos which are considered amusing to some and/or controversial to others. She never missed the opportunity to make herself heard in the Haitian music arena in some subjects that most people tend to ignore. She felt that some Haitian promoters were being sexists and were not giving exposures to female Konpa artists especially at the numerous Konpa Festivals. She also took a stand against bootleg copies of Haitian music. In her song *Gaçon Vicieux* she talked about lazy men living at the expense of hard working women, a subject that had outraged members of both sexes but still remain a reality especially in the Haitian diaspora. In 2006 Patricia Juste who is also a proud

New York City Police Officer, a devoted mother and a recording artist surprised the Haitian music society when she opened a couple of music stores, one in Queens and one in Long Island. Her company, Real Biz Music, is also producing and distributing records in the U.S., Haiti, the Caribbean and Europe. Patricia Juste is the younger sister of the drummer and actor Ricky Juste.

Juste, Ricky - Drums
Ricky is the well-known drummer of the band K-Dans. He also had at least one solo CD in the market. He is also an actor. Ricky Juste is the older brother of the singer/producer Patricia Juste.

Juste, Roland - Singer

Jwilavi entertainment
Production company based in Haiti, their website jwilavi.com provides information about Konpa events.

K

K-Dans - Band

The band K-Dans was created in the late 1990s. The band introduced many young talents that would later be known as some of the top stars of the Haitian music business by the turn of the century. In their first album, titled S.O.S, many of the songs quickly became the favorite of the teenagers. Their song *Graduation* has made K-Dans the band of choice at almost every high school and universities graduation parties. The sad song *Touman*, about the premature death of a young married woman also has reached the heart of anyone who has lost a love one.

The singer Michael Guirand, the guitarist Glenny Benoit, the keyboardists Carlo Vieux and Richard Cavé as well as the conga player Alex Thébau will later became members of the popular band Carimi.

K-Dans also released in four years the albums *Nou Pa Normal, Big Boss, Bagay Yo Changé* as well as some live albums showcasing the talent of their singer Jude Jean.

While Jude Jean had a beautiful voice and has attracted many young women over the years, the band members and management felt that he was not able to move the crowd and make them jump like most singers were doing at the turn of the century at the live shows. K-Dans wanted to introduce some new blood and offer to Jude the idea of adding someone else in the front line and Jude didn't welcome the idea and refused the offer.

In the year 2006 Jude Jean was replaced by a much younger musician name Markenzy Talon (Mac –D).

Jude Jean moved on by creating the band known as "Chill" while K-Dans released the album *Easy Fit* at the end of the year with Mac- D on lead vocal. The album quickly became a success and the band was able to move forward by touring the U.S. and Canada only a few months after the album first hit the shelves. K-Dans old and new followers filled up the ballrooms and clubs to see the young charismatic singer. However after the tour Mac-D left the band and moved to Florida with his parents in May 2007.

K-Res - Band
This band is also known as Caress.

K-Sou Coupé - Band

Kahara, Georges - Congas
Georges played with the band Latino

Kaliko Productions
Show and record production company - It is owned by the promoter and club owner Gérald Firmin aka Gérald Kaliko.

Kam, Frantz - Singer

Karlil, François - Keyboard

Kaskad - Band
This band came out in Montreal under the name Volny Orchestra, under the direction of the Volny Brothers before changing the name to Kaskad.

Katalog see: Etienne Vladimir

Kassav - Band
Popular band from the island of Guadeloupe, Kassav is known for playing Konpa and Zouk music.

Kazak Eksperience - Band
Band based in Cap Haitian.

Kébrau, Béatrice - Singer

Kébreau, Gérald - Bass
Gérald is the talented bassist of the band T. Vice.

Kéké see: Bélizaire Clement

Kelly, James - Trumpet
James played with Tabou Combo.

Kepopoz - Band

Kersaint, Pierrot * - Congas
Ti Pierrot was one of the conga players who used to perform with three congas at a time. He started his career with Les Difficiles and his best years were with

D.P. Express.
During the 1980s he came out with a series of solo project with a group of friends under the title Gamma Express. Ti Pierrot was not only a great drummer; he was also a great Konpa composer. He tried many times to come out with Gamma Express as a performing Band, but unfortunately the attendance was never enough to balance the group budget.
Ti Pierrot was among the musicians who left D.P Express in 1985 to create the band G.P. Express in Silver Spring Md. a suburb of Washington. D.C. Pierrot did not last long in the U.S. He returned to Haiti, but he did not rejoin D.P. Pierrot Kersaint died in Haiti in the late 1980s.

Keslin, Almondo - Drums
Born in Port-au Prince Almando started his professional career with Bossa Combo. He participated in different music projects in Haiti with Haitian music giants like Weber Sicot , Ansy Dérose to name a few but Almando's career really shine with D.P. Express in the late 70s and early 80s. In the mid 1980s he was replaced by Edner Couloutte. Later on in the late 80s he joined Les Frères Dejean where he continued to show his talent as a great drummer. While many Haitian musicians left Haiti to continue their career in other parts of the world, Almando spent his entire career playing music in Haiti. He is also the creator and leader of the band "Omni Band".

Keslin, Carmelot - Drums
Carmelot played with Cadence Rampa, Super Choucoune, and later on with "Coupé Cloué".

Keslin, Chandler - Drums

Keslin, Frantz - Congas
Keslin, Yvens - Gong

Kessy see: Lubin Jean Samuel

Khal Mah - Band

Kiko see: Paul Frantz

King Kino - see: Divers Pierre Raymond

Kita Combo – Band
Band of the Mini Jazz era created in 1973.

Klean - Band
Konpa band based in Montréal

Klinik - Band
Discography includes *Emergency* and *Kréyol Mix U.S.A*

Koldjensen, Sabrina - Singer
Played with System Band, Superstar, Riské and Caress

Kompamagazine.com
Konpa Magazine is a popular online magazine where Konpa fans discuss issues regarding Konpa music on a daily basis. It reports Konpa news 24/7 on the website music forum as it happens. It is owned by the journalist and Konpa news reporter Patrick Desvarieux.

Kompamania - Band

Konpa
Other name for the rhythm Compas Direct invented by Haitian saxophonist Nemours Jean Baptiste. With the advancement of the Creole movement, modern Haitians changed the spelling from the French word "Compas" to the creole word "Konpa."
Some people tend to spell it "Kompa" with the letter "M". However, based on the studies of the Créole language the rule of "M" before the letters "B" and "P" does not apply in Créole unlike in languages like French and English because Créole is a phonetic language. Writing Konpa with the letter M would change the sound of the word, therefore the proper spelling is: **"Konpa"** with the letter "N", not "M".
The word Konpa is also used to describe the way people dance the rhythm, even though at first it started as the dance "Dansé Carré" which later was changed to a dance called "Bourèt", and finally to the "Konpa Dance" as we know it today.

Konpa Festival or Konpafest
A concert with one or many Konpa bands, most Konpa festivals are done outdoor with vendors selling food, flags, shirts, music and other novelties under canopies. Major Konpafests are broadcast live on Haitian websites and on Haitian television stations in Haiti and in the Haitian diaspora. Konpa festivals can attract from 10.000 to 30.000 people. The yearly Miami Konpa Festival is known as one of the top 10 largest gathering of people in the East Coast of the United States.

Konpa Kréyòl - Band

Created in Haiti Dec. 3rd 1998, Konpa Kréyòl was composed of only five members they called themselves "*jazz la jeunesse la*" meaning the band of the youths because they like to sing about adolescent issues.

After a misunderstanding during a tour in Miami, the members of the band moved away from the management and the band leader David Dupoux to create the band Kréyòl La.

Konpa Manba - Band

This band was created in New York playing the Konpa Manba style of Coupé Cloué.

Konpa Manba

The style of Konpa played by Coupé Cloué, a rhythm based also on the modification of the conga beat.

Kool Konpa - Band

Their album Caréssé Mwen was released in 2005.

Kréyòl La - Band

This band was created by some ex-members of Konpa Kreyol

The two leaders of the band went separate ways in the Konpa world. The lead singer Ti Joe Zenny rallied around him all the original musicians to create the band Kréyol La, while the keyboardist and band leader David Dupoux came out with his band Krézi Mizik.

Krézi Mizik - Band

After the lead vocalist of Konpa Kréyol came out with his own band Kréyol La, his partner David Dupoux did not waste any time creating another band. With the help of star singer Michael (Mika) Benjamin and other talented musicians the band Krézi Mizik was born first under the name "Plézi". Shortly after the name was made public another group in Haiti went to the media and said that they had the right to the name Plézi. David Dupoux and his managers were forced to change the name to Krézi Mizik. In 2006 Krézi released the album *Haiti San Manti.*

Krik Krak - Band
This band was created in Florida by Loubert Chancy after he left Skah Shah

Kunkel, Kevin – Trombone

L

La Ruche (La Ruche de Léogane) -Band
This band was created in the town of Léogane in 1970. Their only hit song *Deux Jumeaux* was remixed by the band Top Vice in the 1980s.

Labadie, Emilio - Trombone

Labissière, Jean Claude - Sax
Few are the people who really know that the band Les Difficiles de Petion Ville had a saxophonist when they first came out in the early 70s. Jean Claude Labissière is indeed the only saxophonist that ever played with the band.

Labossière, Didier - Sax

Lacroix, Willy - Singer
Willy Lacroix left his mark in the Super Ensemble de Nemours Jean Baptiste in the 1960s. In the 1980s he took part, alongside the singer Carlo Claudin, on a Mini Record Project to honor the works of Nemours Jean Baptiste in an album featuring the 15 golden songs of the great maestro.

Ladouceur, Méjuste - Radio Personality
Ladouceur is the host of the popular show "Caraïbes By Night" aired Monday to Saturday from midnight to 3 am on Caraïbes fm in Haiti. In November 2007 he received the award as the best Konpa show host of the year.

Lafond, Kétly - Singer
Kétly is one of the few female artists of the pre Mini Jazz era even though she only played for a very short while with Jazz Des Jeunes.

Lafond, Wilfrid * - Guitar

Lafontant, Cédrick - Keyboard
Cédrik is the leader of the band Rafrechi.

Lafontant, Edouard - Drums
Played with the band Super Ensemble de Webert Sicot, Edouard was part of the members who tried to keep the band alive after the departure of the great maestro with the Super Choucoune project with André Dorismond as the lead

singer.

Lafontant, Joseph - Congas

Lafontant, Louis Philippe - Gong/Percussion
Philippe played with Bossa Combo in the 1980s.

Laguerre, Cathélius - Congas

Laguerre, Jean - Singer

Laguerre, Jean Claude - Congas

Laguerre, Richard - Bass

Laguerre, Serge - Congas
Serge is also a talented musician who moved back to Haiti after living and performing in the New York area. He played with Lakol and Skah Shah before joining the band Stings of Jacky Ambroise. When the band Konpa Kréyol split, Serge became a member of the group Krézi in 2005.

Laguerre, Ulrick - Singer
Ulrick played with the band Thamad Fever.

Lahens, Louis - Singer
Louis Lahens was known as one of the top singers of the 1960s. He played with the bands Jazz des Jeunes, Orchestre Citadel, Ensemble Aux Calebasses, but really found fame in his days with Super Ensemble de Nemours Jean Baptiste.

Lahens, Serge - Singer
Serge played with the band Méridional des Cayes.

Lainé, Joseph (Blagueur) - Singer
In the early 70s the band Super Choucoune was created by some members of Super Ensemble de Webert Sicot who have stayed in Haiti after most musicians moved to the U.S. with their leader Webert Sicot. That band introduced the powerful voice of the young Joseph Lainé to the public. After the dissolution of Super Choucoune the young man tried in vain to find work in the musical arena until he was discovered by Rodrigue Milien who made him a popular singer when he featured him on lead, especially in the hit song *Ti fi Kriyé* and later in the song *Grimèle*. The public had known the artist by the

name of "Blagueur". In the late 70s he was one of the founding members of the band Shooblack, (which would later become Shoogar Combo), in which he increased his popularity with songs like *Lèlène Chérie* and *Zoklo*.

In the 1980s one of Skah Shah's top composers the hit maker Arsène Apollon moved back to Haiti where he created the band Skah Shah d'Haiti with Blagueur on lead vocal because Blaguer's voice was considered to be in the same range as Cubano and Zouzoule. By the next decade Blagueur moved to the U.S. where he joined the band Volo Volo in Boston where he also worked on a few more projects without ever regaining the fame of the 1970s with Rodrigue, Shooblack and Shoogar.

Lainé, Rolls (Roro) - Drums / Gong

Roro was already a well-known football player (soccer) in Haiti more so than he was known for being a musician in the early days of his career, even when he was playing the gong for Ensemble Select, the band of the popular Coupé Cloué. During that period Roro took the time to learn the techniques of the percussion line, especially by watching and playing next to Ernest Louis (Ti Nès)

After the death of Coupé Cloué his career took a step back, but he offered his services to Mizik Mizik where he showed his talent as a drummer. Then he started to perform with Djakout Mizik. In the new century Roro has finally become one of the superstars of the Haitian music world as Djakout became one of the bands that dominated the Konpa world. With his partner Shabba on Congas, Roro is often seen as one of the showmen sometimes leaving the drum set to step up on the microphone to hype up the crowd. Sometimes he plays the drums while standing up. In any case no one could have imagined that the shy gonguist of Ensemble Select was going to become such a charismatic Konpa artist.

Lakansyèl - Band

Lakol - Band

No band ever took the Haitian music world by surprise as Lakol did in the early 1990s. The band's marketing plan was unheard of until then. Lakol came out with an album accompanied with a well-produced video introducing the new stars in the song *Olé Olé* which is considered by many as one of the best Haitian videos ever released. For more than a decade after its release no Haitian video came close to the success of the Lakol video *Olé Olé*.

The marketing plan worked so well for the band that within only a few months of the album release Lakol was already touring every town in the U.S. with a large Haitian population. When the band arrived for the first time in Haiti they had a very warm welcome as people lined up in the airport route to get a glance at the entertainers as the motorcade moved on toward the hotel. The shows were extremely packed as the public welcomed the charismatic lead singer Stanley Toussaint (Tantan) and his brothers the late Patrick Toussaint on drums and Vladimir assisting with some background vocal. In the following years Lakol also released the albums *Difé- Kolem and Something Special* as well as albums with compilation of the best hit songs of the band. If Lakol was always able to produce very good albums as well as good and catchy videos, their live performances were not always up to par and one of the problems faced by Lakol over the years is the fact that the group seems to be constantly changing musicians and that inconsistency has not worked in their favor.

 In 2004 Stanley Toussaint released the album *Pam Pam Pam* as a solo album and not as the leader of Lakol. He went on tour in the following years as a solo artist accompanied by contracted musicians and this time without his brothers, thus putting an end to the Lakol projects. In 2006 the band's management was considering changing the name of the band to Bang but never did. In 2007, they make it known that the name is Olé a name base on their 1990s hit song *Olé Olé*. That also was put on hold as Tantan released another album in the spring of 2008 titled *Machandiz La*.

Lakol D'Haiti - Band

This band came out in Cap Haitien in the 1980s. During a tour in the U.S., many of the members decided to stay and were recruited by other active bands in the Diaspora. Some of them have managed to become well-known superstars and songwriters like Jean Max Valcourt who gave his services to the band Phantoms until he created his own band "Dola". Jean Max is also the owner of Maximum Studio in Brooklyn. The talented drummer Shedly Abraham took part in countless projects with different artists and bands until he too built his own recording studio in New York. Shedly is the producer the album series "Djazz La" with the collaboration of several Haitian stars. The keyboardist Arly Larivière moved to Miami where he found fame in the band D-Zine at first and with the band Nu Look later. Arly became one of the best songwriters and respected singers in the business. The singer Delly François also went to Miami and was one of the top showmen of the band D-Zine. He also has worked with System Band in his career and returned to Miami to try desperately the D-Zine project. The bassist Joseph Perrin has played for bands like Lakol de New York, Phantoms Bazouka and System Band among others while the other bassist Nixon Mésidor has played for D-Zine and Top Vice.

On Aug. 4th 2007, the guys of Lakol d'Haiti had a successful get together where they surprised the Konpa fans at the nightclub Marabou Café with a wonderful performance. The show was called Le Grand Nord (The Big North) where they honored some musicians of the previous generations that are from the Northern part of Haiti.

Lalanne, Brune - Trumpet
Brune played with the band Les Formidables de St. Marc.

Lalanne, Gardner - Guitar
One of the star guitarists of the Mini Jazz era, Gardner played with the band Les Loups Noirs in the 1970s.

Lalanne, Grégoire - Keyboard

Lalanne, Waag - Keyboard
Wagg made a name for himself in the family managed band Les Loups Noirs. Later on he continued his career with Les Frères Déjean and Magnum band before calling it quits.

Lalanne, Wagner - Keyboard
One of the names that were definitely a household name in Haiti in the 60s and 70s was the name of the Lalanne Family. We can say that if the name was so popular in the Konpa music arena, it is because of the success of Wagner. Wagner was a regular of the Casino International Nightclub, one of the places where music was king in the 50s and 60s giving the opportunity to musicians to perform for local and international audiences as well.
During that period Wagner performed as a substitute to other keyboardists. When Nemours felt that there was a possibility that the Duroseau brothers were working on getting their papers together to move definitely to the U.S. he called on Wagner to substitute his star keyboardist Richard Duroseau.
By the time Richard moved to the U.S., Wagner was ready to feel up the vacancy by becoming the lead keyboardist of the popular band. If Richard was known in the early days of the band as a great wonder on the Accordion, Wagner showed to the world that there is even more magic in the organ/piano keys. He delivered a good job at each show, and he found a way to win the heart of the maestro and the fans by coming up with innovating sounds, solo and grooves and has therefore revolutionized the music and remains even today the role model that designed and mapped out the way Haitian artists play the keyboard.
Wagner Lalanne tried his best to keep Nemours' band alive and not succumb to the pressure of the Mini Jazz in the early 1970s. Even after Nemours has

called it quits, and try to find work in the U.S., Wagner Lalanne was the man who came out with the band Top Compas in a courageous effort to keep the dream alive. When the maestro returned to the country the name Top Compas was eventually changed to Super Combo de Nemours Jean Baptiste. However when it was Wagner Lalanne's turn to move to the U.S., Nemours made it clear to everyone that he would retire if Lalanne was not going to be by his side.

Wagner Lalanne moved to the U.S., where he became a music instructor in Florida.

Lalanne, Widy - Keyboard

Laleau, Constant - Congas

Lamarre, Lyonel - Drums
One of the star drummers of the Mini Jazz era, Lyonel played with the band Les Fantaisistes de Carrefour. He had developed a style that is up to now never been imitated.

Lamarre, Paul - Guitar

Lamothe, Dionne - Singer
Dionne played with Bossa Combo in the 1980s. Dionne excelled in the song Caroline, a song she did in duo with the legendary Raymond Cajuste.

Lamothe, Félix - Keyboard
Félix played with the bands Les Diables Bleus du Cap and Ascenda in his native town Cap Haitien before joining Les Loups Noirs in Port-au-Prince.

Lamour, Katty - Singer

Lamy, Ernst "Nono"- Keyboard / Accordion / Bass
Nono is a legendary musician of the 1940s and 1950s who have played with many artists. He helped several bands and stars by arranging their songs. He played respectively with Issa El Saieh, Orchestre Radio du Commerce, Dòdòf Legros, Guy Durosier Raoul Guillaume, Orchestre Casino International, and Edner Guignard. Although he spent some times in Canada in his younger years, Nono returned has lived most of his life in Port-au-Prince Haiti until his death in 1994 at the age of 71.

Lapierre, Jonas - Trumpet

Lapointe, Elie - Guitar
Besides his solo album titled Talent, Elie Lapointe has worked with the band New York All Stars and later Fahrenheit until he joined Djakout Mizik in the spring of 2007. He left Djakout in the spring of 2008.

Laporte, Gabriel - Guitar
Gabriel Laporte is a talented musician who made his mark in the Haitian music industry especially with the Miami-based band Nu Look. After he released his solo album in 2007 titled *Leave Me Alone*, he announced his resignation from Nu Look, citing lack of respect and low payment.

Laporte, Grégory * - Keyboard
Played with Magnum band

Laporte, Pierre - Keyboard
Pierre is the leader of Tap La Band.

Laraj - Band

Laraque, Jean Alix (Jan Jan) - Drums
Jean Jean was also a drummer of the Mini Jazz era who developed his own style while playing with Les Blousons Noirs. He also played with Les Corvingtons in Haiti before moving to New York where he proved himself once again in the band Ibo Combo. Back to Haiti in the 1980 he joined the band Caribbean Sextet. Unfortunately Jean Jean died at the tender age of 36 years old.

Laraque, Michel - Guitar
Michel started his career with his band Les Shelberts in the Mini Jazz era in Haiti. He became the regular guitarist of the glorious years of the band Ibo Combo in New York.

Laraque, Pascal - Keyboard

Laraque, Philippe (Toto) – Singer / Guitar
Toto Laraque moved to Canada where he continues to perform with his band Harmonic 5. Toto played in his younger years with bands like Ibo Combo, Gypsies and Pepsi Jazz. He had the best days of his career however with the band Caribbean Sextet. His songs *Chatte Fifi*, and *La Revanche de Joli Bois* although fill with words that have shocked many people, remained until today the songs that made Toto Laraque one of the popular artists in the history of the Haitian music. Toto Laraque is also an actor. He appeared in the

movies *La Peur D'aimer* and *Coup de Foudre* among others.

Larèce, Frantz - Bass

Larece, Frantz - Keyboard / Guitar
Best years with Partners.

Larèche, Saillens - Keyboard

Larivière, Arly - Keyboard / Singer
Born and raised in Cap Haitien, the son of the "Tropicana" composer Daniel Larivière, Arly started to get recognition as a member of the band Lakol d'Haiti based in Cap Haitien. During a tour in the U.S. the band was completely dismantled and most of the members·decided to try life in the U.S. Some stayed in New York while Arly and some others moved to Florida working as freelancers on other bands as needed.
Soon after, the band D-Zine was created and it is there that Arly started to get some recognition for his hard work and devotion, and eventually became the leader of the band. After an intense argument among the members, the band was split in two different groups. While some members moved on with the name D-Zine, others created the band Nu Look which Arly later joined and once again became the band leader after a few shows.
Arly Larivière is known for super hits like: *Avenue de la Passion, Souvenirs, Why Do You Say You Love Me* and *Loving You.*
Unable to manage his fame and popularity with the band Nu Look the once hard working Arly has after a few years became an undisciplined individual. He was known to be chronically late for his shows. After several complaints from the fans and the media, he made the commitment to be on time for work especially after his tardiness has caused the brawl at the Djounbala nightclub in Pétion-Ville Haiti by impatient people that got tired of waiting for him and his lead singer Gazman to arrive. Nevertheless no one can contest that Arly Larivière is one talented musician and one of the best composers in the Konpa community.

Larivière, Daniel * - Keyboard / Conga
Played with Tropicana for many years, he was mostly known for his albums of the compilation of boleros made with the band Tropicana.

Larieux Farah -Administrator
Manager of the band Zenglen

Laroche, Jhonny – Drums

Played with Septentrional du Cap

Larose, Fito Jr - Singer

Larose, Joseph Dieudonné - Singer

Dieudonné Larose is known in the musical world simply as "Larose". He became popular when he shook the Port-au-Prince Carnival parade route with the band Shoogar Combo after the departure of Ti Kit and Musset Darcy. Shoogar introduced its new star to the general public with a wonderful performance in the carnival song *Pigeon*. In 1985 the band D.P. Express called on Larose to replace the singers who had left the band to reside in the U.S. Larose wasted no time to take the lead on D.P. Express front line and hit the Haitian music chart of the late 1980s with songs like *Grann Nanna, Négrié*, among others. By the early 1990s Larose moved to Montreal Canada where he found the band Méridional de Montreal struggling without a competent lead vocalist. Larose agreed to work with the band, but also said that he will make some changes and do things the way he feels was the best. The band that was incognito suddenly turned out to be one of the top Haitian bands of the 90s with some hit songs like *Mandela, Jolie Minou, Mission, and Accident* among others. Larose eventually left his partners of Missile 727 and moved on with the creation of his own band "Larose et son Super Sonic 747". The 747 didn't have the success of the 727 despite the releases of a couple of good albums by the super sonic like: *Guantanamo* and *Vivre En Enfer*, Larose was unable to find work and to manage his musicians. He eventually went back to work with the musicians of Missile 727 and during that decade the public was kind of confuse with the releases of several albums with the name Larose either with a 727 or a 747. Finally the public seems not to care which number or name of device or weapon that followed his name, they were just happy to have another album of Larose. Larose finally let go and moved on by having his next albums like: *Ou va L'humanité, Respect, Larose Chante Pour Les Coeurs Brisé*s as a solo artist under the name "Larose."

Larose, Jean - Singer
Jean played with the band Les Diables du Rythme de St Marc.

Larose, Louis - Keyboard

At an early age Louis Larose was already a superstar in his native town of St. Marc as a member of the band Dragon in the 1950s. Before long he created with some friends the band Les Diables du Rhythm de St. Marc, one of the most popular band ever out of St. Marc.
When he moved to New York, he joined the band Tropical Combo de Ti Jacques in the 1970s and later as an innovator he introduced the band Gran Pan Pan in Brooklyn in the 1990s

Las Fargas, Frederick - Keyboard
Frederick is a non-Haitian musician who played with Tabou Combo in the 1990s.

Last Stop - Band
That band was created in New York in the 1970s.

Lataillade, Alfred - Keyboard
Alfred spent most of his musical career with the band K-Dans.
He is a very talented and respected keyboardist in the Konpa society. He is the author of many K-Dans hit songs to include but not limited to: *An Tout Franchise Revokasyon, Kazwel, Coraline, Internet,* and *Bagay Yo Changé.*

Latino - Band
Another band of the Mini Jazz era based in New York.

Latino d'Haiti - Band
This Mini Jazz came out in 1967 in the Place St Anne neighborhood with the Jean Robert Damas on saxophone and Bertholini Jean François on guitar as well as the gonguist Jean Michel Ulcena. A few years later all three of them joined the band Bossa Combo.

Latortue, Ernst - Saxophonist

Latorture, Eddy - Keyboard

Latouche, Joseph Surppris - Guitar
Joseph played with the band Do Ré Mi Jazz before joining the band Les Ambassadeurs in the Mini Jazz era.

Latus, Evens - Drums

Laurenceau (Les Frères Laurenceau) - Band

Laurenceau, Guy - Bass
Guy played with the band Les Frères Laurenceau.

Laurenceau, Lyonel - Saxophone
Lyonel played with the band Les Frères Laurenceau.

Laurenceau, Serge - Saxophonist
Serge played with the band Les Frères Laurenceau.

Laurent, Bob - Singer
Bob is one of the singers of the New York-based band Gran Pan Pan.

Laurent, Raymond – Radio Personality
Raymond had for the many years entertained the Haitian community of Montreal with the best songs and information about Konpa music.

Laurent, Roger (Marechal Tito) - Congas
Marechal became a star musician when he played with the bands Super 9 and Scorpio in Haiti. In New York in the early 1980s he once again showed his ability to entertain in the early days of the System Band. Marechal left New York and moved to Montreal, Canada. He became a freelance musician taking part in different projects for many artists in Canada and the U.S.

Laurole, Etienne - Keyboard

Laurore, Edzer (Bazz) - Gong /Singer /Producer
Edzer worked as a freelance musician for several bands like Lakol, Eric Virgal, Tania St Val, Djet-X, Phantoms. In 2002 he released Edzer Bazz with several guest artists Armstrong Jeune, Shedly Abraham, Kenny Desmangle, Jocel Almeus, and Ronald Smith among other. In the spring of 2008, he released his second album titled *Divorce*.

Laurore, Henry - Gong /Percussion

Lauvanis, Jean Pierre Placide - Singer
Jean Pierre played with the bands Les Jokers and Super Soline in the Mini Jazz era.

Lavaud, Joseph (Joe Atomic) - Singer
Joe was a well-known musician of the 50s and 60s. He was born in the Dominican Republique of a Haitian father. He did most of his musical career in Haiti and Martinique.

Lavaud, Wilfrid - Guitar

Lavelanet, Lesly - Drums
Lesly played with the New York based band Djet -X in the 1970s.

Lavelanet, Lesly (Kòkò) - Bass
One of the most respected bassist in Konpa world, Kòkò did countless shows and many albums with the popular bands "Skah Shah" for more than three decades from the 70s to now.

Lavelanet, Philippe - Producer/Promoter
Philippe is the owner of the record company Antilles Mizik based in Queens New York.

Laventure, Frantz - Congas
Frantz played with Skah Shah in the 1970s

Lavil, Philippe - Singer

Lavoile, Frantz (Frantzy) - Bass

Le Corps, Robert (Bob lekò) * - Promoter
In the 1980s Bob Lekò was a well-known promoter in Miami. His name was heard by many people from the shout outs that he received from Isnard Doubi, the singer of System. Bob Lekò was killed in Haiti in 2007.

Leal, Eddy - Trumpet

Léandre, Ernst (Papou) * - Singer /Guitar
Papou was a star guitarist playing with the popular band Septentrional and at the same time a well-known troubadour singer and composer in his band Les Charmeurs du Cap. He left us with his remarkable hit "Bénita".

Léandre, Fritz (Fito Léandre) * - Guitar
Fito Léandre may have been known to many as the sprinter and the very fast right wing soccer player of Racing Club Haitien, a team that dominated the sport in general in Haiti. Fritz who was one of the National Football Team players moved to New York after the world cup of 1974. He played with the band Tropical Combo de Ti Jacques until his death at a young age in New York

Léandre, Napoléon – Guitar
Napoléon was the father and mentor of the late star guitarist of Septentrional Ernst (Papou) Léandre.

Lebon, Fritz - Singer
Fritz played in Haiti with the band Les Shleu Shleu in the Mini Jazz era.

Lebon, Serge - Trumpet

Lefranc, Georges - Guitar

Legagneur, Adrien - Bass /Tuba
Adrien, who started as a Konpa Bass player and has also played with Emeline Michel, has upon completing high school toured the world with a punk rock band and later in his career played with many American superstars including Billy Ocean and Harry Belafonte.

Legagneur, Carrie (Youyou) - Bass
One of the best bassists in the Konpa business, Youyou played with many bands as a substitute. He used to play in the U.S. and Canada for Sweet Micky until Welton Derosier was able to travel outside of Haiti. In Connecticut he came out with his own band Zoum in the 1990s, but soon after the band came out Youyou became a regular of the New York based band Zin. In Aug. 2007, he introduced the band Connecticut All Stars (C.A.S) in a well organized show in Connecticut; however he continued to perform with Zin on a regular basis.

Legagneur, Gary - Bass
Gary is the brother of Youyou.

Legagneur, Guery - Accordion
Guery played with Tabou Combo in the late 1960s and early 70s.

Legagneur, Junot - Guitar
Junot played with the band Les Fantaisistes de Jérémi in the Mini Jazz era.

Legagneur, Kenny - Keyboard
Kenny played with System Band for a short while in his career. Kenny continue his musical career by performing with non-Haitian bands

Legend - Band
Legend is a very good band with talented musicians that did not however get much recognition. Legend has changed the way some Haitian bands produced

carnival music when they came out with the carnival *Pren menw*. This style is now being adopted by many bands like Mizik Mizik and Konpa Kréyol, but few people really know that the style was created by the group Legend in 2001.

Legendaires (Les Legendaires de Delmas) - Band
This band came out in the Delmas neighborhood on Dec. 20, 1967
Their star saxophonist Pierrot Romain later joined the band Astros in New York in the 70s, and went back to Haiti to play with Arsène Appolon in the band Skah Shah d'Haiti in the early 1980s.

Leger, Fabiola Dupoux - Band Manager
Fabiola Dupoux Léger is the manager of the band Krezi. Prior to the band Krezi, she managed the band Konpa Kreyol.

Léger, Francy - Guitar
Francy played with the band Washington Express in the 1980s.

Léger, Nancy - Singer

Legitime, Patrick - Drums

Legros, Alexandre *- Percussion*

Legros, Archibald - Guitar

Legros, Rodolphe * (Dòdòf) - Singer /Guitar
Dòdòf Legros was one of the artists that left his trademark in the Haitian music business. His Troubadour style and hit songs like *Marabou De Mon Coeur* and *Manman Nanotte* to name only those are being played until today by several musicians. Dòdòf Legros was one of the first Haitian artists who were in demand outside of Haiti. He had the chance to play in several islands including Cuba as well as the U.S. and Canada. One day while performing, Dòdòf fell on stage in front of a live audience. He was transported to the hospital and later was hospitalized at a Brooklyn hospital where he died at the age of 51. Dòdòf Legros is the uncle of the famous brothers Tico and Dadou Pasket.

Legros, Frantz Henry - Drums

Legros, Fritz - Guitar
Fritz played with his cousins Dadou and Tico Pasket in their band Magnum

Band in the 1970s.

Legros, Jean - Guitar

Legros, Richard – Singer

Lejeune, Jean - Gong / Percussion

Lejeune, Jean - Congas / Percussion

Lelain, Ernst - Guitar

Lemans, Hans - Singer

Lemonier, William - Sound Engineer

Lemorin, Michel - Guitar

Leneus, Adler - Singer
Adler played with Gamma Express.

Léon, Edouard - Guitar
Edward played with Skah Shah in the 1980s.

Léonard, Roland - Singer

Lerebours, Pierre - Drums
Pierre played in different musicians' projects including Mini All Stars of the producer Fred Paul. Pierre also gave his services for some time to Skah Shah in the mid 1990s under the leadership of Jean Elie Telfort (Cubano).

Leroy, Eddy *-Trumpet
Eddy played with Septentrional du Cap.

Leroy, Harry - Saxophone / Trumpet
Harry is a well-known studio owner and sound engineer in New York for many decades.

Leroy, Henriot - Singer
Henriot played with the band Les Ambassadeurs in the Mini Jazz era. Henriot marked his passage in the Haitian music by singing the super hit "*Bobine*" as well as several boleros.

Leroy, Jean Pierre Petit * - Singer
Leroy played with Scorpio in the 1980s, filling the gap left by the very popular Gracia Jean Phillipe (Ti Kit) with a voice quite similar. Unfortunately just like Ti Kit, Leroy lost his life at an early age.

Les As - Band
This band came out in the early 1980s in Petion-Ville.

Les As De La K-Dans-Band

Lestage, Jean Robert - Sax

Lespinas, Joe - Drums
Joe played the drums for the band Les Beatniks de Queens in the Mini Jazz era.

Lespinas, Smith - Guitar/Keyboard
Smith played the guitar for the band Les Beatniks de Queens in the Mini Jazz era. He later worked as a keyboardist when the guitarist Ronald Smith joined the band.

Letemps, Erna - Singer
Erna is the daughter of the singer Ernst Letemps who played with Jazz Des Jeunes and the band Les Astros in the late 1970s.

Letemps, Ernst - Singer
Ernst played with Jazz des Jeunes and Les Shleu Shleu. In the mid-70s he joined Yves Arsène Appolon and Antoine Rossini Jean Baptiste (Ti Manno) in the creation of the band A.A. Express which later became Les Astros. While many people tend to think the hit song *Bingo* was sung by Ti Manno on lead, it is actually Ernst Letemps who did the lead vocal on the Astros album. Ti Manno added *Bingo* in the D.P. Express medley *Ensem Ensem* in the early 1980s on the album titled *David*.

Lévêque, Jacky - Keyboard

Levy, Max - Congas
Max is one of the founders of the band Bossa Combo.

Lévy, Nikol - Keyboard
Nikol is a great music arranger and he is also a mentor to many musicians.

Lévy, Paul - Singer
Paul played with the band Les Vikings in the Mini Jazz era. During his shows and recording he used to say "Banm Boule" a slogan he created to remind people that he was not only a singer but also a well-known football (soccer) goalie playing for Violette Athletic Club.

Lhérisson, Yves - Congas
Yves played with Djet-X in the 1970s.

Libérus, Dieuseul - Congas

Lilavois, Hammerton (Tony) - Singer
Tony played with the band Les Ambassadeurs in the Mini Jazz era. He really excelled in the song *"Obsession"*.

Limage, Maggie - Singer
Maggie is one of the star singers of the all female Konpa band Riské.

Lindor, Luigy - Singer
At a very young age Luigy Lindor charmed the Konpa community when he started to perform with the band Papash. He became the star singer of the band Zig Zag which released the music video *Roche Nan Soley* in the 1980 which helped many to recognize the talent of the young Luigy. Luigy moved to the U.S. where he continued to sing and produce music. In 2007 he became the member of the band Kagé based in Florida.

Lindor, Rodney - Singer

Lionceaux (Les Lionceaux Des Cayes) - Band
This band which was created in 1971 but really became popular when they moved to Port- Au Prince and the population got to discover their talented singer Léon Dimanche. With songs like *Nostalgie, Vas-T-En, Nelly,* and *Agoyé* among others the band captured the attention of not only people in Haiti and the Diaspora but the French Caribbean Island as well.

Logik - Band
New name of the band Compas Manba under the leadership of Yves Léon Paul (Ti Guy) former singer of Ensemble Select de Coupé Cloué.

Lominy, Hector -Trumpet

Lopez, Marcos - Singer - Trumpet

Born in Puerto Rico, Marcos played with the band Mini All Stars under the direction of the producer Fred Paul in the 1980s. He excelled in the song *"Anastasie"* and made a name for himself as the man singing the Konpa with a Spanish accent. He participated in other Konpa projects notably with Skah Shah.

Lopez, Mia - Journalist

A native Floridian, Ms. Lopez, also known as Mia Lopez-Kebreau as her married name, was brought up in a diverse community where her roots were spread far and wide. The product of a Cuban father and a Haitian mother, she was always proud to be a tad different from those in her environment, as if because she was bi-racial and multi-ethnic she had an added spice that was unique.

After pursuing a Degree in Broadcast Journalism in 1998, her and her cousins realized how rare it was to see a Haitian geared community site on the now ever growing World Wide Web, thus together they decided to launch a simple website that catered to Haitians abroad and of course the Diaspora called www.Sakapfet.com. Focusing on Live Broadcasts, Updated News direct from Haiti and Photo's from the countryside and the ever popular Haitian Bals, Sakapfet.com has continued to thrive.

It was through her work with Sakapfet.com that Ms. Lopez found her niche for Public Relations and began lending her talents to the "community", primarily with the Haitian Compas Festival as a Media Coordinator in 2000. This became the motivating force that compelled her to establish M.I.A. Media, Inc., one of the first official Public Relation Firms in the Haitian Music Industry.

Working with some of the top Haitian artists, including T-Vice, CaRiMi, Krézi Mizik, Nickenson Prud'Homme, as well as some of the major events in the community such as the Rasin Festival and the Haitian Independence Festival, Ms. Lopez continues to excel with all her clients be it non-profit organizations or the best producers in the industry.

When asked why she focuses more on her Haitian roots than her Cuban traditions she says "I was raised in Miami, and dominated by the Cuban culture when I stepped out of my home, by the music on the radio, the language on the streets. I want to give all that is Haitian the same voice in Miami and everywhere, the same way my mother and grandmother did in our home. But do not be misled, I love both cultures, when asked where I am from, I say "100% CubAitian."

Lopez, Michel - Drums
Michel played with the band Les Mordus in the Mini Jazz era.

Lorquet, Joseph (Jojo) - Producer
Jojo is the presenter of the Konpa community gossip show Exit; he is also the manager of the all female Konpa band Manmzel based in New York. He was also the manager of the bands Exit and Summer in New York in the 1990s. During the 1990s Jojo was also the representative and booking agent of Sweet Micky. He also produced a few albums for different artist including Sweet Micky and did perform as a singer and a songwriter at times in some of his productions.

Louis, Carmel - Piano
Carmel played on Les Frères Dejean's album *"Léon sou Broadway"*.

Louis, Dougone - Singer
Dougone played with Meridional des Cayes.

Louis, Eddy - Gong
Eddy played with Les Gypsies and he was also part of the squad led by Robert Martino that turned into Scorpio in the mid-70s.

Louis, Ernest (Ti Nès) - Drums
Ti Nès played for most of his career with Ensemble Select de Coupé Cloué.

Louis, Fresnel (Nènè) - Singer
Nènè played with the band Shupa Shupa in the Mini Jazz era.

Louis, Gregory - Drums
"Tabou est un groupe qui demande beaucoup d'energie sur scene et j'aime ca. Pour moi tabou combo est le groupe de Konpa par excellence," said Greg Louis, the young drummer who joined Tabou Combo in July 2004. Greg was born in Paris, on Feb. 2, 1980. He moved to Guadeloupe when he was 9 where he continued to learn the drums. Greg is a self-taught drummer. He started playing at the age of 2, bought his first drum set when he was 11, and became a professional at 19. "Music for me is a passion... it's my life", said Greg. "I always wanted to make music my career." And, what a career it has been... On his musical journey he has met and played with Jacques D'Arbaud, Tania St Val, Jean Phillipe Marthély, Jocelyne Berouard, Willy Salzedo, Harry Diboula, New York All Stars, Dozz, Jocelyne Labylle, and many others. Greg said he is opened to all styles, and plays every form of music he can. "Je suis avant tout un musicien du coeur; j'aime faire groover la musique et faire vibrer le publique qui m'ecoute; le toucher," said Greg. His expertise includes Funk, Salsa, Reggae, Zouk, Konpa, Jazz, Soca, Hip-Hop, and others. The musicians that have influenced him the most are Dave Weckl, Dennis Chambers, Hormar

hakim, Jean Phillipe Fanfan, and of course his father, the piano player Roland Louis with whom he had played in various cabarets throughout the Antilles when he was a young boy. Greg is now looking forward to make his contribution to the continuing success of Tabou Combo.
Bio from: www.taboucombo.com

Louis, James – Gong

Louis, Jean Claude - Saxophone
Jean Claude played with band La Ruche de Léogane

Louis, Jean Eddy - Singer
Eddy played with the band Volo Volo de Boston.

Louis, Jean Robert - Bass
Jean Robert played with Scorpio.

Louis, Joseph Eddy - Guitar
Eddy played with the band Combite Créole de Rodrigue Milien filling the gap left by Marcelus Victor.

Louis, Marc Antoine - Drums
Marc Antoine played with the band Les Ambassadeurs in the Mini Jazz era.

Louis, Marie Carmel - Singer

Louis, Patrick - Singer

Louis, Pierre - Trumpet
Pierre played with the Léogane based bands Norma and La Ruche respectively.

Louis Records
Haitian owned record company

Louis, Samuel - Keyboard

Louis, Shiller - Guitar

Louis, Sony (Ti Boeuf) - Drums
Star drummer of the band Les Difficiles de Pétion Ville in the Mini Jazz era. Now living in Florida, Ti Boeuf is known in the Haitian music community as a

sound engineer. He also participated in the "Flash Back" projects with his younger brothers Eddy and Patrick Louis playing at least once a year in Haiti. Flashback plays the music of Les Gypsies and Les Difficiles reminiscing of the good old Mini Jazz days.

Louis, Yvon - Trumpet /Trombone
Yvon played with Bossa Combo.

Louissant, Alex -Trumpet
Alex played with the band Les Formidables de St Marc.

Louissant, Carlo - Singer
Carlo played with the band Les Morphées Noirs in the Mini Jazz era. Carlo is the older brother of the late Yvon Louissaint, former singer of Les Frères Déjean.

Louissant, Harry - Drums

Louissaint, Riverson (Sonson) -Drums
Sonson is a member of the band T. Vice.

Louissant, Ronald - Saxophone
Ronald played with Jazz des Jeunes on sax tenor.

Louissant, Yvon * - Guitar /Singer

Yvon started in the early 60s as a Troubadour playing here and there at different places to make some money. As the Mini Jazz movement was taking off he first joined the band "Morphées Noires" and later he moved to a more popular band of the same neighborhood of Place Jérémi/Bas Peu De Chose, called Shupa Shupa, as a guitarist.
After the dissolution of Shupa Shupa, Yvon found himself once again playing solo at private parties and sometimes serenading for very little money. However, his break came when one day the popular singer Guy Durosier was playing at a private party, and while Guy was singing inside Yvon stood outside with his guitar and gave a replica to Guy Durosier's songs to the amusement of the people who couldn't enter the private party. When the guitarist Fritz Léandre, (the late Fito Léandre), who used to play soccer for Racing Club Haitien, found out

what was going on outside he called on Yvon to join him at the party. This is how Yvon Louissaint started a relationship with Guy Durosier who wasted no time to make him his sidekick in his band "Guy Durosier et Son Système". At the nightclub Cabane Choucoune, Guy introduced the street performer Yvon Louissaint to the elite crowd as the "New Star of Haitian Music".

When Guy Durosier left the country, the rising star Yvon Louissaint joined the band Les Frères Déjean de Pétion Ville; this is actually the band that will turn Yvon into a superstar. Frères Déjean recorded Durosier's song *Léogane* with the "nasal voice" of Yvon Louissaint on lead, and the song was being played on radio station all over the country to the delight of the population. In the years that followed many people were going to Frères Déjean to watch Yvon perform live. Yvon also had the ability to sing easily in Spanish which was appreciated by many fans.

In the mid to late 70s Yvon excelled on another folk song called *Latibonite*, which Frères Déjean played in a Latin music fashion. During that period Les Frères Déjean had moved to New York, where they recorded their first album in the Diaspora. In that album Yvon once again proved that he was one of the best at that era as he left his mark in the song *"Bouki ak Malice"*.

Yvon Louissaint was a star singer, but he was also an artist who was hard to manage. Yvon saw the world according to Yvon, and he was always ready to plead his case and to prove others wrong even when he was at fault. Many would refer to him as "moun fou" or crazy guy, and things degenerated as Yvon was using most of his money on drugs and booze. The musicians couldn't keep up with his lifestyle and on top of it he refused to get help, Yvon was eventually let go by Les Frères Déjean, who replaced him with Harold Joseph, another singer who like Yvon could sing easily in Spanish and perform the Latin styles Salsa and Mambo. In the meantime Yvon was heading to even more self-destruction. One day he passed out in the streets of New York on a snowy day. In that incident he lost some of his fingers to frostbite. The snow had done some damage beyond repair and the doctors had to amputate many fingers on both hands of the guitarist.

Yvon was often seen in Florida and New York in very bad shape, and he was often being avoided by his fellow musicians. Although many would greet him, some were sad to see him, but still happy to lend a helping hand sometimes. However his appearance and argumentative attitude were not welcomed by many. At one time it looked like he was coming out of his mess, as he recorded a couple of solo albums which made it a total of three solo albums since he had done one previously in 1978 called *Cé Sa*.

In one of his albums he talked about the accident and also how he was mistreated by many people. Yvon was also getting some live shows, but not enough for him to bounce back to being a star as the market had already shifted to the more in demand digital bands and above all some new stars.

The story of Yvon Louissaint is, in itself, another chapter of the life of a popular artist that went the wrong way due to the lack of support in the Haitian music industry for ill musicians. In the early 1990s, Yvon Louissaint was no longer the worry of anyone in the business. The fans had moved on following other artists and producers and promoters were no longer interested in people who can sing in Spanish and the Twoubadou style was on pause at the time.

Yvon Louissaint died in New York in 1993 leaving behind him a whole world of memories to many music lovers. His discography includes the albums: *Yvon Louissaint et Les Antillais, CéSa,* and *Yvon Louissaint Chanteur des Frères Déjean,* but his best years and recording remains those that he did with Les Frères Déjean.

Loups Noirs - (Les Loups Noirs) - Band

No other band in the 1970s era had the popularity of Les Loups Noirs (The Black Wolves) in the French Caribbean Islands. At one time the band was practically living in the small Antilles.

Created on Dec. 4th 1968, they were also known for their beautiful boleros as music lovers of the 60s and 70s will for the rest of their lives remember great hits like *Doudoune, Pourquois Betty,* and *Manman* etc... Besides the boleros Loup Noirs also left us with some good Konpa songs like *Anana, Belle Martiniquaise, La Sirene* and many more. In the late 70s Les Loups Noirs added a trumpet and a Trombone to their lineup. The band finally collapsed in New York in the late 80s with very few of the originals members.

Lov - Band

This band came out of the New York/N.J area in the 1990s with Emmanuel Obas and Vardy Pharel on lead vocal with some other ex-members of the band Mizik Mizik.

Lovelace, Arthur - Singer

Arthur's voice was used as one of the machines that help moved the Compas Direct movement of Nemours Jean Baptiste. Many Haitians grew up listening to the voice of Arthur Lovelace in memorable songs of the 60s like *Les Trois Dangers, Boule Malachong,* and *Immortel Compas,* among others.

Lovinsky, Jean André - Keyboard
Played with Safari Combo, he was part of the squad that changed the band to Super 9 with the star singers Assade Francoeur and Harold Joseph.

Lozamar, Ed - Radio Personality

Lubin, Emmanuel - Guitar /Keyboard
Emmanuel played with the band Les Loups Noirs.

Lubin, Gesner - Singer

Lubin, Ronald - Guitar
Ronald replaced Alex Tropnas in Sweet Micky's band. He later joined the Miami based band Hangout.

Lubin, Jean Sammuel (Kessy) - Singer /Drummer
The young Samuel, who grew up in the Fontamara neighborhood, showed an interest in music as an adolescent. However after trying with some unknown bands, he became the drummer of the popular band Scorpio. The name Kessy was given to Samuel for his aptitude to play the drum as many Haitians call the instrument "Caisse" or in the Créole language "Kès".
In April 1986, Kessy changed gear leaving the Konpa music to move on with the Rasin music genre by creating the band "Koudjay". The band became known to the public in the early 1990s, when they did the song *Manman Poule La*, a song that basically targeted then President Ertha Pascal Trouillot, the first female president of Haiti. At that same time Kessy introduced in the band's video his two sisters the singers/dancers Mirlande and Nerlande Marcelin the latter was only 12 years old. That formula will be imitated by many Rasin band in the years that followed as Mirlande and Nerlande would become exemplary performers and role models to many female artists of the Rasin music movement.
In the years that followed Kessy continued to show his interest and loyalty to the Lavalasse Movement and President Aristide which has caused him many problems with the Haitian Army. Kessy, who was persecuted while the president was in exile in the early 1990s, had to hide until the return of his leader to power in 1994. Kessy re-emerged with some songs that rocked the nation like *Zo Popé and Coco Rat*. By 1996 René Préval became president and Kessy took upon him in songs like *Gran Majè, Bwa Maré, Rat Do Kalé* to denounce government employees that according to him were taken advantages of their power by oppressing others and stealing. After president Aristide returned to power Kessy and his sister Mirlande were employed at the National Palace, while he continued to play music and coming out with

more hit songs. When President Aristide was exiled the second time in 2004, Kessy and his sisters left Haiti and moved the band to Florida.

One of his musicians and closest friend a conga player name Luksèrne who also played for the Rara band "Raram" stayed in Haiti and was seriously persecuted and at some times had to hide in the mountains to survive.

In 2006 Kessy, his sisters and the members of the band filed for political asylum in the U.S. Kessy continue to play music. He still takes part in many festivities in the Diaspora, especially at the Haitian participation at the different Caribbean Carnival notably in New York, Florida, Boston and Washington D.C.

Kessy who on many occasions was the champion of the carnival in Haiti put on a memorable show on the streets of Washington, D.C. at the 2002 Caribbean Carnival. In 2005 his band Koudjay was the first Rasin band ever to take part in the Labor Day Caribbean Parade in Brooklyn, where he showed once again that he is one of the best Haitian performers by putting on good shows and by having one of the bands with the most followers which is an indication of his popularity. In 2006, Koudjay gave back to back wonderful performances first at the Caribbean parades in Boston Massachusetts and a week later at the Labor Day parade in Brooklyn N.Y. On both occasions the band had more followers than some of the popular bands on the parade route, again showing to music lovers all over the world that Samba Kessy and his band Koudjay is still one the best choices of most Haitians.

Luc, Necker - Guitar

Lucien, Féquière - Singer
Féquière played with Volo Volo de Boston.

Lucien, Ismael (Tipa) - Guitar
Musician of the band Take Off, Tipa played earlier for the band Sakad.

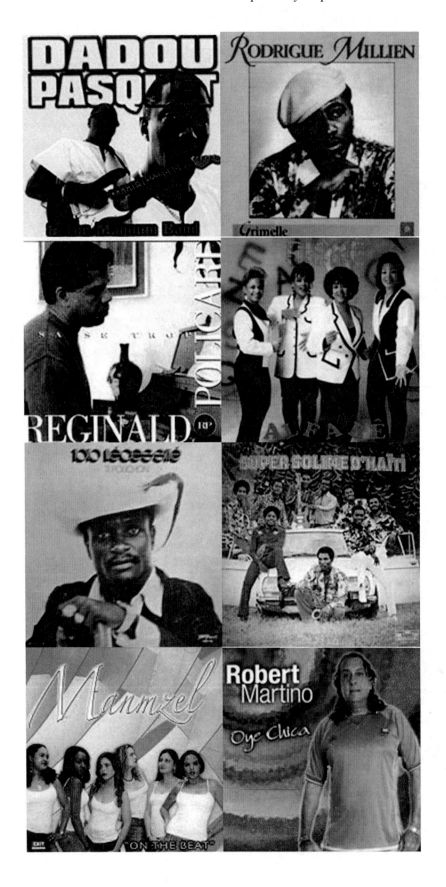

Michel Martelly   Isnard Doubi - Alan Cavé

Carmelo Frederique   Almando Keslin

Roger M. Eugene   Mario de Volcy

Lukson, Estiverne - Keyboard

Lynch, Eric - Singer

Lynch, Michel Melton – Bass

M

M.G Force – Band

M.I.A. Media Inc
Public Relation Firm in the Haitian Music Industry created by the journalist Mia Lopez

Mac-D see: Talon, Mackenzie

Macaya Record
One of the top Haitian record labels of the 1970s

Macho Band - Band
This band came out of New York in the late 1980s.

Maggy Records
Records Productions Company.

Magic Compas Band – Band
Konpa band based in Michigan

Magic Connection - Band
Based in Haiti in the 1980s this band did not last long, but their album released by mini record in 1984 was another good work that did not get enough exposures.

Magloire, Evelyne - Singer
Evelyne is the female singer of the band Septentrional since the 1990s.

Magnum Band - Band

(Dadou-Laurent and Tico)

One of the goals of the creator of Magnum Band was to change the course of the Haitian music as Magnum Band never stops to innovate in term of creativity and finding new sounds and beat throughout their existence.

The band came out on June 24th 1976, a date that has a special mystical meaning for the creator of the band, the guitarist André (Dadou) Pasket. The date is the day of St. John, a day celebrated in Haiti with great ceremonies in every Masonic Temple by the Free Masons.

When Magnum first came out, they didn't intend to play Konpa music. Dadou who freshly came of Tabou Combo encouraged his older brother Claude Pasket (Tico) who was still working with Les Frères Déjean to join him in his new project. When the band first came out they were playing Haitian folk music like the music of their popular late uncle Dòdòf Legros in a modern jazz fashion. Unfortunately the public that was used to following their idols both in Tabou and in Déjean was not ready for the sudden changes. They expected that a band with Dadou and Tico was going to rock the house and set the roof on fire with mad Konpa. No need to say that many people were very disappointed at the direction that the band was heading, and eventually didn't follow the brothers in their adventurous route. For that matter the brothers head for California in quest of another audience. There again they face many obstacles, but stayed loyal in their commitment of not working for any other bands but their own. After the North East and the West, the band moved to the South and found their new home in Miami. It is at that juncture that many people started hearing of the band as they regrouped with some musicians with a good past in the Haitian music world like the singer Eussed Fungcap and the bassist Nasser Chéry. They went to work and released their first album titled *"Experience"* with some mega hits that marked the late 70s like *Magnum Dehors, Trahison, La foi,* and of course *Experience.* In the song *Experience,* the Chinese Haitian Euseud Fungcap showed to the world that he was still one of the best performers and that he had not lost a bit of the skills that he used to demonstrate so well with the band Les Ambassadeurs in the Mini Jazz era.

In the middle of the song he delivered a super jam using the word "Experience" *"Experience gran moun nan sé nan tèt li- Experience gran moun nan nan sèvo li etc…while the band answered: Pigaw bétizé - fok ou pa ransé".* The album was influenced by some of the flavors of the American beat of the 70s like the horn sound style of *Cool and the Gang, the Commodores, Earth Wind and Fire, and KC and the Sunshine Band*. The band had a couple of Americans in their lineup like the trombone player Russ Harden and the saxophonist Bob Curtis with the spicy Konpa beat of Tico on drums and Serge Cicéron on Gong while Dadou Nasser assisted with the Hispanic American Hernandez Gutierez provided a rhythm that sounded new to the ears of Konpa music lovers. Dadou has realized his dream of being different from all the other Konpa bands and up to now no band has managed to copycat the Magnum formula….None has even come close to it, thus giving Magnum Band the right to declare themselves "LA SEULE DIFFERENCE" a slogan they choose claiming to be the only difference in other words a very Unique Konpa band playing a style that only Magnum and the Pasket Brothers have the secret.

In the years that followed some of the top musicians have left the band including the singer Eussed Fungcap who had moved on with his own dream and has become one of the top Haitian painters and Haitian art distributors in the world. But Magnum never stop innovating and surprising the Haitian music society with one hit after another as they introduced the singer Yvon Mondésir who has in previous years played with Dadou in the band Tabou Combo.

Their second album, *Jehovah* was a tribute to the Almighty. On that album cover the band showed once again their mystical style as the album had on the top of it an eye inside of a pyramid among other symbols many people still have trouble comprehending. The album also had the songs *Congo Nan Vodou and l'Amour*.

The band lost some momentum in the years that followed, but continued to produce. Even in the most difficult conditions they released the album *Zouké* followed by *Adoration*. When the brothers realized that their music from the previous albums were still getting some serious airtime and that many young fans were talking about the music of Magnum in Haiti while the Haitian community of the Diaspora were not giving them much credit, they decided to relocate in Haiti, and it is there that they were going to become the real superstars that they had dreamed of all the time. They had their own band and the band was on top of the charts with Dadou as the sole singer of the band, and had above all many loyal followers. It is in that line of idea that the slogan *Paka Pala* was created in other word *"You got to be there"*. Magnum did a song call *Paka Pala* which was the title of their next album even when the song talk about a girl, many people however do know that the title was inspired by the famous slogan of the 1980s.

After they had done it all in Haiti, the mid to late 1980s saw an Haiti with terrible political instability, and many who had their permanent visa and/or U.S. citizenship were returning to the U.S. and the Pasket brothers found themselves back in New York City. There the public that didn't want them a decade earlier was more receptive as Magnum introduced their new lineup which included the French Caribbean singer Nestor Azérot and was getting some nice gigs. They released a very good album which showed again that they are still the most mystical Haitian band ever, as they came out with the song *Ashadei*. In that album Magnum gave life again to another Haitian folk song, *Trois Feuilles Trois Racines*.

Ironically, Magnum returned to Miami where they struggled, but still remained productive and also never stopped looking for work even outside of the Haitian community as they often traveled to the French Caribbean islands. One of the greatest additions to Magnum Band is the talented bassist Laurent Ciceron who had acquired his experience in his years with Les Loups Noirs and his band Les Deutz. Without wasting any time the band came out with the album *Difé* which also included the songs *Africa, Rève and Ansanm Ansanm*. During that period the music of Magnum would take them as far as Europe while they continued to compete with more new bands in the state of Florida. To mark its territory Magnum released an album with the title *"We Are The Best In Town"* and to show their popularity around the world the band made yet another statement in their next album titled *San Fwontiè* which basically means that in 1996 the band had No Frontier. Who would dare to say differently to Magnum Band, the only Haitian band that was chosen to perform at the Olympic Games in Atlanta. In that album Magnum also gave us the songs *Vérité* and yet something mystic in *Allah or Akbar* and the remake of a Tropicana song *Superstition* and a Konpa feeling of the Marvin Gaye's song, *Close The Door*. Just like history kept on repeating itself with the band moving from town to town and country to country, after Florida the band moved back to Haiti again.

Magnum and the Pasket brothers Dadou and Tico have over the years worked days and nights to bring to the music industry some of the best Konpa songs ever recorded and continue to be La seule difference as we have experienced it in their many albums. The discography of Magnum band also includes: *Islam, Tèt Ansanm, Adoration* (which include the mega hit *Libèté*), *Pure Gold, Revelation, Chèché Lavi, Cross Over, Pardon, Anthology 1-2 and 3* and some albums recorded during live concerts among others. In 2004 Magnum Band signed with the record label Hibiscus record as they released the album *Oulala* which include songs like *Magnum Band Phenomenal, Bel Ti Womans* and *Gasson Gwo Vant*, they also released the video *Magnum Band Phenomenal* which was shot in the French Antilles as Magnum continued their journey by performing in the French Caribbean and in Florida especially.

In 2006, the band went on their 30th Anniversary tour with a squad of respected and talented musicians that included the great Haitian trumpet master and former boss of Tico Pasket the legendary André Déjean and congas player Camille Armand who has played most of his career with Skah Shah. After more than 30 years Magnum Band have entertained millions of people and for three decades their songs have been played and are still being played by radio stations and DJs at many clubs and at countless private parties all over the world, and even now no bands Haitians or non-Haitians, have been able to duplicate the work of Magnum Band, the band that still remains after all these years: *"LA SEULE DIFFERENCE."*

Maignan, Camille - Saxophone
Camille was the band leader of Meridional des Cayes.

Malette, Yvon - Trumpet

Malval, Georges (Foufouille) - Gong
Foufouille played with the les Gypsies de Petion-Ville in the 1970s.

Mamane see: Absolu Louimane

Mamina see: Jacquet, Elizabeth

Manfoubens - Band
Band of the Mini Jazz era, which later became Les Shleu Shleu de Dada Jacaman.

Maniak - Band
This band was based in New York in the late 1980s, and early 1990s.

Manigat, Eval - Bass
Eval Manigat is one of the most respected Haitian musicians. This talented bassist is a very good music composer and arranger. At a very young age, in the town of St. Marc in the 1950s he played with the bands Dragon, Palace and Crystal until his services were requested by the Cap Haitien-based band Tropicana. Later he really became a star when in Port-au-Prince he joined Cadence Rampa, one of the most popular Haitian bands ever working under the leadership of Webert Sicot.
In the mid 70s Eval Manigat moved to Canada. Unlike many Haitian artists who simply call it quits once they left the country, Manigat continued to excel in his musical career by creating the band "Buzz" with some Haitian and Canadian musicians. As if he would never get tired of music Manigat moved on with the creation of the band "Tchaka", a band that won a "Juno", one of the most prestigious music award, in Canada.

Manigat, Evens - Guitar

Manigat, Guy - Drums /Gong /Percussion
Guy played with Septentrional du Cap.

Manigat, Imgart Garry – Singer

Manigat started his professional career when he joined Ti Manno's band, Gemini All Stars. His voice resembled the voice of Ti Manno so much that often Ti Manno would let him start the shows. However when it was time for Gemini to travel to the U.S., Ti Manno left Manigat in Haiti fearing that if he traveled with him the squad might end up staying in New York, since they would have a singer. Soon after Manigat came out on lead on the Gamma Express' album, the solo project of Pierrot Kersaint. The world soon discovered that he was going to be one of the top Haitian singers in the market as he excelled in the song "Confiance". After the success of the album, Pierrot wasted no time to showcasing the highly desired voice of Manigat on a couple more albums.

When the guitarist Gary Résil was putting together his band Exodus in New York, in the early 1980s, he managed to have Manigat on lead vocal. Manigat took part in several Mini All Stars shows and recording projects with his cousin Fred Paul the owner of the Mini Records label company.

In 1985 he was solicited by Maryland entrepreneur Bob Baltazar as the lead singer of the band G.P. Express. He recorded two albums with the D.C. based band G.P. Express. He lived in Rockville Md with his wife and kids until 1990, when he moved alone to Montreal, Canada where he came out with a couple of his own solo projects and created a new family as well. He felt that people took advantage of him in his early days, for that reason even though many have contacted him, he categorically refuses to take part in projects that are not his own. Moving from Canada the U.S. and the Caribbean, Garry is not playing live shows but is constantly trying to come out with the song that will once again bring him to the top of the Haitian music chart.

Manmzèl - Band
Just like Riské, this band is an all female band.
The band came out in 2004 and did not get the popularity of Riské. Some of the members are not Haitian.

Manno, Mathieu - Bass
Mathieu played in New York based band Tropical Sextet.

Marabou Café
Haitian owned club in Miramar Fl.

Marc Records
One of the top record production companies, Marc Records has produced records from the 1960s to the late 1990s. The owner and president of the company, Marc Duverger worked until his death for the advancement of Konpa music not only as a record producer but as a show promoter as well. Marc Records has given exposures to bands and artists that were ignored by most producers and eventually contributed to the success of many Konpa superstars.

Marcel, Raymond - Trumpet
Raymond played with the band Latino.

Marcelin, Claude - Guitar
Claude Marcelin is one of the top Haitian guitarists who have dominated the market for more that three decades. Ti Claude as he is known in the Konpa world started his career in the early 70s as an adolescent when he joined the band Les Difficiles de Pétion Ville which he later left to revive the band Gypsies after the original Gypsies had left Haiti for the U.S. In that band he collaborated with his partner and friend Denis Nozil (Ti polis) and they both became household name after the band under the guidance of their manager Pierrot Al Khal released the song Roi Baron.
At the creation of the band D.P. Express Claude Marcelin moved on to work with Eddy Wooley and Ti Polis. When Claude left D.P, he helped several artists and bands with their project. The fact that many Haitians didn't comprehend the concept of being a freelancer had made Ti Claude Marcelin the subject of many critics.
He played with some of the greatest bands in his career as needed and would move on with the next band that offered more money. Ti Claude has worked also with Magnum band, the Caribbean Sextet, Gamma Express, Top Vice and Djakout Mizik and many studio projects with several artists. In one of his solo project he wrote the song *Relax Ti Mal* which is one of his memorable hit songs. After Claude Marcelin left the band Caribbean Sextet, the band leader Réginald Policard was so upset that he wrote the song *Dr. Claude* to show that Ti Claude Marcelin was just going around selling his music services. If at that time the song got Claude Marcelin upset, we can say that today we have more than too many "Claude Marcelin" as Haitian artists now understand much

better the concept of collaboration and freelancer. Haitian artists and fans now can understand much better that the musician is a worker, a professional who doesn't have to stay in any particular band/job for a lifetime and that he/she is free to move around and advance in his/her career.

After Ti Claude Marcelin left Djakout Mizik, he moved to Canada where he is living with his family. In January 2008, he was baldly wounded as he escaped form a kinapping attempt in Haiti.

Marcelin, Emmanuel - Keyboard

Marcelin, Ernst * - Keyboard
Ernst Marcelin was also known as the man who saved Tabou Combo. In effect the popular Tabou Combo was losing their grip in the mid 1980s until Ernst Marcelin joined the band and brought with him some new sounds and a complete new feeling to the music of Tabou Combo with the solos and grooves that he provided on the keyboard with his magic fingers. The man who was always quiet was just starting to enjoy fame by traveling around the world with the most popular Haitian band was gunned down in Brooklyn in 1989. Someone put an end to the life of one of the most promising Haitian musicians that many believe was going to change the direction the music was heading. From what he had done, many of the keyboardists that came to the business after Ernst Marcelin did try to follow his style.

Marcelin, Lesly (Samba Zao) - Percussion /Congas /Gong

Marcellus, Jean Junior (Money G) - Singer
With his friend Ti Linèt, the singer Money G created the band Gabel in Miami Fl. However in April 2008 during an argument he was beaten by some of his fellow musicians. When his request that his aggressor be removed from the band was not met, he and the band leader his friend Ti Linèt decided to move on under the name 5 Etoiles as they released the single *Abu*.

Marcellus, Prosper - Saxophone

Marchant, Ronald - Drums

Mardis, Yves André - Singer
Star singer of the Mini Jazz era, Yves André Mardis' voice is one of those that left a mark on the 1960s and early 70s in Haiti singing super hit songs like *Ti Claudette, Ti Zoizo* and the slow song *Ou Seul*.

Maréchal Tito see: Laurent Roger

Marothière, Virginia (Nia) - Singer
Musician of the New York based band Zin, Nia didn't waste time to take over
the lead of the band next to Alan Cavé and at the same time filling the hole left
by the singers Maggy and Georgy. The band did some new songs in order to
put her on the spot light as she excelled in the live performances on *Hasta la
vista and Boubout*

Martelly, Michel (Sweet Micky) - Singer/Keyboard
Michel Martelly, better known as "Sweet Micky", was born in Port-au-Prince,
Haiti. He grew up in the Port-au-Prince suburb of Carrefour with his brother
and four sisters. Micky credits veteran Compas bands, Skah Shah, Frères
Dejean, Tabou Combo and Cesaria Evora, a singer from the Cape Verde
Islands with being influential on his music.
Micky first began performing as a one man band in 1988 in the casinos in
Haiti. He released his first hit "Ou La La" in 1988. Two years later Micky
expanded the band to include a bass player and a percussionist and by the
release of the album "*I Don't Care*" in 1994 Sweet Micky was a household name
in Haitian communities at home and abroad.
Over the past decade, Martelly has won the hearts of the Haitian people
through his musical talent and charismatic persona. His music blends Haitian
music with new interpretations of compas, roots, salsa, Caribbean Soca and
jazz-fusion. His persona and satirical lyrics ignite great controversy
throughout the Haitian diaspora. The only thing which is predictable about
Sweet Micky is that he is completely unpredictable. He has been known to
wear diapers, mini-skirts and other shocking outfits onstage.
When Wyclef Jean of the Fugees needed someone to spark the flames for his
Carnival album, it was Martelly whom he called upon to record the title song.
As Wyclef proclaims while the "Carnival" tempo rises tumultuously,
"Surprise; it's Sweet Micky, y'all!"
Sweet Micky is often referred to as the "Bad Boy" of Haitian music, but this
description is music more appropriate in its American slang definition where
"bad" means really, really good. In 1997, Michel Martelly showed the world
that his musical talent is a continuous means toward a very positive end by
donating his time to participate in "Knowledge is Power", an HIV educational
music video with a powerful message about preventing the spread of HIV.
Based in Haiti, Martelly tours incessantly performing throughout the U.S.,
Haiti, Canada, the Caribbean and Europe. His wife Sophia handles the
business affairs of the band. Together they have 4 children. In his spare time
Micky enjoys playing soccer.
Information from www.afiwi.com
His discography includes *I Don't Care, Tout Sé Martelly, An Ba Rad La ,Dènié*

Okazion, Men Kozé Ya, The Sweetest, 100.000 Volts, Woulé Woulé, Jojo Banm Nouvel Mickey, and *Aloufa* among others to include remixes and live recordings.

Marthély, Jean Philippe - Singer
One of the star singers of the Guadeloupe based band Kassav, Jean Philippe lived in Haiti for a while where he learned to master the Konpa rhythm.

Marthély, Serge - Singer
Serge was the singer of Raoul Guillaume's band.

Martial, David - Singer

Martineau, Patrick - Keyboard
One of the musicians that started the band Zenglen in Haiti, the album Atò N'Alez is release with his signature like if it was his own project.

Martinez, Raymond - Keyboard
Raymond played with Les Ambassadeurs as an accordionist.

Martino, Ramond - Congas
Ramond played with the band Latino. He is the older brother of Robert Martino.

Martino, Robert - Guitar / Singer
At an early age Bob Martino started his career with his neighborhood band Les Difficiles de Petion Ville in the 1960s under the leadership of the guitarist /singer Henry Celestin. However, after an animated dispute with Henry, Bob Martino left the band and moved on by creating his own band "Les Gypsies de Petion-Ville" with the assistance of Pierrot Al Khal.
Before long the band Gypsies became one of the top bands of the country as Robert Martino continued to innovate by creating one hit song after another. Before long the band had several albums on the market to include the first one released in 1972 with songs like *Haiti, Vrai Bonheur, Gypsies en Douce.* By the following year, 1973, Gypsies occupied the airwaves with songs like *Patience, Gagotte, Express Way, Prier and Reproche.* In 1974 the band continued to be the king of the airwaves with songs like *Courage, Cassa* and the slow song *Imcapable D'aimer.*
The band leader kept his band on top of the chart in 1975 with songs like: *Fièrté Vacances Azakidam Kélélé, Viré Rond* in the album titled *"Fièrté."* We must note also that some of the hits of Gypsies in the mid-70s include songs like *La Tulipe, Espoir* and *Dime* the band also did some great carnival songs and the hit songs *A Coté* and *Pa Colé* that always kept people on their feet every time the

band hit the first notes.

Robert Martino is known as one of the greatest Haitian music composers and a legend for the work that he did over in the period of four decades and counting. He has, over the years, resided in Haiti and in the U.S. but never stopped working for the advancement of the Konpa music. In the mid-70s, when he left his band Gypsies to try life in the U.S., the band was kept alive by his brother-in-law and manager Pierrot Al Khal with the help of Ti Polis and Claude Marcelin. When he returned to Haiti, the music was taking another direction as the influence of the French Caribbean bands was taking a toll on the Mini Jazz movement. There again, Bob Martino came to the rescue as he introduced in his band some new instruments like the trumpet and the trombone and a keyboard synthesizer with some serious musical arrangements. The band was introduced to the public under a new name, *Scorpio.*

By the year 1977 the band introduced their first album "Ensem Ensem" with songs like: *Ensem Ensem, Tacombé* and *Tandé.* In 1978, after the band shook up the streets of Port-au-Prince with the carnival song *Colé sou Yo,* the band quickly release their second album with songs like *Pélérinage* and *Bling Guin Ding* in that album the band played a reggae song *Roots Rock Reggae.*

By 1979 the music of Robert Martino and his band Scorpio was on top of the chart as the band continued to travel around the Caribbean and in the Haitian diaspora. In that year the band came out with two albums. The first was *"Min Yayade La"* with two catchy phrases *Min Yayade La* and *Pa Kité'l Alé* the latter was the official title of the song. In that album, released by Macaya Records, Martino did a remix of his Gypsies song *Tandé.* The second one was going to be the song of the summer of 1979 as in every party and on the air no DJ could afford not to play the song *"Map Mandé Courage"* which was released as a Big Single by Mini Records. The other side the Big Single had the song *Vin Pran Piyaye;* however it is the song Courage that was on the lips on every Konpa lovers including the fans of the rival band D.P. Express as the many chorus part of the song with the word "Attention" like: *Attention tout moune nap ralé mouchwa etc... Attention tout moune nap dansé'w Rara etc...* were not only entertaining but easy to sing along.

In 1980, the band rocked the street of Port-au-Prince once again with the carnival song *Pran Sanw.* Soon after, Martino introduced his next album titled "1980".

In 1981 with the voice of Gracia Jean Phillipe (Ti Kit) the band continued its journey with the memorable carnival song *Kaskèt sou Tête.* By the spring the band came out with one of the songs that would show that Scorpio had matured not only their new style but also in their delivery as everyone could see the professionalism of the band in the hit song *Christiane* in the album *"Gypsies Fever".* That album also had a remix of another Gypsies song called

Azakidam Kélélé.

By 1982 Robert Martino moved away from his own band to reside in the U.S. where he releasedthe album *"Opa Opa"* with Rotel Records while keeping the name "Scorpio de Robert Martino". However at the same time the musicians of Scorpio in Haiti under their new leadership released the album *"Vacances"* with the songs *Kèdèk Kèdèk, Aprann Viv* and *Vérité* under the label Chancy Records with their new name "Scorpio Fever". In the years that followed the Konpa world saw a series of bands with the name Scorpio without Robert Martino. Some of them are Scorpio Fever, Scorpio Universel, Scorpio d'Haiti, Scorpio La Crème.

By the end of the decade Robert Martino reappeared in force with the band Top Vice in Miami. There again he continued his musical career with a band playing a completely different format as the music of Top Vice is played mostly by a digitalized keyboard with most of the song already sequenced and ready to be played. The job of Robert Martino was simplified but still he delivered at each show the thing he did best which is playing the guitar.

With Top Vice he did the albums *"Men Nou"* in 1987 and many more followed to include: *Sinfoni Damou, Haiti Mon Pays, Miami Mon Ami,* and *Konpa Avèg La* among others that include some live recordings.

Robert Martino has contributed in the work of many artists and he has always been a great support to his children band the musical group T. Vice. On several occasions he helped them with their musical arrangements and also lent a helping hand during the carnival parades in Haiti and the Diaspora. Robert even managed to lend a helping hand to Sweet Micky the arch rival of his kids' band, even after Sweet Micky had on several occasions used the name of the legendary musician negatively in his dirty jokes. Robert Martino joined his friend Robert Charlot Raymondville in the formation of the band Nu Vice, a band that has all the musicians of Top Vice with the exception of Freddy, the lead singer.

After four decades of live performances and many studios and live recordings Robert Martino who have worked in the Konpa business from the Mini Jazz era of the 1960s to the Full Band years of the late 70s to the 80s and to the Digital reduced format of the 1990s and tirelessly continue to surprise the Konpa world with his guitar solos, his innovative music and the releases of new songs. In 2007 Robert Martino released the album *Oyé Chika*. He also during that time gave a super performance on the float of T. Vice at the 2007 carnival.

Martino, Roberto - Singer / Guitar

The older of the two sons of legendary guitarist Robert Martino, Roberto is the lead singer and guitarist of the band T. Vice. When he first started to sing and play, many people didn't believe that he would last in the business and that his days were numbered. However, Roberto continued to improve day by day and eventually became one of the top Haitian performers with the ability to animate the crowd. Roberto managed also to develop his own style and show the world that he is one hell of a guitarist.

Martino, Reynaldo - Keyboard
The younger of the two sons of legendary guitarist Robert Martino, Reynaldo is the leader of the band T. Vice. He is a very hard working musician who continued to surprise the public with innovative grooves and solos.

Mascari, Jean Léon - Singer
Léon played with Volo Volo in Boston.

Mascary, Maxime * - Singer
Maxime played with Scorpio in the 1980s.

Mass Doudou see: Damelus, Jean Junior

Mass Konpa - Band
This band was created in Haiti in 2003 by the popular singer Gracia Delva.

Massac, Andrew Duroseau - Drums

Massac, Fritz - Keyboard
Fritz Massac was one of the most popular musicians of the 1960s. He was the Accordionist and leader of the band Sublime D'Haiti that did the super carnival tune "*Sublime en Pin Pan*". Fritz Massac moved to the U.S., and despite his old age, he is often seen in Florida at many Haitian parties and concerts.

Master Dji see: Herard Georges Lys

Masterful (Les Masterful) – Band
Band based in the Washington D.C. area from the late 70s to the 1990s. Masterful played not only Konpa but reggae and calypso as well. They mostly played for non-Haitian crowds.

Mathelier, Jean - Claude - Keyboard

Mathias, Fred - Bass

Mathieu Edner - Guitar

Mathieu, Harold - Bass
Played with Bossa Combo in the 1980s

Mathieu, Levelt - Guitar
Levelt played with the band Channel 10 and later with Les Frères Déjean in Haiti. In New York he also played with the band Djet-X.

Mathieu, Lutsen - Congas

Mathieu, Wilner - Saxophone

Mathieu, Yves Mary - Congas

Mathou, Jn Marie - Keyboard
Jean Marie Played with the band La Ruche de Léogane.

Mathurin, Eric - Keyboard

Mathurin, Gino - Media Personality / Photographer
Gino is the owner and manager of the internet site echodhaiti.com.

Mathurin, Jean Maurice (Ti Jean) - Drums
Better know as Ti Jean, Jean Maurice Mathurin appeared in the musical scene in New York in the early 1980s. He became the drummer of System Band and has managed to make his mark in the Haitian Music Industry as one of the most talented drummers. For one reason or another he often left the band sometimes for many months or even years, but every time the band's management will welcome him back putting on the side whosoever has replaced their favorite drummer.
Some people make the mistake of thinking that Ti Jean Mathurin is also called Ti Jean Marassa. The answer is No…Ti Jean Marassa is a well-known fan of the band; he is not the famous drummer.

Mathurin, Jean Michel (DJ Jean Michel) - Radio Personality
Jean Michel, known as Jean Jean or DJ Jean Michel, is also one of the owners of the internet site echodhaiti.com. He was, for many years, the most popular Haitian DJ in Washington D.C. He was also the radio host of the show Echo D'haiti in the early 1990s. Jean Michel was for many years the news director of WUSA TV (CBS) channel 9 in Washington D.C. Jean Michel Mathurin is the brother of the singer Carmelo Frédérique (Frédy).

Mathurin, Noé - Guitar

Mauzoul, Gary - Sound Engineer
Gary has been mixing band in the H.M.I since the mid-1980s. He started with Jamming Jacky in Long Island and has worked over the years with Phantoms, System Band, Carimi, among others.

Maxima All Stars - Band

Ma Maison
Haitian-owned record label and show production company based in New York in the 1980s.

Mayala, Daniel * - Drums
Daniel is the father of the late Mario Mayala, guitarist of Skah Shah. Daniel Mayala played most of his career as the drummer of Jazz des Jeunes.

Mayala, Dufont - Congas
Just like Nemours depended on Kretzer Duroseau to deliver the Konpa rhythm on congas, his counter part was non other that Dufont Mayala on Cadence Rampa the band of the legendary maestro Webert Sicot. Legend has it that Mayala created the tempo necessary to make the difference between the two rhythms. However many people including Nemours Jean Baptiste felt that Cadence Rampa was none other but Konpa with a different pattern.

Mayala, Edward - Congas

Mayala, Mario Joseph * - Guitar
Mario Mayala practically grew up in the Haitian music scene since his father Daniel Mayala used to play the drums for the popular band Jazz Des Jeunes while his uncle Dufont Mayala used the play the congas for Cadence Rampas one of the most popular band of the 1960s. Contrary to the previous Mayala generation, Mario didn't become a percussionist. His love, however, was for the chords and at an early age he took part on a small neighborhood band as a guitarist with some of his cousins. However the talent of the young teenager was going to be noticed when he joined the band "Les Morphés" in which he was grabbed by the band Les Shleu Shleu to be a substitute for the lead guitarist Serge Rosenthal. Since his cousin Jhonny Frantz Toussaint (Ti Frè) was also part of the band, the young Mario didn't have any problem to become friend of the second squad of Les Shleu Shleu that will later become as Skah Shah.
In 1974 the band left their manager Dada Jacaman and moved to New York

just like the first Shleu Shleu squad that became Original Shleu Shleu. Since there was already a Shleu Shleu in New York, the second version with Mario Mayala, Ti Frè, Cubano, Loubert Chancy and Arsène Appolon called themselves Skah Shah. It is in that band that the world will see the true face of Mario Mayala as he became the only lead guitarist of the band and making a super match on the chords line with his cousin Ti Frè on rhythm guitar.
In 1980 he collaborated with his friend the saxophonist Gerard Daniel in releasing the album "G.M. Connection", an album that carried the initials of the first name of the two musicians and also their signature on some wonderful Konpa songs.
Mario Mayala died in New York in 1996 at the age of 42. He left behind him a whole world of memories for his friends as the author of some of Skah Shah's greatest hits like *Voisine Françoise, Anba Rozo, Les Dix Commandements, Men Numéwo Wa, La Vie Belle* and *Piprite* among others.

Mazarin, Erick - Singer
Erick played shortly with Les Ambassadeurs and later joined Scorpio in the 1980s. When Arsène Appolon moved to Haiti to create his band Skah Shah d'Haiti, he called on Erick Mazarin to make a solid duo with the singer Joseph Lainé (Blagueur).

Mazarin, Ricot - Singer
In the 1970s Ricot Mazarin was not only one of the star singers of the island, he was the winner of a local singing competition that gave him the opportunity to represent Haiti at an international competition. The young singer was in-demand by many Mini Jazz groups including Los Incognitos, the band that would later be known as Tabou Combo, and also by Les Diplomats. Ricot did try to work with both bands for a very short while. However, he was going to be one of the most followed artists of the 60s and one that give strength to the Mini Jazz movement when he came out next to Yves André Mardis in the band Les Fantaisistes de Carrefour. His voice was all over the airwaves as Les Fantaisistes had some of the greatest hits of the late 60s with songs like *Tristesse, La Femme, Rêve Bleu, Haiti, Création, L'homme* and *Contemplation* with the sweet and warm voice of Ricot Mazarin on lead. In the early 70s Ricot Mazarin left Haiti and immigrated in the U.S. In the mid 70s he contributed to the success of the band Volo Volo de Boston, playing next to Ti Manno.

Médard, Fabrice - Singer
Fabrice played with the band K-Dans in the 1990s.

Médard, Mathieu - Singer
This talented drummer started his career with Septentrional has over the years

also helped many others in their solo projects and live performances including Rodrigue Milien, Emma Achilles and Roger Colas.

Melodie Makers
Haitian owned record label company based in Miami Florida.

Menard, Charles Paul -Trumpet*
One of the founders of Centre D'acceuil De Carrefour, he was the mentor and professor to many musicians. He died in Liberia during a revolt against the Liberian government a few years after he was invited by the President of Liberia to manage the Liberian government orchestra.

Ménard, Edwige - Singer

Ménard, Mirline (Mei Mei) - Singer
Mei Mei is one of the singers of the band Hangout. Mei mei is also a professional dancer. The pretty face and sexy body of the entertainers attract young men to her performances. Her loyal fans call themselves the M.M.S Club.

Ménard, Samuel - Singer
Samuel played with Tropicana.

Menau, Robert – Bass

Ménélas, Claude - Bass / Congas
Started his career as the Congas player of the Band Les Ambassadeurs, and later became a talented bassist.

Ménélas, Ernst - Saxophone
Ernst Ménélas is known as one of the greatest band leaders of his generation. He is also a guitarist, a keyboardist and a congas player, but he made a career as a saxophonist.
Ernst had a unique way of putting the softness and great feelings to the sound of his saxophone. If Ambassadeurs was known for the beautiful love songs it was not only for the vocalists but also to the sound of Ernst Menelas' saxophone
In the late 70s he moved to the U.S., and was only seen in the music arena at Les Ambassadeurs reminiscent parties.

Ménélas, Henry Robert * - Bass
One of the star musicians of the Mini Jazz era, Henry later became the

manager of Les Ambassadeurs moving his younger brother from the congas to the bass. He died in New York in a car accident.

Ménélas, Jean - Trumpet

Ménélas, Ralph - Guitar
Ralph became popular when he joined Zenglen in the 1990 but left the band to move on with other musical projects.

Ménélas, Reynold - Trumpet / Trombone
Reynold Menelas is one the musicians that contributed in the return of the full horn section in the Konpa music a movement that put end to the Mini Jazz era in Haiti. As the influence of the French Caribbean band like Les Aiglons, Exile One and Gramaks was felt by Haitian bands it took horn blowers like Reynold to save the day for Scorpio in the album *Ansam Ansam*.
Reynold, however, had some experience in the business since he played earlier in his career for Doremi Jazz Simalo and he was also know for blowing the trumpet at the services of the church Eglise St. Gerard. After the release of Scorpio's first album, Reynold left Haiti and moved to New York where he joined the band Astros. He collaborated also with Thamda Fever. He became popular; however, in the Diaspora when he joined the band Accolade de New York, a band that had a wonderful horn section that also included the saxophonist Jean Robert Damas and Jules Pagé.
Reynold used to play both the trumpet and the trombone during most of his live shows and studio recordings. He was often seen with a hat, many people think that it is because his role model was none other that the great trumpet player Chuck Mangione.

Mennau, Jean - Guitar
Jean is one of the founders and the first guitarist of the band Septentrional.

Mentor, Josh - Drums

Mercier, Ansyto (Ti Ansyto) - Keyboard
Son of legendary musician Hans Mercier who took it upon himself at a very young age to take over the legacy of his father by creating the band "Top Digital" after his father had put an end to the band Digital Express. Ti Ansyto also became over the years an assistant to his father in the studio productions especially during the carnival season.
In the year 2005 he left his own band to join the newly formed "Kreyol La" which was an emerging band with former members of the popular group Konpa Kréyol. In 2006 his dad became also a member of the band Kreyol La.

This father and son combination is considered by many as one of the best ever experience in the history of Konpa as they are both two great musicians sharing the same style and love of music.

Mercier, Hantz (Ansyto) - Keyboard

 Ansyto is considered as a legend by many people in the Haitian music business. Ansyto, as the producer, has helped many artists to advance in their career.
The man basically started as a conga player when he was only a schoolboy. However, people started to notice the artist in his band Compas Express. He left Compas Express to join Ti Manno in the creation of the band Gemini All Stars in the early 1980s. His father provided a space at his home as the band's headquarter, and his contribution to the success of Gemini was awesome. Ansyto left Gemini to join the band D.P. Express in the mid-1980s and in 1985 he was part of the squad that left D.P. and moved to Washington D.C. to create the band G.P. Express (Gemini Plus Express) a combination of the defected members of D.P. Express, like Edner Couloutte, Pierrot Kersaint, Marc Bellande Jacquet (Choupitte), Ti Polis, Lyonel Simeon, and some ex-members of Gemini like Patrick Casseus, Imgart Manigat, Claude Cajuste, as well as Mario Germain and Ansyto who were members of both bands.

By the late 1980s Ansyto returned to Haiti where he was re-integrated in a D.P. Express with some new members. He revived the D.P. song *"Exactement"* which he turned into a complete new hit by adding a super jam and chorus part with the word DIGITAL as the music was moving to more digitalized instrument. The song was being played all over the country. His parent's home which is located in a residential neighborhood has also become not only the new headquarter of D.P. Express, but also a Nightclub call the Ansyto Fan Club/Club 50.

By the early 1990s Ansyto created his own band "Digital Express', he also took with him some members of D.P. Express and he recorded the song *Digital* in his first album. The song, which was a complete remix of the D.P. song *Exactement* was an instant hit in the Konpa community and has, above all, granted the band many contracts to perform outside of Haiti notably in the French Caribbean, the U.S. and Canada.

In the years that followed, Ansyto became a successful businessman by converting a room at his house to a recording studio. He helped many bands in their music production. During the carnival season Ansyto was usually the most sought-after producer in the country and musicians often wait for hours to work with the demanding music programmer. In the meantime he continued to perform live and to travel with his band and, of course, to release his many albums with his band Digital Express. He has, in the late 1980s to early 2000's produced a multitude of songs for Digital Express, his albums include *Digital, l'Homme Digital, Top of the world, Ansyto, Collection Live, Yo Paré, Vol.8, K2000, Wache Wache,* and *Invasion* among others.

The magical fingers of Ansyto were for many years one of the secrets that contribute to the success of the artist Sweet Micky. After the release of the album *Aloufa,* Sweet Micky was unable to perform live all the difficult keyboards parts that Ansyto had done on the album. In other to satisfy the fans who wanted to dance the new songs Mickey made Ansyto an offer to join his band. Ansyto who was getting tired of managing his own band and producing at the same time for others take the opportunity to work with Michel Martelly. He performed with Sweet Micky for many years, and in 2006 he made the move that shocked many people when he joined his son "Ti Ansyto" in the band Kreyol La.

Méridional (Méridional des Cayes) - Band

Meridional is a popular band that came out in the town of Les Cayes on July 28, 1965. Their song *Manman Zo* was one of the great hits of the 70s. In the 1980s many members of the band stayed in Canada while the band was on tour. They struggled and performed under the name Meridional de Montreal until the singer Dieudonné Larose freshly from the band D. P Express decided to stay in Canada and join the squad. The name of the band was eventually changed to Missile 727. In the meantime the original members who went back to Haiti continued to perform as Meridional. Over the years aging members were replaced by much younger musicians.

Meridional de Montreal - Band
The name Meridional was later changed to Missile 727 when star singer Joseph Dieudoné Larose joined the band.

Merilus, Jude - Singer
Played with the band Super Soline formerly known as Les Vautours and Samba Jazz, Jude played with the band under all three names in the Mini Jazz era.

Méroné, Reynald - Bass

Reynald played with Les Diables du Rythme de St Marc.

Méroné, Martial - Guitar
Martial played with Les Diables du Rythme de St Marc.

Merry, Sergo - Singer
Sergo played with Shupa Shupa in the Mini Jazz era.

Mesidor, Farol - Drum
Farol is a very good drummer and also a polite and very quiet person. He played with Skah Shah, Les Frères Déjean, and Bazouka during his career.

Mésidor, Nixon - Bass
Nixon moved to the U.S. with the band Lakol d'Haiti in the 1990s. Nixon played with a series of band in the Miami area including D-Zine and Top Vice.

Messeroux, Dominique - Trumpet

Messois, Ulysses - Percussion /Congas

Métellus, David (Ti Koka) - Singer
Ti Koka played with a few Konpa bands before moving definitely with the twoubadou style music playing his tunes and mostly the most popular Konpa hit of other artists/bands as well as the folks songs of Haiti. Ti Koka is one of the best Haitian entertainers. He represented Haiti at the Smithsonian Institute in Washington D.C. at the Folks Life Festival in 2004, where he made people of all nations dance to his tunes. A year later he was invited by another American Association to tour several cities in the U.S. with some other Caribbean artists including the mighty Sparrow.

Métellus, Marie Georges (Georgy) – Singer

 Georgy came to the Konpa business at an early age, when she joined the group Zin the late 1980. Her very first hit was *Haiti*. Georgy sang Zin's hit song *Haiti* so well that at every performance the fans cried for more. Always well dressed at every show, people sometimes would go to Zin's shows to watch not only her performance, but also to see how sexy she looked and what she was wearing. The young popular performer was a real role model to many young ladies that tried to imitate her. They would come to the shows but they would spend most part of the night just standing in front of the band watching Georgy's moves. Some men would just not move in front of her until the show was completely over.

Georgie was, however always complaining of being over-worked and under-paid, and in the late 1990s she left the group to join Phantoms another band based in Brooklyn New York. Her journey with Phantoms did not last long, but she did not return to Zin. Instead she moved to Florida and in 2003 she joined the band Hangout. Georgy who was one of the top female artists and who has earned the title of Princess Georgy from her fans became, however, in Hangout the Drama Queen of the Haitian Music Industry. It seems like she couldn't stay out of the news and she was often found in the middle of many dramas and she also has developed the attitude of "Let's give them something to talk about". Georgy is known to many band leaders as an artist hard to manage, but no one can contest that she is a great performer and a charismatic musician who has forever marked the Haitian music world with songs like *Coq* that she did with the band Zin and songs like *911* which she did with the band Hangout.

Météor - Band

Metrosonic - Band

Méus, Lucien - Saxophone
Lucien is a member of the band Tropicana.

Mews, Fréderic * (Dodo) - Bass
Dodo played with Shupa Shupa and later on with Shleu Shleu under the leadership of Loubert Chancy. He was with the Shleu Shleu squad that later became Skah Shah.

Mezifils, Delices - Guitar
Delices struggled with many bands before joining Krézi, a more popular band in the Haitian music market.

Miami Hit - Band

Michaud, Jhonny (Joujou) - Singer
Joujou played in New York with the band Gran Pan Pan.

Michel, Douglas - Congas /Percussion

Michel, Emeline - Singer
Although she is not considered as a Konpa artist, Emeline, however, took part in several Konpa shows. She is considered as one of the best and most respected artists of her generation.
Emeline has become a star in the French Caribbean by emphasizing complex themes, conscious lyrics, and a broad palette of musical styles, including the native Haitian konpa, Twoubadou, and rara.
Born in Gonaives, Haiti, Emeline's first experience in music was singing gospel music at the local church. At 18, she won a song contest in Haiti, with the grand prize being a one year music scholarship at the Detroit Jazz Center. She landed there not knowing a lick of English and became the first in her family to ever leave Haiti. She returned to Haiti and developed a career as the country's most prolific singer/songwriter. Emeline remains one of the few women bandleaders in Caribbean music. In 2007 she released *Reine De Coeur*, her 9th album, but her 4th CD as record producer. She has lived in France and Canada, and currently resides in the U.S. She has toured five continents and become one of the best-selling Haitian artists worldwide.
Visit: www.emeline-michel.com

Michel, Emilio - Bass
Played with Rodrigue Milien's band Combite Créole in the 70s

Michel, Jacques Gérard - Singer
One of the singers of the band Tropicana, he is also know as the sound engineer of the band.

Michel, Gérard *- Saxophone /Trumpet /Guitar /Singer
Gérard played with the band Jazz des Jeunes in Haiti and later with Tropical Combo in New York.

Michel, Paul - Sax

Michel, Ronald - Drums /Percussion
Started as the gonguist of Gemini all Stars de Ti Manno, Ronald Michel moved to the drums to replace Edner Couloutte in D.P. Express when Couloute moved to Washington D.C. as one of the creator of the band G.P. Express.

Miel - Band

Milar, Eric - Trombone

Milbrun, Claudie - Guitar
Claudie is the guitarist of the group Shadow Band de Connecticut.

Milbrun, Lisa - Keyboard / Singer
Lisa is the singer and keyboardist of the group Shadow Band de Connecticut.

Milbrun, Whitney - Singer
Whitney is the band leader of the group Shadow Band de Connecticut.

Milford, Pierre Richard - Congas /Percussion

Milford, Wilson -Trombone
Wilson played with Bossa Combo.

Milfort, Hans (Doc) - Gong /Percussion
Doc played with the band Samba Creole in the Mini Jazz era. Doc is presently living in Florida with his family.

Millet, Ralph - Guitar

Millien, Léon - Guitar
Léon Millien came out with the band Les Manfoubens which would later became known as Les Shleu Shleu. He became before long one of the top guitarists of the Mini Jazz era, especially known for a guitar move known in the Konpa society as "Grajé." Léon left Haiti and moved to the U.S. where he continued to study music. In the late 70s he tried to make a comeback on the Haitian music scene with a band call Sham Sham in New York. However, the band didn't make if far in the demanding market.

Millien, Rodrigue - Singer /Guitar
Rodrigue Milien was at first an actor playing with Troupe Alcibiade in the 1960s. He and his partner Jules Similien (Toto) were good additions to the

company of the popular comedian.

One of their roles was to entertain the public with some Twoubadou songs as a warm up prior to the comedy shows. However, the songs that were mostly funny songs got the attention of more than just the crowd because somehow a scout must have discovered the talent of the actors/musicians and encouraged them to record their first album titled *Nécéssité* with some memorable songs like *Fète Ménage Mwen, Dassoman, Zoclo* and *Tchoul Suportan* and of course the hit song *Nécéssité*. The word 'Nécéssité" would forever become the last name of the actor singer Jules Similien as he will be known as Toto Nécéssité for the rest of his professional career as an entertainer.

 The duo continued to charm the Haitian music world by performing under their new name as a band "Combite Créole". By their second album the band was already performing outside of Haiti, and during a tour in New York the band decided to stay to perform in area restaurants and by doing some special gigs. After trying life in New York Rodrigue decided to go back home while his partner Toto stayed in the Big Apple. That was the automatic split of the band which resulted in having two bands call Combite Créole, one in Haiti as Combite Créole de Rodrigue Milien and Combite Créole de Toto Nécéssité. Since the Combite of Rodrigue was doing wonders in Haiti, Toto in the following years decided to drop the name Combite Créole and go simply on his albums as Toto Nécéssité.

The day of the return of Rodrigue Milien in Haiti, many fans went to the airport to see their idol getting out of the airplane. It was during the pre-carnival season and a float was waiting for the artist at the band's headquarter, and Rodrigue completely block the streets of Port-au Prince living major traffic jams in the Lalue and Rue Pavée neighborhoods a few blocks from the National Palace.

In the years that followed Rodrigue Milien captured the heart of the nation by coming out with one hit song after another. The artist was always busy playing in the provinces and in the nation's capital and his regular shows at the club Chez Maguy was most of the time successful.

Rodrigue has over the years recorded many albums in Haiti as well as in the Diaspora. He also recorded albums with popular artist and bands like Les Frères Déjean, Gemini All Stars, Océlito, and Joseph Lainé also known as Blagueur. Among his many songs the album recorded in New York in the mid-70s with Toto will remain one of his best as the song *Lougarou* was the one that took the band to the level of superstars, which was the reason both artists were able to go different ways and still find success equally. While on his own Rodrigue Milien continued to shine in Haiti with the albums *Croyance* and *Kout Ba Résidence*

His discography also includes *Pa Fèm Sa, Separation, Nostalgie, Lakay, Bien Jwen Ak Bien Kontré, 14 Février, Ambiance Samedi Matin, Raket, Grimelle, Rodrigue*

Milien Les Meilleurs Boleros, Map Tan Ou, Palé Kréole, Rodrigue En Twoubadou and many more.

In the 70s the music of Rodrigue Milien was so popular in Haiti and the French Caribbean Islands that the television and video producer Claude Mancuso, a French citizen living in Haiti and president of the popular production company HTN did a movie on the artist called "**A La Mizé Pou Rodrigue**".

In the movie many of Rodrigue songs are featured as well. This was one of the first Haitian movies with a popular singer that was shown on big screen throughout the country. At the turn of the century Rodrigue Milien continued to live his life in Haiti where he also worked as a radio announcer, he was honored on several occasions especially during the *Haiti Twoubadou* tour in 2004.

On April 4th 2007 in a radio interview on the show "Matin Caraïbes" in Haiti Rodrigue Millien said that in the early days of the band , he and Toto were invited to play at the movie theater Bel Air Ciné, they had to borrow some instruments from friends and they had to walk more that four miles carrying an amplifier borrowed from the band Samba Creole because they couldn't afford public transportation which was one Gourde the equivalent of 20 cents/U.S. Rodrigue said after the show they were paid $3.00 for the two of them. He also said that they only got paid $350.00 for their first album titled Nécéssité that became one of the mega hit and best sellers of the 1970s. Rodrigue said that he finally made some serious money in music when the singer Wyclef Jean paid him for using sentence of one of his songs in Wyclef's hit *24 hours*. In the song *24 hours*, the voice of Rodrigue is heard from the original recording of Combite Créole saying the words *"Mwen ta Renmen konnen dat e jou map mouri."*

Milord, José Nikès - Bass
José played with Phantoms.

Mini Records
One of the top Haitian record labels of all time, the owner/president of the company Fred Paul is one of the most respected producers ever in the history of Konpa music. He has over the years turned many Haitian artists into superstars. He was the first producer to introduce to the Haitian music market a collaboration album when he did the successful *"Mini All Stars"* with the help of some of the best artists that he had produced. The album was such a success that a series of M.A.S collaboration followed over the years.

Minuty, Frantz - Saxophonist

Mirak - Band
This band was created by Mario de Volcy in the late 1980s. Their hit song *Madéla Lagué* introduced to the world the talent of the singer Sylvie D'art.

Missile 727 - Band

Mitchell, Tom - Saxophone
Tom is a talented non-Haitian Konpa musician who played in several Konpa albums especially in the 1980s He was for many years part of the squad of the Magnum Band. He also played with Tabou Combo and System Band in his career.

Mitton, Jean (Jean Jean) - Saxophone

Musique En Folie
One of the greatest music festivals in Haiti where artists can showcase their talents, sell their products. The annual music fair the year 2000 in Pétion - Ville and it moved to "Cercle Bellevue" in Bourdon in 2003 and in 2006 it was moved to "Parc Historique de la Canne à Sucre".

Mizik Mizik - Band
The public's first encounter with the name Mizik Mizik was at the American Airlines music competition in the mid-80s. That competition introduced the famous keyboardist Fabrice Rouzier to the world. As the band leader and creator of the group moved to the U.S., where he attended the University of Maryland the band basically was dormant. While Fabrice was in the U.S., he mastered his musical skill by playing with Tabou Combo and the band Zépon of Washington D.C. When he returned to Haiti he quickly put back Mizik Mizik as a competitive band in the Haitian music arena.
The band got the attention of the public with songs like *De Ger* and *Farinen* with Vardy Pharel and Emmanuel Obas on lead vocals.
By the second half of the 1990s the two singers moved to the U.S., where they created the band Lov. Mizik Mizik bounced back and survived the storm by recruiting the singer Eric Charles from D.P. Express. The arrival of Eric Charles changed the course of the band as the fans and members didn't waste any time accepting Eric as their new front man. With Eric Charles on lead vocal the band released the albums *Blakawout* with the hit songs *Blakawout, Ayizan* and *Sa Poum Fè* which put the band right back on top of the music scene in Haiti and in the Diaspora.
The members of Mizik Mizik also took part in the successful Haiti Twoubadou albums and tours.
In 2007 Mizik Mizik celebrated their 20th Anniversary on a successful tour.

Moïse, Alfred - Trumpet
One of the greatest Haitian musicians of all time Alfred Moise was also the band leader of Septentrional along with Ulrick Pierre-Louis. He is also the composer of many hits of Septentrional like *Fredeline, Ti fi ya levé, Padoné Mwen,* and *Marie Josée* among others.

Moïse, Michel - Bass

Moïse, Tony - Saxophone /Guitar
Tony Moïse started his career with the band Les Frères Laurenceau. He later joined the band Les Manfoubens that later became Les Shleu Shleu. Tony was the first maestro of Les Shleu Shleu and he also directed the band in New York for many years under their new name Original Shleu Shleu since the band owner Dada Jacaman has recruited new members to continue his business after the squad led by Tony Moïse had moved to the Big Apple in search of a new life.
Tony Moïse tried on many occasions to give new life to Shleu Shleu but unfortunately fell short of reviving the band that has created so much fun and left many memories of Haiti to millions of fans all over the world. One of his attempts also was to come out with a new name as he tried with *"Essence"* that once again didn't survive for long. Tony Moïse will always remain a great saxophonist a mentor and a great band leader. Many have followed his footsteps and his leading style throughout the history of Konpa music.

Molière, Jules - Singer

Molière, Léopold - Bass /Keyboard
Léopold started to play music at a very young age. He played with different bands before becoming a star in the 1960 when he joined the band Cadence Rampas of Webert Sicot. He also played with the band Les As and the popular Ibo Combo. He moved to Canada in the 70s where he is also known as a remarkable musician.

Molière, Serge - Saxophonist
Serge played with La Ruche de Léogane and later in his career with the band Gemini All Stars de Ti Manno.

Molin, Robert - Singer/Guitar
Robert played with the band Etoile du Soir.

Mollentiel, Henry - Saxophone

Mombrun, Hubert - Saxophone
Hubert played with the band Missile 727.

Momplésir, James (Ti Linèt) Keyboard
Ti Linèt created the band Gabel in Miami Florida with the help of the singer Jean Junior Marcellus (Money G). In April 2008, after a dispute with the other members that they have recruited, the two founding members of the group left to create the band 5 Etoiles as they released the single *Abu*.

Mompoint, Georges - Percussion /Congas

Mompoint, Ronald - Percussion /Congas

Mompremier, Jacques - Trumpet
Jacques Mompremier is also known as the first band leader of the band Septentrional.

Morphées (Les Morphées) - Band
Band of the Mini Jazz era

Moncelet, Dominique - Singer

Mondésir, Guy - Congas /Percussion

Mondésir, Réginald - Singer
Musician of the band Ju Kann

Mondésir, Yvon (Biassou) - Singer
In the mid-70s Yvon Mondésir took the Konpa music world by storm with his unique voice and his charisma when he joined the popular band Tabou Combo singing next to Shoubou. He took part in the albums *8eme Sacrement* and *The Masters*. He excelled in the album the Masters in songs like *Lovely Mama* and the slow song *Loneliness*.
Later in his career, he collaborated with Dadou Pasket in Magnum Band to replace Fung Cap. He also worked with Mini All Stars and he came out with his own band called First Class in the late 1980s. One of First Class hits is the song *"Computer"* with the catchy phrase *"Mété'l Sou Computer"*.

Monfiston, Gérard - Singer
Gérard is one of the first singers of the band Septentrional du Cap.

Monfont, Philippe - Percussion

Montès, Jeannot * - Bass
Jeannot played with the bands Les Copains and Ibo Combo in the Mini Jazz era.

Montinat, Jean - Keyboard

Montreuil, Charles - Keyboard

Montreuil, Claude - Keyboard
Claude is one of the members of the famous Montreuil family that has given to the Konpa world many talented musicians. He preceded his brother Nathan in the band Scorpio, and later his late brother Guy was going to be one of the best known keyboardists of the 1980s as one of the stars of Coupé Cloué's band. Prior to his days in Scorpio, Claude played with the famous maestro the saxophonist Webert Sicot, and the great drummer Almondo Keslin in the band Zotobré. After he left Scorpio he moved to New York where he helped put together the band Astros. He also helped Assade Francoeur with the band Wanga Negess and later he has worked in a project call *Konpamania*.

Montreuil, Gérald - Keyboard
Gérald played with the band Les Ambassadeurs.

Montreuil, Guy * (Ti Guy) - Keyboard
Guy followed the footsteps of his older brothers Claude and Nathan by becoming a Konpa keyboardist but it was Guy who became the most popular among the Montreuil brothers. Ti Guy did not play for Scorpio like his older brothers; he played most of his career for Coupé Cloué. He was among the musicians who left Coupe's band to create a group with much younger musician "Compas Manba" The band did not last long because Guy Montreuil died at a very young age before the band even had the chance to record an album.

Montreuil, Nathan - Keyboard
When his older brother Claude left the band Scorpio, band leader Robert Martino quickly called on Nathan to fill the vacant position. Nathan delivered even more and better solo for Scorpio and became a tough act to follow when he left the band also a few years later.

Montreuil, Roland - Keyboard
Roland is the father and mentor of the famous Montreuil brothers.

Montreuil, Rolande - Keyboard/Singer

Montrose, Jean Claude - Trumpet
Jean Claude is a member of the band Septentrional.

Moon Foo Band - Band

Moon Kool - Band

Mordus (Les Mordus) - Band
Band of the Mini Jazz era

Morin, Denon - Singer
Denon played with the band Meridional des Cayes. He excelled in the memorable song *Manman Zo*.

Morissaint, Fritznel - Drums

Morisseau, Fritz - Gong /Percussion
Fritz played with the band Super Soline in the Mini Jazz era.

Morisseau, Guesly - Keyboard/Flute

Morrisset, Maurice - Drums

Moscosco, Jules Edouard - Drums

Mourra, Jimmy - Singer
Jimmy played with Zèklè in the 1990s.

Mozayik - Band

Mulet, Onel - Saxophone

Murat, Antalcidas Oréus -Trumpet
Antal Murat is one of the most respected Haitian musicians of all time. He played for many years with the band Jazz Des Jeunes. He collaborated with Nemours Jean Baptiste in the band Conjunto International. Antal was also the man who introduced the legendary singer Gerard Dupervil to the band Jazz Des Jeunes. Antal is also credited with the super song *Fleur De Mai* one of the greatest Haitian hit songs of all time. Antal Murat died in Port-au-Prince Haiti

in 1988.

Murat, Jules - Saxophone

Musique Des Antilles
Haitian owned record company and show production company.

Musset, Jean - Saxophone

Muzac, Emmanuel - Guitar/Bass

Myrtil, Jean Guyderson (Guyby) - Keyboard
Guyby played previously for the bands King Posse and Sakad. He is presently the leader of the band Take Off.

Myrthil, Joseph - Guitar

Mystic - Band

Mysty Jean see: Misterline Jean

N

Nader, Reynold (Sinsin) - Guitar
Sinsin started his career with the band Super Tabou in the 70s before joining Les Gypsies de Petion Ville where he played next to Robert Martino. He continued his journey with Martino when the band became Scorpio. In the 1980s he joined the band Les Frères Déjean and later in his career he created his own band Panic de Petion Ville.

Nakawout -Band

Napoléon see: Prudent Fritz

Narcisse, Ancelot - Trombone

Narcisse, Pierre Eddy -Trumpet

Narcisse, Willie - Congas / Percussion

Nau, Herman - Drums
The man that would become one of the most popular Haitian drummers and leader of one of the most popular Haitian bands of all time started his career playing the accordion. Born and raised in the neighborhood of Pétion-Ville, Herman Nau learned to play music and developed an interest in becoming a professional musician at the Lycée Pétion Ville a neighborhood high school, the same school that has formed many Haitian talents, including the talented Déjean brothers André and Fred. As they became young adults, the Déjean brothers started their own bands Les Frères Déjean while Herman in 1968 turned a neighborhood band Los Incognitos to a professional band call Tabou Combo that would in the following decades became the most popular Haitian Konpa band ever.
In the 1970s it was Herman Nau who again put the band back together in New York after the members were scattered all over the U.S. Herman has worked over the years to protect the legacy of Tabou Combo and has never stop acting as the band real owner. His style as a drummer is highly respected by many Konpa, and Zouk drummers. Herman delivered a rock feeling to the Konpa beat that only Herman Nau knows how to manage. His contribution to the band musical arrangement is impressive as he also contributed to the chorus line of Tabou Combo with his strong voice. In 2001 Herman Nau moved back

to Haiti where he worked for the Aristide government. In Dec. 2006 and early 2007 he toured with Tabou Combo with some former members. Many fans hope for a permanent return of Herman Nau to the popular band.

Nau, Hushai - Singer

Nau, Rudy - Drums
The son of Herman Nau followed the footsteps of his dad first by filling in for him, and later temporarily replacing him in the Tabou Combo. Rudy became the first drummer of the band Carimi. He left the band after a disagreement with the management during a tour in Haiti. Rudy has also worked with the band Dola in 2007.

Nazaire, Yvon - Guitar
Yvon played in his early days with the band Norma de Léogane before joining Bossa Combo in the 1980s to fill up the vacancy left by Rodrigue Toussaint.

Nazi Roland, Pierre * - Keyboard
Pierre played with Les Diables du Rythme de St Marc before joining the band Super Ensemble de Nemours Jean Baptiste and later the band Jazz Des Jeunes. Later on in his career he was playing with the band of the troubadour star Ti Koka until his died of a cardiac arrest in 1999

Nazie, Georges - Guitar
This talented musician did his time in his younger years in Haiti with several bands including Les Frères Déjean. He found his space in the Konpa society with his Montreal based band T-Kabzy.

Neff, Georges - Bass/Piano

Neff, Jean - Bass
Jean played with the bands Sublime and Super Ensemble de Nemours Jean Baptiste in the 1960s.

Neff, Robert (Bob Neff) - Singer /Drums
One of the star singer of the Mini Jazz era, Bob was the first singer of Les Gypsies de Petion Ville. He moved to the U.S., where he became the drummer of the band Gemini One in Boston.

Neks -Band
This band was created in Miami Florida by the guitarist Ralph Menelas.

Nelson, Darico -Trumpet
Darico played with Jazz des Jeunes before joining the band Super Ensemble de Nemours Jean Baptiste. In his early days he created his own band Jazz Darico a band that didn't have much success.

Nelson, Ronald –Trombone

Nerette, Chenet – Radio/T.V Personality
Nerette is the Chief executive Director of Power 102.1FM WRCX, Radio Continentale in Boston, Massachusetts and General Manager of ACETN Television Network in Atlanta Channel 26 Comcast. **Nerette** is also a show promoter. He does live shows with different bands in Atlanta and in Boston. Nerette other projects is organizing the Miss Black Beauty international Pageant in Boston. He also writes articles on the website Basekompa.com on a daily basis.

Nerette, Raphael - Singer

Nia see: Marothière, Virginia

Nido see: Noel Edner

Noël, Chenet -Trumpet
Played in his early days in the 1960s with Tropicana then became a regular of Super Ensemble de Webert Sicot band before joining Septentrional later on in his career.

Noël, Edner (Nido) - Singer
Nido had his best years with the band Fassad in the 1990s

Noël, Henry Pierre - Keyboard

Noël, James - Drums

Noël, Madsen - Guitar

Noël, Reynold - Bass
Reynold played with Tropicana du Cap.

Nomads - Band
After he left Carimi, the guitarist Steve Derosier created his own band "Nomads" in the year 2004.

Norma (Norma de Léogane) - Band

Normil, Darlene - Singer

Nortil, Jean * - Saxophone
Jean played with Tropicana du Cap.

Nostalgik - Band

Noze, Raymond - Guitar

Nozile, Alix - Congas
Alix is a member of the band Nu Look.

Nozile, Dieujuste Polynice (Ti Polis) - Guitar
Ti Polis at an early age developed a passion for music by playing the congas for a neighborhood theatrical group of young kids. The Nozil musicians are known in the Konpa music world for their aptitude of playing the congas and other percussion instruments, however Ti Polis moved out of the ordinary as he learned in his adolescent years the secrets of the guitar that would become his bread and butter for the rest of his short life.
When Robert Martino and Gypsies moved to the U.S. in the mid-70s, the management of band recruited some new talents and released the Gypsies album *Lwa Baron*. Among the new artists the public was going to discover two of the Haitian guitarists Ti Polis and Ti Claude Marcelin who dominated the late 70s, 80s and 90s.
In 1976, the two were among the members that created the band D.P. Express. However Ti Polis was hired by Les Frères Déjean soon after the first practice sessions with D.P. He moved to the U.S. with Les Frères Déjean in the late 70s and was among the members who had to move back to Haiti after Les Frères Déjean confronted some problems with the U.S. immigration at the U.S./Canada border. Ti Polis played with Les Frères Déjean in Haiti until some of the musicians moved on to create the band "Dixie Band" in the early 1980s under the leadership of the drummer Touco Bouzi and Ti Polis. The band even released a couple of albums titled "Dixie Band/Ti Polis". However Ti Polis left his beloved Dixie to joined D.P. Express and in 1985 he was also among the members who left D.P. Express to create the band "G.P. Express" in Washington, D.C. After two albums with G.P. Express, Raymond Cajuste came on a truck from Florida and moved Ti Polis and his family from their Maryland home to Miami Florida without the knowledge of his best friends Mario Germain Lyonel Simeon and Imgart Manigat who created G.P with him in D.C. Leaving Maryland to start a new project with the guys of Bossa was

241

something that Ti Polis would regret all his life as his wife and kids moved right back to Maryland since the project to revive Bossa in Florida was a total failure.

A few months later Ti Polis moved to Canada where he helped Larose in his "Missile 747" project. Once again his relation with Larose didn't last and he found himself moving from band to band from city to city and working on several artists' solo projects. One thing is true about Ti Polis, it look like everything he touched turned to gold. Around the same time Ti Polis helped Anna Pierre to release her album *Mété Suc Sou Bonbon*. He also worked with Dof Chancy by regrouping the band Super Stars in Florida. He helped the band Zépon of Washington D.C. in their album titled *Yo Palé*. He also released a few solo albums including one titled *"Zinglin "* in 1988 while he was living in Maryland not knowing then that he would later become a member of the band Zenglen Plus in Miami. At the end of the century he rejoined the band Les Frères Déjean which was also a failed attempt to revive a great band of the past. At the turn of the new century he found a steady job with the band Nu Look. On April 9 2003, the music world was shocked by the news of the sudden death of Ti Polis one of the most talented and famous Konpa guitarists of all time.

His body was transported to Haiti where he is buried.

Let's note also Ti Polis had changed his first name from Dieujuste to Dennis.

Nozile, James - Percussion / Gong
James played with Fassad prior to Zenglen.

Nozile, Robert (Ti Robert) - Congas
Ti Robert played with the bands les Widmaiers and later with Les Frères Déjean among other bands in his career.

Numa, Faubert - Singer
Faubert was the star singer of the band Volcan des Gonaives

Nu Faze – Band

Nu Look - Band

This Miami based band was created as some members of the band D-Zine decided to move along without some of the original members. Ever since its creation the band managed to stay as one of the busiest bands in the Haitian music industry. Despite their success the band often left a bad note to the followers and promoters as the musicians of Nu Look are known as the most undisciplined ones in the HMI due to their chronic lateness. Nu Look is known to show up late for work and have irritated many people over the years. The band sometimes showed up to work two hours late, which is considered a lack of respect to the paying public. Nu Look was blamed for chaos and damage done to the night club Djoumbala in Haiti as frustrated fans started to protest when they saw no signs of the musicians after waiting more than three hours for a show that Nu Look was supposed to open for the band Zenglen. While the artists where on stage ready to perform, the band leader Arly Larivière and the singer Gazzman Pierre were no where to be found. When they finally showed up they found a riot of angry people and some even got injured due to their lack of discipline and respect to the public. When they returned to the U.S., they issued a statement saying that they would work on their chronic lateness. However that didn't stop the guitarist Ralph Condé to walk away from the band that almost cost him his life according to the singer Gazman Pierre in an interview to Konpamagazine.com on September 11, 2007. Even when the band Nu Look only released two studio albums (*Big Mistake* and *Sill News*) in six years, they managed however to put out a series of live albums with some of their best hit songs *Avè'w Map Maché, Loving You, Gran Dépensè* and *Why Do You Say You Love Me*.

Nu Look has been one of the most popular bands of the new century.

Nu Poz - Band

Nu Stars - Band
Konpa band based in New York

Nu Vice - Band

This Miami-based band was created as the members Robert Martino and Robert Charlot Raymondville moved along without their star singer Carl Frederique (Frédy). Frédy was replaced by a singer name Herly that was acquired from Atlanta.

New York All Stars - Band
New York based band of the 1990s

O

Obad - Band
Konpa band of the 1990s

Obas, Beethova – Singer/Guitar
Although he is not considered as a Konpa artist, Beethova took part in several Konpa shows.
Over the last decade, Beethova Obas has built an international reputation as one of the most important and compelling young musician from the Caribbean. This modern troubadour is a core of a new generation of musicians who have combined the traditional Haitian music such as Konpa, Rara, Voodoo music with conscious lyrics and a whole range of musical influences.

Obas, Emmanuel - Singer
Emmanuel first made contact with the public when he won the second American Airlines music contest with the song "Lagel", written by his brother Beethova Obas. In the 1990s he became one of the vocalists of the band Mizik Mizik in Haiti, and in New York with "Lov". He replaced Gracia Delva in the group "Zenglen", but his journey with the Miami-based band only last a few months.

Odyssey One - Band

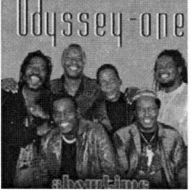

The band Odyssey One came out in 1979 with some ex-members of the band Les Deutz. The discography of Odyssey One includes the following albums: *Beaucoup De Gas, Deutz In Miami, Show Time, Nèg Guinnen* and *Alleluia*

Omni Band – Band
After his days with Bossa Combo, Zotobré, D.P. Express superstar drummer Almando Keslin came out with his own band Omni Band. Almando joined

later in his career joined the band Les Frères Déjean, replacing Touco Bouzi.

Opamizik.com
Opamizik.com is a popular online magazine where Konpa fans discuss issues regarding Konpa music on a daily basis. It reports Konpa news 24/7 on the website forum "Opa Music Section" as it happens.

Orelien, Valentin - Trumpet

Orchestre Compas du Nord d'Haiti - Band
Their discography includes *Nagé Pou Soti*, released in 2000 and *Fo Pastè* released in 2003.

Orchestre Ibo Lélé - Band

Orchestre Super Sonic - Band

Original H - Band
Konpa band based in Paris, France, the discography of Original H include the albums *Wè Pa Wè Tout Moun Jwen, Tout Moun Dakò,* and *Men Konpa (live)*

Oriol, Lyonel - Bass /Guitar
Lyonel played with Ibo Combo in the 1970s.

Oscar, Raymond - Singer
Raymond played with Meridional des Cayes.

Osias, Gerald - Keyboard

OSS. Record
Haitian owned record company

Osselin, Antoine - Drums
This drummer is known to be the role model for the 60s generation. He played with the band of "The Casino International", and he was also known as a great showman.

Ovide, Florant Jr - Drums

Ovide, Ingrid - Singer

Oui Band - Band

This band came out in New York in the 1980s, the discography of Oui Band includes *Perspective Imagine* and *Cherché La Femme*.

Ozone - Band

This band came out under the leadership of Gary Didier Perez the former lead singer of Zenglen.

P

Pachas (Les Pachas du Canapé Vert) - Band
Les Pachas du Canapé Vert, created in 1969, quickly became one of the top Mini Jazz of the early 70s. Their song *La Messe Sou Boulevard* was an instant hit. Other songs like *l'Orage Calé, Yamaha, Siro Miel, Ingrid, Samba Pachas, Calipso Pachas, Imitation* and *Desorde musical*, were also well-appreciated by their fans. In the 1980s the band leader Pierre Richard Baltazar, with the help of his brother Robert Baltazar, tried his very best to revive the band in the Washington Metropolitan area with some new blood, like the singer Jean Claude Vivens, the drummers Mario Jean Gilles of Scorpio the guitarist Daniel Samedi of Samba Creole, the gonguist Nixon Clermont, the guitarist Joseph Louis (Fanfan Alexis) and Felix de la Cruz as well as some former members of the band, like the late singer Antoine Alexis. The band did some gigs in the U.S., especially in some cities on the East Coast. However, the singer Antoine Alexis died in Maryland and the younger musicians have moved on with other musical activities. The Baltazar brothers were involve in the creation of the band G.P. Express and later on Richard became one of the sound engineers in the business until his equipment was stolen after he did a show in Philadelphia.

Pachou Combo – Band
Band of the Mini Jazz era created in 1973

Pageot, Guy - Guitar
Guy Pageot has helped several artists in their projects. His discography includes *Hommage à Gérard Dupervil and Next Level.*

Pagié, Jules - Saxophone
Jules Pagié played with Bossa Combo on sax tenor next to Jean Robert Damas. Jules Pagié was among the musicians that moved to New York to create the band Accolade de New York.

Palace - Band
Former band of the town of St. Marc

Palmiès, Marc – Gong

Pamphile, Fritz* - Promoter /Club Owner
Fritz was the owner of the popular club Cabane Créole.

Panic de Pétion Ville - Band
This band came out in Pétion Ville under the leadership of Reynold Nader (Sinsin).

Panorama des Cayes –Band
This band was created in 1965 in the town of Les Cayes.

Pantal see: Guilbaud Pantaléon

Papa Jube see: Altino Jhon Jube

Papash - Band

This band came out in the 1980s; Papash was one of the bands that made their mark in the Nouvel Jenerasyon movement with stars like the singer Wydens and the singer/guitarist Ralph Condé. The song *Feeling Papash* was an instant hit in the 1980s and quickly got the band some serious airtime and gigs in and out of Haiti.

Papillons (Les Papillons) - Band
Band of the Mini Jazz era created in the early 70s

Papillions Jaunes (Les Papillons Jaunes) Band
Another band of the Mini Jazz era created in the mid 1960s.

Papillon, Ralph - Singer
His discography includes *Réglé Kozé'w*, *Downtown* and *Sheriff Trankil*.
Papillion is known for wearing a hat in public and on his album covers.

Paquette, Anthony - Trombone

Parent, Beatrice
Musician of the Konpa/Ragga band Black Parent

Parent, Clark
Clark is a member of the band Black Parents.

Parent, John Clark - Singer/Guitar
John Clark is one of the musicians of the band Black Parents. Unlike his cousins, John Clark lived in New York and not in Montreal, Canada which made it difficult for him to perform with the band since he constantly needed to provide a petition in order to work as a musician in Canada. He was eventually replaced by other guitarist for the local shows. However, he never missed the occasion to tour with the band and to work with them, arrange some of the songs and show his support and contributions in any form as soon as the band called for his help.
In 2005 John Clark Parent released his solo album *"Tashou"* under the label AC Records of the singer Alan Cavé.

Parent, Lydie
Lydie is a member of the band Black Parents.

Parent, Majorie
Marjorie is a member of the band Black Parents.

Paris, Achilles * (Ti Paris) - Guitar /Singer
Although he never played in a Konpa band the music of Achilles Paris (better know as Ti Paris) has helped many bands and artists in their journey. For more than 50 years of Konpa history the list of entertainers who have remade his songs really long.
The music of Ti Paris was heard all over the country as the man from Jacmel never missed the occasion to keep it real in his writing even when he added a sense of humor to most of them.
From the time of Jazz des Jeunes to Sweet Micky and Beethova Obas, in more recent years we have heard his tunes over and over being done by different entertainers. In the 1960s the bands Ibo Combo and Shleu Shleu have used some of his songs. In the 1970s the band Bossa Combo used some of his lines in their hit song *Te Quiero,* Coupé Cloué and his famous band also used some of the work of Ti Paris and it continues with Boulo Valcourt, Beethova Obas and Sweet Micky among others. Ti Paris died in 1979 at the age of 46 but some of his songs like *Mon Ideal (Lina), Banm Pam Ladan'l* and *Ladan'l Poum Mouri* to name a few are still being used by today's artists.

Paris, Max - Keyboard

Partners - Band
This band is known by many as the very first New York-based band of the new generation movement. The band was created in the mid-80s by Jean Claude Provilus (James) Jensen Derosier, Lemy Raymond, Frantz Larece and Pierre Provilus. A few years later the band became "Phantoms" with Pierre Raymond Divers (King Kino) as the lead vocalist replacing James. The style of the band changed completely and the Provilus brothers' dream for a new generation genre of Konpa music in New York was forever shattered as Phantoms is nothing short of a hard Konpa band. James' song *Lumiere de la lune*" still remain a good hit played by Phantoms.

Pascal, Alix (Tit Pascal) - Guitar /Keyboard
Tit Pascal was in the 1970s one of the best musical arrangers. Many bands including Tabou Combo have used his services and savoir faire in terms of the chord lines. He started as many young men in the Mini Jazz revolution of the 1960s. He played for the band "Les As". After a live performance he was shot by a Macoute and has been paralyzed since that unfortunate incident. Tit Pascal moved away from the Konpa scene in the 1980s and has produced some solo albums and has also worked with some jazz artist as well as the Rasin music movement.

Pasquet, André (Dadou) - Guitar /Singer
Dadou Pasket is one of the legendary Haitian musicians of all time. Unlike many musicians, he didn't start his career in Haiti. He basically learned how to play Haitian music by hanging out with older and well-known musicians in the 1960s. Dadou basically was introduced to the public when he joined the New York based band "Tropical" one the first Haitian bands created outside of Haiti.
The name Dadou Pasket would become known to the world when Dadou was chosen to play the lead for the popular band Tabou Combo in New York. The guitar skills and speed of Dadou were automatically noticed as guitarists all over the world were trying to match up his speed. Dadou's style dominated the early 1970s as Tabou Combo's song *New York City* from the album *8em Sacrement* was the first Haitian album to turn Gold .The song was on top of the International hit parade in Paris, France and was being played in Discos all over Europe. Dadou also excelled in the album *Canne à Sucre* and he proved that he was again one of the masters of Konpa music as he delivered in the Tabou Combo album "The Masters" some guitar solos that, after all these years, most guitarists can't even copy.
On June 24, 1976 with the help of his brothers Carlo and Claude (Tico), he

created his own band, Magnum Band. Dadou continues with Magnum his journey as a great guitarist a singer an exemplary band leader and one of the best Konpa Composers of all time. In 2006 he toured with his Band with some well-known Haitian musicians on the 30th Anniversary of Magnum band. Besides his many albums with Magnum Band and Tabou Combo his discography also included, his solo albums like *Islam* and *Dadou En Troubadour*.

Pasquet, Carlo - Congas

Older brother of Tico and Dadou Pasket, Carlo played under the leadership of Webert Sicot, replacing Dufont Mayala in Super Ensemble de Webert Sicot.

Pasket, Claude (Tico) - Drums

Tico, the older brother of Dadou Pasket, was also discovered in New York. During a tour of the band Gypsies in New York the drummer left and Tico was called to replace the vanished musician. He impressed the guys so much that they invited him to move with them to Haiti. No one would imagine that this young Haitian musician discovered in a very strange way was going to become one of the best Haitian musicians that the Konpa world would ever know and also one of the most imitated Haitian drummers of all time.

After his years with Gypsies, Tico impressed his followers as he showed that he continued to be one of the best when he lined up with the full band Les Frères Déjean. When his younger brother famous guitarist Dadou Pasket decided to create his own band, Tico left his job with the Déjean Brothers to engage in his own adventure and on June 24, 1976, his career took a new direction forever as he created with his brothers the band that would be known as Magnum Band.

After four decades behind the drums, Tico Pasket is still a proud musician who has devoted his life to what he believed in: being one of the ambassadors of Konpa music, as he is continuing to work as a professional musician and taking Magnum Band all over the world.

Passion - Band

This band was based in Montreal in the 1990s, and helped discover the talent of Stanis Eders (Pipo).

Paul, Frantz (Kiko) - Congas

Kiko was known in the 1970s as a very good percussionist and showman of the band Super Soline. He became even more popular when he joined Les Gypsies replacing Marc Edmé. He traveled with the band to the U.S. While some of the musicians stayed in the States, and moved on with their lives, Kiko went back to Haiti with Robert Martino and was one of the original members of Scorpio. However, he was replaced by Marechal Tito in the early days of the band.

Paul, Fred - Producer / Promoter
Fred Paul is the owner/President of the record company Mini Records. He is one of the most respected producers in the history of Konpa music. He has over the years turned into superstars many Haitian artists. He was the first producer to introduced to the Haitian music the collaboration style of album when he did the successful Mini All Stars album in 1977 putting together some of the best artists that he had produced. The album was such a success that in the years that followed Fred Paul produced over 30 All Stars albums.
Born in Petite Rivière de l'Artibonite, Fred Paul has produced over the years more than 300 albums. The first album he did with the band The Bougaloos de Montreal was released in 1971 and ever since, he never look back producing many bands and artists.
Fred Paul doesn't produce albums recorded at live shows. To him, it's not fair to record an artist while he /she is tired performing all night. To him, that's not a good way to immortalize an artist.
Fred also did a few live shows to promote his artists; he was the impresario who went to Africa with Coupé Cloué as well as the performers Claudette & Ti Pierre.

Paul, Gerard - Congas / Percussion

Paul, Jean Robert - Keyboard

Paul, Julien - Singer / Bass
Julien Paul is the man that is considered as the pioneer singer of the rhythm Konpa Direct. He was with Nemours Jean Baptiste in the band Aux Calebasses as a singer and as a bass player. His voice carried the songs *Trou Panno* and *Tipiti Calebasses.*

Paul, Patrick - Keyboard

Paul, Sergo - Singer
Sergo Paul was the funny and charismatic singer of the band Super Soline.

Paul, Nemline - Singer

Paul, Rossely - Keyboard

Paul, Wilner - Singer

Wilner played with Omni Band.

Paul, Yves Léon (Ti Guy) - Singer
Ti Guy played with Coupé Cloué in the 1990s in the last days of Ensemble Select. He is also the founder and leader of the band Compas Manba of New York which later became a band playing in Haitian-owned bistros and restaurant in New York under the name Lojik Manba.

Paulipap, Jean - Guitar
Musician of the New York based band Gran Pan Pan.

Pauyo, Lyonel - Saxophone

Payne Alfredo - Singer
Played with Tabou Combo

Payoute, Eddy - Guitar

Peddy See: Pierre Charles, Jean Claude

Pè Guiguit see: Roche, Guitary

Penm see: Evens, Ignace

Penson, Sergot - Singer / Drums

Pepignan, Jacques - Guitar

Pepsi Jazz - Band

Perez, Gary Didier - Singer
Gary Didier Perez's voice appeared with the creation of the band Zenglen as the band shocked the Konpa world with a new style and they were proud to sing about it the song *Fidel*. The strong voice of the new singer as well as the charming and charismatic feelings that he put in the songs *Eva, Ou Mèt Alé* and *Tambou Nou* contributed to make him the new sensation of the early 1990s. However, the original band broke down in the middle of a tour in the U.S. and Gary moved on with other bands like "Mizik Mizik" and his own band "Ozone" Even after the band has regrouped in Miami with new members, Gary has moved on with his career and didn't take part in the success of the movement of which he was one of the creators.

Perl, Maryse - Singer

Pérou, Charlie - Gong
Charlie played with the band Les Vikings in the Mini Jazz era.

Perrin, Ernst - Singer
Ernst was next to Wiener Smith one of the star singers of the band New York based Latino in the Mini Jazz era.

Perrin, Joseph - Bass
Moved to New York from the band Lakol d'Haiti, Perrin as he is know in the Konpa community has been working with different bands as a bassist to include Lakol of New York and System Band among others.

Pétion, Gaston - Gong

Pétion, Jean Claude - Guitar
Jean Claude Pétion was one of the guitarists with the fastest fingers in the Mini Jazz era. He played with the band Super Tabou and later became one of the leaders of the band Les Cougars de Pétion -Ville.

Pétion, Pierre Richard - Keyboard

Pétion, René * - Bongos / Percussion
Those who had the chance to see Ensemble Select de Coupé Cloué playing live will also always remember that one of the musicians was always seated on the floor with a pair of bongos between his legs. René Pétion was an indispensable musician for the band since his instrument was vital to the rhythm Konpa Manba, thus making him the most famous Haitian bongo player ever. René died in 2007.

Phantoms - Band

This band was created in Brooklyn New York after some of the members of the band "Partners" decided to break away from their leader the bassist Jean Claude Provilus (James). The band came out with the singer Pierre Raymond Divers, also known as King Kino, as they shocked the Konpa world with some surprising and daring political and social lyrics like the song *Haiti en Cowboy* and the song *Vagabon*. The discography of Phantoms includes among others some of their most famous albums like *Ouvè baryè, Résurection, Pa bougé Dix ans Déja,* and *Frèt Kash,* as well as some compilations and live recordings including one of the first live Konpa recordings on the market. The album *D.C. Sou Konpa* was released by Geronimo Records after a show not in Washington, D.C., but in Silver Spring, Md (a suburb of the District of Columbia) by promoter Jean Claude Vivens of JCV Productions.

The band Phantoms has been up and down in the Haitian music business, and the ins and outs of their star singer King Kino have affected the band stability. In the spring of 2007 the band released a statement announcing that the name of the band would be changed to "Sak Passé". However, the fans and the media reacted and in September the band voted that the name would remain Phantoms and assured the fans that there will not be a name change.

Pharel, Edouard (Vardy) - Singer
Vardy played with the band Mizik Mizik in Haiti. He moved to New York where he created the band Lov with the singer Emmanuel Obas. Vardy moved to Porto Rico where he studied medicine.

Philibert, Pierrot - Guitar
Pierrot is credited with developing the guitar groove and rhythm style of the famous band Les Frères Déjean which is also played by System band and followed today by many. The famous guitarist Réginald Benjamin followed in the footsteps of Pierrot in the band Les Frères Déjean in the 1970s. Many people that were around in the early days of Frères Déjean will remember the famous chorus *"Filibè mété ou grann"*, which is however from a popular Haitian dirty joke and has nothing to do with Pierrot Philibert contrary to popular belief.

Philippe, Camille - Singer /Guitar
Camille played with the band Les Manfoubens.

Philippe, Eddie Pierre - Gong
Star gonguist of the Mini Jazz era, he played with the band Les Ambassadeurs.

Philippe, Johnson - Keyboard

Philippe, Luc - Timbales /Drums /Gong /Percussions
This polyvalent musician was known as one of the showmen of the Super Ensemble de Webert Sicot.

Philippe, Mario - Drums

Philogène, Benito (Bénito d'Haiti) - Singer
One of the star singers of the band D.P. Express who made his mark in the music arena with a voice that reminded people of the popular singer "Ti Manno". He didn't have any problem filling the gap left by Manno in D.P. Express. Benito became schizophrenic and later died in Port-au-Prince.

Philosca, Mireille - Singer

Pierre, Alet - Congas
Alet played with Septentrional.

Pierre, Andrien - Singer
Original singer of the band Jazz Capois which is now known as Tropicana du Cap.

Pierre, Anna - Singer
Author of the super hit song of the 1990s "Mété Suk Sou Bonbon'm", a very daring song that got the attention of everyone. The song was followed by a music video that introduced the artist. However, Anna Pierre is a professional nurse who never had the intention of making music a fulltime career. She was happy to enjoy her short-lived fame by making some appearances as a guest artist on some special occasions and fund-raising parties.

Pierre, Charles Joseph - Trumpet
Charles played with La Ruche de Léogane.

Pierre, Chesnel - Gong

Chester played with Les Frères Déjean.

Pierre, Cheyna - Writer
Owner/Administrator of the internet site Opa Mizik.com

Pierre, Claudette - Singer
Claudette came out in the 1970s as a surprise to the Haitian music world as her sweet voice took over the airwaves. With the help of the blind keyboardist Ulrick Pierre (Ti Pierre), the duo became the entertainers of choice of many groups organizing private functions and fundraisers. Her song *Camionette* was an instant smash hit in Haiti and will always remain one of the most popular songs by a Haitian female artist. Her discography also includes the albums *Camionette, Haiti, Collaboré, Tour 79, Noel, Zanmi, Hello Africa,* and *Pa contrarié'm.*

Pierre, Cléona (Cléo) – Singer/Model/Actress
Cléo started her career in the band D'Sire and later she joined the band Hangout. In 2006 she left the band to start her own business and to embrace a career in the Haitian movie industry as she continues to show that she is a talented actress.
She has worked as a model, actress, and was also the Miss-Haiti-Florida 98. She is well-known for her passion for music. She has appeared on Pyramide Magazine, Tambour Battant Magazine, and Island TV. She played with Zenglen, Harry Brice, Alaye, Miraj, Nu-Look, Larose, Top Vice, Wyclef and Sweet Micky
In 2007 Cléo released her solo album titled *"Lanmou Dezièm Men".*

Pierre, Danny - Singer /Keyboard

Keyboard player, songwriter, composer, vocalist, Danny P. became a member of Tabou Combo in 1996. He left the band in 2002 to pursue his career in the American music industry. Since then he has signed to EMI Publishing along, with names like Usher, Alicia Keys, Jay Z, P. Diddy, and Sean Paul to name a few. Danny P. co-wrote the #1 smash hit "Come Undone" with Robbie Williams, selling over 18 million records and has been seen on E TV, MTV and VH1, escorting the multi-platinum soul singer Joss Stone to the Grammy Awards in Feb. 2006. Despite the Hollywood parties and his #3 Billboard hit "Saturday Night" for Aaron Carter, he says "My best time in music has been with Tabou Combo".
Bio from: www.taboucombo.com

Pierre, Daphney - Keyboard

Pierre, Ernst Frantz - Bass

Pierre, Ferrat
Ferrat played with Jazz Des Jeunes.

Pierre, Fritz - Trumpet
Star musician of the 1960s

Pierre, Garcia - Trumpet / Trombone

Pierre, Gazzman (Gazzman) – Singer

The artist became popular with the emergence of the Miami based band D-Zine in the 1990s. He was among the members who revolted against the management and moved on to create the band Nu Look. Gazman's unique voice helped carry the success of Nu Look and he also took part of some management responsibilities and looked out for the best interests of the band. He worked also in public relations as he is the one who does most of the interviews for the band.

Gazzman, who is very tall, is also known as a good soccer player, which has helped him in keeping a good athletic shape. He is also known as a teaser and he often used his practical jokes on other musicians particularly on Ritchie, Gracia Delva and Pipo. Most of the time the public found the jokes not to be funny as Gazman sometimes used words that are considered inappropriate in the Haitian society. In the fall of 2007 he apologized to Richie by saying that if he could turn back the clock he would have not said nasty things toward the famous drummer of Zenglen. He had for many years kept a colorful hair style which is the reason that many people call him "Couleur" which is the French word for "color".

Pierre, Gehoboam - Drum / Percussions
Gehoboam played with Ozone and the band Compas Manba.

Pierre, Gérard - Singer

Pierre, Ghislaine - Singer

Ghislaine played with the band Partners.

Pierre, Harold - Gong /Percussions

Pierre, Harry * - Trumpet
Harry played with Tropicana and Les Frères Déjean.

Pierre, Henry Joseph - Drums /Percussion /Keyboard

Pierre, Jackenson * - Guitar /Singer
Jackenson played with Digital Express in the 1990s.

Pierre, James Alex (Black Alex) - Singer
Although he is known for being a rap singer, Black Alex has participated in several Konpa projects, notably with his friends Ralph Papillion, Fabrice Rouzier, Sweet Micky, T. Vice, and Carimi. With the success of the Ragga Muffin band King Posse in 1996, Black Alex became one of the favorite stars of high school kids of the mid-90s.
Unable to manage his fame, he abused his body with alcohol and other substances, which eventually almost took his life in 2003. Many musicians especially Fabrice Rouzier, gave their time and money to save his life. A couple of years later Black Alex survived an assassination attempt when he was shot multiple times in Petion Ville after a poker game. He was robbed of an expensive gold necklace that was given to him by his friend Wyclef Jean, the popular Haitian-American Hip-Hop superstar.
Black Alex rebounded in the Haitian music scene by being a guest artist on several bands and artists albums as well as live shows including the Konpa Festivals. In 2007 during the carnival he was awarded his own float and was not part of the King Posse's squad for the carnival even after he shot the video with his former band mates.

Pierre, Jean Claude - Singer

Pierre, Jean Ulrick - Singer

Pierre, Jodnerson (Kiki) - Singer
Kiki is the singer of the band Rafrechi.

Pierre, Josias - Radio Personality
Josias has over the years made several interviews with different Konpa artists in his popular radio shows in Haiti.

Pierre, Julmiste - Congas

Pierre, Kennelly - Bass

Pierre, Lerida - Drums /Percussion
Lerida is a member of the band Tropicana.

Pierre, Leslie – Gong
Leslie played for the band Les Beatniks de Queens in the Mini Jazz era.

Pierre, Louis - Trumpet
Louis played with La Ruche de Léogane.

Pierre, Louis - Percussion

Pierre, Lucky - Singer /Guitar

Pierre, Lyonel - Singer

Pierre, Marcel * - Singer
Marcel is one of the first singers of Jazz Capois. He perished in a boat accident in the northern part of Haiti.

Pierre, Milo - Congas

Pierre, Muller - Guitar

Pierre, Murat - Saxophone /Guitar
Murat is one of the pioneers of the Haitian music and a mentor for many Konpa artists.

Pierre, Philippe - Singer /Keyboard
Even thought Philippe spent most of his career in the religious music arena he has helped many artists in their projects. The artist, who is blind, is known as a very good keyboardist, and music arranger.

Pierre, Prémilus Thélusmé - Trumpet
Thélusmé played with Arsène Appolon's band Skah Shah #1 Plus in the 1980s.

Pierre, Romny (Don Roro) - Singer
Roro played with Triomecs in the 1990s.

Pierre, Saint Harry - Singer
Harry played with Sweet Coupé.

Pierre, Sergot - Percussions

Pierre, Stanley - Singer

Pierre, Stefy - Singer

Pierre, Ulrick * (Ti Pierre) - Keyboard / Drums / Bass

Ti Pierre was born blind and like many handicapped musicians, he learned to play many instruments including the drums, the bass and the keyboard at the school St. Trinité. He played numerous concerts for the school, which eventually made him popular. However, like many musicians formed by the Catholic institution, he had moved on with his life working as a professional entertainer, making people dance in area club and private functions, with the singer Claudette Pierre, with whom he created the duo "Claudette et Ti Pierre". Their album with the song *Camionette* was a hit that took many by surprise, especially that the sweet voice of Claudette was new to music lovers. Their discography includes *Camionette, Haiti, Collaboré, Tour 79, Noel, Zanmi, Hello Africa* and *Pa contrarié'm.* The blind musician Pierre Ulrick (Ti Pierre) was killed in 1991 while he was playing at a house that presumably belonged to a Macoute. The artist was only doing a gig with his fellow blind musician, the violinist Pierre Fleuvil (Amerik). They were both killed because they couldn't see their way out while other people were fleeing the massacre. Ti Pierre was only 38 years old.

Pierre, Vanel - Gong / Percussion
Vanel played with Magnum band

Pierre, Varnel * - Congas
Varnel played with Tropicana until his death.

Pierre, Wilbert – Bass

Pierre Charles, Jean Claude (Peddy) - Singer

Peddy is a pioneer of the Mini Jazz era. He started with the band Les Diplomats, but he gained his popularity with the band Les Shleu Shleu where he made a perfect duo with Gross Bébé. He sung some memorable hits with Les Shleu Shleu like *Vacanses, Maria Del Alma, Colline*. He left Haiti to immigrate to New York, but soon after, other musicians from the band came to New York and they reunited as Immortel Shleu Shleu and continued to make beautiful Haitian hits like *3 Fois 3, Minui Sonnen, Frankie Tête Chòv, and Moun Damou*.

Pierre - Louis, Brunel - Gong / Percussion

Pierre-Louis, Fréderic (Frédo) - Singer
After trying with some Konpa bands Frédo made his mark in the music scene with the group Kanpèch.

Pierre-Louis, Jean Berdy - Radio Personbality
Berdy is a radio host and the founder and President Director of Basekompa.com.

Pierre -Louis, Jean Marie - Singer
Jean Marie played with Les Lionceaux des Cayes next to Léon Dimanche.

Pierre-Louis, Lucien - Trumpet
Lucien played with Septentrional.

Pierre -Louis, Mérilus - Guitar

Pierre-Louis, Serge - Bass

Pierre - Louis, Ulrick - Saxophone
Ulrick Pierre Louis could be described not only as one of the greatest Haitian band leaders, but also as the keeper of the Septentrional legacy. In effect he has devoted all his life to making sure that the band kept a good profile, a positive image, discipline, and conduct that should be an example and a model to generations of musicians to come.
Ulrick started his professional career at the age of 18 years old playing from the "Quatour Septentrional" to "Trio Symphonia" that would later become known as "l'Orchestre Septentrional" du Cap Haitien. In the 1960s he led the band to one of the most popular Haitian bands, competing hard with the top bands of Port-au-Prince, like Compas Direct of Nemours Jean Baptiste, Cadence Rampas de Webert Sicot as well as Jazz des Jeunes under the direction of René St Aude. In the 1970s all those top saxophonists and band

leaders had succumbed to the power of the Mini Jazz revolution as the idea of the big band was fading away, Ulrick Pierre Louis was the only one of the top maestros that was able to keep his band above water and kept on working hard by making some super-hit songs that kept the band busy in Haiti and overseas. The songs *Mariana* and *Caridad* are among the super hits composed by Ulrick Pierre Louis for the band Septentrional.

Pierre -Louis, Victor - Guitar

Pierre -Louis, Yves - Congas
Played with Les Loups Noirs

Pierre Pierre, Gary - Show Promoter/Journalist

Pierrot, Dante - Saxophone
Dante played with Nemours Jean Baptiste in the 1960s along with his brother Max.

Pierrot, Laguerre - Guitar

Pierrot, Max - Saxophone
One of the two Pierrot Brothers, who next to his brother Dante, played with the saxophonist Nemours Jean Baptiste.

Pignat, Henry - Keyboard
Henry played in the Mini Jazz era with the band Les Loups Noirs. He was later hired by the band Les Vikings de la Martinique.

Pipo see Stanis, Eders

Piquion, Max - Saxophone

Piquion, Genevieve - Singer

Piquion, Géraldine - Singer

Pirogue - Band

Pitzies (Les Pitzies) Band
Band of the Mini Jazz era

Placide, Carlo - Guitar

Planet Malibou
Popular club in Long Island New York in the 1990s, the club was known as Imagine until it was sold to the late Gardy Celestin who changed the name to Planet Malibou.

Platinum - Band

Plaisir, Jean – Keyboard

Plaisir, Jean Robert Ludner - Radio Personality
Plaisir, as he is known to most people, is a popular radio announcer working for the promotion of Haitian music in the Diaspora. Plaisir has worked in New York on Radio Tropicale in the 1990s until he moved to Florida where he has worked on several radio stations over the years. In 2003, he created the show Plaisir Ambiance on the radio station Planet 17 and in 2005 he moved the show to Radio Mega. His show is heard not only in Florida but in the Bahamas as well. Plaisir is known as one of the masters of retro music bringing his audience the oldies and goodies of the past decades as well as the new hits in his variety show.

Plen Pip - Band

Point du Jour, Paul - Guitar
Played in the 1960s under the leadership of maestro Webert Sicot

Point du Jour, Paul Jr - Keyboard
Played with Toto Nécéssité in New York among other bands throughout his career

Policard, Dominique - Singer

Policard, Gaëtan - Bass

Policard, Jeff - Singer
Founder and singer of the band Ti Doz, which later became known as Fahrenheit based in New York

Policard, Réginald - Drums/Keyboard
Réginald Policard, who became one of the most respected Haitian keyboardists, actually started his musical career as a percussionist in the 1960s New York based band Ibo Combo. In the 1970s he returned to Haiti after he

completed his studies abroad. When he realized that most of his musical partners had also returned home, they recreated the band under the new name the Caribbean Sextet, this time with Réginald Policard on the keyboard. With the Caribbean Sextet Réginald has worked on the following albums: *Forte Dose, En Gala, Madougou,* and *Caribbean News,* he also had his solo albums *Lessé, Sasé Twòp, Ki sa Nou Yé, Sérénité, Vinn Avèm, Tradition* and *Gadé'w.* His sons, Jeff and Gaëtan, are members of the New York-based band Fahrenheit.

Pompilus, Yvon - Singer

Porky see: Herissé Jean Robert

Pouchon: see Duverger Auguste

Poular, Michael - Promoter
Michael is a well-known personality in the Haitian music industry. He was in the 1990s the manager of the club Planet Malibou in Long Island New York.

Poular, Steve - Singer

Pozé - Band
Konpa band based in Miami with some former members of the band D-Zine including the singers Ello and Delly François.

Pressage, Nadia - Singer

Pressoir, Michel - Singer
Michel Pressoir was one of the star singers of the 1950s. He played for the band of Edner Guignard, which had a regular show at the famous hotel El Rancho. Michel Pressoir had a strong voice and he delivered some powerful notes in the song Ti Jocelyne, which had made him popular in the early days of Haitian recordings. He was quickly recruited by Nemours Jean Baptiste. However, his days with the famous maestro didn't last long, because Michel Pressoir left Haiti to immigrate to the U.S. He had the time to record one of Nemours' most famous songs of the 1960s, the song *Infidélité.* In the 1970s and 1980s Michel lived in Hyattsville, Md, a Washington, D.C. suburb, with his Salvadorian wife. During that period he often performed in a local restaurant called the Versuvio which was later turned into a Chinese restaurant and nightclub called King Kong, one the spot that have seen the evolution of the singers Jean Claude Vivens (Agi) and Carl Frederique (Freddy) under the mentorship of Michel Pressoir. Besides playing music Michel Pressoir has earned his living as a professional truck driver and a recording studio owner.

Michel Pressoir moved to Port St Lucie Fl. where he retired.

Previlo, Jeannette - Singer

Prézau, Lesly - Guitar
Lesly played in the Mini Jazz era with the band Les Vampires.

Pri-Vice - Band

Prud'homme, Nickerson (Nicky) - Singer / Keyboard
Nicky is highly respected for his contribution to the Konpa music, especially to the Miami-based band Zenglen. He showed his support to many artists on their musical projects including the popular singer Gracia Delva. In 2005 Nicky's song *Zanmi* was a super hit that dominated the airwaves in Haiti for many months. In 2007 Nickerson left Zenglen and started to work as a solo artist. In the spring of 2008 he announced the name of his new band Harmonik with the singer Mac D on lead vocal. He also released at the same time a single titled *Jerem*.

Pro Domo Sua - Band
This band came out in New York in the late 1970s.

Prophète, Eddy - Keyboard
Eddy is a very talented musician who has played around the world as a solo artist and with other orchestras. He played in his early days with Webert Sicot as well as the band "Latino".

Provilus, Jean Claude (James) - Singer / Bass
James was one of the creator, band leader, and songwriter of the New York-based band "Partners" in the 1980"s. However James was not part of the group when the name was changed to "Phantoms". In the late 1990s he did a few shows with Phantoms, a sign that the former maestro does have a good relationship with his former band mates.

Provilus, Jean Pierre (Captain Jean) - Keyboard / Singer
Musician of the band Phantoms, Jean Pierre was actually one of the first artists with a successful rap inside of a Konpa song when he did a rap over an old Haitian tune: "*Ti fi ya ki kuit ou poule...poule la vole chodyè...*" that song got him the recognition of many in the Haitian music business. He was known as "Captain Jean" because he wore a boat captain's outfit on the album cover of the Partners. He tried ever since to dress like the Captain on many future shows.

Provins, Guy - Keyboard

Prudent, Daniel Justin - Bass

Prudent, Fritz (Napoléon) - Drums
Just like all the Konpa conga artists are playing the tempo and musical Konpa measures left by Kretzer Duroseau, we can also say that the many drummers played the tempo, measures and style left by Fritz Prudent (Napoléon) until it was modified by Smith Jean Baptiste of Les Shleu Shleu in the mini jazz era. This talented showman of Nemours' band was also known for his multitude of drum sticks in almost every pocket of his pants.

Prudent, Yves - Singer

Puissance 8 - Band

Pyronneau, Elysée - Guitar
One can say that Tabou Combo really has the secret when it comes to finding a talented guitarist to replace another one. If they were able to find Dadou Pasket to replace Albert Chancy, history basically repeated itself when it was time to fill the hole left by Pasket.
In 1976 they found a young guitarist who was studying music at Brooklyn College, even when he was very religious. Elysée Pyronneau took the opportunity to perform and eventually traveled around the world with the famous Haitian band. Elysée took control and had contributed to the many changes of Tabou Combo. The formula used by the band for a decade was changed as the band added a horn section that included saxophone-trumpet and trombone. From the mid-70s to the 1990s Elysée Pyronneau has used his guitar to make Tabou mania jump out of their socks in songs like *Mabouya, Voyé Monté, Baissez Bas, Juicy Lucy, Zap Zap* and *Tabou Mania* among many other hits.
In 1981 Elysée released his only solo album titled *Colito* under the label Marc Records.
In the 1990s Elysée quietly retired from the musical arena. Once again, Tabou Combo was able to fill the new hole with Ralph Condé.

Q

Q-Style - Band

When famous guitarist Ronald Smith left System band after many years of success, he joined his partner Réginald Benjamin in the creation of the band Rolls Royce. However, after only a few shows, Réginald went right back under the leadership of maestro Isnard Douby and the manager Marc Arthur Chevalier. Ronald Smith, on the other hand, moved on with his career with his own band "Q-Style".

Queen Dada - see Dary Daphney

R

Rafrechi - Band
Konpa band based in Maryland

Rameau, Rosler - Singer

Ramponeau, Ernst - Drums
Ernst Ramponeau had some good years with Les Frères Dejean, but his best years were with Skah Shah in the 1980s.

Rangon, Viviane - Singer

Raphael, Géroboam (Géronimo) - Producer /Promoter
Show and record producer, Géroboam Raphael is also the owner of Géronimo Records based in New York. He was also a radio announcer in the New York City Haitian community in the late 1970s. Geronimo has produced 360 Haitian albums over the years. To him the artist that brought the most profit to his company is Coupé Cloué.
At the turn of the century Geronimo moved from record productions to the production of Haitian movies.

Ravaj -Band

Ravix, Gilbert - Singer

Raymond, Alexis - Percussion

Raymond, Bernard - Bass
Bernard played with the band Super Soline in the Mini Jazz era.

Raymond, Robert (Bobby) - Bass
Bobby is a very talented and in-demand musician. He gave his expertise and services to many artists on their solo project including the late superstar Ansy Dérose. In the late 1970s he made his mark in the Konpa world with the New York based band Les Astros. He reappeared later in the next decade with the group Zin. Bobby moved on with his career as a professional musician working with non-Haitian musicians and playing other styles of music.

Raymond, Claude - Saxophone
One of the star saxophonists of the Mini Jazz era, Claude Raymond started his career with the band Les Vautours at a very young age. He stayed with the squad with the different name change over the years from Vautours, Samba Jazz (not Samba Créole), Les Fantaisites d'Haiti to Super Soline, and has shown that he was not only a talented saxophonist but a leader who was able to survive difficulties, bounce back and keep his head high. Like many in the field Claude eventually left Haiti and migrated to the U.S. where he played in Boston with the band Gemini One in the late 70s.

Raymond, Lemy - Guitar
Lemy is also a musician that stands out because of his height. Lemy is one of the original members of "Partners" which became "Phantoms". He is immortalized by the guitar performance he did in Phantoms' hit song "Vagabon".

Raymond, Max (Ti blan) - Guitar
Ti Blan started is musical career with the band Les Eperviers also at a young age before becoming one of the rhythm specialists of the Mini Jazz sensation Super Soline playing next to his brothers Claude, Bernard and Roland. He was also among the members who tried to revive the good old days in the late 70s in Boston with the band Gemini One.

Raymond, Michel - Guitar
Michel played with the band Norma de Léogane, and later with Webert Sicot.

Raymond, Roland - Bass /Congas
Roland played with the band Super Soline in the Mini Jazz era first on congas and later on bass working next to his brothers Bernard, Claude and Ti Blan.

Rayon X - Band

Reflex - Band
The albums *Blazé* released in 2004 and *Reflex live* are their only known recordings.

Regis, Mario - Drums

Rejouis, Fontane - Singer

Relaxx Band - Band

In the early 1980s a group of young men of Erasmus High School put together a Konpa band in the heart of Brooklyn, called Relaxx Band. One of the purposes of Relaxx Band was to replace the platinum bands like Skah Shah, Accolade, System Djet-X and Tabou in their regular shows while they were on their summer tours. The band didn't waste any time to having their first and only hit *Puela,* and suddenly the band that was supposed to be a substitute to others became the competition.

The song "*Puela*" really helped in the discovery of the singer Patrick Sammy (Pachouko) and the saxophonist Jean Vonksy who is now a medical doctor. Jean worked also for System Band in the 1980s.

Rempler, Kedner - Gong / Percussion
Kedner played with Les Ambassadeurs in the Mini Jazz era.

Rémy, Jean - Congas
Jean played with Jazz Des Jeunes.

René, Alix - Violin
When Tabou Combo first came out in the 1960s the band formerly known as Los Incognitos was playing with both violin and accordion thus making their sound very different from any band of the Mini Jazz era. The violinist Alix René was the man who provided that sweet sound in the mist of the rhythm of Tabou Combo.

René, Richard - Keyboard
Richard played with the band Jazz Des Jeunes and later with Webert Sicot. He created the troubadour band Les 7 Vedettes, maker of the mega hit song *2 chances* in the 1970's.

Renélique, Sarah - Singer

Reshka Promotion - Show Promotion Company
Reshka stands for: Respect-Elite, Satisfaction, Knowledge, Achievement
It was founded by the show promoter Réginald Roseme, the company is based in New York.

Résil, Gary - Guitar
Gary Résil is one of the musicians who were not a star in Haiti prior to making it big in New York in the 1970s. He came out with the band Les Gypsies de Queens and he later played with Skah Shah as a third guitarist, working under the shadow of Mario Mayala in the late 70s to early 1980s. He spent a few years with Skah Shah, during which he put a serious contribution in the album *Forever/La Vie A Belle*. By the end of the 1980s he joined Tabou Combo to fill the hole left by Jean Claude Jean, there again the guitarist proved that he was not only a good guitarist but also a good music composer and arranger as he put his touch in the albums *Aux Antilles, Zap Zap* and *Kitém Fè Zafem*. The Tabou Combo song *Laura* is considered one of his most well-known works.

Reynold, Joseph - Bass

Richard, Edouard - Guitar
Edouard Richard started his career with the Mini Jazz Shupa Shupa when he was only a teenager. He moved to New York where he became the star guitarist of the band Original Shleu Shleu for many years. He also took part in some of the Mini All Stars albums and world tours. His band, "Fwèt" didn't make it big, however Edouard Richard will always be a respected guitarist who contributed to the popularity of the Konpa. Edouard Richard also played with the bands Mystik, Bazouka and Skah Shah.

Richard, Faniel – Guitar

Riché Jean - Guitar

Riché, Pierre - Singer
Pierre Riché is one of the pioneers of the Haitian music and founder of the "Trio des Jeunes", which later became Jazz des Jeunes. Pierre Riché's voice was heard for many decades in the country, as the song *Madan Marié* was a hit in the country and is still a classic remembered even now by music lovers. The artist moved to the U.S., where he eventually abandoned the professional music scene for other interests.

Ricken, Ulysse - Guitar
Ulysse is a freelance guitarist who has worked for many years with different artists and bands.

Rigaud, Jean Lesly - Bass

Rimpel, Kedner - Gong / Drums
In the Mini Jazz era Kedner played with Les Ambassadeurs, one of the platinum bands of the Mini Jazz era. He later became a drummer.

Riské - Band
This all-female Haitian band was the very first in that format in New York. The band took the music by storm with the song *Alphabet*. However the project didn't last long because the band was poorly managed. Note that the first all-Haitian female band was Top Girls in the town of Cap Haitien. Unfortunately there are no recording or pictures available.

Rivera, Althée - Singer
Played with jazz Des Jeunes

Robergeau, Charles - Congas

Robert, Frangel - Singer
Frangel is one of the first singers and star of the band Jazz Capois.

Roc, Hans - Keyboard

Roc, Jimmy - Drums

Roc, Réginald - Saxophonist
Réginald showed the Konpa world that he was in the 1970s one of the best tube blowers as many saxophonists in the French Caribbean Islands imitated his style. Under the leadership of Réginald Roc the band Les Loups Noirs dominated the airwaves and many live shows, particularly in Martinique.

Roche, Guetary (Pè Guiguit or Guito) - Drums
Guetary is better known as "Pè Guiguit", a name that was given to him by his friend, the singer Michel Martelly. At a young age Guito had the chance to be a substitute for Herman Nau in the popular band Tabou Combo. At the turn of the century he helped created the band 718 Boys. After a misunderstanding among the members 718 Boys became two separate bands. Some members moved on by creating the band Tempo, while Guitary worked on his own band G-5. In 2007, Pè Guiguit lent his services to his friend Sexy Frantzy. He is known in the Konpa music arena as one of the best dressed Haitian artists.

Rockmasters.com
Popular website about Haitian music and upcoming shows

Rodrigue, Jhonny * - Singer

Rodrigue, Ronald – Singer
In 1991 with the help of Konpa icons Claude Marcelin and Ansyto Mercier he released his album *"Vini Danse"*.

Rodrigues, Georges - Congas

Roger, Nicolas - Bass

Rolls, Frantz - Guitar

Romain, André - Singer
André is one of 1970s star singers of the band Ibo Combo.

Romain, Emile - Drums
Emile played with the band Les Fantaisites de Carrefour in the Mini Jazz era.

Romain, Joseph Yves - Saxophonist

Romain, Pierrault - Saxophone
Pierrault was the star saxophonist of the band Les Legendaires de Delmas in the Mini Jazz era. In New York he resurfaced in the Konpa scene on sax tenor next to Daniel (Ti Sax) Alcé on alto sax in band A.A. Express under the leadership of the drummer/composer Arsène Appolon. He stayed with the band when the name was changed to Astros. In the 1980s he followed Arsène Appolon to Haiti leaving his home and family in Queens New York to create the band Skah Shah d'Haiti. Unfortunately that band only lasted a couple of years and Pierrault went back to New York and has moved on with other priorities.

Romain, Thony - Saxophone
Thony played with Shoogar Combo in the 1980s.

Romain, Tony *- Guitar
Tony played with Bossa Combo.

Romulus, Colson - Singer

Romulus, Jacques - Drums

Rosefort, Rulx - Congas

Rulx played with the band Sakad.

Roseman, Joshua - Trombone

Roseme, Réginald - Promoter
As far back as he can remember he idolized his grandfathers, who were exceptional businessmen, and their demeanor and ethics in business relations. The first one worked as the Director or Product Quality Assurance for a major Haitian sugar manufacturer and the other was a self-made businessman. Another significant influence was his uncle, Andre Dorismond, who was a member of Sicot's band - one of the innovators of Konpa music. Each of these men contributed to building the environment that would mold him into the man that created Reshka Promotions/Marketing.

Rosemond, Guy - Guitar
In the 1970s Guy Rosemond led his band Samba Créole to victory at two different carnival music competitions. Samba Créole won first place for the songs *Caporal* and *Colé Boyo*. Guy was known among his musician as a "No Nonsense Maestro", he was the author and arranger of most of the songs of Samba Créole. Under his leadership many musicians known as superstars in the business like Mario de Volcy and Frantz Joseph (Fanfan Kè Kal) have learned the fundamentals of the Konpa business and have acquired a certain degree of discipline from the young leader. Guy Rosemond is the author of songs that describe the social life of the Haitian people His songs also carried a message or advice to the public especially when one take into consideration songs like: *Ti Paul, Chance et Malheur, Silly Girl* and *Principe Pa Nou* among others. However it is the song *Caporal* that has contributed the most to the success of Guy Rosemond and the popularity of the Mini Jazz Samba Créole.

Rosental, Serge - Guitar
Although Sergo is a well know guitarist and band leader he is also a good accordionist. He was recruited to be the guitarist of the band Les Manfoubens which later became Les Shleu Shleu. When his partners Tony Moise, Smith Jean Baptiste and others left the country and moved to New York, Sergo stayed in Haiti and led a new squad of young musicians to a second version of Shleu Shleu that included Loubert Chancy, Cubano, Zouzoule, Ti Frè, Mario Mayala, and Arsène Appolon. Unfortunately history repeated itself as the second squad followed the footsteps of the members that became known in New York as the Original Shleu Shleu by also moving to New York themselves where they created the band Skah Shah. Sergo Rosenthal also took part in the Zotobré project with the legendary saxophonist Webert Sicot and the drummer Almando Keslin.

Rosier, Wilner - Saxophone

Rossignol, François (Fanfan) - Singer
Star singer of the band La Ruche de Léogane, Fanfan showed the world that he can really sing as good as the bird "rossignol" in his delivery in the song *2 Jumeaux*, the band's most popular song ever.

Rossignol Noirs - Band
The album Kaloj Kok, released by Mini Records, is the only known recording about the group.

Rotel Records
Records production company.

Roumer, Maxime - Guitar

Rousseau, Hercule * - Congas
Hercule has played with the band Jazz des Jeunes for most of his career. He then became one of the most popular show producers in the business of the 1970s and 1980s

Rousseau, Vaillant - Singer

Rouzeau, Gina - Keyboard

Rouzeau, Richard - Singer
Richard came out as one of the three star singers of the band Papash, next to Wydens and Ralph Condé.

Rouzier, Fabrice - Keyboard / Producer
Fabrice first got the attention of the public when he appeared on the televised music contest organized by American Airlines in the second part of the 1980s. That was the first time he introduced his group Mizik Mizik. A few years later Fabrice became not only a musician but a music producer as he helped Michel Martelly to achieve stardom in the release of Micky's first hit song *Ou La La*. By the early 1990s Fabrice left Haiti and moved to the Washington D.C. area where he resided in Laurel Md while attending the University of Maryland. With music still in his blood, Fabrice used a corner of his apartment and turned it into the "Bois Moquette Studio" and it is in that period that he also sequenced albums for a few bands and artists, like Jacques Sauveur Jean, Zépon a Washington, D.C. based band that Fabrice also performed live with

while residing in Maryland.

During that period of the first half of the 1990s, Fabrice Rouzier was also called by Tabou Combo to replace Ernst Marcelin, who was assassinated in Brooklyn. Fabrice would not only do the studio work for Tabou Combo, but also managed to travel around the world with Tabou despite his classes at University of Maryland.

Once he graduated in the mid 1990s, Fabrice returned to Haiti where he is working in the family owned automobile business "Sunoto". Fabrice didn't waste any time upon his return to putting his band Mizik Mizik back on the rail and in the front burner of the Haitian music scene.

Under his label, Bois Moquette, Fabrice released the Mizik Mizik album *Farinen*. However, the next album of the band titled *De Ger* was sold to Hibiscus Records a non-Haitian company. After the album *De Ger*, Mizik Mizik lost their lead singers as both Vardy Pharel and Emmanuel Obas moved to the U.S., where they created the band "Lov". Fabrice continued to produce other unknown artists and put them on the map in the Haitian music arena while he also had to deal with damage control of his own band. He introduced to the world Eric Charles who he recruited from a dismantled D.P. Express. Eric proved that Fabrice had made the right choice in the Mizik Mizik album *Blakawout*. In the album *Blakawout*, Fabrice made a turn by putting a Twoubadou feeling in some of the songs on the album. That move was very appreciated by the music lovers and Fabrice capitalized on the idea by releasing the album *Haiti Twoubadou* with the collaboration of some of the top Haitian superstars. The album *Haiti Twoubadou* was such a huge success that many artists left their own work to be part of the Haiti Twoubadou world tour, making Fabrice Rouzier one of the most respected and innovative Haitian music producers of his generation.

His new company Soley Sound is a record label that is proudly producing new artists like Belo, Jah Nesta, and Tifane among others

In 2007 Fabrice traveled to Cameroon Africa with the singer Bélo to represent Haiti at a yearly musical contest organized by Radio France Inter. With a squad of musicians led by Fabrice Rouzier, the artist that he produced, Bélo walked out of Africa with as the winner of the international music contest.

Rythmo Band d'Alfred Moise – Band

S

S.S One - Band
This band came out in the early 1980s and they released a total of three albums. Their song *Manman Zizi,* released in 1985 got the attention of many people.

Safari Combo - Band
This band came out in the Carrefour neighborhood in the 1970s with star singer Assade Francoeur who made several hits for the band including the song "*Wi Parrain*" and with the voice of the young Harold Joseph the band delivered one of their best hit songs *"Dé ba ba".*
When most of the stars left the band to created Super 9, Safari Combo didn't survive long and eventually ended all operation while Super 9 became one of the best bands of the 1970s.

Saget, Pierre - Guitar /Singer

Sakad - Band
Band of the Nouvel Jenerasyon era

Sakaj – Band
Band of the Nouvel Jenerasyon era

Sainsmir, Martivel - Congas
One of the most popular congas players of the band Septentrional, the man who kept the tempo going for the distinguished sound of the band Septentrional.

Saint Aimé, Jean Mécène - Keyboard

Saint Aude, René Charles * - Saxophone
The legendary saxophonist Charles René St Aude was born in St Michel de l'Attalaye in 1909. His family moved to Gonaives in 1911 where he also went to school. His music instructor and mentor was Ostra Bernier and his first instrument was the flute. In 1935 he joined La Fanfare des Gonaives and by 1943 he was already playing popular music with the band Quinteto Des Jeunes, which later became Conjunto Des Jeunes. The name was changed to Jazz Des Jeunes under the leadership of Rene St Aude.
His music rival was Nemours Jean Baptiste, the founder of Compas Direct and

the two started something that musicians have passed on from generation to generation, "The Haitian Music Polemic" even when Nemours is known for casting the first stone.

In 1972 Jazz Des Jeunes moved to New York since most full bands couldn't compete with the Mini Jazz Movement with bands like Tabou Combo, Gypsies, Samba Creole, Difficiles, Les Ambassadeurs, Les Pachas, Shupa Shupa, Les Fantaisistes, Les Shleu Shleu, Les Loups Noirs and others were getting most of the gigs and radio airtime.

Suffering from hypertension and being a diabetic, Rene Saint Aude was ordered by his doctor to stop playing music. Even after he retired from playing live he was still managing his record store and signing the rare and few contracts for his band.

Charles Rene Saint Aude died in Kings Brook Jewish Hospital of New York in 1995.

Saint Fleur, Mackenson - Guitar
Musician of the band Hangout, he played in previous years with Koudjay, and 509.

Saint Victor, Jean Michel (Zouzoule) - Singer
Zouzoule came to Port-Au Prince at an early age from Cap Haitien. He joined the school St. Louis de Gonzague and became a member of the all-boys school choir. His sister Nicole St Victor was already a well-known singer/music instructor at St Trinité a well-known Catholic school in Haiti. However, Zouzoule started to hang out around the Mini Jazz music scene particularly with Les Shleu Shleu in which he eventually became one of the background vocalists.

Zouzoule got his break to move on as a lead singer of the famous band when the singer J.C. Pierre Charles (Peddy) moved to the U.S. with some members of the first squad like Smith Jean Baptiste and Tony Moise to create the band Original Shleu Shleu in New York.

As the new lead vocalist of the second version of Les Shleu Shleu, Zouzoule made his mark in the musical arena of the early 70s with songs like *St Valentin, Machann Yo, Cap Grandou, Joumou Pa Donnen Kalbass, and Solanges* among others. Shleu Shleu made the acquisition of another star singer Jean Elie Telfort (Cubano) and just like Peddy and the first squad did a few years earlier, Cubano and the second squad moved to New York and created the band Skah Shah in 1974. Zouzoule once again had the hard labor to keep the Shleu Shleu project alive in Haiti by being the lead vocalist of a third version. With the success of Skah Shah in the Haitian diaspora, Zouzoule made the choice to leave his country in the mid-70s to collaborate with his former partners of the second squad and enjoy the glory days of the new Kings (Shah) of New York sharing the front line of the band once again with Cubano.

By the 1980s Zouzoule was already one of the superstars on the Haitian music industry and one of the two voices that identify the popular Skah Shah # 1. Since he was a more disciplined musician than Cubano, he often had the duty to start the shows, even at times singing some of the songs that were recorded with Cubano on lead vocal. Many people who used to follow Skah Shah know that Cubano had the bad habit of being late for work.

The hard work of Zouzoule paid off as the band leader and composers of the band made him the singer of choice in hit songs like *Men Numéwo A, This Is It, Doing It, Caroline* and *America* among others. When the band broke up in the early 1990s, the voice of Zouzoule once again had the duty to lead some musicians in the Bazouka project on several albums like *Zo Pèlin, Plézy Gayé, Kann Kalé* and *Soleil*.

At the turn of the century the musicians of Skah Shah managed to get back together, trying to patch up their differences and to revive the good old days. Zouzoule didn't waste any time giving his services once again and went on tour with the musicians who have over many years shared the best years in his musical career. In 2006 Skah Shah released the album *Lagué Diazz La* and despite his gray hair Zouzoule still has his wonderful and strong voice.

Saint Victor, Lyonel - Congas
Played with Les Difficiles in the 1960s

Saintil, Alix - Drums

Saintilus, Max - Bass

Saintine, Edner - Singer
Edner played with Ensemble Select de Coupé Cloué.

Saint Val, Tanya - Singer
Although she was not born in Haiti, the French Caribbean Diva took the Haitian music scene by storm in the 1980s with the song *Ti Chalè*. During her successful career she even lived in Haiti in the 1990s, where she became a member of the group Magnum Band. Tanya moved on with her career and left Haiti, but continued to be part of the Konpa scene.

Saint Vil, Eddy - Guitar
Eddy is known as one of the guitarist and founders of the popular New York based band Zin. He is the author of some of Zin's hit songs. In 2007 Alan Cavé released his solo album titled *De La Tête Aux Pieds*. Ironically one of the best songs of the album the song *Happy Birthday* was written by Eddy St Vil.

Sainvil, Alix - Congas

Sainvil Fleuvius - Singer /Congas

Sainvil, Lycius - Saxophone
Lycius played with the band Septentrional.

Salgado, José - Guitar
José played with Gypsies in the Mini Jazz era

Salvant, Tinès - Singer

Samba Créole - Band
One of the popular bands in the 1970s, Samba Créole came out with one great carnival song after another like *Caporal* and *Colé Boyo.* It is the band that popularized the catchy phrase "*Padi sa, padi sa - padi sa padi sa sé lwanj o - alam poko mouri yo poté kod pou yo maré samba*". The song was originally made by the Band à Pié "*Le Peuple S'amuse.*" The administrators of the hospital Asile Français sent the police to stop a Samba Créole practice session at the Rosemond family's home next door. Since this incident Samba Créole resumed practice on Rue Chareron in the back yard of Antonio Milfort the President of Le Peuple S'amuse, and many believe that the song was made to show support to Samba Créole which later put the catchy phrase on their album in the song "*Caporal*". Samba Créole was the band in which some great artists started their careers like the drummer Mario de Volcy, the bassist Joseph Tabutau (Djo Light) the guitarist and band leader Guy Rosemond, the drummer/gonguist and now sound engineer Ernst Denis, among others.

Samba Jazz - Band
Samba Jazz started as Les Vautours. The band didn't last long nor didn't have the success of Samba Créole. Some members moved on to create the band "Super Soline d'Haiti" which had much success in the 70s.

Samedi, Daniel - Guitar
If Guy Rosemond was the motor of Samba Creole, Daniel Samedi was the transmission of the band. Daniel developed a unique style that until now is never imitated. He retired from Konpa music when he moved to New York in the 1980s.

Sammy, Patrick (Pachouko) - Singer
In the early 1980s a group of young man of Erasmus High School put together

a Konpa band in the heart of Brooklyn call Relaxx Band. One of the purposes of Relaxx Band was to replace the platinum bands like Skah Shah, Accolade, System Djet-X and Tabou in their regular shows while they were on their summer tours. With the voice of Pachouko, the band wasted no time to have their first and only hit, *Puela* and suddenly the band that was supposed to be a substitute to others has became the competition.

Most of the kids couldn't resist the heat of the New York Konpa scene of the 1980s and eventually moved on with their lives by going to college while others joined other bands. In the 1980s Pachouko traveled to many other cities playing with different bands from G.P. Express in Washington to Frères Déjean in Haiti, but for some reason never regain his minutes of fame of the early 80s.

Sanon, Agazou - Congas

Sanon, Ilgane - Singer / Percussions
Musician of Les Frères Dodo

Sanon, Michel Antoine - Guitar

Sansarick, Pradel - Promoter
Pradel was in the 1980s the manager of the band Washington Express.

Sansasyon - Band

Sarita, Champagne - Singer

Sauveur, Jean Sony - Promoter / Radio Personality

Sauvignan, Carlo - Congas
Carlo played with Les Fantaisistes de Carrefour in the Mini Jazz era.

Sauvignon, Justin (Tonton Noel) - Singer
Tonton Noel played with the band Super Soline in the Mini Jazz era.

Savius, Ludovic (Chinois) - Gong
Even though he is known for playing with many bands from his days with Les As de Carrefour to being seen of the video of the song Moun Damou of the New York based band Les Shleu Shleu, Chinois will always be known as the showman of the band Channel 10. He also played with the bands Sexy One and Macho Band in New York in his long musical career as a percussionist. Savius Ludovic has a Chinese look, which is the reason he is called 'Chinois",

which is the French and Creole translation of the word "Chinese."

Scorpio - Band
Universel – d'Haiti - La Crème

The band Scorpio started in 1977 as Robert Martino returned to Haiti to give a new life to his band Gypsies. However the music was changing and under the influence of the French Caribbean bands horn sections and new keyboard sounds the management team decided to change the name of the band from Gypsies to Scorpio. The name came up in the middle of a practice session as the guitarist Reynold Nader (Sinsin) was bitten by a Scorpion.

The first formation of Scorpio consisted of the guitarists Robert Martino and Reynold Nader (Sinsin) the percussionists Patrick Louis, Georges Jean Louis and Frantz Paul (Kiko) and the singer Olson Jean Louis on lead vocal. The horn section had Jules Pagié who would later joined Bossa Combo, Reynold Menelas and Fritz Dorvilien. The last two moved to New York with the keyboardist Claude Montreuil to be part of the band Astros.

The first album of Scorpio captivated the heart of many and gave the band a new breed of fans. Before long, the public started to found out that the rivalry between Difficiles and Gypsies has been turned to D.P/Scorpio. The battle started in the late 70s with the same teams under new names and new sounds to the benefit and amusement of the fans.

In their first album titled *Ensem Ensem* under the label Macaya Records, Scorpio offered a total of 7 songs that include *Ensem Ensem*, *Tandé* and the carnival song *Pa Colé* as the hit songs. By the second album, some of the musicians have moved to the U.S. Patrick was replaced by Eddy Louis and the horn section was completely new with Mario Denis (Ti Chouk) and Saur Gelin (Samsonito). The keyboardist Nathan Montreuil replaced his brother, Claude. On that album, produced in 1978 again by Macaya, the band offered six songs with *Pélérinage*, *Bling Ding Guing* and the 1978 carnival song *Colé Sou Yo*.

By 1979 the new team was in full control of the market and knew which direction they wanted to go as they released two albums during the year with two different record labels. The album *Min Yayade La* was released under the label Macaya and the album *Map Mandé Courage* came out under the label Mini Records. By the end of the year the singer Olson Jean Louis moved to the U.S. and put an end to his short musical career, he was replaced by the star singer of Shoogar Combo Gracia Jean Philippe (Ti Kit) who will became the principal rival of D.P. Express singer Ti Manno putting even more spices in the musical polemic of the two top bands of Pétion Ville.

In 1980, Scorpio released the album titled *1980-M'pap Krazé,* like a statement to say that, despite the changes in personnel the band was there to last. One thing that was in Scorpio's favor is the loyalty of the Scorpio fans to the band. The name Scorpio and the Blue & White flag of the band meant so much to them. By 1981 the singer Ti Kit was in full control of the band's front line and Scorpio was at its peak time. The band was extremely busy traveling throughout the country to play even in the remote areas to please their fans. The band also was in demand in the Haitian diaspora and the Caribbean Islands. The album *Gypsy Fever* had a huge success with the song *Christiane* and the carnival song *Kaskèt Sou Tête.* With success come a lot of money and finally the band leaders found a problem that they were unable to manage. The leaders were being accused of not being fair to the hard-working musicians when it come to profit sharing. That troubled time came with the resignation of the band leader and hit maker Robert Martino. Martino left the country and he released an album with the name Scorpio under the label Rotel Records in 1982 with the song *Opa Opa.* In the meantime Martino was brutally attacked in the song *Aprann Viv* in the album titled *Vacances* by the musicians of the band who had regrouped under the new name **Scorpio Fever** and found a replacement for Martino in the guitarist François Mary St. Preux. Scorpio Fever's first album was released by Chancy Records in 1982 also. In 1983 the band released the album *Homage à Claudy* in loving memory of their keyboardist the late Claudy St. Jean Marty, who had played earlier for Panorama des Cayes.

 In the years that followed most of the stars of the band had moved on with their careers, and the country has seen many musicians being part of a band named Scorpio or with the Scorpio tag in their names: Scorpio Universel, Universel Scorpio, Original Scorpio, Scorpio de Robert Martino, Scorpio D'Haiti, Original Classic Scorpio D'Haiti, and Les Scorpios which had success with the song *Ké Makak La (Ti Moune Yo)* after the downfall of President Jean Claude Duvalier in 1986. The band **Scorpio La Crème,** created in New York by some of the superstars of the early 80s, like the singer Gracia Jean Philippe (Ti Kit), Mario and Samsonito. The band Scorpio La Crème was very promising and was apparently going to change the direction of the musical scene in New York. Unfortunately the premature death of the singer Ti Kit also put an end to the dream and the career of his fellow members, who decided to let go of the Scorpio legacy.

In 2007 a band out of Canada released a carnival song under the name Scorpio. The song had all the elements and the proper ingredients of the real Scorpio formula. Many observers were asking if the Scorpion was about to bite again. Maybe we have not seen the end of it yet after 30 years.

Seducteurs (Les Seducteurs de Pétion -Ville) - Band
Band of the Mini Jazz era

Séjour, Harry - Saxophone
Harry played with Webert Sicot in the band Cadence Rampas. He was part of the squad that stayed with the singer André Dorismond in the creation of the band Super Choucoune 70 when Webert Sicot moved to the U.S. In 1985 Harry Séjour, while living in Maryland, created with Jean Claude Vivens and other young musicians of Washington, D.C. the band Washington Express. A couple of years later he decided to quit and has been playing ever since for a community church in Washington, D.C.

Séjour, Weiner - Singer

Select (Select de New York) - Band

Sénat, Charles - Guitar

Sénatus, Alphonse - Congas

Sénatus, Bobby - Keyboard

Sénatus Guerino – Congas
Musician of the Miami based band Gabel

Séney, Evens – Congas

Septentrional du Cap (Septen) - Band

While the big bands of Nemours, Sicot and Jazz Des Jeunes were not able to compete with the success of the Mini Jazz movement, the big band Septentrional managed to be as popular as the mini bands of the 1960s and 1970s. Septen was the only band with a special radio show on Sundays on M.B.C, one of Port-au- Prince's radio stations with the most listeners at the time. The show *Club Septen De Port-au-Prince* used to air with not only music, but other forms of entertainment like jokes, games, trivia, and more. Septen, in the meantime, was also the king of Cap Haitien and, as a company; the band had a restaurant, and a movie theater, among other businesses. Septentrional was created in 1948 by musicians of two different groups. In the early to mid 1940s there were some groups playing at the neighborhood parties call "Fètes Champètres". Most of these parties, which are part of the Haitian culture, usually take place to celebrate a saint of the Catholic religion in different part of the country. The two well-known bands of the Northern part of Haiti were the "Trio Symphonia" with Jacques Mompremier, Jacob Germain, and Ulrick Pierre Louis who was only a school-boy. The second band was the "Quatuor Septentrional", with Raymond Jean Louis, Fidele Léandre, Théo Pierre and Jean Meneau. It is that collaboration that led to the creation of the band Septentrional the longest-working Haitian band of all time, the band that many fans call "La Boule De Feu Du Cap Haitien" (The Ball Of Fire Of Cap Haitien).

It would take the arrival of the late producer Marc Duverger, of Marc Records, in the field of music recording to release the band's first album in the 1960s. Since the band was around more than a decade, they had many songs already prepared, so a series of albums followed which made it impossible for any Mini Jazz to keep up with Septen in the 1960s as Haitian record productions and Haitian songs getting radio airtime was something quite new to the population.

Septentrional took the country by storm with their style of music that sounded different from the Port-au-Prince based bands. It had in it a reminder that the music is somewhat original and typical to the life of the Northern provinces with the congas and percussion lines bringing the feeling of the rhythms of the natives. The band was playing some hot songs and some nice boleros that were new to most people, but not to those that used to follow the band in the early days in the town of Cap Haitien. Therefore hit songs like *Mambo Bossu, Ti Yayi, Vent Tempète, Chauffeur Automobile, Tambou Frapé, Ti Fiya, La vie Gaçon, Mona ,Giselle, Fredeline, Septen Tu Vois La Mer, Cité Du Cap Haitien, Louise Marie,* and *Marie Josée* among others were déja vu to the followers of the band, but new to the new acquired fans of Port-au-Prince and other provinces. By the end of the 1960s Septentrional was so popular that they were chosen to provide music on the float of one of Port-au- Prince's most prestigious social club that often came out as the band "Diabolo" of the "Bas Peu De Chose" neighborhood.

The band captivated the music world outside of Haiti and began their regular trips outside of the country particularly to the U.S. and Canada. Today in the Haitian diaspora the band has a committee called "Co-Septen", based in New York that looks over the interest of the band in the diaspora.

Septentrional is one of the first Haitian bands, if not the first, to perform at

Madison Square Garden one of the largest entertainment arenas in New York City. The band has backed up many visiting international artists in Haiti and was the band of choice of the legendary Haitian comedian Languichatte Débordus to record his albums. Many great Haitian musicians are part, or have been part of Septentrional. Among them we can name Guy Durosier, Roger Colas, Jacques François, Alfred Moise and Ernst Léandre among other great artists. The band leader, guardian and mentor Maestro Ulrick Pierre Louis retired, but at times traveled with the band or made a special appearance. The singer Michel Tassy, despite his old age continued to perform and tour the world with the band that has in this 21st century, a new squad of musicians who are, for the most part less than half the age of Septentrional. That lead us to say that Septentrional is not only a band it is an Institution.

Septen Junior - Band
This band was a group of young men in the town of Cap Haitien playing the style of Septen.

Sévere, Hubert - Bass

Sexy Band - Band

Shadow Band - Band
This band is based in the state of Connecticut. It was created in the 1990s by the Milbrun family.

Shamba # 1 de Boston - Band

Sham Sham - Band

Sharp Records
Haitian owned record company

Shleberts - Band
This band was created in the Mini Jazz era by the Walker brothers. They never released any record, but Les Shleberts was the first Mini Jazz to appear live on Télé Haiti in the 1960s. The band didn't last long because the brothers moved to Washington, D.C. where they continue their musical career playing with Hispanic bands, thus some of them are married to Hispanic women. The singer Georges Walker became a keyboard player and he often used to perform with Zépon. In 2004, with his help, the singer Jean Claude Vivens (Agi) created the band Trankill in Washington, D.C. His son Micky Walker is a

well-known sound engineer in the Washington metropolitan area and also the lead keyboardist of Trankill.

Shleu Shleu - Band

In the mid-60s, the young men of Haiti took control of the destiny of the popular music by starting a music revolution by reducing the number of musicians on stage in a new format that was baptized the "Mini Jazz" by Nemours Jean Baptiste himself. In the forefront of the revolution was the band Les Shleu Shleu. The band started as Les Manfoubens, and by the time they came out with their first album in 1967, the name Shleu Shleu was already a household name since the band was created on Dec. 22, 1965 under the leadership of their manager/owner Dada Djackaman.

In their first album the band offered to music lovers a multitude of hits that will forever immortalize the artists. Songs like *Vacances, Alfredo, Péché A La Ligne, Dada 4/3,* and *Haiti Mon Pays,* to name a few. In the years that followed Shleu Shleu proved that it was not by chance that they captured the attention of the world as they released in 1968 an album with ten memorable hits that included *Maille, Deviné, Café Au Lait, Ti Came, Dans La Vie, Boutillier* and the slow song *Haiti Terre De Soleil* a song that has over the years made many Haitians living in the diaspora cry as they feel nostalgic and remember the motherland. By 1969, Shleu Shleu released another album that included the hits *7 jours De La Semaine, Moun Damou* and *Ceremony Loa.* Once again Shleu Shleu proved that they could write some of the best slow song in *Grille Ta Cigarette* and *Minuit Sonin.*

As the music of Shleu Shleu dominated the airwaves at the end of the decade, the band started to travel outside of the country and decided to stay in New York, where they released the album *Tête Chauve.* When the band members found out that Dada Djackaman had regrouped in Haiti with some new musicians under the same name, the first squad of Les Shleu Shleu composed of Tony Moise, J.C. Pierre Charles and Smith Jean Baptiste decided to call themselves the **Original Shleu Shleu** in order to show to the world that they were the members that started the Mini Jazz revolution and the authors of the super hits of the late 60s.

Dada Djackaman wasted no time replacing the departed musicians and introduced to the world in 1970 some new talents that were going to become some of the top Haitian superstars of all time.

In effect, the new Shleu Shleu came out with the album *Cé La Ou Yé* with the saxophonist Loubert Chancy, the guitarists and cousins Mario Mayala and Jhonny Frantz Toussaint, and the singers Jean Michel St Victor (Zouzoule) and Jean Elie Telfort (Cubano), as well as the drummer Yves Arsène Appolon, all supported by the band leader the guitarist Serge Rosenthal, who decided not to follow the first squad in New York on the adventurous road.

In 1971 Dada celebrated the 6th Anniversary of the creation of Les Shleu Shleu with an album titled *6eme Anniversaire* with another nine songs that include *Sept Péchés Capitaux, Trois Bébé, Quatre Saisons* and *Cap Grandou.*

In the meantime, in New York the Original Shleu Shleu continued to perform mostly the hits of the 60s and introduced in 1971 some new songs like *Observé La Cadence* and *Cé Vérité* in an album with a female name *Sandy.* Around that time the New York based band started to use the acronym "O.S.S" for Original Shleu Shleu. With one Shleu Shleu in New York and one in Haiti there began a silent competition. Even when neither of the bands had ever launched any attack on the other, people were anxious to see which one was more productive.

In 1973 the second squad living in Haiti got the attention of the public when they released a song for the National Football Team on the occasion of the CONCACAF soccer tournament a Pre-World Cup Qualifier Games held in Haiti in 1973. The motivation song with the name of the football stars like Manno Sanon, Philippe Vorbes, Claude Barthelemy among others was played on the radio every day prior to, and during the tournament as the nation sang to the catchy chorus parts "*Al Bay Goal*" and "*Nou Pral A Munich*" referring to Munich Germany where the Haiti National team played against Italy, Argentina and Poland in the 1974 World Cup Finals. The band also released the album *Acé Frapé* with the songs *Solanges, Belle Ti Machann* and *Banda.*

As the band started to tour the world they released in 1974 the album *Succes Des Shleu Shleu A Paris* with a picture taken in front of the Eiffel Tower. That album had the songs *Yola, Reviens, Douceur La Vie* and *Caroline.* After their success in Paris, the band set foot in New York where they decided to make their new home base. However, there was a problem. New York already had a band with the name Shleu Shleu so the newcomers had to brainstorm to find a new name and the band Skah Shah was created with Loubert Chancy as the band leader.

To mark their territory the first squad Original Shleu Shleu released two albums back to back: *En Filant Les Aiguilles* in 1974 and the album *Les Shleu Shleu A New York* in 1975 with the hit songs *Trou Crabes, L'amitié* and *L'évangile.* In those two albums the original members put on a lot of energy and tried their best, as the New York market that they had been in control for more that five years was now being shared by other stars arriving from Haiti, not only the newly-formed band Skah Shah but also another great competitor and hit maker by the name of Tabou Combo.

While the bands in New York continued to produce wonderful songs, the courageous Dada Jacaman tried another time to pick up the broken pieces and introduce the saxophonist Gerard Daniel and a third new squad in the album *Toujours Le Même 4/3* with mostly songs that were made by the second squad prior to living the country. By 1976 Dada was working with some members that were not able to get the name Shleu Shleu on the upper level of the music charts in the competitive market. The music was taking another turn with the addition of the full horn section and modern keyboards, which put an end to the Mini Jazz era. Nevertheless Dada Jacaman managed to release a few more albums in the late 70s with his fourth version of Les Shleu Shleu and also introduced to the world some more talented musicians, like the gonguist Joseph Durandis (Joe Gong) and the late singer Gracia Jean Philippe (Ti Kit) in the song *Crapeau.*

Ti Kit also made it big in the industry with the bands Shoogar Combo and later with Scorpio prior to his death in New York.

The Original Shleu Shleu made several attempts to revive the success of the good old days. However, the music had made a turn that the pioneers of the Mini Jazz movement failed to comprehend and they were not able to keep up. Unlike Tabou Combo, Skah Shah, Bossa Combo and others, Original Shleu Shleu didn't modify their style. They didn't add younger members nor introduce the new sounds cards that attract younger followers. The members were mostly interested in playing their past successful hit songs or, at least attracting nostalgic fans of the Mini Jazz generation. It shows not only in their live performances but also in the titles of some of their latest albums, like *Pioniers, La Tradition Continue* released in 1991 and *Souvenir* released in 1994. In the year 2006 a Shleu Shleu album was released with the title *40th Anniversary,* with a total of eight songs. It looks like the name Shleu Shleu is here to stay after all, and that the tradition may continue for generations to come.

Shoo Blak - Band

This band was created in the mid 1970s and helped discover the talent of the singer Joseph Lainé (Blagueur). Their album released in 1978 with the songs *Lèlène Chérie, Kenbé Dom,* and *Shoo Black Zin* captured the attention of music lovers in and outside of Haiti. Before the release of the second album titled *Michou* in 1979, with the band's popular song *Courage,* most members moved on and created the band "Shoogar Combo", which eventually was more successful. Shoogar Combo has also re-mixed some of the hits of Shoo Blak like *Kenbé Dom, Pimbèche* and, of course *Lélène Chérie,* which they have turned into a hit song in the 1980s.

Shore, Garry - Saxophone
Gary Shore played with Skah Shah in the 1980s. The young American moved to Haiti, where he played with D.P. Express and he also took part in many Konpa artists' studio projects. His drug addiction was the subject that inspired the song *Dékolé* by Beethova Obas.

Shoogar Combo - Band

Shoogar Combo was created in 1979 from the remains of Shoo Blak by Gérald Chéry the manager of Le Lambi Nightclub/Hotel. The band became an overnight sensation and another successful group coming from the south side of Port-Au Prince. The band was considered the house band of the popular nightclub, which has kept the entertainers busy for many years. Despite the departures and returns of the lead singer Blagueur over the years, the band managed to hire some talented individual that they have turned into Haitian Superstars like the singers Gracia Jean Phillipe (Ti Kit) who left his mark in the band for his performance in the song *Kraché Difé*. Musset Darcy (Vava) captured the world in *Vivine* and *Matinette* before he left the country to join Les Loups Noirs in New York and Dieudonné Larose rocked the streets of Port-au-Prince when he was introduced to the crowd by doing a great show with the carnival song *Pigeon*.

In 1979 Shoogar Combo surprised the world with the song Gro Lobo, a carnival tune that is out of the ordinary. That same year, the band released two albums back to back with one called *Sweet and Jumpy,* with the songs *Gro Lobo* and *Cé Sa Ou Kwè*. But it is the second album with the work put together by the singers Ti Kit and Vava, in songs like *Kraché Difé, Matinette* and *Vivine* that was going to take the band outside of Le Lambi and moved on around the Caribbean and other countries. By the summer of 1980 the band released *Deception,* an album that was recorded in Montreal.

The band lost both lead vocalists as Ti Kit was hired by Scorpio and that Vava had left the country. The singer Blagueur moved back to his fellows and put the band back on the map with a big single released by Mini Records: the re-mix of the song *Lèlène Chérie*. That same year the band released another album with five more songs showcasing the talent of Blagueur in the song *Zoclo*. On that same album, Shoogar Combo paid tribute to the pioneers Nemous and Sicot in the song *Hommage à Nemours et Sicot*. The drummer Jean Félix (Jean Mò) proved that he also had singing ability in the song *St Cécile*. By the years 1983 and 1984 the singer Dieudonné Larose carried the band down many successful roads, and songs like *Caresé'm En Bas, Toto Sou La Coi (Carnival 83), Déméléw* and *Pinceau (Carnival 84)* were songs known by all the Konpa fans.

To many people, Shoogar Combo was a star-making factory, as the musicians of Shoogar Combo, once they become popular was hired by other bands. Ti Manno did it when he was creating his band Gemini by getting some members of the horn section. Scorpio took the singer Ti Kit in his prime with Shoogar. Yves Arsene Appolon took the singer Blagueur, the congas player Léon Beauvais and the guitarist Jean Roosevelt Chatelier, among others to create his band Skah Shah d'Haiti. When D.P. Express needed a popular singer in 1985 they went straight to Shoogar Combo and recruited Joseph Dieudonné Larose.

By the end of the decade to the 1990s Shoogar Combo was traveling from the U.S. to Haiti and some musicians often stayed in the U.S. during those tours, either to join other bands or to find other jobs and put and end to their musical careers. In the mid 1990s there were so many musicians of Shoogar in the U.S. that they made an attempt to create a Shoogar Combo in the Big Apple. Despite a couple of albums released in the diaspora, the band only survived a few live shows.

Besides the albums and songs noted earlier, Shoogar Combo has released over the years a multitude of albums including but not limited to: *Pitié Pou Fanm, Shoogam Cé Pam, Le Malouk, Les Plus Grands Succes, Malouk 97* and some live recordings.

Show Off - Band
This band, based in Haiti, has the ability to play the Konpa as well as the Ragga music.

Shupa Shupa - Band
One of the top bands of the Mini Jazz era, the band came out of the Bas Peu De Chose neighborhood on July 13, 1968, with Yvon Louissaint and Edouard Richard on guitars. Yvon Louissaint later became one of the singers of the band. Their songs *Voisine Came, Epoque Chaleur* and the slow song *Pardon Incertain* has marked the late 60s and early 70s.

Sicot, Raymond - Trumpet
Raymond Sicot was respected in the Haitian musical scene of the 60s and 70s. Many know him as the younger brother of the legendary maestro, but those who had the chance to work with him or to see him perform understand that he is as great musically as his older brother. In 1960, they started as Les Frères Sicot (the Sicot Brothers) or La Flèche d'or des Frères Sicot. However,

Raymond chose to move on with his career by working with other musicians on other adventurous roads rather than working with his difficult brother Webert. Later Webert changed the name of the band to Super Ensemble de Webert Sicot.

Sicot, Webert - Saxophone

In the 1940s two young brothers, Webert and Raymond Sicot went to the school Centrale Des Arts et Métiers, which was, at the time, under the direction of Augustin Bruno. The school was part of a government program for needy children and has over the years created some of the best Haitian musicians. By the time Webert became a teenager he was already known as a good saxophonist, and his mentor, the great François Guignard, managed to find him and his brother some jobs with the band Jazz Capois in the town of Cap Haitien. However, the brothers didn't make a career in the northern part of Haiti, as they returned to Port-au-Prince where they worked in the early 50s with Jazz Des Jeunes, the Orchestre Saieh as well as the Conjunto International alongside his friend Nemours Jean Baptiste. Sicot was a complete musician. Besides the saxophone (baritone-tenor and alto) he played the trombone, the flute, guitar and congas. The elder Nemours Jean Baptiste around that time had the chance to learn some tricks and acquired some saxophone skills from the young Webert Sicot.

By the second half of the 1950s Nemours Jean Baptiste became one of the stars of the Haitian music scene creating a lot of buzz with his new band and by attacking the country's most popular band Jazz Des Jeunes. In 1960 the Sicot brothers came out with their own band called La Flèche D'or des Frères Sicot. Raymond, however, couldn't keep up with the attitude of his demanding brother and eventually left the band. Webert Sicot moved and introduced his new style accentuated by the conga beat as the "Cadence Rampas" and suddenly the rhythm Compas Direct, which was getting momentum had a serious match as Sicot cast the first stone in the song "Sispann Voyé Roch". When Nemours realized that Jazz Des Jeunes basically was not interested playing his game, he quickly turned on Sicot's band and thus started the musical polemic Nemours/Sicot.

Sicot is known as one of the best Haitian musicians and the greatest Haitian band leader of all time. With the help of talented and charismatic singers, like Gary French, Gerard Thézan and André Dorismond in the 1960s he delivered a series of hit songs and sold-out records with his band known as "Super

Ensemble de Webert Sicot". Sicot was also known as the Difficult Maestro and as the King of Carnival Songs. Some of his carnival songs were a reference to many artists and bands many years after his death. He was the role model of 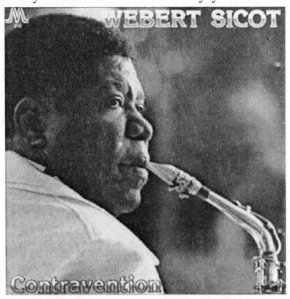 many saxophonists; however none so far had ever reach the popularity of the great maestro. Among the memorable songs left by Webert Sicot we can cite: *Deux Guidons, Zépon, Ti Male, Ti Georges Counan, Crab Mal Zorey, Jet Rampas, Point Final, Bon Anniversaire, Joui La Vie* and *Catalina* among others.

In the second half of the 1960s, a series of young musicians emerged around the country and started the Mini Jazz movement. The reduced format was very appealing to the new generation and took a toll on both Nemours and Sicot, as well as the famous Jazz Des Jeunes. At the same time many people were leaving the country for the U.S. and Webert Sicot followed the new route and found his new home in the Big Apple. In New York he created the band "Orchestre Le Jeune" with some of his former musicians and other experienced artists who were already living in New York. That project however didn't last long.

He then released a solo album, titled "*Just For You*" in 1971, and by the mid-70s he returned to Haiti, where he also recorded some more solo albums including *Webert Sicot The Greatest*. He also took part in putting together the band "Zotobré' with some younger musicians, like Claude Montreuil, Serge Rosenthal and Almando Keslin to name a few. He also released an album with his longtime rival but best friend, Nemours Jean Baptiste titled *L'union*.

Webert Sicot has also worked in his life for some great musical organizations like C.B.S in the U.S. and for the orchestra of the government run radio station "Radio Nationale" in Haiti.

While Haitians all over the country were enjoying themselves in the streets of Port-au-Prince during the Mardi Gras parade in Feb. 1985, they were hit by the news of the sudden death of Webert Sicot, the man who was, for many years, known as the King of Haiti's Carnival. On that occasion the band D.P. Express paid tribute by playing during the Mardi Gras parade some tunes written in previous years by the famous maestro.

Silencieux, Jean Clotaire - Singer
The singer Jean Clotaire Silencieux is also the owner of the Haitian Television

company Tele Citronelle. Since 1996 he organized the beauty pageant Miss Télé Citronelle showcasing the talent of young Haitian women living outside of Haiti.

Simeon, Lyonel (Yonyon) - Trombone

Yonyon is one of the talented trombonists who have played the instrument eloquently for many years. Lyonel played with Caribbean Sextet and Zèklè as well as D.P. Express in Haiti. He was part of the squad that left D.P. Express to create the band G.P. Express in Washington D.C., a band that later became Zépon and represented Haiti at different activities in the DC/MD area. At the turn of the century Lyonel became a well-known cook in the D.C. area and he opened his restaurant Chez Yonyon in Hyattsville Md.

In 2004, as the Smithsonian Institute was celebrating the 200th anniversary of the Independence of Haiti, the food provided for the two week festival by the restaurant Chez Yonyon was one of the greatest attractions.

In the fall of 2006, he escaped death as he and his young daughter Phabiene were held hostage by armed bandits. Lyonel who is a former acrobat jumped out of the window into the arms of awaiting police officers as one of the bandits was distracted by a noise from the first floor.

A year after the robberty, he decided to close the restaurant to the surprise of his clients.

The restaurant Chez Yonyon is also mentioned in the Trankill song *Ma Debatte*.

Similien, Jules (Toto Nécéssité) - Singer

Toto started his career like Rodrigue Millien as a comedian on Troupe Alcibiade in the late 1960s. With his partner Rodrigue, he used to warm up the crowd with some nice twoubadou songs. He got the name Toto for playing the character Odié Bénito on the Alcibiade shows. In the early 70s the duo came out with their first album entitle *Nécéssité* and with the success of that album the artist added the name Nécéssité to his given stage name and became ever since known as Toto Nécéssité.

The success of the album also gave the artists the opportunity to move on with their musical careers and put an end to their theatrical stage life. The band traveled outside of Haiti and their second album, *Lougarou* was recorded in New York. There again, the superstars were getting a lot of exposures and unlike Rodrigue who returned to Haiti, Toto decided to stay in New York where he played for many years with a complete new group of musicians. He released, in 1977, the album *An Ba Besment,* a mega hit that showed that Toto can move on with his career without Rodrigue. Toto was so popular that he was chosen by producer Fred Paul to launch the Mini All Stars projects and what a job he delivered in the songs *Cé Péché, Debrouillé* and *I'm Laughing*. The success of than album encouraged Fred Paul to continue with the project and over the years Fred Paul produced more than 30 other albums with different artists on the Mini All Stars projects. In 1978 Toto surprised the Konpa world with the album *Thank You Africa,* in which he showed his skills in the song *Coq La Chanté.*

The artist was so popular that in 1979 he released two albums with two different labels. One titled *Aux Enfers* with Mini Records and another one *Tripotage* under the label Marc Records.
By the early 1980s Toto took his popularity to Haiti where he had so many shows that the artists barely had time to rest. In 1982 Toto repeated the same scenario by releasing two albums in the same year with two different labels. That time he came out with *Azoumounou,* produced by Cine Records and *Ti Pouchon,* produced by Mini Records. The song *Ti Pouchon* took the country by storm as it was on the lips of almost all the Konpa music fans of all ages. In the years that followed Toto continued to perform in Haiti, the Caribbean and the Haitian diaspora.
 Besides the album noted above his discography also include: *La Pophetie, L'amitié Pap Trahie, Haiti Libéré, Révélation, Liména, Bann Nan Cho, Tripotage La Fini, Louange A Dieu, Lougarou, Magouilleurs, Message, Nécéssité, Pa Excitém, Prié Poun Nou, Sida Titine,* and *Tout Moun Sou Blof* as well as some Best of Toto Nécéssité.

Simon, Alphonse -Trumpet
Star trumpet player of the previous decades - professor and a mentor to many musicians.

Simon, Frantz - Singer
Singer of the band K-Sou Coupé in New York

Simon, Prosper - Saxophone
Simon played with the band Les Lionceaux des Cayes in the 1970s.

Simond, Rigaud - Bass
Rigaud, as a business person has played in his career as a freelancer with many groups especially the gospel band Heavenly Citizens, among others. He also plays at some Konpa shows as needed. He was for many years the manager or agent of many artists including Emeline Michel, Jacques Sauveur Jean, Orlane and Eric Virgal.

Simpson, Serge - Keyboard
Serge in the 1960s created the bands Les Gilbreteurs and Horse Back. In his

career, he has played with Nemours Jean Baptiste for a short while, before moving on with much younger musicians in the band Ibo Combo.

Sinik Mizik - Band

This band based in the town of Port de Paix really shocked the world by putting a great show at the eight edition of Music En Folie in Haiti on Nov. 18, 2007.

Siwel - Band

This band was created in New York in the 1990.

Skah Shah – Band

After the departure of the first squad of Les Shleu Shleu to the U.S., the band's owner/manager Dada Djackaman wasted no time recruiting some new members and kept his business moving. He introduced to the Konpa world some new talents that include the saxophonist Loubert Chancy the singers Jean Eli Telfort (Cubano) Jean Michel St Victor (Zouzoule), the guitarists and cousins Mario Mayala and Jhonny Frantz Toussaint (Ti frè) the drummer Yves Arsène Appolon six musicians that would in the next four decades dominated Haitian Music industry. In 1971 Dada celebrated the sixth Anniversary of the creation of Les Shleu Shleu with an album titled *6eme Anniversaire* with nine songs that include: *Sept Péchés Capitaux, Trois Bébé, Quatre Saisons* and *Cap Grandou*.

In 1973 the band got the attention of the public when they released a song for the National Football Team on the occasion of the CONCACAF soccer tournament as the World Cup Qualifier Games held in Haiti. The motivation song with the name of the football stars like Manno Sanon, Philippe Vorbes, Claude Barthelemy among others was played on the radio every day prior to, and during the tournament as the nation sang to the catchy chorus parts *"Al Bay Goal"* and *"Nou Pral A Munich"* referring to Munich, Germany where the Haiti National team played against Italy, Argentina and Poland in the 1974 World Cup Finals. The band also released the album *Acé Frapé* with the songs *Solanges, Belle Ti Machann* and *Banda*.

With such success the band was also touring the French Caribbean Islands and Europe. They recorded the album Shleu Shleu à Paris with hit songs like *Aie*

Tiou Aie (a successful chorus part that they used in the 1973 carnival) *Yola*, the slow song *Reviens* and *Caroline* that would be over the years be played by many bands of every generation. When the band finally made it to the U.S. the members decided to follow the route of their predecessors by staying in New York to continue their musical career. However there was only one problem. New York already had the members of the first squad using the name Shleu Shleu, so the newcomers had to let go of the name that gave them fame and move on with a new name for their enterprise. After many names were considered the drummer Arsène Appolon came up with the name Skah Shah meaning "Little King" and indeed a new king was born in New York in 1974 with the exception of the singer Jean Michel St Victor (Zouzoule) who would later joined the band in the following years.

The buzz was so high in New York that most fans couldn't wait for the first show. From that day forward, Skah Shah took the forefront of the Haitian music in New York putting Original Shleu Shleu on the back burner and created a serious challenge for Tabou Combo. The band released the album *Guèpe Pangnol* with the words "Skah Shah ex Shleu Shleu d'Haiti"on the cover. Guèpe Pangnol was released under the label Maggy Records, and in the same year they released the album Les *Dix Commandements*, under the label Marc Records with the new name Skah Shah # 1. That album includes the song *Haiti*, one of the most popular Konpa songs of all time which moved the musicians from stars to superstars. The song still makes anyone living outside of the motherland to feel nostalgic, and the chorus part "*Mézanmi kòman nou yé*" showed that the artists cared and worried about family and friends left back home.

In the following decades, more than 60 albums with the name Skah Shah appeared in the market, and the band has seen many changes in the personnel as well. In the late 70s the band added more musicians to their horn section and a keyboard to the lineup in order to keep up with the changes of the time. From that day on Skah Shah was no longer a Mini Jazz but a full band as they released the album *Message,* an album that include their mega hit *Zanmi*. Many great musicians have worked for the company, like the drummer Ulrick Bouzy (Touco) the trumpet player Anderson Cameau, the keyboardist Jean Acindor, the guitarist Gary Résil among others. Some members that were not part of the eight have showed their loyalties and proved that they are also real Skah Shah like the gonguist Rodrigue Gauthier (Ti Crane), the drummer Ernst Ramponeau and the congas player Camille Armand, who have worked for many years with the band and maintained the balance of the percussion line. After the success of the 70s and part of the 80s, most members were unable to cope with their fame and the band suffered some serious damage as some members left to create their own bands, each holding on to the name Skah Shah. Suddenly the "little king" was turning into a whole bunch of little kings fighting for the same last name. At one time Cubano had his own Skah Shah, Loubert Chancy had his own Shah Shah, and Arsène Appolon also had his own Skah Shah, as if they couldn't let go of the name that they cherished so much. Besides the albums released as Skah Shah #1 with the band as the solid team, there are also some albums like Shah Shah D'Haiti, Skah Shah # 1 Plus, Skah Shah #1 Plus Alliance released by Arsène, Skah Shah Number One by Cubano, as well as Georges Loubert Chancy, Skah Shah #1 and Jhonny Frantz Toussaint du Skah Shah. During the many breakups, a new band by the name of Bazouka, with Zouzoule on lead vocal was also created in the 1990s. At the end of the day the public was tired of all the new bands and most people couldn't keep up who was doing what. The division was prominent, many feelings were hurt. The show promoters couldn't picture who they should work with in order not to offend their other best friends, and basically none of the bands ever found the success of the good old days of Skah Shah # 1 as a team playing the best Konpa.

At the turn of the century the original members come to their senses and put their egos aside and regrouped for a tour. The tour was successful as fans from all over the world packed the house wherever the band was playing, like in the early days of the band. That reunion led to several other shows and to the release of some live albums with the hit songs of the past and the album Skah Shah # 1 *Lagué Jazz La* released in 2006 with 10 new songs.

Skandal - Band
Skandal was one of the first bands of the Nouvel Jenerasyon movement in the second half of the 1980s. In the 1990s the band was basically not active, until it showed some signs when they released the album Lakou Lakay in the year 2000 under the label Crossover Record. Despite the release of the record, Skandal was still not active playing live.

Sky Band - Band

Smith, Joel - Congas
Joel played with the band Latino in the Mini Jazz era.

Smith, Ronald - Guitar /Bass
Like other members of his family Ronald played in the 70s with the New York based band Latino. He started as a bassist and later he became the guitarist of choice of the band. He also played for the band Les Beatniks de Queens next to the talented guitarist Jean Robert Castel. However, it is with the band Astros that he proved his talent as guitarist and composer. When the band Les Frères Déjean got in trouble with their visa situation, and many musicians were forced to stay in Haiti during a tour in the early 1980s, the rest of the squad

who returned to New York, collaborated with some musicians of Astros in the creation of System Band. Ronald Smith was one of the Astros members who took part in the project.

In the years that followed, the world saw one of the best guitar duos ever, if not the best, in the partnership and chemistry in Konpa Music provided on stage and in studio with the combination of Ronald Smith and Réginald Benjamin. The two were able to change roles from solo to groove without anyone noticing when the changes occurred during the songs.

In the 1990s the duo left System Band after a disagreement with the band administration and created their band Rolls Royce. As the Rolls Royce project found too many obstacles to survive in the Konpa competitive market, Réginald returned to System to work under the same management that he has walked away from a few months earlier. Ronald Smith, however, moved forward with his life until he created his band, Q-Style.

Smith, Wiener - Singer
Next to Ernst Perrin, Wiener was one of the star singers of the New York based band Latino.

Solitaires (Les Solitaires) - Band
Band of the Mini Jazz era

Sony Bel Anfòm see: Zulerion, Jean Sony

Speed Band - Band

Spice Band - Band

Solo, Elsie - Singer
Elsie palyed mostly in duo with her partner Judin Solo

Solo, Judin - Singer
Judin did most of his shows playing with her partner Elsie Solo. He is also one of the first Haitian artists to use the drum machine.

Souffrant, Juanito - Guitar
Juanito performs in Chicago, his album Chaka was released with Freddy on lead vocal.

Souffrant, Yves - Trumpet
Yves Souffrant was known for his ability to hit high notes. He played with the legendary maestro Webert Sicot.

St Aude Records
Haitian owned record production company

St. Cyr, Edler (Cliff) - Congas/Gong
Musician of the band Take Off, Cliff played with the band Back Up prior to joining Take Off.

St. Eloi, Patrick - Singer
Patrick is known as one of the talented singers of the Guadeloupe-based band Kassav, a French Caribbean band which became extremely popular in the 1980s.

St Hillaire, Archile – Band Manager
After the musician of the Miaim based band Zenglen disagreed with their manager Bellande Georges on some issues, they turn to Archile St.Hillaire to keep the business going. However Archile and Zenglen also went separate ways as he took side with the singers Reginald and Frerot to create the band Fasil in Haiti. That project also didn't work in his favor as he and Frero returned to Florida living Reginald in Haiti. Archile continued to offer his assistance to bands and artists in their live shows and record deals as an inverstor in the Haitian music business.

St. Jean Martyr, Claudy * - Keyboard
Claudy played with Scorpio in the 1980s. The band released a song after his death titled *Homage à Claudy* as a tribute to his work in the popular band. Claudy also worked in previous years with the band Meridional des Cayes.

St. Juste, Michel - Keyboard

St. Louis, Prosper - Bass
Prosper is one of the founders of the band Trio Select, which later became Ensemble Select de Coupé Cloué.

St. Louis, Ambroise - Bass

St. Louis, Harold – Keyboard

St. Louis, Moses - Journalist
Moses reports to the best of his ability all the news about the Haitian music on a daily basis on the website Opamizik.com

St. Louis, Objet - Bass

St. Louis, Rony - Guitar

St. Louis, Wesner - Congas

St. Paul, Pierre Richard - Guitar

St. Pierre, Maxime - Trombone

St. Pierre, Serge - Drums
Serge played in the Mini Jazz era with the bands Do Ré Mi Jazz Simalo and later in his career with the band Channel 10.

St. Preux, François Mary - Guitar
François is the talented guitarist who replaced Robert Martino in Scorpio after the members moved away from the leadership of the maestro and the management to create their own band. In the late 1980s he moved to Maryland, where he joined the band G.P.Express and by the 1990s he moved to Boston, where he continued to live with his family. He made an attempt with the Boston-based band Tiz. However, that project was not successful and François is no longer being seen in the Konpa music arena.

St. Prix, Dédé - Singer
Dédé is another French Caribbean Singer who has resided in Haiti and also found success and increased his popularity among Haitian music lovers.

St. Vil, Fleuviliste - Singer

St.Vil, Jean Edwin - Keyboard

St. Vil, Raphael – Singer

Staco Harold – Promoter / Producer / Radio Personality

Staff - Band

Stanis Eders (Pipo) - Singer
Pipo made a name for himself in the HMI with the band Passion de Montreal. He moved to Florida to join the band D'zine, and later he became the lead singer of the band Hangout.
In September 2007, during a tour in Haiti, he decided that he would leave the

band to work on other music projects. In the spring of 2008, he introduced his band Bel Jazz at a live show at Club Boca in Boca Raton, Fl.

Stars (Les Stars) - Band

Star Combo – Band

Stil – Band
This band based in Haiti was created at the end of 2007 by three former members of K- Dans the keyboardist Alfred Latallaide the singer Jude Jean and the guitarist Didi Santana.

Steel Groove - Band

Strings - Band
This band was put together by the guitarist Jacky Ambroise in 1996. After trying with the digital format and the troubadour orientation, Jacky finally found the formula that worked for him when he created a band which the music focused on the strings.
Strings discography includes *Flamenco Tropical, Island Follies, Tropical Mood* and *Coconut Groove*.

Stupart, Erold - Bass
Erold is the original bassist of Les Frères Déjean.

Styl -Vice -Band

Sublime d'Haiti - Band
Under the leadership of Fritz Massac on accordion, the band Sublime created on Nov. 13, 1962 made one of the most memorable carnivals of the 1960s with the song *"Sublime En Pen Pan."*

Summer - Band
This band was created in New York in the 1990s by the promoter/producer Jojo Lorquet with Clark Cajuste, the son of the singer Raymond Cajuste, on keyboard.

Super 9 - Band
When the band Safari Combo was split in two after an argument among the members and the management, the members who left created the band Super 9 with the star singer Assade Francoeur. Assade did not waste any time

making the band popular by creating mega hits like "*A ma femme*". Their 1974 carnival was a song was made to honor the National Soccer Team players after Haiti's qualification to the 1974 World Cup soccer tournament.

Super Channel 10 - Band
This band was created by some former members of the band Channel 10.

Super Combo - Band
This band was created by Nemours Jean Baptiste in an attempt to revive his band Super Ensemble de Nemours Jean Baptiste. Unfortunately super Combo never had the popularity of the great band that dominated the Haitian music scene for almost two decades.

Super Choucoune 70 - Band
This band was created in Haiti after the departure of Maestro Webert Sicot to the U.S. While many musicians followed their leader to the U.S., some of the musicians of Sicot's band chose to stay in Haiti and created under the leadership of the singer André Dorismond the band Super Choucoune. The band, however never got the popularity that was expected, and most of the musicians including André Dorismond, ended up leaving the country as well by the end of the decade.

Super Ensemble de Nemours Jean Baptiste - Band
Many people know the band as Compas Direct, but the official name of Nemours Jean Baptiste's band was Super Ensemble de Nemours Jean Baptiste.

Super Ensemble de Webert Sicot - Band
Many people know the band as Cadence Rampas; however the official name of Wébert Sicot's band was Super Ensemble de Wébert Sicot.

Super Princes - Band

Super Soline - Band
Created from the remains of Samba Jazz, Super Soline became more popular than the musicians ever dreamed of. Unfortunately, the band didn't have a management team that could capitalize on the success of the songs. Some people felt like the band tried too much to sound and imitate Les Fantaisistes de Carrefour that even the album cover *Super Soline d'Haiti* was a complete reproduction of Les Fantaisistes' album *Volley Ball*.
Super Soline got the attention of the population when they released the song *Cé Gérard Ou Rélé*. The song is very funny and created a buzz and a new slogan among young people. Besides *Cé Gérard Ou Rélé*, the band also released other

albums including *Haiti* and *Plaisir Musical*.

Super Sonic 747 - Band
After he left the popular band Missile 727, Dieudoné Larose created his own band which came out as a rival to Missile. The Super Sonic didn't last long as a performing band, but Larose continued with his career as a singer.

Super Stars - Band
This band was created in Haiti by Adolphe Chancy (Ti Dof) and Jean Claude Jean after they left the band Tabou Combo in the 1980s. However, the political situation in Haiti caused Jean Claude Jean to return to the States and continue to work with Tabou Combo while Dof Chancy moved the band, around first in New York and later in Miami.
In the early days of its creation the band had many successes with the singer Michel Batista in the songs *Alpha* and *La Familia*. In the U.S., the band continued, under the leadership of Dof Chancy to perform in many towns with Michel Batista, and later with the singer Harold Joseph who Dof Chancy took out of System Band. Harold proved himself in the song *La Vie A Belle* one, of the best songs of the band.
The band has over the years produced many albums. Some came out under the name Super Stars Music Machine, Super Stars D'Haiti and others under the name Super Stars de New York. The discography of the band includes: *Music Machine, La Vie Ya Belle, Modern Compas, Champagne Sur La Savanne, Business,* and *Raché Yo Ak Mizik.*

Super Star Records
Haitian owned record company

Super Tabou - Band
After the quick success of Tabou Combo de Petion Ville, another group of young musicians under the leadership of the guitarist Jean Claude Petion appeared under the name Super Tabou, still in Petion-Ville. Later the name of the band was changed to Les Cougars de Petion-Ville.

Surpris, Lesly - Congas

Suspense - Band
The band introduced the talented guitarist Gerald Balan. Their song *Ti Pa Ti Pa* was a very catchy one.

Sweet Coupé - Band

Sweet Groove - Band

Sweet Micky see: Martelly, Michel

Sweet Micky - Band
This band was created by star singer Michel Martelly in the late 1980s. While playing a regular gig in Pétion Ville, a friend shouted that this is sweet music by Sweet Micky, and Michel Martelly decided to call his band "Sweet Micky" a name by which many refer to the artist, as his stage name as well.

Sweet Natal - Band
Sweet Natal is another band in the New York area that based their style on the Konpa played by Coupé Cloué.

Sweet Vibe - Band

Swell, Steve - Trombone

Sylné, Madsen - Trumpet
Madsen is a member of the band Septentrional.

Sylva, Edgard - Singer
Edgar was the star singer of the band Les Vikings in the Mini Jazz era.

Sylvain, Gerald - Congas

Sylva, Garçonnet - Keyboard
Garçonnet played with the band Les Diables Du Rythme de St Marc.

Sylvain, Bernier (B.S)
B.S is a popular radio announcer.

Sylvain, Carl (Jojo) - Drums / Timbales / Percussion
Jojo is a musician of the band phantoms. He started by playing next to Jensen Derosier on timbales on the early days of the band. Later he moved on to playing gong, however he can, as needed, play the congas also. Jojo also owns and manages a record store in New York.

Sylvain Clifford (Ti Guy) - Congas/Singer
Clifford played with the bands Accolade de New York, Skah Shah and his band, Rara Machine. In the Skah Shah song *Men Numéwo A*, it was the voice of Clifford that called the numbers and it was his idea also for the song. Today

Clifford is involved in show production and he is also working as a Realtor in New York.

Sylvain, Harry (Tico) - Drums
Tico played with Bossa Combo in his early years in Haiti, but he left the band and moved with his family to the U.S. He later was reunited with some of his Bossa Combo partners in New York in the creation of the band Accolade de New York.

Sylvain, Jean Elie - Singer

Sylvain, Marcel - Singer

Sylvie d'Art see: Darléus Sylvie

System Band - Band

In the late 70s, the band Les Frères Déjean was one of the bands on top of the Haitian market, making one hit song after another when we consider *Marina, Koté Ménage Ou, l'Univers, Débaké, Gladia etc.* The band was on top of their game in New York City just like Tabou Combo and Skah Shah until trouble came their way at the U.S./Canada border, where some members were told that they would not be able to return to the U.S. The band went to Haiti while the members with legal documents returned to the U.S. after playing with the brothers for a few weeks. Upon their return they faced the reality that they would have to move on with their career without their bosses and mentors.

A left-handed gonguist by the name of Frantz Avin (Fanfan Avin), until then unknown in the business volunteered his house as headquarter for the band to practice. The name System Connection was chosen but was later changed to System Band.

Among the member, who took part in the transition we can cite the Douby brothers, Isnard and Lesly, on vocal, as well as the singer Harold Joseph, the bassist Ernst Vincent the guitarist Réginald Benjamin and the saxophonist Lucien Céran. Along with the drummer Ernst Ramponeau, who played with Les Frères Déjean in Haiti, and the conga player Roger Laurent (Marechal Tito), former member of Super 9 and Ronald Smith recruited from Les Astros.

The band started by playing the hit songs of Les Frères Déjean, but after only a few shows they saw some members moved on in other direction. Ernst Ramponeau joined Skah Shah and Marechal moved to Montreal, Canada. Ramponeau was replaced by Jean Mathurin and Marechal left his place for Eric Charlier (Manatan), another musician from Les Astros. He too left the city and was replaced by Martial Bigaud.

A few years later the former gonguist of Les Astros, Fritz Frederique (Ti Mitou) joined System band replacing Frantz Avin who had moved to Florida. The contribution of the late Ti Mitou was remarkable in the history of System, as the man who started as a gonguist was going to become one the best showmen of the band and of the business as a singer and a crowd pleaser.

In 1982 Les Frères Déjean moved back to New York and the members of System who were part of the band quickly joined their former bosses, leaving behind the loyal musicians who joined them in making System Band a reality. Isnard Douby, Ernst Vincent (Ti Nes), Réginald Benjamin and Harold Joseph took part in the album *Sans Rancune* with some super hits like *Maléré, Haiti* and *Belle Déesse*. Despite the fact that they did a great album and created the opportunity for Les Frères Déjean to get back on top of the market in New York, the move had outraged many New Yorkers, who felt that System Band was on the right track after the releases of two very good albums. The band was already creating its fan base with songs like *Manman* and *Banm Passé* which the followers were getting used to.

On the advice of many people and especially the firm position of Lesly Douby, (the younger brother of Isnard) who refused to go back to work, as he put it, in other people's band after creating System.

Eventually System came back stronger than ever and found their own identity and respect on the market, which was confirmed as they released three hit songs *Anita, Innocent,* and *Vacances.*

Besides the talented musicians, the band was also lucky to get the support of qualified music arrangers to help in their albums. Among them we can note Nikol Levy, Jean Baptiste Edouard and Dernst Emile. Their horn section also always included some of the best blowers in the Konpa arena from Lucien Céran, Frantz Carriès, Isnard Douby and Mario Collin to the non-Haitian musicians like Daniel Block, Paul Henegan, Steve Swell, Joshua Rosemond and Tom Mitchell.

Other known musicians who took part in System band we can also name the singers Perez Alvarez, the singer/drummer Michel Blaize and the gonguist Fritz Bonheur, who later became a sound engineer.

System Band identified their style as the "Machiavel Caramel". The band is also known as the master of slogans in the Haitian music world. It seems like they always have something new for Konpa fans to repeat all year long once an album is released. System Band has over the years produced many hit songs. While we will not enumerate all of them, we will note the song César, written by Michael Ange Bazile, a friend of the band. Other hits worth noting are *Aveg La, Beeper-Ingratitude, Chagrin d'Amour, Péyi Ya Pa Pou Vann, Jan'l Passé'l Passé* and *Bel Kado*

Like in any company, employees and founding members are expected to move on and to grow outside of the company at some times. Some members left and returned to System after some failed attempts. Ronald Smith, however, had created his own band, Q-Style in New York, while the bassist Ti Nes Vincent became the leader of the band Hangout in Florida.

T

T.Dozz - Band
This band was created by Jeff and Gaëtan Policard the sons of the keyboardist Réginald Policard. The brothers later changed the name of the band to Fahrenheit.

T.Kabzy - Band
The band T.Kabzy which struggled in the early days of its creation had find the way to success with a couple of songs like *Sim Alé, My Name is,* and *Nap Relax.* The Montreal Canada based band has been on tour in many major towns in America and the Caribbean islands where there is a large population of Konpa fans.

T.Strong - Band
This Konpa band based in Paris France since Jan. 15, 2001. In 2006 the band release a CD titled *3eme Etaj La* with 11 songs.

T.Tabou - Band
This Miami Fl. based band was created by the bassist Adolphe Chancy in the 1990s.

T. Vice – Band

Reynaldo & Roberto Martino

In 1990 the sons of the famous guitarist Robert Martino surprised the musical world by coming out with the band T. Vice. The name of the band in itself showed everyone that the boys were determined to follow the footsteps of their legendary father and role model as they chose a name based on their father's band Top Vice.

With Roberto on lead vocal and guitar, and his younger brother Reynaldo on keyboard, the band T. Vice, with the support of friends and family members, became a reality. The Martino Brothers managed to accomplish what many thought would have been the impossible by taking over the lead of the digital music movement and by getting most of the best gigs of the popular Michel Martelly (Sweet Micky). When Michel realized that T. Vice was moving him to the back burner he quickly went into a series of attacks on the band and their parents. T. Vice didn't get intimidated and went on a counter-attack in the song *Gaçon Makòmè* and some responses through their carnival songs.

By the turn of the century T. Vice had managed to take over the lead of the digital movement and Sweet Micky was no longer able to compete with the two brothers. Around that time the full band Djakout Mizik which had for many years launched some attacks on T. Vice, was becoming popular and T. Vice chose to shift the musical polemic to Djakout. However, T. Vice made their mark on the carnival scene in 2002 when they came out with the carnival song *Elikoptè*. During the whole parade the thousands of fans following the band received from Roberto the order to wave their shirts or any other clothing articles like the blades of a helicopter. In the following four years the band basically controlled the carnival scenes as well as being the band of choice of the Konpa Festivals throughout the world as they continue to improve.

In 2005 the band introduced the drums in their format and in 2006 they added another percussion piece the Gong making the band a seven-member band with James Cardozo, Olivier Duret on vocal and Gerald Kebreau on bass. The discography of T. Vice includes but is not limited to: *Konpa Kontak, Dim Saw We, Vinn Pran Note, Kité'm Vive Banm T. Vice Mwen, 4 Las, Pren Plezi Ou, Kitém Viv* and a series of live recordings as well as some compilations of their best hit songs. The band that started as a trio is now an eight member Konpa band.

T. Zee - Band

Tabou Combo - Band

"Rhythm is the essence of Tabou Combo," says Tabou Combo's co-founder and ex-drummer Herman Nau. The infectious rhythm of Haiti's national dance music, Konpa (con-pah), has propelled the country's preeminent dance band around the world. The 12 members of the band have covered many territories since leaving Haiti and relocating to New York City in 1971. By that time, Tabou had already established itself as Haiti's number one group, and as the "Ambassadeurs of Konpa." Tabou Combo now has worldwide fans and followers from London to Paris, Holland, Switzerland, Japan, South America, throughout the Caribbean and in North America.

It is easy to understand why Tabou Combo's relentless and high-energy style of Compas dance beat knows no language barrier. Singing in English, Spanish, French or their native Creole, Tabou serves a hot mix of grooves and textures with roots from around the world. You will hear a strong dose of the Dominican Republic's national dance music, meringue. In addition, there is Haiti's dance-till-you-drop carnival music, rara, the hypnotic drums of Haitian voodoo rituals. Add to that quadrilles and contra-dances from Haiti's French colonizers and funk from the American soul era to James Brown for good measure. The mixture of all these influences makes for a serious bass line that brings new meaning to the word bottom; layer upon layer of accents courtesy of drums, percussion and congas, the constant intertwining of two guitars with the feel of West African Soukous, topped with bright piano riff and the brassy sound of a three man horn section.

Tabou Combo got started in 1968 in Petion-Ville, a town just outside Port-au-Prince, by Albert Chancy and Herman Nau and some friends, all in their teens. They began by naming themselves "Los Incognitos", because they were unknown at that time. They changed to Tabou Combo in 1969, in order to bear a name closer to the Haitian culture. That year, the band won first prize in a televised talent contest, gaining a national reputation in Haiti, and by 1970 it was one of the island's leading bands. Then the Chancy's parents stepped in, and Albert, the band's guitarist and original leader was sent to college in Montreal, and gave up music. The band dissolved and its members drifted to the United States. Early in 1971, however, an unexpected meeting led to a Tabou reunion with rhythm guitarist Jean-Claude Jean as the leader and the band has been together, with a few changes, ever since.

Employing the repetition and breaks of Afro-American gospel music, Tabou Combo entices the listener to become listener and dancer. Almost four decades after Tabou Combo's establishment, the band has audiences dancing everywhere from concert halls to the streets and in nightclubs around the world. Says Fanfan, the band's background vocalist and main songwriter, "We want people to dance and forget their sorrows."

There is no doubt, the music is made for dancing, but Tabou also features lyrics that focus on social issues of the day. For example, the lyrics from the title cut of the group's 1991 release *Zap Zap* deal with uplifting the image of Haitian people in the wake of bad press connected to the AIDS epidemic.

It was 1974 when the band captured Europe's attention with its million selling hit single *New York City*. Tabou steadily has been building its international followers ever since. The 1989 release, *Aux Antilles* (The Antilles), topped European and Caribbean charts for six consecutive weeks. *Aux Antilles* also won Best Album for Haitian Dance Music at the 1991 1st Annual Caribbean Music Awards at New York City's famed Apollo Theater. Tabou's release, *Kitem Fè Zafem* (Let Me Do My Things), was voted among Beat Magazine's Best of 1988. In 1989, Kitem Fè Zafem, along with *Zap Zap* were used by the film director Jonathan Demme in his movie Mystery Date. The song Juicy Lucy was chosen by French movie maker Maurice Pialat for his movie Police (1985). In 2002, world known guitarist Carlos Santana recorded the song Mabouya (Foo Foo) on his album Shaman.

After traveling around the world with Tabou, Fanfan says he has found that people everywhere are all the same and they all love music. Tabou Combo seduces the people with rhythm that does not let go. Konpa's unrelenting dance beat is contagious and there are plenty of witnesses. Many of the thousands of Tabou Combo fans around the world eagerly will testify... that is, if they can stop dancing long enough to talk
Bio from: www.taboucombo.com

Tabutau, Joseph - Bass
Ti Djo played for the band Samba Créole in the 1970s; he later created the band Formule H. When he moved to New York he became known as Djo Light because he left the bass for his lighting shows at different functions and clubs.

Take Off - Band
Konpa band based in Haiti

Talon, Mackenzie (Mac-D) - Singer
Mac - D played with K- Dans in 2006. Mac D was the singer of choice who replaced the popular singer Jude Jean. While K-Dans thought that they found a gold mine in Mac D, the young singer quietly moved to the U.S. in the spring of 2008, he collaborated with Nickenson Prud'homme in the creation of the band Harmonik.

Talles, Emmanuel - Trumpet
Emmanuel Jaboint Talles played with many groups before making his mark in the Konpa music by playing in the band Super Ensemble de Nemours Jean Baptiste in the 1960s.

Talles, Frantz - Bass
Played with the band Latino in the 1970s

Tam Tam - Band

Tam Tam Records

Haitian owned record company

Tandans - Band

Tap La - Band
This band is based in Miami Fl.

Tassy, Jean Claude - Singer
Jean Claude played with the band Ju-Kann in the early 1990. He is also a cargo plane pilot living in Florida.

Tavernier, José - Singer / Drums
José started his career in the mid-60s in the Mini Jazz era with Les Mordus and Les Copains, but he found fame with the band Ibo Combo in New York in the early 70s. After a long absence from the musical scene, many people were happy to see him perform and crack some jokes during the *Haiti Twoubadou* tour in 2004.

Taxi Kréol - Band

Taxil, Gerard - Guitar

Tchaka - Band
This band was created in Montréal by the bassist Eval Manigat.

Tchaka - Band
This band is based in Chicago

Teesfeel, Harry - Guitar

Telcide, Martial - Drums
Martial was a tough act to follow for many musicians of the Mini Jazz era because he dared to be different. While many artists were following the Nemours Jean Baptiste style of back lines, Martial was playing more of a Cadence Rampas, which made him stand out among others, and gave Les Ambassadeurs other flavors. Martial was known as a showman and was able to change his style to bring the sweetness on the slow songs. Les Ambassadeurs dominated their generation for producing more slow songs.

Telfort, Jean Elie (Cubano) - Singer / Harmonica

In the 1960s the town of Port de Paix had three young singers who many considered potential superstars. They were Guy Jean who would end up singing in area bistros in Washington, D.C. The others were Roger M Eugene (Shoubou) and the third one is Jean Elie Telfort (Cubano).

Jean Elie started to get the attention of the people of Port de Paix first as a soccer player and later as the singer of the band La Perle Des Antilles. However, Port de Paix was going to lose all three singers as the guys moved on to bigger cities. Shoubou joined the band Tabou Combo based in Pétion Ville while Jean Elie who is three years younger went to complete his last years of high school at Lycée Pétion in Port-au-Prince.

Tabou Combo was the passion of young people at the end of the 1960s and they had a regular gig at a movie theatre called Ciné Paramount. Jean Elie, like other young men became a groupie of Tabou, hanging around his successful friend Shoubou. Since he had very good diction and was fluent in t French, Shoubou got him a job as Tabou Combo's Master of Ceremony at the weekly show. Shoubou's dream was that his childhood friend Jean Elie could be next to him as the lead singer of Tabou, but it was only a dream because Shoubou himself was walking on thin ice and was not even at that time fully accepted by all the members. The star singer of Tabou at the time was Sergo Guerrier the man that was the main attraction of the young ladies and the favorite front man of the band.

When the first squad of Les Shleu Shleu decided to move to New York the band's management had to do some damage control and started to audition some new talents. Shoubou suggested to his friend Jean Elie to try for the job and among the 20 finalists maestro Serge Rosenthal chose the young man from Port de Paix Jean Elie Telfort as the new front man of Les Shleu Shleu, and from that day forward the world would know one of the best vocal duo in a band as Cubano and Zouzoule would dominate the Konpa scene with their powerful voices for many years.

Jean Elie was a great fan of the Cuban singer Celia Cruz and he often talked about her talent. People started to see him as a male version of the legendary Cuban singer, especially in the way he moved while he was playing. Since they couldn't call him Celia, which is a female name, the guys started to call him "**CUBANO**" which means the Cuban.

By the early 1970s Cubano quickly became a star. His voice was heard all over the airwaves in hit songs like *Reviens, Cérémonie Lwa, Acé Frapé, Aie Tchou Aie, Quatre Saisons, Sept Péché Capitaux, Caroline, Belle Ti Machann* and *Yola* among others. In 1973 Shleu Shleu did a song of support for the National Soccer Team in preparation for the 1974 World Cup. It was the voice of Cubano that delivered the song that was played all over the country as a mean of motivation to the CONCACAF games final held in Haiti at the end of 1973. In the song, Cubano called the name of each soccer star while the band answered *"Al Bay Goal"* in other words *"Go and Score"*.

In 1974, after successful tour in Europe and the Caribbean, most members of the second squad of Les Shleu Shleu followed the footsteps of their predecessors by moving to New York where they became known as Skah Shah.

It is in New York that Cubano would reach the status of superstar as Haitians living in the diaspora would travel for many miles to come and experience the new Konpa sensation of New York. Cubano, then the only singer of the band showed that he not only had a great voice, but also had the ability to entertain and that he had no reason to envy Sergo Guerrier, Shoubou and others. He became the ladies favorite in his new home base and the source of attraction to his band as soon as the band released the album *Les Dix Commandments* with the mega hit song *Haiti*. The words in the song written by Arsène Appolon were delivered eloquently by Cubano who created the feeling of being nostalgic especially in the Jam he dropped on top of the chorus part *"Mézanmi Kòman Nou Yé"*.

When Zouzoule joined Skah Shah a bit later, it only motivated Cubano to work even harder and the perfect duo delivered in every album a state of the art Konpa that many bands tried to imitate but could not.

Cubano also made his mark in songs like *Racine Corré, Zoute, Zanmi, Manman, Macho Man* and *This Is It* among many others.

By the early 80s Cubano started to be a problem for the band leader and administration as he was chronically late and sometimes even absent. He, at times, would be in the room but spend time talking to his friends and letting Zouzoule do some of his work.

By the mid to late 80s Skah Shah continued to be a band with too many stars doing their own things and was difficult to manage. Some members showed more interest in their solo albums with the name Skah Shah tag to them. Loubert Chancy, Jhonny Frantz Toussaint (Ti Frè), Arsène Appolon all had their projects. Cubano got some members and other musicians and moved on with his own Skah Shah also. Instead of writing the name of the band as Skah Shah #1, Cubano chose to use only letters and called his project Skah Shah **NUMBER ONE.** Now as a band leader and a more mature musician, he quickly learned to manage his time and carried the responsibility of directing and managing a squad of musicians. In the 1990s he tried his best to keep the Skah Shah legacy alive, in the middle of the confusion of the many Skah Shahs. He, as well as his former band mates, who had moved on to create their own bands including Bazouka with Zouzoule on lead vocal, were all struggling and fighting to get jobs playing the same old hit songs of Skah Shah. At that time the music had shifted to the digital movement and bands like Top Vice, T-Vice, and Sweet Micky were getting most of the gigs. In New York the Konpa market was dominated by more structured full bands like Tabou Combo, System Band, Zin and Phantoms.

Cubano managed to survive by releasing some competitive albums under the title Skah Shah Number One as well as some live recordings. His albums El Cuban, l'Essence and Knockout are among his best as a songwriter and a band leader. At the turn of the century he agreed to be part of a reunion tour that included all the original members and some that became part of Skah Shah along the way. The matured musicians finally realized that they were only strong when they worked as a team and all those egos and hunger for power would only result in chaos for everyone's career.

In 2006 the band released the album *Lagué Diaz La*. Cubano once again continued to tour the world with his partners of the early days as some of the most perfect groups of musicians that the Konpa society has ever known. They bring the flavor of the good old days to many nostalgic Haitians in search of reminiscing and enjoying well-organized parties as Skah Shah continued to attract people who love to dress to impress, with the voice of Cubano still strong and leading the way.

Telfort, Rousseau - Guitar
Rousseau worked mostly as a freelance musician for most of his career. He played with Konpa and Gospel artists alike and delivered the best of himself in studios and live shows as well.

Tempo - Band

Termitus, Moise - Bass

Termilus, Sachel (Ti Papy) - Guitar
Ti Papy played with his band Groove La as well as Sweet Micky and has participated in several Konpa studio projects with different groups, especially in Miami Fl. In the spring of 2008, Ti Papy joined the band Nu Look.

Terribles (Les Terribles de Pétion Ville) –Band
Band of the Mini Jazz era

Terry, Sue - Saxophone
She is a non-Haitian female musician who played the saxophone next to
Loubert Chancy in Skah Shah.

Tezil, Jean Edner - Singer

Thadal, Walter * - Trumpet
Walter played with the band Super Ensemble de Nemours Jean Baptiste.

Thadent, Bernard Jr. - Singer

Thamad Fever - Band
This band came out in New York in the late 1970s.

Thamar, Ralph - Singer
Ralph is a French Caribbean superstar that made his mark in the Konpa world,
and has captivated Haitian music lovers all over the world.

Thébaud, Alex - Singer /Congas /Gong
Musician of the band K-Dans who later joined his former K-Dans partners in
the band Carimi, based in the Haitian diaspora. Alex played the congas in
K-Dans but he moved on to the gong when he joined Carimi.

Thélémaque, Louis - Saxophone
Louis Thélémaque is another genius from Super Ensemble de Nemours Jean
Baptiste. Like most of the musicians of the group, he eventually moved to
New York where he spent the rest of his musical life playing for the Christian
community.

Thelismond, Francis - Singer
Did his best years with Les Frères Déjean in the 1990s

Thelus, Andre - Congas

Thelusma, Adeline - Singer
Adeline played with the band Papash in the early 1990s

Thelusma, Thedile - Singer

Théo see: Jadotte Théophile

Théodat, Turgot - Saxophone

Théodore, Jimmy - Percussion

Théodore, Joel * - Singer
This talented singer had his best years with the band Bossa Combo in the early 1980s with the success of the songs *Notre Dame* and *Société* and the interpretation of the late Ritchie Valens' song *Donna*. Just like Ritchie Valens the young singer Joel Théodore died too young to enjoy his God-given talent.

Théagène, Pierre - Singer

Théophile, Benoit - Congas

Théophile, Emile - Trumpet

Théophile, Rosny - Singer

Thézan, Gérard - Singer
Gérard Thézan was one of the star singers of the 1960s that helped take the band Super Ensemble de Webert Sicot to the level of one of Haiti greatest bands ever.

Thibault, Wilfrid -Trumpet

Thibert, Sergot - Bass
Sergot joined the band Les Fantaisites de Carrefour after the Charles Brothers Gersaint (Mama) and Pierre (Pèdè) left Haiti to immigrate in the U.S.A. in the early 1970s.

Thibulle, Renand - Drums
Renand was the star drummer of Djet-X, a New York based band in the 1970s under the leadership of maestro Gerard Daniel.

Thimoté, Gabriel - Saxophonist
Gabriel was, next to Prosper Simon the other star saxophonist of the band Les Lionceuax des Cayes, a band that dominated the south of Haiti and later the whole country in the 1970s with the powerful voice of Léon Dimanche.

Thimothé, Frantz - Drums

Thora Combo - Band

Thozin, Emmanuel - Bass
Emmanuel Thozin was mostly known during his best days as a showman who played in Haiti with one of the late version of Scorpio and later in New York with Carlito Coupé.

Ti Blan see: Charles Octavius Claude Cinna (Sax)

Ti Blan see: Raymond Max (Guitar)

Ti Guy see: Montreuil Guy / Paul Yves Léon / Sylvain Clifford

Ti Kabzy - Band
This band, based in Montreal, came out in the 1990s finally get some recognition at the turn of the century. Under the direction of the guitarist Georges Nazi and the bassist Joe Fortuné, the band managed to make some hit songs and was able to make people of every generation enjoy their Konpa.

Ti Linèt see: Momplésir James

Ti Mitou see: Frederique Fritz

Ti Nes see: Louis Ernst / Vincent Ernst

Ti Nes see: Vincent Ernst (Bass)

Ti Papy see: Termilus Sachel

Ti Pouch see: Charlemagne Edzer

Ti Régi see: Bastien Réginald

Ti Yale see: Jean Baptiste Roger

Ticket Magazine
Ticket magazine is a product of Le Nouveliste Newspaper. The magazine produced in Haiti often featured Konpa artists on the cover.

Tico Pasket see: Pasket Claude

Timmer, Alix - Show Promoter / Record Producer / Distributor

Tiz - Band
Konpa band based in Boston

Top Adlerman see: Gaston Jean Adler

Top Compas - Band
When Nemours moved to the U.S. with some of his musicians, the remaining members created the band Top Compas. That didn't help them much as the Mini Jazz movement was gaining momentum and eventually kept Top Compas on the back burners. When Nemours returned to Haiti, he changed the name to Super Combo de Nemours Jean Baptiste and quickly released the hit song *Gasson Nou Nan Ka* with the voice of the singer Carlo Vieux.

Top Coupé - Band

Top Digital - Band
After the dissolution of Digital Express,(the band of legendary Konpa keyboardist Hans "Ansyto" Mercier) "Ti Ansyto" kept the flame of the family owned band alive by creating the Top Digital Band with the support and the blessing of his famous father. The band Top Digital finally came to an end in 2005, as Ti Ansyto was called to be a member of the newly formed band Kréyol La. Ironically, in 2006 his father also joined the squad of Kréyol La.

Top Girls - Band
This band, which was created in Cap Haitien in the Mini Jazz era, is known as the first all Haitian female bands in the history of Konpa music. There are no recordings or pictures of the band.

Top Gyps - Band

Top Master - Band
This band is based in West Palm Beach Florida.

Top Shleu - Band

Top Vice - Band

Top Vice came out in Miami in the 1980s. At first no one took the idea seriously, the band playing in a reduced format and playing mostly the hit songs of other bands. However, little by little the public started to show up at their shows and the buzz was out that a new format was created and that the musicians were talented and knew what they were doing.

With the experience of the guitarist Robert Martino, who had been unemployed since he left Scorpio, and the magic fingers and the computer knowledge of the keyboardist Robert Charlot Raymondville, the lead singer Carmelo Frédérique (Freddy) a new comer in the Miami area from Washington, D.C. carried the band and the new system to another level.

Later the band added a bass player with the arrival of Joe Charles in Florida. Over the years many changes occurred in the band. In 2003 Robert Martino was replaced by the guitarist Ralph Condé and later Robert returned to the band. In 2005, Robert Martino and Robert Charlot walked away from Freddy to create the band Nu Vice and later Martino went back to Top Vice. Courageously Freddy continued to fight to keep the band busy and the name alive by adding the drummer/composer Ulrick Bouzi to the lineup.

Top Vice's discography include but is not limited to the following albums: *Min Nou, Carnaval, Sinfoni D'amou, Compas L'an 2000, Grove Mania Top Vice Gold, Haiti Mon Pays Miami Mon Ami, Compas Avèg La, Iya Iya Oh Oh (Let's make love tonight), Steady and Ready, Tcho Tcho* and a series of live recordings as well as some best of and compilations of the selected hit songs of the band

Toussaint, Hilarion - Trumpet

Toussaint, Jhonny Frantz (Ti Frè) - Guitar

Ti Frè grew up in a family where music was king. He had the chance as a teenager to play with his cousins Milot Toussaint at first and Mario Mayala later in the band Les Shleu Shleu in Haiti. He was also part of the second squad that would later be known as Skah Shah. In his years in Skah Shah, he showed the world that he was not only a good guitarist, but also a very good songwriter as he composed for the band some memorable hit songs like: *Manman, Racine Coré, Macho Man,* and *Forever Number One* among others. Ti Frè also released his solo album with the title *Aida*. In the 1990s he was part of the musicians that left Skah Shah to be part of the band Bazouka. At the turn of the century the members of Skah Shah got back together and the fans were happy to see that Ti Frè was back playing with their favorite band. In 2006,

Skah Shah released the album *Lagué Diazz La* and once again the contribution of Ti Frè in that album showed the world that despite his four decades in the Konpa, he had kept his touch as one of the best Konpa guitarist of all time.

Toussaint, Milot Guitar - Guitar
One of the pioneers of the Mini Jazz movement Milo was one of the first guitarists of Les Shleu Shleu. He is credited with creating the "Bouyon" groove style, which was common and imitated by many guitarists over the years. Unlike a solo, where the note seems to be detached and played in a sequence, the bouyon sounds like a combination of notes being played at the same time. It takes a skilled guitarist to be able to do it as it can be confusing and requires the ability to change chords quickly. Milot Toussaint left Haiti at an early age and he was replaced in Les Shleu Shleu by his cousin Jhonny Frantz Toussaint who was able to follow in his footsteps in every way possible and has even became a more popular musician and real master of the bouyon groove. In the late 70s he tried to make a comeback in New York with the band Last Stop, but the Last Stop project was also been the last stop for Milot Toussaint as he quietly retired from the music scene.

Toussaint, Patrick *- Drums
One of the Toussaint brothers who helped put together the band Lakol. Patrick died at a very young age.

Toussaint, Rodrigue - Guitar
Rodrigue played with the band Bossa Combo during the best years of Konpa in the 1970s. As the lead guitarist, he was more of quiet person who, like Mario Mayala, Ronald Smith and Réginald Benjamin, let his guitar do the talking.

Toussaint, Sergot - Guitar

Toussaint, Smith - Drums
Smith played with the bands Washington Express and later with G.P.Express in Washington, D.C.

Toussaint, Stanley (Tantan) - Singer / Guitar / Keyboard
Tantan took the music scene by surprise in the early 1990s with the release of the video of his hit song *Olé Olé,* which also introduced his band "Lakol". Suddenly there was this voice and this young dancer that got the attention of every music lover in what is considered by many the best Haitian music video ever released. No video had made an impact on the public like the *Olé Olé* video that showcased the talent of Tantan. Before long the name Stanley Toussaint and the band Lakol was known not only in the Haitian diaspora but

all over Haiti and the French Caribbean Islands.

At the band's first tour to Haiti, people lined up along the route from the airport to take a glance at Tantan and the members of Lakol. The band played in front of a large audience at every show. In the following years Tantan continues to show that he is one of the best Haitian songwriters and that the success of *Olé Olé* was not just by chance as he released *Difé, Kolem* and *Something Special,* among others. However, Tantan suffered some serious losses over the years as some of his best musicians were constantly being recruited by more popular groups, and sometimes he even played the guitar while singing at some shows. The death of his brother, the band's drummer Patrick Toussaint, had a serious impact on him as well. However Tantan managed over the years to continue to work and to produce good songs with his band Lakol.

In 2004 he released the album *Pam Pam Pam* that once again surprised many people in the Haitian Music Industry. The *Pam Pam Pam* album was released not as a Lakol album, but simply as "Tantan", showcasing the famous entertainer this time as a solo artist and not like the leader of a musical group. Once again history repeated itself as the song won the first prize in the Song of the Year and Video of the Year categories at several Haitian music awards in 2005. The *Pam Pam Pam* album, just like the Olé Olé album was sold out and has been reprinted by the production company as the public continues to demand the record, even several years after it was first released, thus making Stanley Toussaint one of the best Haitian entertainers of his generation. In the spring of 2008 Tantan released the album Machadiz La

Toussaint, Vladimir - Singer
Vladimir was mostly a support as a background vocalist to his star brother Tantan. At the turn of the century he lost interest and eventually faded away in the Konpa music scene.

Toussaint, Webert – Guitar

Toussaint, Yves (Ti Yves) - Drums
Yves Toussaint was one of the founders of the band Samba Creole. However, before the band became successful with the carnival songs *Caporal* and *Colé Boyo*, Yves had left the country and moved to Canada where he became a professional drummer playing in Canadians and other international bands.

Traffic - Band

Trak - Band
A band that was mostly known for mixing the Konpa with the Latin styles of

music, especially Salsa and Merengue.

Trankill – Band

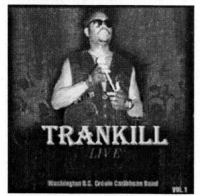

When the musicians of Zépon decided to voluntarily put an end to their live performances as they moved on with other careers, the Washington, D.C. area was left without a band from the year 2000 to 2004. The singer/promoter Jean Claude Vivens came back to the scene in full force with the creation of a new band with the support of the father and son keyboardists, Georges and Micky Walker, as well as the guitarist Jean Gardy Hypolitte. On April 2004 he introduced the band Trankill to the public of Washington in front a sold-out crowd at the Napoli Nightclub in Silver Spring Md. In 2005 the band released the album *Trankill Live* as well as the video of the song *Sonson*.

Tredling, Jean –Trombone
Played with the band La Ruche de Léogane in the 1970s

Trenard, Francis - Saxophone
Francis was one of the star saxophonists of the band Jazz des Jeunes who played next to maestro René St Aude.

Tricheurs (Les Tricheurs de Manhattan) - Band
This band came out under the leadership of the keyboardist Reynold Duverglas in New York City with the brothers Arthur & Ricardo Lovelace on lead vocal. Boulo Valcourt on guitar, Alix Corvington on bass, Jean Alix (Jeanjean) Laraque on the drums, Claudy Jean on congas (tambours), Gaguy Dépestre on Saxophone, and Guy Jean on gong. When the band leader moved out of New York, both singers followed his footsteps by moving to Washington D.C. and the rest of the musicians moved on with their career and changed the name of the band to Ibo Combo.

Triomecs - Band

Tropnas, Alex - Guitar
Alex came out very shyly in the late 1980s playing with Michel Martelly (Sweet Micky), but by the early 1990s he became one of the most imitated guitarists of his generation. At the turn of the century he vanished from the Konpa scene leaving Sweet Micky no choice but to look for someone who could replace the hard working musician and ex-administrator of his band. Many have tried over the years to fill his shoes from star guitarist Ronald

Lubin and the musical icon Robert Martino to some newcomers in the game like Ti Papy of the band Groove La, and Jean Gardy Hypolitte of the Washington, D.C-based band Trankill who really has the same style as Alex, and often said that Alex was his role model. However, none of those good guitarists was able to put up with the attitude of Sweet Micky and eventually left the band leaving empty the hole left by Alex Tropnas who, after all, seems to be the one who had the formula for the rhythm behind the success of the popular star.

Tropical - Band
This band is considered after l'Orchestre de Pépé Bayard the second Haitian band created in New York in the 1960s. That was the band that also helped the talent of the legendary guitarist Dadou Pasket which was later recruited by Tabou Combo.

Tropical Combo de Ti Jacques - Band
This band was created in the 1970s in New York by Jacques François musician of Septentrional. Their song *Information* was an instant hit and has kept the band weekly show at Chez Julie Restaurant a success and a win win situation for the band and the restaurant. The international soccer, star the late Fritz Léandre (Fito), also played guitar for the band in the late 70s.

Tropical Sextet de Garry French - Band
This band was created in New York by Gary French one of the singers of Super Ensemble the Webert Sicot.

Tropical System – Band

Tropicana – Band

Even through Tropicana was created on Aug. 15, 1963 the story of the band began before that date. Tropicana is basically a continuation of Jazz Capois, which later became known as Caribe, in the 1950s. When musicians got together to form a more solid group that could be more competitive in the growing market by recruiting other talented musicians, a Cuban exile named Basil Conti (who ended in Cap Haitian fleeing Fidel Castro) suggested the name "Tropicana" in memory of a famous club in Cuba.

The meeting was put together by Claudin Toussaint, who became the first leader of the band. Some other members of the early days of Tropicana were the horn blowers Emmanuel Turenne, Chenet Noel, André Butoix, the late Emanuel Figaro (Ti Sax), and notably the famous trumpet player Désilon Voltaire. The singers Coignard Bonny and Michel Fleurantin and Rosny Jasmin (Momo) the latter would become the star singer of the band Etoile Du Soir in Port-au-Prince. Besides Momo, some other musicians of the band were also recruited by more stable bands like the bassist Eval Manigat, who was snatched by maestro Webert Sicot for his band.

The early days of Tropicana were very troublesome, as musicians were coming and leaving and the members had trouble managing the group. In the middle of all this chaos, the guitarist Charlemagne Pierre Noel came with some powerful members of the government including Reynold Dominique (the brother of Max Dominique who was married to the president's daughter) and Tropicana would forever be known as the favorite band of the Macoutes. Toussaint tried his best to get back the control of his band until he realized that it would be better for him to leave the country and he ended up in New York. The band at the time, was playing a style called Cadence Plaké, and was basically not getting many gigs, but with the addition of some new members, the band quickly changed direction and moved on to play more danceable tunes. With the addition of some younger members with new ideas like the singer Parisien Fils Aimé, Geordany Joseph the conga player and composer Daniel Larivière, Louis Jean Lubin on trumpet, Pierre Lesca on drum and of course Ti Blan on saxophone, the big band happened to survive at a time when the Mini Jazz had basically put an end to the reign of both Nemours and Sicot big Ensembles. From that time on Tropicana, also known as Tropic or La Fusée D'or du Cap has become a super force in the Haitian music world both, as the best-managed band, but also as a hit maker.

More than forty years after its creation, Tropicana continued to tour the world, and songs like *Yolande Mizè Maléré, Adrienne, Doux Tropic* and *Angelique* will remain for many years to come songs that dominated the Haitian music scene as Tropicana continue to surprise the world as a band that has no reason to envy any group of any generation, for it has survived all kind of changes and storm in the Haitian music arena for more that forty years.

Tropidisc - Records Company

Trouillot, Joseph André - Singer / Bass
Joe Troillot was one of the star singers of the 1950s. He played with the top bands of the time, like the Orchestre of Issa El Saieh, Raoul Guillaume and The Casino International band. He left Haiti in the late 1960s and in the 1970s he created his band Le Combo Express in Montreal, Canada. Joe Trouillot, born in 1922 continues, despite his old age, to perform live at several fundraisings events, concerts and private parties in the 21st century. He was also honored on several occasions as one of the pioneers of the Haitian music.

Turenne, Emmanuel - Saxophonist
Emmanuel Turenne is known in the Haitian music arena as one of the star saxophonists and former leader of the band Tropicana. He had developed the horn section style of the band keeping the saxophonists busy almost throughout the songs compared to other bands, where the saxophone's parts are used only in the introduction and the end of the songs, besides a few solo in between. Next to Ti Blan and Yaffa, Emmanuel Turenne has managed to show that the saxophone line of Tropicana's horn section is really unique.

Twoubadou
Basically the word troubadour was commonly used in Europe in the 11th century as the people living in southern France, eastern Spain and northern Italy used the word to describe artists that compose and sign verses and ballads about courtly love.
The word which came from the Old Latin verb "trobar" is translated as "to find" in English or "trouver" in French and later the word "trobador" was used to describe the folks singers who were able to find, to compose, to improvise, to invent their own songs.
This culture was carried in the Americas due to colonization and eventually made it to Haiti as well as Haitian folks singers were also call Troubadours. Many Haitian Troubadours used to serenade their girlfriends with love ballads at night, sometimes to the delight of friends and family members. The singers Rodrigue Millien and Jules Similien (Toto Necessité) were known troubadours in the country before reaching stardom as comedians and later as

recording artists. Gesner Henry (Coupe Cloue) was also a troubadour early in his career.

If Archille Paris (Ti Paris) remain the most popular Haitian troubadours of all time, he was however not the first troubadour to entertain the population, because people of the previous generations often talk about a man name Canjo who used to amuse the public with his ballads.

In the town of Les Cayes a man name Robert Molin is believe to have created many songs that were later used by Coupe Cloué, the band Etoile du Soir and many other artists. Robert Molin was the troubadour who entertained the south side of the country.

In Port-au-Prince the Legros family was well known for creating songs that were loved by the public. Jean Legros and Archibal Legros were famous guitarists, but they couldn't reach the popularity of the troubadour Rodolphe (Dodof) Legros author of the songs *Marabout de mon coeur*, *Manman Nanotte* and *Mademoiselle je vous aime* among others.

The troubadours who entertained the crowd in the yearly cultural activities at the town of Saut d'eau also known as ville Bonheur located in the Plateau Central Haiti have inspired Nemours Jean baptiste in the creation of the rhythm Compas Direct.

The word was widely used in Haiti and a band even came out under the name Les Gais Troubadours. However, with the invasion of the mini jazz in the country the style of music played by the troubadours simply vanished for more than two decades in the country with the influence of amplified instruments. The acoustic guitars and accordions were quickly replaced by the electric guitars and organs. Many young troubadours have also found fame by joining the mini Jazz movement.

At the end of the century, Mario de Volcy released his album Super Mario IV in which he included the song Marie La Folle with the sound of all the instruments used in the past by the Haitian troubadours. This song started a trend in the Haitian music scene as it sounded new to the ears of younger Haitian music lovers. Fabrice Rozier took advantage of the situation by releasing the album *Haiti Twoubadou* with the collaboration of several Haitian stars. He writes the word in his native Creole language by changing the first **r** to a **w** and dropping the last **r** in accordance with the creole grammar.

After the release of the album, the new generation simply called the style of music "**Twoubadou**" as well.

Today in the Haitian society the word "Twoubadou' is use to describe not only the artist but the style of music as well.

U

U-Nik - Band
This band came out in N.Y with superstar guitarist Ronald Smith and the singer Moise Juste. Most of the members are from Ronald Smith's band Q-Style. To many people U-Nik is basically the new name of the band Q-Style. The band was introduced to the public by the music video titled *Lyllie* released in December 2007.

U-Turn - Band
This band came out in New York in the mid 70s

Ulcena, Jean Michel - Gong
Played with Bossa Combo, and was also one of the musicians of the group who left Haiti to create the band Accolade de New York. Prior to Bossa Combo he played with the band Latino D'Haiti.

Universel Channel 10 - Band
This band was created by some former members of the band Channel 10.

Urbain, Richard - Promoter / Producer
One of the top show Haitian show promoters, Richard did most of his shows in New York. He is also the booking agent of several Haitian bands. He is also a record producer.

Ulysse, Anthony (Ti Mèt) - Gong

Ulysse, Rosemond -Saxophone

V

V.M Band - Band
V.M was another name that used to be used to identify the band Velox Machine.

Vag - Band
When Ralph Condé left Haiti to immigrate to the U.S., he created the band Vag. The band did well for a few months but did not survive when Ralph moved on with his career by playing with more popular bands like Lakol, Tabou Combo and Nu Look.

Valbrun, Claude - Guitar

Valcin, Hugo - Bass / Drums

Valcourt, Henriot (Boulou) - Singer
Boulou is one of the artists who started his musical career at a very young age. In the 1960s, he was only a teenager when he joined the band Les Copains. He left Haiti to study in Canada, where he became a member of the band Caribe. After his experience in Canada, he moved to New York where he collaborated with Réginald Polycard, the Laraque Brothers Michel and Toto, as well as the singer José Tavernier in the band Ibo Combo in the early 70s. As a fan of Ti Paris, he spent his career trying to keep the music of the deceased artist alive by performing at least a song of Ti Paris from his days to Ibo Combo to his current performances.
In the mid-70s Boulou returned to Haiti where he started his T.V. show, "The Boulou Show". During that period some more members of Ibo Combo returned to the country as well, and the musicians regrouped this time under the name Horizon 75 which later became known as Caribbean Sextet. In the 1980s the band Caribbean Sextet became very popular and their Sunday shows at l'Auberge in Boutillier were one of the main attractions in the country.
In the 1990s Caribbean Sextet lost its grip and Boulou tried his best to save the band, until he desperately created the band Djanm. He later changed the name to Caribbean Djanm. Finally, Boulou decided to move on as a solo artist and tour the world while he continued to also be active in broadcasting. Boulou has over the years received many awards and he continued to represent Haiti as an artist at different international festivities in different countries in the Caribbean, Europe, Africa and the Americas. He took part in the Smithsonian Folk Life Festival in Washington, D.C. in 2004, where his performances were

appreciated by people of all nations who experienced the yearly tourist attraction in which every year a different country is showcased in the U.S. capital.

Boulou also took part in different artist projects, notably Réginald Polycard and the Haitiando albums produced by Mini Records.

Valcourt, Jean Max - Keyboard

Jean Max became a star in his native town of Cap Haitien at an early age. He showcased his talents in the band Lakol d'Haiti in the early 1990s. He moved to New York, where he became a member of the band Phantoms as the second keyboardist of the group.

As a song producer, the services of Jean Max were often requested by other artists and bands of the 1990s, including the band Zépon in Washington, D.C. By the turn of the century Jean Max decided to build his own recording studio and ever since he has been one of the busiest Haitian music producers, as his studio "Maximum Studio" is one of the favorites of Haitian artists in New York.

Valdez, Bedo - Keyboard

Valerius, Hernst (Doudou) - Saxophone
Doudou is like, Harold Joseph, another musician who was educated by the school Frères Adrien. Just like Harold he showed his talent in the band Safari Combo and moved on to create the band Super 9. His style on the saxophone was quite unique, which put him in a class by himself in the 1970s. He left Haiti in the 1980s. He joined of the band Thamad Fever in New York, an adventure that didn't last long. In the early 1990s he gave his help to Skah Shah, replacing Loubert Chancy and later he gave his help to the squad of the band Bazouka.

In New York, just like the singer Jean Claude Dorsainvil (Charlie), Doudou worked for many years as a bus driver in the Linden Boulevard corridor in Queens. He also used to provide transportation from New York to other towns for many Konpa bands based in New York.

Valmé, Bernard - Gong / Percussion
Bernard played in New York with Djet-X before becoming a regular musician of Phantoms.

Valmé, Reynald - Congas
Reynald was snatched out of Haiti by Tabou Combo to replace Fanfan Ti Botte

on Congas as Fanfan moved on to the front line supporting Shoubou on the vocal lineup of the band.
Prior to the popular Tabou Combo, Reynald played in Haiti with D.P. Express as a double for Pierrot Kersaint, and also with the band Caribbean Sextet.

Valmé, Ricardo - Keyboard

Valmé, Serge - Singer

Vampires (Les Vampires) – Band
Band of the Mini Jazz era

Vautours (Les Vautours) - Band
This band came out in the Mini Jazz era, the name was later changed to Samba Jazz and some members moved on to create the band Super Soline d'Haiti.

Vava see: Dascy Jean Musset

Vega Band - Band
Haitian band that was based in Paris France

Velox Machine – Band
That band also identified itself as V.M. Band.

Venelin, Velouse - Singer

Verault, Andre - Trombone

Verdier, Daddy - Guitar / Keyboard

Verdier, Jean Claude - Promoter / Producer
Jean Claude Verdier is one of the most popular Haitian music producers. His company, Musique Des Antilles, has produced many Haitian bands and artists especially in the 1980s. Jean Claude Verdier moved back to Haiti in the late 70s where he continued not only to produce some artists, but managed to become one of the top show producers of the country, working not only with Haitian bands and artists but with some of very popular foreign stars as well. His company provides the sound system for many bands in their live shows, concerts, festivals and carnival floats.

Vertières - Band

Vertilus, Fritz - Congas

Vertus, Jacques - Trumpet
Jacques played in the 1960s with the band Super Ensemble de Webert Sicot.

Viaux, Didier - Gong

Viaux, Eddy - Gong
Eddy is a musician of T. Vice. He played previously with Hangout.

Victor, Jacques - Congas

Victor, Marcel - Singer
Marcel is a well-known radio announcer in Boston, but in the Mini Jazz era he had his days as the singer of Les Eperviers and later joined the band Les Papillons.

Victor, Marcelus - Guitar
Marcellus is another very quiet guitarist who let his fingers do the talking. Marcellus played the guitar at an early age for churches only, but in his teenage years he became the star guitarist of the band Les Animateurs. When Les Animateurs created the hit song *Ti Machine*, Konpa lovers started to notice the talent of the young guitarist. Marcelus later joined the band Combite Créole de Rodrigue Milien when Rodrigue returned to Haiti after trying life in the U.S. with his partner Jules Similien (Toto Nécéssité). Marcelus, playing guitar solo next to Rodrigue and Almajik Belot created the trio that moved the nation with the unique style of the Combite Creole's chord line. In the 1980s Marcelus joined Les Frères Déjean, playing with Casimir Alliance and Francis Thelismond on lead vocal. In the 1990s, while the band was on tour in the U.S., some musicians decided to call it quits and stayed in America as the music business and night life in Haiti was almost non-existent due to the embargo and insecurity in the country. Marcelus regained his fame of the 1970s when he became one of the founding members of the Miami-based band D-Zine. After a series of good live shows and successful albums, a dispute among the members ripped the band apart as some members moved on to create the band Nu Look. Marcelus and some others stayed loyal to the D-Zine projects, but unfortunately, didn't succeed.

Victor, Paul * - Guitar
Paul played with the band Channel 10 in Haiti.

Victor, Staford - Keyboard

Vieux, Carlo - Singer

Carlo Vieux helped Nemours to keep the Compas Direct dream alive in the early 70s as the Mini Jazz movement was at its peak in Haiti. Nemours Jean Baptiste tried to regroup his members who were living Haiti to find life in other countries, especially in the U.S. Carlo Vieux delivered an excellent job in the song *Gasson Nou Nan Ka* with Nemours' new band Super Combo. The idea of keeping the dream alive was a good one, but the reality was facing Nemours that the good times were behind him and Carlo Vieux moved on with his career by joining Rodrigue Millien in the band Combite Créole replacing Jules Similien (Toto Nécéssité) who had decided to stay in New York. There again, the career of Carlo Vieux took a dive as he never became as popular as Toto was in the Combite Créole band and he finally moved on with other careers.

Vieux, Carlo - Keyboard /Singer

Carlo Vieux is one of the founders of the band Carimi. He plays the keyboard and he also sing during live shows and on the studio recordings. He was previously a member of the band K-Dans in Haiti, he met in New York with two other members of K-Dans and the trio used the first two letters of their first name to form CARIMI the name of their new band **CA** for Carlo Vieux **RI** for Richard Cavé and **MI** for Michael Guirand.

Vikings - Band

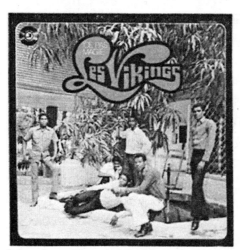

Vikings was one of the popular bands of the Mini Jazz era. Vikings was known for coming out with many slogans. Levy, one of the singers of the band, was also at the time of the goal keeper of the soccer team Violette. While playing he used to say the catchy phrase "*Banm Boul*".

Vikings made the song *Teuleuleu* which is even now one of the memorable hits of the 70s. When Mariela, a young schizophrenic lady, made the news in the 70s by climbing the "Sans Fil" telephone tower in the "Post Marchand" neighborhood, Vikings was quick to make a song titled *Mariela* which was also a popular tune of the era.

Vilamil, Ernie - Keyboard

Vilejoint, Merlot - Guitar

Villard, Marc - Trumpet

Villevalex, Leconte (Choubouloute) - Singer
Choubouloute got his name for singing the song *Choubouloute* a popular hit of
the 1940s made by the band Les Gais Troubadous. He later joined the band
Citadel before becoming popular as one of the singers of Super Ensemble de
Nemours Jean Baptiste.

Vilsaint, Lesly - Guitar

Vilson, Georges - Singer

Vincent, Ernst (Ti Nes) - Bass
Ti Nès was not one of the superstars in Haiti like many musicians of his
generation. He played the congas for a small band in his neighborhood in
Wanhey/Carrefour, a suburb of Port-au-Prince. He joined the band Les Frères
Déjean in New York in the late 70s and the young bassist had no problem
proving that he was able to fit in with the band which was already full of
professionals. When the band Les Frères Déjean had trouble with their visa
situation and was forced to stay in Haiti during a tour, Ti Nès was among the
group of musicians who returned to New York to create the band known as
System Band.
It is with System that Ti Nès was going to show his ability to create mega hits
and a Konpa arranger that the band has learned to count on. He has over the
years complemented the work of the famous duo of guitarists Ronald Smith
and Réginald Benjamin by providing the System Band with one of the best
chord lines ever in the history of Konpa Music.
At the end of the 1990s Ti Nès moved to Miami Fl. with his family and found
worked with the band D-Zine. In 2004, he was one of the members of D-Zine
who walked away from the rest of the team to create the band Hang Out. Ti
Nès was also named the band leader of Hang Out.

Vincent, Lyonel - Gong / Percussion

Virgal, Eric - Singer
Eric Virgal is a French Caribbean Music star who has captivated and charmed
the music lovers and had the chance to perform with many Haitian Konpa
superstars at shows in Haiti and in the Haitian diaspora. He is often
accompanied by Haitian Konpa artists at most of his shows.

Virtioses de St Marc - Band
This band of the Mini Jazz era came out in the town of St Marc in 1970.

Vital, Daddy - Singer
Daddy was the lead singer of Magic Connection in the early 1980s.

Vital-Herne, Jacques - Singer
Jacques played with the band Les Blousons Noirs in the Mini Jazz era. He left Haiti and the music business to study medicine. He is presently working in New York as a medical doctor.

Vivien, Fritz - Gong
Fritz played with Scorpio and Djakout Mizik in Haiti. When he moved to the U.S. he created his own Rara band in Brooklyn.

Vivens, Jean Claude (Agi) - Singer / Producer / Promoter

Born in Port-au-Prince Haiti, Jean Claude used to amuse his family and friends by singing and imitating all sorts of animals, even before he went to kindergarten. By the time he was a teenager he was already a good storyteller, always surrounded by friends who wanted to hear him crack jokes. Besides story telling, Jean Claude also developed two other passions: his love for radio broadcasts and music. He was often seen with a radio, either listening to music or the news. When he was 10 years old he saw the band Les Loups Noir perform at his cousin first communion party and after that day he became an avid Konpa fan and wanted to play music as well.

As a young man growing up in the Mini Jazz era, besides the Sunday afternoon kermesses and festivals, Jean Claude was too young to go watch his favorite bands perform at night, so he hung around some day practice sessions of bands like Samba Creole, Les Diamants and Les Pitzies, mimicking the artists and later found himself making songs of his own, beating all kind of cans and drums with friends in his backyard.

In 1976 he moved to New York where he started to follow bands like Original Shleu Shleu Astros, Les Frères Déjean, Djet-X, Skah Shah, Tabou Combo, and later System Band and Accolade. He and his late brother, Ambroise Vivens Fils (Fanfan), made new friends in their Cambria Heights, Queens' neighborhood and they became a well-known group of Konpa fans known to all the Konpa musicians and fans as the "Agimals", for the young men were often seen with different beautiful women at several parties. Contrary to the other members of the group Jean Claude was often invited by musicians to jam with them and he often entertained the crowd with his Konpa skills and some of his improvisations were even put on records by some of the bands. In 1981 he moved to Washington, D.C. where he joined the band Choc Combo as the lead singer. The band was turned to Les Pachas de Washington and by 1985 Jean Claude Vivens, known in the music arena of Washington, D.C. as Agi (short for Agimal), created with some fellow musicians the band Washington Express. He often cracked a few jokes to amuse the public during his live performances. He was invited by radio announcer Albert Massillion (Konpè Zin) for an interview about the band and to tell some jokes as well. During that Saturday night show on WPFW he took it upon himself to announce the upcoming songs on the radio show, and his voice and skills were discovered by Radio Host Jean Claudel Fleurival, who invited him to co-host his Sunday afternoon Konpa show "Radio Metropole Inter" on WNTR. Jean Claudel Fleurival is a very experienced broadcaster who had worked in Haiti on Radio Nouveau Monde (R.N.M) in the 1970s and was the host of the popular show "Le Rhytme Bat Dans La Caille". He became the mentor of the young Vivens.

By the end of the of the 1980s the voice of Jean Claude Vivens was already the voice of the Haitian community of Washington, D.C. being heard on live broadcast, radio jingles, commercial advertisings, on music recordings. He also was the Master of Ceremony of choice of the concerts and special events of the community, making him the most popular figure in the entertainment business in the DC/Maryland area. He became also at that time one of the singers of the band G.P. Express, playing next to the talented singer Imgart Manigat. In 1985, while he was playing with Washington Express eight musicians of the band D.P. Express as well as some former members Gemini All Stars de Ti Manno moved to Washington to create their own band, G.P. Express on the invitation of show promoter Jean Robert Baltazar, Jean Claude was approached a few years later by the keyboardist Ansyto Mercier, who saw in him a charismatic performer, to become part of the more professional squad that included popular artists like Ti Polis, Mario Germain, Lyonel Simeon, among other well-known stars of the 1980s. Jean Claude saw it as an opportunity to travel and show his skills outside of the DC/Maryland area. In 1988 Jean Claudel came up with the idea of starting the first Haitian T.V. show in the Haitian diaspora. Once again he called on Jean Claude Vivens to co-host the show with him. The two, without any experience in television production, besides being eloquent speakers and being fluent in the French language, started the show "Télé Metro", but without enough sponsorship, the show eventually didn't succeed.

In the following years Fleurival moved to New York but Vivens decided to keep the dream alive as he met a local politician, the council member Gregory Hamilton, who agreed to help him take some television production classes, computer graphics and editing workshops. Hamilton saw in Jean Claude a young man with a vision as Jean Claude explained to him that there was a need to promote, entertain and introduce other cultures in the area while educating foreigners in their native languages about immigration laws, fair housing laws, health issues, drug prevention and other concerns not quite understood by non- English speaking residents.

On Dec. 2nd 1990, Jean Claude Vivens started his own T.V. show "Haiti A Suivre" and he received, at the end of the year, the Bruce Moyer Award for his dedication and vision as a young entrepreneur. By the next year he was already named the assistant program director of the TPCT, a government-run station in the city of Takoma Park. With the help of council member Hamilton and the mayor of the city, he also created shows for other nationalities living in the Washington, D.C. area. Jean Claude created the shows "French Caribbean Music and Variety", and later he created the show "Africa Plus" which he turned over to the African community and left the production to his student Yves Hemou Acka Diaz, a native of the Ivy Coast.

In 1992 a new band was created in DC/Maryland from the remaining members of the G.P. Express and Washington Express squads who had merged into one group called Zépon. Without the support of promoter Jean Robert Baltazar the band relied on Vivens to do the job because he had been involved in some local shows and a successful yearly picnic since 1989. Jean Claude took it upon himself to use his contacts to bring other Konpa bands, Rasin bands and performing artists to Washington, D.C. and Maryland to perform with Zépon, not knowing that he was going to become one of the top show promoters of the Haitian diaspora of the 1990s. Haitian bands and artists from all over the world relied on him to promote their work in DC/Maryland. Jean Claude organized numerous shows with almost all the Haitian bands and artists on the planet. His yearly picnic was used as a model in New York as his brother in law the late Pierre Valbrum, and his friends started the Labapec picnic in New York which lead to numerous Konpa festivals in the Haitian diaspora.

Jean Claude with a degree in business administration and in psychology started his company, J.C.V Productions in 1995 and at that same time built his television studio in Wheaton Md.

Jean Claude became also a member of the D.C. Caribbean Carnival Committee (DCCC) and a registered member of the Caribbean Band Leaders Association (CBLA) of Washington, D.C. representing Haiti at the yearly Caribbean parade in Washington, D.C. He has over the years received 12 musical trophies and three television awards with two for the Best International T.V show. His song *Lanmou Pou Haiti* was nominated in 1996 for best lyric at the Haitian Music Award.

In 2004 he created the band Trankill. In 2005 he became a member of the Haitian Online Community under the name STaFF PoZé. He writes article about Konpa history, Konpa education, trivia, and anecdotes on Kompamagazine.com Haitinetradio.com, Opamizik.com, Kompatv.com, Basekompa.com, among others. He had also run at the turn of the century a real estate office in Wheaton Maryland, a record store in Silver Spring Md and the family-owned Nursing School VMT Education Center in Washington, D.C. In 2005 he collaborated in the creation of the school Centre D'Etude Classique De Meyer (CECM), in a suburb of the town of Jacmel, Haiti.

In 2007 he became the cultural correspondent for Radio Caraïbes FM, one of most popular radio stations in Haiti, which can also be heard online on caraibesfm.com. He is also the correspondent for the show Plaisir Ambiance on Radio Mega of Miami. Jean Claude is the author of the book Konpa Encyclopedia.

Vixamar, Norma - Singer

Vixamar, Smith (Siro) - Trumpet
Musician of the band Tropicana

Vod-K - Band

Volant, Maggie - Singer

Volcan (Volcan des Gonaives) - Band

Volcan des Gonaives was one of the few bands of the town of Gonaives.

Volcy, André - Singer

Volcy, Ernst (Nènè) - Bass
Nènè started his career with Les Morphées. He later joined Bossa Combo, where he showed the world that he is also an excellent music composer, as he is credited with some of Bossa Combo's early hits including *Importance Musiciens*.

Volcy, Marc Yves - Singer
Marc Yves Volcy was one of the idols of the 1970s, with his wonderful voice. He replaced the popular Fung Cap, but before long he managed to win the

heart of the followers of Les Ambassadeurs as soon as the band released the song *Fini*. In his live performances Marc Yves Volcy showed the fans that he had the charisma necessary to move the band forward. But during a tour the newly popular singer decided to stay in Canada, and that is where he continued his career, as well as doing other jobs. Marc Yves Volcy has, in the years that followed, managed to release some solo albums in which he expressed that life outside of Haiti is far from being easy for nostalgic Haitian entertainers. He also took part in some of the reminiscing shows by Les Ambassadeurs which often reunite some of the ex-members to perform for some of the fans of the good old days of the Mini Jazz era.

Volcy, Mario (Mario de Volcy) - Drums /Singer /Broadcaster /Promoter.
In recent years, many people have known Mario de Volcy as a broadcaster both on radio and television, as well as a show producer and record distributor, especially in New York. However to people who have been in the game awhile will tell you that Mario has, over the years, been one of the most innovative musicians for having played in the Mini Jazz era and his contribution to the Rasin music movement, as well as the return of the Twoubadou rhythm to the scene.
At an early age Mario Volcy already made up his mind that he would be a musician as his house was like the hangout spot of many artists in the early to mid 1960s, but when he witnessed Luc Philippe one of the showman of Super Ensemble de Webert Sicot on timbales, he automatically knew the instrument he wanted to play.
As a teenager he became a member of Les Cougars de Pétion Ville, and later Les Pachas du Canapé Vert. When the drummer Ernst Dennis was let go by Samba Créole, he was quickly replaced by the young Mario Volcy. Mario who is close to the Milfort family, was no stranger to the members of Samba Créole because the band used to rehearse at the gonguist Hans Milfort's (Doc) home in downtown Port-au-Prince. Mario was seriously in-demand as many bands were requesting his services. Finally he joined the band Les Loups Noirs in the mid-70s. Before Tico Sylvain left Bossa Combo he chose Mario to replace him. Mario became by the second half of the 1970s one of the best assets ever to the band Bossa Combo, not only with his skills as the drummer that changed the style of the percussion line, but also as one of the band's top composers.
His contribution to the albums *Accolade* and *Racines* are remarkable even today. In the song *Chère Madame*, Mario made some of the most famous breaks ever recorded in the history of Konpa music. By the first half of the 80s Mario already had two solo albums in his discography, which included the superhit Konpa songs *Premiere Communion* and *Viva Carnaval*.
Mario later did the song *Mandela Lagué* with his band "Mirak" after the release from jail of Nelson Mandela, the South African leader, political activist and

Nobel Prize winner. The song showcased the talent of the singer Sylvie D'art. Mario moved to New York where he continued to work in the Haitian music industry. His contribution to the promotion of the Haitian culture in New York is enormous. He is known as someone who is always ready to do what it takes for the advancement of Konpa and the promotion of the country culturally. In 1997, he released the album Super Mario IV, in which he showed his skill in playing different styles of Haitian music. The feelings he put into the song *Marie La Folle* has contributed to the reappearance of the Twoubadou style music on the Haitian music market in later years.

Mario is known in the business today as a mentor and an adviser to many musicians and bands.

Volcy, Pierrot - Singer
Pierrot became popular in the 1980s when he joined the band Accolade de New York.

Volcy, Romeo - Percussion
Musician of the New York based band Zin, Romeo is the younger brother of legendary drummer Mario de Volcy. With his friend, the drummer Patrick Appolon, he released the album *Patrick & Romeo Sé Zin* at the end of the 20th century.

Volcy, Roberto - Percussion

Volcy, Yves Michel - Singer

Volel, Emmanuel * (Picho) - Singer
Picho is one of the pioneer musicians of the Haitian community of Washington D.C.

Volel, Emile - Singer

Volel, Fred - Guitar

Volel, Lyonel - Saxophone / Keyboard
Lyonel played the sax for the band Ibo Combo in the 1960s, but he is also known as a great keyboardist and musical arranger.

Volny, Carl Henry – Guitar

Carl Henry is one of the brothers who created the band Volny Orchestra in Montreal Canada.

343

Volny Orchestra - Band
This band was created in Montreal by the Volny Brothers. The name was later changed to Kaskad.

Volny, Patrick - Singer
Patrick is one of the brothers who created the band Volny Orchestra in Montreal, Canada.

Volny, Ronald - Guitar
Ronald is one of the brothers who created the band Volny Orchestra in Montreal Canada.

Volo Volo-(Volo Volo de Boston) - Band

In the mid-70s the band VoloVolo took the Konpa community by storm as the first successful Haitian band coming out of the town of Boston. With the singers Antoine Rossini Jean Baptiste (Ti Manno) and Ricot Mazarin ex-star singer of Les Fantaisistes, the band came out with a series of hit songs like *Rivièm Simalo, Piece Nan Do, Hep Camarade* and off course the mega hit of the 70s *Carésé*.

By the late 70s Ti Manno moved to New York where he joined the band Astros and later he moved to Haiti to be with D.P. Express. Volo Volo then had to make some major adjustments and found some new front men. Over the years that job was done successfully by Christ Bazile, who the band had taken from Afro Combo, another band in Boston, and later the singer Joseph Lainé (Blagueur) also worked with the band.

The discography of Volo Volo includes the following: *La Nature, Vive Konpa, 14 karat Gold, Met Kafou, Volo Is The Best, 20 Ans De Succes, Gigika Rara, Carésé* and a series of live recordings and remixes. However, we must note that songs like *Bagay La Dominém, Melodie* and *Nou Nan Route* has kept Volo Volo on the Konpa charts for many years.

Voltaire, Desilon - Trumpet
One of the pioneer musicians of Cap Haitien from the band Jazz Capois who later created the band Tropicana

Voltaire, Pierre – Bass

Volume - Band

Vonksy, Jean - Saxophone
This talented musician joined the Konpa music world as a member of the Relaxx Band while he was still in class at Erasmus High School in Brooklyn. It is, however, with the group System Band that he would later find fame in the Konpa society. He abandoned his musical life to continue with his school projects. Today Jean is a medical doctor.

W

Wainwright, Frantz (Kiki) - Singer / Guitar
One of his memorable songs is the hit *Haiti Terre de Soleil* which he wrote for les Shleu Shleu.

Wanga Nègès - Band
This band was created in New York by the star singer Assade Francoeur after he left Ensemble Select de Coupé Cloué.

Washington, Andrew - Trombone
Andrew played with Tabou Combo in the 1980s. The young African-American surprised many Konpa fans with his ability to do all the background vocal parts of Tabou in Creole during the live shows. He also did a rap part in the song *Juicy Lucy,* which was a combination that wasn't the norm in Konpa music at that time.

Washington Express - Band
This band was created in Washington, D.C. in 1985 by Jean Claude Vivens and the promoter Pradel Sansarick. The band entertained the public in Washington, Maryland and Virginia from the mid to late 1980s, even after the departure of Jean Claude Vivens, who had joined the band G.P. Express.

Watters, Ken - Trumpet
Ken first joined Tabou Combo in 1989, where he performed for 5 years. He then rejoined the band in August of 2003. "Tabou Combo is a world-class band," said Ken. "Their triumphs at world music festivals around the globe prove this (nobody, from any country, ever wants to follow Tabou in a program). They are absolutely the best and hardest grooving band in their genre of music and it's a thrill to contribute my part... I am looking forward to the future with the band."
Bio from: www.taboucombo.com

We - Band

Wesner, Charles - Congas

Widmaiers (Les Widmaiers) - Band

Widmaier, Ansy - Bass

Widmaier, Goose Mushy - Piano

Widmaier, Herby - Singer
Herby is the founder of the famous radio station Radio Metropole. He is the
father of the well-known singer drummer and guitarist Joel Widmaier.

Widmaier, Joel - Drums - Singer /Guitar
The son of Herby Widmaier, Joel found fame as a vocalist with the band Zèklè
in the 1990s. He was later a member of the group Strings. Joel is one of the rare
musicians who were doing double function during his performances, being
the lead singer and the drummer at the same time.

Widmaier, Richard - Guitar

Wilfred, Alnatas - Trombone

Wooley, Eddy - Guitar
Born in Cap Haitien where he played with different local groups early in his
career, Eddy became notable when he replaced Robert Martino as the lead
guitarist of Les Difficiles de Petion Ville.
When the band became D.P. Express in 1976, Eddy was promoted to band
leader, a position he held until he left Haiti in the 1990s to live in Canada with
his family.

Wowoli - Band

X

X-Factor - Band

X-Tra - Band
Solo project of Brutus Dérissaint guitarist and one of the leaders of Zenglen

Xplicit - Band

Xsussa - Band

Y

Yaffa see: Domingue Liautaud

Yah Fah Band de Miami - Band

Yama Records
Record Productions Company

Yanvaloo Entertainment
Show Production Company based in New York, the owner Rudy Colas is known in the Konpa community as Yanvaloo. He often takes pictures of live Konpa shows that he posts on the different Konpa internet sites.

Yonyon see: Simeon Lyonel

Youyou see: Legagneur Carrie / Besson Byrneste

Z

Zabala, Nestor - Trombone

Zagalo see: Désir Jude / Belizaire Atkinson

Zam – Band

Zamor, Eddy * - Radio Personality
Eddy was a popular radio personality and one of the pioneers of Haitian radio broadcasting in the Diaspora. He introduced in the 1970s the show *Eddy Publicité* in New York. Eddy did for Konpa in New York what Ricot Jean Baptiste did for the Mini Jazz in Haiti. His two-hour show was for a long time the only resource to hear Konpa music on the airwaves in New York and the best place to promote all the Konpa events. Eddy Zamor was a great radio announcer. He had a wonderful and clear voice and was a true professional. His show is mentioned on the System Band song *Vacances*, in which Isnard Doubi said: *"J'envois des Lettres Eddy Publicité"*. In the 1980s he retired from radio broadcasting as he witnessed a complete invasion of the airwaves by many underground Haitian owned and operated radio stations in New York and in Miami by some people who didn't have any skills, nor the love for the profession that he cherished all his life. Eddy never returned to radio broadcasting. He died in New York.

Zatrap -Band

Zèklè - Band
This band is credited with being the innovator of the Nouvel Jenerasyon music movement in Haiti. Their album *Stop* was an instant success and got the attention of people of all ages. It also introduced to the world the talent of the singer/drummer Joel Widmaier who would become the role model of many musicians of the years that followed. Zèklè was basically quiet from the mid 1990s until they reappeared on Dec. 1st 2007 at a concert at the Park Historique de la Canne à Sucre with the original members at a well advertise concert.

Zèl - Band
This band came out in Florida in the 1990s

Zenglen - Band

One of the bands that basically tried hard to change the course of Konpa history would definitely be the band known as Zenglen. As the members were getting ready to create a band by practicing the songs of Zèklè and Kassav, playing rock and other styles of music while looking for their own identity, some empty beer bottles placed on top of the speakers fell and broke into several pieces on the floor. The next day, as the members returned to practice, they found that the homeowner wrote the word "Zenglen" on the floor with the broken pieces. From that day on, the band was known as Zenglen (which basically mean pieces of broken glasses).

The band became one of the wonders of the early 1990s as they released the song *Fidel* on the album *An Nou Alèz*. In the song the band said that "change" is never easy and always faces obstacles and resistance, but that they pledge to remain faithful (*Fidel*) to their mission, which is to improve and modernize the Konpa rhythm. The Konpa world was introduced to their newfound stars like the guitarist and singer Brutus Dérissaint and the lead singer Gary Didier Perez, among others. Unfortunately during a U.S. tour most of the band's members abandoned ship and the band broke up like a real Zenglen.

In Miami, Brutus never stopped caressing the dream of keeping some of the pieces alive and had moved on with some attempts like the Zenglen Plus and a few solo albums in the 1990s. Many musicians tried to help him to collect the pieces, but they often moved on with their own projects like the creation of the band D-Zine. Nevertheless, Brutus never lost faith and still remained fidèl (Faithful) to his mission by hiring more talented musicians each and every time. At the end of the century the acquisition of the drummer Richard Herard (Ritchie) and the singer Gracia Delva took Zenglen to the level of a very competitive Konpa band in the demanding market as they released the album *Easy Konpa,* with nothing but major hit songs that were going to move the band to the front burner of the industry and ever since that time Zenglen haven't looked back despite the so many changes of personnel that continued to occurred.

The album *Easy Konpa* was introduced to the public with the release of the video of the song *5 Dwèt* which helped discover the singing talent of Gracia Delva and the many skills of Ritchie not only as a high-class drummer but also as a songwriter. The song *B.S. Productions* got the attention of the public as the song was about unqualified show producers damaging the reputation of bands. On the same album the band touched some subjects until then taboo.

They talked about lesbians in the society in the song *Flannè Femèl* and drug use in the song *Ti Poud*.

In the following years, Zenglen continued to amaze the Konpa fans all over the world with the releases of the albums *Let It Groove* and *Do It Right*.

In 2002, while the band was returning from a tour in Europe, the singer Gracia Delva was sent back to Haiti by the U.S. Immigration Services and the band had to deal with damage control as the management quickly brought Emmanuel Obas, the ex-singer of Mizik Mizik to the team. When that attempt failed they moved on by hiring Réginald Cangé and Edouard Jean Baptiste (Fréro), two new singers, to replace their charismatic front man. Réginald and Fréro, two young men fresh out of Haiti, tried their very best but were unsuccessful at making the public forget about Gracia, despite their tremendous effort and the good job they both delivered in the album *5 Etoiles* which also included the songs *Child Support* and *F.K.D.*

The band's internal problem always seems to take precedent however, and at the end of 2006 both singers decided to boycott the band's next show in N.J. The word got out and the band leader Brutus called the singer Kenny Desmangle to the rescue. Kenny put on such a good show that he, was by the beginning of 2007 the new singer of Zenglen. By March 2007, the band released the single *Ou Fè Fot (O.F.F)* with the voice of Kenny Desmangle on lead. Over the years the Konpa observers have seen broken pieces that continued to break in even more pieces, but the band remains solid and true to their mission: Zenglen don't change…Zenglen improve…like they often say in their songs *"Sé pa changé nou change se pi bon'n vin'n pi bon."*

Zenglen Plus - Band

As a few members of Zenglen moved on with their career, they continued to play some of the music of Zenglen at their live shows until they eventually became D-Zine. The name Zenglen Plus first appeared on a solo album of Brutus, the band leader of Zenglen.

Zenith - Band

Zenny, Joseph Junior (Ti Djo) - Singer

Ti Djo is the lead singer of the band Kréyòl La. The native of Jacmel came out of his shell in 1998 as the lead singer of the band Konpa Kréyol. The video clip of the song *"Li pa vini"* has shown to the world that Ti Joe Zenny has some serious acting talent. Soon after the release of the clip he was contracted to be the villain in the movie "I love you Anne", in which he played alongside the comedian Daniel Fils-Aimé better known as "Tonton Bicha". The movie was an instant hit with sold-out showings in many movie theaters in the country, especially at Ciné Capitol in Port-au-Prince, throughout the summer of 2003. Ti Djo is a very charismatic person, very talkative, and fun to be around.

Zipe - Band

Zépon - Band

This band was created in 1992 in the suburb of Washington, D.C. by some former members of G.P. Express. Compared to the other Haitian bands, Zépon had a different marketing plan as they mostly looked for work outside of the Haitian community. As the only band playing French Caribbean music in Washington, Zépon had the chance to represent Haiti at many international concerts and balls in the nation's capital. They even played at the French embassy for Bastille Day among other major concerts including Africa fete, D.C. fete, Kunta Kinte festival in Annapolis, Md. and at the international shows of the History Museum in Washington, D.C. and the Baltimore Museum of Arts in Baltimore Maryland.

Zépon had a line of great musicians including Fabrice Rouzier on keyboard and Dieujuste Nozil (Ti Polis) on guitar. Mario Germain, the band's leader was also a former bass player of D.P. Express and Gemini All Stars de Ti Manno. Lyonel Simeon, another member of D.P. Express and the Caribbean Sextet, was on trombone. With a line of such great musicians and the singers Jean Claude Vivens, Jacky Bois and Micheline Joseph Parks, the Haitian music was well- represented in the U.S. capital.

On stage Zépon played their music as well as the great hits of Gemini and D.P. Express. In the 1990s their performances at the DC Caribbean carnival were so remarkable that many spectators would not leave until they had seen Zépon. The band has received more than a dozen Caribbean music awards and trophies.

Zic Band - Band

Zig Zag - Band
The band introduced in the 1980s the talent of the singer Luigy Lindor in Haiti.

Zig Zag - Band
This band, unlike the 1980s Zig Zag, was put together by Chrisostome Bazile and friends in the U.S.

Zigge - Band

Ziltik - Band

Zin - Band
Created in New York in the mid-1980s this band did not waste any time in becoming one of the most popular bands in the Haitian music industry. From their very first hit *"fèm volé"* Zin continued to make one hit after another.
Zin was one of the first bands of the Nouvel Jenerasyon movement and people often traveled many miles to attend their shows. With hit makers like Alan Cave (singer), Alex Abellard (keyboard/guitar) and Eddy St. Vil (guitar) the band always had something new to attract the public, including the songs from Alan's solo albums like *Sé Pa Pou Dat, Ma Rose,* and *De La Tète Aux Pieds.* Before the coming of Zin in the New York City Haitian music market, the Haitian night shows used to attract mostly the nostalgic Haitians. Zin is credited for encouraging college students and young working adults for attending Konpa shows in the Haitian Diaspora.
The discography of Zin includes but not limited to: *Fèm Vole, Opa, Manyen'w, Yo Pou Zin, Sa Zin Guen La, 3 Lettres Seulement, Kanpe Sou Bit,* and a series of live albums and *the best of Zin.*

Zinglin
 A solo project of the late Dieujuste Nozil (Ti polis) released in 1988.

Zotobré - Band
 This band was created by the great Webert Sicot at the end of his career. It was supposed to be a come back for the creator and leader of Cadence Rampa, but the band did not last long. Famous musicians like Almando Keslin, Serge Rosenthal and Claude Montreuil were part of the project.

Zoum - Band
This band was created in the 1990s in Connecticut, but it did not last long. The

project failed when the creator and star Bassist of the band joined the New York based band Zin.

Zouti - Band

Zshea - see: Caze Florence

Zulerion, Jean Sony (Sony Bel Anfòm) - Radio Personality/Promoter

1ˢᵗ Class - Band
This band based in New York came out at the end of the century and should not be confused with First Class the band of Yvon Mondésir of the late 1980s.

2 Nice - Band

2 Sweet - Band
This band came out in New York in the 1990s

509 - Band
This band came out in Miami in 2004 with star singer Kenny Desmangle. Their song *Fake* released in 2004 on their first studio album titled *Shake* got the band some airtime and a trip to Haiti. In 2005 the band came out with the song *509 Police*, which brings a message of peace, law and order to bands that tend to preach violence in their songs.
The band openly criticized the Carimi's song *Nasty Biznis* and the Konpa Kreyol song *Gen Gen Gen* while they try to educate the public not to support bootleg materials and bad promoters in the vidieo *509 Police* released in 2005. At the end of 2006 the band suffered a loss as their lead singer Kenny Desmangle was hired by Zenglen.
The name 509 was chosen because the number 509 is the area code of Haiti.

7 Vedettes (Les 7 Vedettes) - Band
This twoubadou/Konpa band of 7 members really got some serious recognition in the Konpa world when part of their song "2 Chans" was being played by many Konpa bands, including the great Tabou Combo in the early 1980s.

718 - Band
This band came out in New York at the turn of the century, but it didn't last long, as the members moved on by creating other bands like Tempo and G-5. The numbers 7 1 8 represented the area code of Brooklyn and Queens, two major cities in New York with a large concentration of Haitian.

ACKNOWLEDGEMENT

Special thanks to the people and organizations that have one way or the other contributed to the realization of this book.

Jessica Steinmann
Jonathan Vivens
Mario Germain
Ludner Plaisir
Albert Decady
Antonio Vilmenay
Carlito Douyon
Paul Henegan
Taboucombo.com
Opamizik.com
Haitinetradio.com
Kompamagazine.com
Afiwi.com
Konpa.info
Basekompa.com
JCV Productions
VMT Education Center
Haiti A Suivre T.V Show
Patrick Devarieux
Philippe Lavelanette
Alex Abellard
Mario de Volcy
Géroboam Raphael
Geronimo Records
Mini Records
Fred Paul
Marc Records
Fritz Duverger
Serge Bellegarde

This book is a dedication to the loving memory of my dear brother Ambroise Vivens Fils (Fanfan).

To all my radio listeners, T.V viewers and my students of the Konpa forums who have inspired me to complete this book, I say many thanks for your patience and blessings.

To our readers: You too may contribute to the Konpa Encyclopedia. If you feel that we have missed your name, a relative, a band or your favorite "KONPA" artist please provide us with some information at:
konpabooks@yahoo.com

ISBN 142516368-8